The Poetry of Boethius

The Poetry of Boethius

Gerard O'Daly

The University of North Carolina Press

Chapel Hill and London

First published in the United States 1991
by The University of North Carolina Press

Library of Congress Cataloging-in-Publication Data

O'Daly, Gerard J.P.
   The poetry of Boethius : studies in the Consolation of philosophy
/ by Gerard O'Daly.
    p. cm.
   Includes bibliographical references and index.
   ISBN 0–8078–1989–1
   1. Boethius d. 524. De consolatione philosophiae. 2. Boethius
d. 524—Poetic works. 3. Latin poetry—History and criticism.
I. Title.
PA6231.C83035 1991
100—dc20

90–25028
CIP

First published in Great Britain 1991
by Gerald Duckworth & Co. Ltd.
The Old Piano Factory
43 Gloucester Crescent
London NW1 7DY

Photoset in North Wales by
Derek Doyle & Associates, Mold, Clwyd.
Printed in Great Britain by
Redwood Press Ltd, Melksham.

Contents

Preface

The *Consolation of Philosophy* is a literary and philosophical masterpiece of late antiquity, but the poems which alternate with prose passages throughout the work have too often been considered to be mere interludes in the argument or decorative embellishments of it. This study seeks to show that they form a vigorous and sophisticated sequence in their own right, reflecting and elaborating the Latin poetic tradition from Lucretius to Seneca's tragedies, and adapting that tradition's imagery, myths, and motifs to the work's overall structure. The poems of the *Consolation* should be read in context: to that extent this book is a study of the work as a whole, but it does not pretend to deal with its philosophical themes any more than is necessary for the appreciation of the poems under discussion. Nor is it a commentary on all the poems of the work, though most are analysed in varying degrees of detail.

In Chapter 1 a brief account of Boethius' career and other writings is given, and the *Consolation*'s problematic generic affiliations are reviewed, as are the questions of its completeness and the (to some) perplexing absence of overt Christian themes and sentiments in the work. Chapter 2 is central to this book's dominant purpose: to show that the poems of the *Consolation* are an integral part of the work's poetics, and that Boethius' uses of poetry can only be understood against the background of Greek and Roman literary criticism. This chapter also considers the problem for a Platonist of poetry's value, and speculates about the influence of the most comprehensive defence of poetry accessible to Boethius – that of Proclus in his *Commentary on the Republic* – upon the *Consolation*. Chapters 3-5 are a series of studies of individual themes and poems: tyrants and the tyranny of the passions (Chapter 3), order and disorder in nature (Chapter 4), and the uses of myth (Chapter 5).

I have written throughout with two main classes of reader in mind: those who are interested in the literature and thought of Classical and Late Antiquity, and those who are concerned with Boethius' considerable influence in the Middle Ages and Renaissance. A consequence is that I have attempted to combine detailed discussion of Boethius' relation to his literary antecedents with the kind of description and extensive quotation of those antecedents that

vii

Classicists may not need, but for which I hope that medievalists and others may be grateful. All Latin poetic quotations are given in the original and in translation; prose quotations are usually given only in translation, with key terms added in the original. All translations of Boethius are my own, as are those of other authors where no translator is named: but I have generally preferred to quote from accessible and reliable translations of other authors, as readers may wish to consult the context of quoted extracts. My own translations have no literary pretensions, aiming above all at accurate rendering of the original.

The idea of this book germinated in the winter of 1984-5, when I lectured on Boethius in Heidelberg and Würzburg, and conducted a seminar on the *Consolation* at Würzburg University. Work on it was made possible through the generosity of the Alexander von Humboldt Foundation, which awarded me a Fellowship, held in the summers of 1986 and 1987 at Heidelberg University. I am deeply grateful to the Humboldt Foundation for this unstinting support.

Professor Albrecht Dihle encouraged this study from the start, and also read and made valuable comments on an earlier version of it: my debt to him is immeasurable.

I should also like to thank Dr Anna Wilson (née Crabbe), who scrutinized an earlier version of Chapters 2-5 page by page. Her painstaking and detailed criticism has enabled me to improve the book in several respects, and I have changed my mind, or modified my views, or stubbornly tried to articulate them more convincingly, many times in reaction to her comments.

My Nottingham friend and colleague Professor Robert Markus read and commented upon a draft of this study, enabling me in particular to clarify my ideas on Boethius' career and social environment.

I am also indebted for generous help of various kinds to Professors Jean Doignon and Siegmar Döpp, as well as to Herr Franz Scherer, Classics Librarian at Heidelberg University, for assistance in procuring books and articles.

No writer on the *Consolation of Philosophy* can be unaware of the immense debt owed to his forerunners. This book could not have been written without the help and inspiration provided by the works of Alfonsi, Chadwick, Courcelle, Crabbe, Gruber, Lerer, Scheible, and Shanzer, to name only those most used. Scholarship thrives on debate: let me stress here my respect and admiration for the contributions of those whose interpretations have stimulated me to occasional disagreement with them.

Grateful acknowledgement for permission to reproduce copyright material is due to the following: Edizioni dell'Ateneo; The President and Fellows of Harvard College; Oxford University Press; Francis Cairns (Publications); Chatto & Windus; Penguin Books; Jonathan Barnes; G.P. Goold; D.A. Russell.

A final debt remains to be acknowledged, and it is the greatest of all: my wife Ursula has once again typed and corrected the entire manuscript, acquiring word processing skills in order to do so. She has also been a perceptive and frank critic throughout, and has sustained me during the tedious phases from which work even on so delightful an author as the Boethius of the *Consolation* is not exempt: *amor mi mosse, che mi fa parlare.*

G.J.P. O'D.

PARENTIBVS OCTOGENARIIS

Abbreviations

AG	Allen and Greenough's *New Latin Grammar* (Boston 1903, often reprinted)
ANRW	H. Temporini/W. Haase, *Aufstieg und Niedergang der römischen Welt* (Berlin/New York 1972-)
CCL	*Corpus Christianorum. Series Latina* (Turnhout 1953-)
CSEL	*Corpus Scriptorum Ecclesiasticorum Latinorum* (Vienna 1866-)
DHGE	*Dictionnaire d'histoire et de géographie ecclésiastiques* (Paris 1912-)
DK	H. Diels/W. Kranz, *Die Fragmente der Vorsokratiker*, 6th edn. (Berlin 1951-2, often reprinted)
ILS	H. Dessau, *Inscriptiones Latinae Selectae* (Berlin 1892-1916)
LCL	*Loeb Classical Library* (London, etc. 1911-)
Long/Sedley	A.A. Long/D.N. Sedley, *The Hellenistic Philosophers*, 2 vols. (Cambridge 1987)
LP	L. Duchesne, *Liber Pontificalis* (Paris 1886-92)
MGH	*Monumenta Germaniae Historica. Auctores antiquissimi* (Berlin 1877-1919)
Nisbet/ Hubbard	R.G.M. Nisbet/M. Hubbard, *A Commentary on Horace: Odes Book 1, Book 2* (Oxford 1970 and 1978)
ODP	J.N.D. Kelly, *The Oxford Dictionary of Popes* (Oxford 1986)
PL	J.-P. Migne, *Patrologiae cursus completus. Series Latina* (Paris 1841-64)
PLRE	J.R. Martindale, *The Prosopography of the Later Roman Empire*, vol. 2: A.D. 395-527 (Cambridge 1980)
RAC	T. Klauser *et al.*, *Reallexikon für Antike und Christentum* (Stuttgart 1950-)
RE	*Paulys Realencyclopädie der classischen Altertumswissenschaft*. Neue Bearbeitung begonnen von G. Wissowa (Stuttgart 1894-1978)
SVF	H. von Arnim, *Stoicorum Veterum Fragmenta* (Leipzig 1903-24)
ThWNT	G. Kittel *et al.*, *Theologisches Wörterbuch zum Neuen Testament* (Stuttgart 1933-79)

TLL   *Thesaurus Linguae Latinae* (Leipzig, etc. 1900-)

The following abbreviations are used for Boethius' works:

arith.   *De institutione arithmetica libri ii*, ed. G. Friedlein
             (Leipzig 1867)
In Cat.   *In Categorias Aristotelis libri iv* (*PL* 64)
Cons. phil. *Consolatio philosophiae.* For editions see Select
             Bibliography, p. 238.
In Int. I, II *In librum Aristotelis peri hermêneias (De Interpreta-
             tione) commentarii* I, II, ed. C. Meiser (Leipzig 1877
             and 1880)
mus.   *De institutione musica libri v*, ed. G. Friedlein (Leipzig
             1867)
Op. sac.   *Opuscula sacra*, ed. R. Peiper (Leipzig 1871); E.K.
             Rand (*LCL* 1918)
In Porph.   *In Isagogen Porphyrii commentorum editio* I, II, ed. S.
   Isag. I, II Brandt (*CSEL* 48, 1906)

The poems (*metra*) of *Cons. phil.* are cited in the form '1 m. 2.4' = Book
1, *metrum* 2, line 4. The prose sections (*prosae*) are cited in the form
'1.1.2' = Book 1, *prosa* 1, section 2 of *CCL* edn.

CHAPTER ONE

The *Consolation* and its Author

(i) A late Roman career[1]

Some time between the later months of 523 and the early part of 526[2] Boethius was found guilty of treason and executed, at the instigation of the Ostrogothic king of Italy, Theoderic. The *Consolation of Philosophy* is the product of his long imprisonment: it was apparently composed at Pavia, the north Italian town which, later in the sixth century, was to become the capital of the Lombard kingdom.[3] Nothing in Boethius' background or career presaged its shocking and terrible end. He was born into one of the wealthiest and most powerful aristocratic families of Italy, the Anicii.[4] The date of his birth is unknown, but the facts of his career suggest that it was early in the 480s. Following the death of his father (who was consul in 487), Boethius, still a boy, was adopted into the no less distinguished family of the Symmachi.[5] His adoptive father, Quintus Aurelius Memmius Symmachus, consul in 485, sometime prefect of the city of Rome, was an important political figure.[6] He was also a cultivated man, the author of a history of Rome in seven books, and the editor of a manuscript of Macrobius' Neoplatonic *Commentary on the Dream of Scipio*, a work which, in

---

[1] This section lays no claim to originality: it is intended as an introductory survey of Boethius' life and times. There is a full discussion in Chadwick (1981) 1-68; see also Barrett (1940) 1-74; Gruber (1978) 1-13; Matthews (1981).

[2] On the problem of dating Boethius' execution see Mathwich (1960) 35f.; Chadwick (1981) 54f., 62.

[3] For the circumstances of Boethius' trial, imprisonment, and execution see (apart from *Cons. phil.* [esp. 1.4] itself) *Anon. Vales.* 85ff.; *LP* 1.276; Procopius, *Bell. Goth.* 1.1.32-9. Cappuyns (1937) 355f. locates the *ager Calventianus*, to which *Anon. Vales.* 87 refers as the place of imprisonment and execution, in Pavia. On the later cult of Boethius at Pavia see Cappuyns (1937) 357f.; W. Bark, 'The Legend of Boethius' Martyrdom', *Speculum* 21 (1946) 312-17; H.R. Patch, 'The Beginnings of the Legend of Boethius', *Speculum* 22 (1947) 443-5. Cf. also Gibbon, ed. Bury, 4.202.

[4] His full name was Anicius Manlius Severinus Boethius: *PLRE* 2.233. On the Anicii see Obertello (1974) 1.3ff.

[5] *Cons. phil.* 2.3.5.

[6] On Symmachus see Usener (1877) 17ff.; Sundwall (1919) 159ff.; *PLRE* 2.1044-6.

turn, was to have a considerable influence upon Boethius.[7] Boethius
would later regard him as one with whom he could have worthwhile
discussions on matters theological.[8]

Boethius married Symmachus' daughter, Rusticiana, whose subsequent loyalty to the memory of her father (like Boethius, executed by
Theoderic) and her husband was impressive. Although the confiscated
estates of Symmachus and Boethius were restored to their family by
Theoderic's daughter, Amalasuintha, in her capacity as regent for her
son Athalaric after Theoderic's death in 526, Rusticiana did not forget
what Theoderic had done to her menfolk. When the armies of the
Byzantine emperor Justinian invaded Gothic Italy in 535, she had the
statues of Theoderic demolished, a vivid affirmation, not merely of
personal hatred, but also of the destruction of the remarkable
co-operation between the Roman senate and the Gothic court at
Ravenna that had characterized the reign of Theoderic until its final
stages.[9]

Boethius was a boy when Theoderic established Ostrogothic rule in
Italy in 493.[10] His career was determined by the settlements, formal or
informal, between Theoderic, the senate, and the Byzantine emperor
in the years which followed. In some cases these settlements
maintained what Theoderic's predecessor as barbarian king of Italy,
the Scirian Odoacer (476-93), had initiated. The Roman aristocracy
was conciliated by diplomatic courtesy, and by the appointment of
Romans to almost all civilian posts. Traditional offices were preserved,
and the hierarchy of Roman administration was largely unchanged.
Military posts, however, were usually in Gothic hands, as well as some
important financial offices. Theoderic nominated Romans to the
consulship, and the eastern emperor normally granted codicils
conferring due rank on the nominees. For the sons of senatorial
families like that of Boethius, an administrative career, which might
lead to the governorship of an Italian province or of the city of Rome
itself, was a prospect as satisfying as it had been under the emperors.
The office of consul, on the other hand, continued to be honorific and
ceremonial, an expensive social duty devolving upon members of
families with wealth and pedigree. Boethius became consul in 510,
when he was not yet thirty years old.[11] His forseeably most important

[7] On the subscription at the end of Book 1 of Macrobius' *Commentary* see Chadwick
(1981) 7; Kirkby (1981) 52. For Macrobius' influence on Boethius see *In Porph. Isag.* I
1.11 (*CSEL* 48.31f.). Courcelle (1967) 116ff. notes the influence of *In somn. Scip.* 2.9f. on
Cons. phil. 2.7: see Gruber (1978) 216; Chadwick (1981) 8. Cf. p. 61 below.
[8] *Op. sac.* 1, praef. (pp. 2ff., Loeb edn.).
[9] Procopius, *Bell. Goth.* 3.20.29.
[10] On Theoderic's rule see Sundwall (1919) 190-259; Ensslin (1947); Stein (1949)
2.107-56. Gibbon's account (ed. Bury, 4.170-204) remains unsurpassed, and has
(197-203) a fascinating and discerning assessment of Boethius' achievements.
[11] On this and later events of Boethius' career see *PLRE* 2.233ff.

task in that office would have been the organization of lavish public games and entertainments at Rome. But Boethius was no ordinary young aristocrat. He opposed an emergency plan, put forward by the prestigious praetorian prefect Faustus Niger, to alleviate famine by the compulsory purchase of food in Campania at prices which would have ruined its farmers. Theoderic upheld Boethius' objections.[12] In his consulship Boethius lived up to the promise that his early writings on arithmetic and music had shown, and yet his first real political gesture on behalf of the Campanians revealed an inclination and a talent beyond the world of learning. For the time being, however, he remained above all a scholar. During his consulship, he tells us, he was able to get some writing done on Aristotelian logic.[13]

Boethius' political career reached its apogee in 522: in that year both his sons became consuls (an exceptional honour in itself), he delivered a panegyric on Theoderic, which became famous, and, finally, Theoderic appointed him Master of Offices (a senior advisory, administrative, and judicial post) in his court at Ravenna.[14] If the first two honours, the consulship of his sons and the panegyric, reflected Boethius' social background and culture, the post of Master of Offices indicated that, in Theoderic's judgement, Boethius possessed the ability that was needed for functions with real power.

In assessing Boethius' achievement, it is useful to distinguish between two kinds of political career open to members of senatorial families.[15] One, the formal 'senatorial' type, might lead through various junior urban magistracies to a consulship or governorship, or to the prefecture of Rome. Boethius' earlier career apparently followed this pattern: it would not usually have led to court office. By contrast, a career of the 'imperial' sort involved direct service to emperor or king, and generally led to the governorship of an overseas province or to court posts. The family of Cassiodorus exemplifies such a tradition of service to imperial and, later, barbarian masters. Cassiodorus succeeded Boethius as Master of Offices at Theoderic's court.[16] Given his family tradition of service, it was a more natural appointment than that of the 'senatorial' Boethius, though it should be emphasized that Cassiodorus was of senatorial background also, and that his period of political service at Ravenna was as brief as that of Boethius. Both men found much time to study and write, and Cassiodorus was no less

---

[12] *Cons. phil.* 1.4.12.

[13] *In Cat.* 2 (*PL* 64.201B).

[14] Sons' consulship and panegyric: *Cons. phil.* 2.3.8; 2.4.7; cf. Cassiodorus, *Ordo generis Cassiodororum*, ll. 14f. (*CCL* 96, p. v). Master of Offices: Theoderic's formula for the appointment is given in Cassiodorus, *Variae* 6.6. See Jones (1964) 1.368f., and, for Boethius, Ensslin (1947) 160f., 307f.

[15] For the following see Matthews (1975) 12ff.; Matthews (1981) 26ff.

[16] For Cassiodorus' career and writings see O'Donnell (1979), critically reviewed by Averil Cameron in *Journal of Roman Studies* 71 (1981) 183-6.

devoted than Boethius to Roman traditions. But it is less likely that
Boethius would have written a history of the Goths, as Cassiodorus
was to do. Boethius suffered Gothic rule as many of his class did, and
co-operated with it out of necessity, without seeking to carve out a
career at the court; but Rome, its senate, and its life were the centre of
his political concerns. His appointment as imperial minister could not
dislodge the senate from its first place in his loyalties, and his instinct
was to protect that same senate and seek help from it, when political
accusations of treason were made against him in 523 or 524. He was to
be cruelly disappointed when the senate, far from rescuing him,
connived at his downfall, but he was convinced of its merits to the
end.[17]

In many respects relations between the Roman senate and the
Ravenna court changed little when the barbarian kings Odoacer and
Theoderic seized power in Italy. The court needed the support of the
Roman aristocracy in order to govern with stability. Theoderic was
concerned to project the image of a ruler who admired and respected
Roman culture, law, and traditions. For Italy his rule meant a welcome
period of relative peace and harmony, despite the large-scale
settlement of Ostrogoths on Italian land, with its attendant tensions
and occasional violence.[18] When he visited Rome in 500 Theoderic was
warmly welcomed by the senate and the Church: the Arian king
worshipped 'like a Catholic' at St Peter's basilica.[19] We do not know the
precise manner in which Theoderic was praised in Boethius' panegyric
of 522, but much of what Boethius said there may have been both
sincere and well-founded. The terrible end of Theoderic's reign, which
swept away Boethius in its wake, was quite unlike its predominantly
peaceful course.

Boethius' support was important to Theoderic: the fall of Boethius
presaged the decline of Gothic power in Italy. In the events leading to
that fall the eastern empire plays a vital, if inscrutable, role. The
details of the events of 523 or early 524 make this clear.[20] The attack
on Boethius followed his support for a fellow-senator, Albinus, who
was denounced to Theoderic for conducting treasonable correspondence with persons close to the emperor Justin. In defending Albinus,

[17] *Anon. Vales.* 85; *Cons. phil.* 1.4.20ff. Barnish (1983) 592f., 596 comments
perceptively on the similarities in the presentation of Boethius as senatorial champion
and martyr in both works.
  [18] See Jones (1964) 1.248ff.
  [19] *Anon. Vales.* 65.
  [20] The following account owes much to Chadwick (1981) 46ff. On Boethius' trial see the
sources and literature referred to in n. 3 above, as well as Sundwall (1919) 230ff.; G.G.
Picotti, 'Il senato romano e il processo di Boezio', *Archivio Storico Italiano* 15 (1931)
205-28; Bark (1943/4); Ensslin (1947) 308ff.; Stein (1949) 2.410ff.; Mathwich (1960); C.H.
Coster, *Late Roman Studies* (Cambridge, Mass. 1968) 46ff.; Tränkle (1973); Obertello
(1979) 1.85ff.

Boethius found himself charged with conspiracy against Theoderic.[21] Letters purporting to be written by him were produced, advocating 'Roman liberty', and he was accused of employing black magic to forward his career, a charge that often accompanied that of treason, but one that was also liable to be levelled against a philosopher with scientific, especially astronomical, interests, such as Boethius had.[22] Informants were found: all were Romans, not Goths. Boethius, even in his short period of office at the court, had made as many Roman as Gothic enemies: his loyalty to the senate was a loyalty to its traditions when these were properly observed, and not one of undiscriminating support for unworthy senators. After Boethius' arrest and imprisonment he was tried in his absence by a Roman senatorial court at Rome. He could not defend himself, and was sentenced to death.

On the face of it, the events leading to Boethius' death are explicable as an intrigue practised by enemies and rivals, possibly jealous of his success at court, and determined to secure his downfall. But two factors call for some discussion. Why did Theoderic turn against the man he had only recently appointed to high office? And what was the role of the eastern empire in the events that led to the death of Boethius? It will be appropriate to attempt to answer the second question first.

Relations between Theoderic's Italian kingdom and Constantinople were changed by the accession of Justin in 518. The loss of imperial control over Italy was exacerbated by religious schism: the eastern and western Churches were in dissension since the Council of Chalcedon in 451 had attempted to resolve the long-standing debate concerning the unity of the person of Christ by pronouncing against the Monophysite doctrine of Christ's single divine nature, and this despite the fact that the Council adopted the views set out in the Tome of Pope Leo I.[23] But divisions were also apparent within the eastern Church, where variant Monophysite tendencies competed with Chalcedonian orthodoxy. In the course of the fifth century it became increasingly obvious to eastern leaders, lay and ecclesiastical, that only abandonment, or at the very least, modification, of the decrees of Chalcedon could achieve eastern Church unity. But such a break with Chalcedon seemed to prejudice the reconciliation of the eastern Church with Rome, which was

---

[21] Barnish (1990) 28-32 speculates that Albinus and Boethius were involved in plans for the installation of Theoderic's ambitious nephew Theodahad as regent or successor with Roman senatorial backing.

[22] See P. Rousseau, 'The Death of Boethius: the Charge of maleficium', *Studi Medievali*, Serie terza, 20 (1979) 871-89; Chadwick (1981) 49f.

[23] Chadwick (1981) 25ff. relates the issues and events to Boethius' career and writings. Cf. L. Duchesne, *L'église au VIe siècle* (Paris 1925) 1-77; Stein (1949) 2.20-7, 31-9, 157-92. H. Chadwick, *The Early Church* (Harmondsworth 1967) 192ff. provides a lucid introduction to the Christological controversy; see also J.N.D. Kelly, *Early Christian Doctrines*, 5th edn. (London 1977) 310ff.

committed to the Chalcedonian definition of Christ's nature. For Rome acceptance of Chalcedon's Christological doctrine was tainted by the Council's insistence that the see of Constantinople had the same patriarchal status as Alexandria and Antioch, and, hence, by implication, as Rome itself. But it was not until the publication of the so-called Henoticon (a conciliatory edict of union aimed at appeasing Monophysite opposition to Chalcedon) by the emperor Zeno in 482, and the growth of Monophysite domination in both Constantinople and Alexandria, that an open break between the Churches of East and West occurred, lasting some thirty-five years, from 484 to 519. At this time, it was easier for Rome to find areas of co-operation with the tolerant Arian Theoderic than with eastern Church and imperial leaders. But the Christological controversy, or at least its political repercussions, played a role in Theoderic's negotiations for recognition as king of Italy by the emperor in 498. Theoderic's title was granted in return for a guarantee by papal legates of the conciliatory Pope Anastasius II that Rome would accept the Henoticon. Pope Anastasius' sudden death in the same year, amidst bitter disputes among his Roman clergy about his eastern policies, led to a papal election fought on the issue of those very policies, which divided the Church at Rome into factions for a number of years, and did nothing to promote reunification of East and West. Despite renewed attempts at reconciliation, and the cultural, diplomatic, and theological links between East and West, it was only after the long reign of the emperor Anastasius (491-518)[24] and the accession of Justin that the schism was ended. Justin's, and his nephew Justinian's, interests were not exclusively, or even primarily, theological: they were persuaded that only through Church reunion on the basis of Chalcedon could the planned recovery of Italy from the Goths be achieved. In ending the schism Rome in effect recognized the Chalcedonian definition of Constantinople's patriarchal status. From Theoderic's point of view, these developments were not necessarily to be welcomed without reservation. Even if the ending of the schism had been a negotiating point in his attempt for recognition by the emperor in 498, the new Catholic orthodoxy of Justin threatened Theoderic's fellow-Arians in the East. Moreover, Theoderic had reason to fear that pro-Byzantine Roman Church groupings, and some Roman senators, looked to the eastern empire as a means of removing the Goths from power in Italy. The pro-eastern deacon John – probably the same deacon John who was a friend of Boethius[25] – was elected Pope in August 523. Though

---

[24] It was not merely Anastasius' Monophysite sympathies (which changed towards the end of his reign) but also the intransigence of Popes Symmachus and Hormisdas (who subsequently negotiated with Justin) that made conciliation impossible.

[25] Boethius dedicated tractates 2, 3, and 5 of his theological writings (*Op. sac.*) to him. His identity with John I cannot be assumed to be certain: see Chadwick (1981) 53 (*ODP*

conciliatory towards Theoderic, he failed, in his capacity as leader of a diplomatic mission on Theoderic's behalf in 526, to secure from Justin religious toleration for eastern Arians. This failure, and the subsequent death of John in Ravenna while detained by Theoderic, led to a drastic deterioration in the relations between Rome and the Goths: open confrontation was only avoided by Theoderic's death in August 526. It is not inconceivable that Boethius was held hostage at Pavia against the outcome of the papal mission to Constantinople in 526, sentenced but not executed.[26]

To turn to the first question asked above. The last years of Theoderic's reign were clouded by uncertainty and suspicion. In the preceding paragraph the changes ensuing upon the accession of Justin as emperor have been outlined. But there were other problems pressing upon the ageing king. His Visigoth son-in-law and, in all probability, designated successor Eutharic Cillica died, probably in 522. Vandal Africa entered into an alliance with Constantinople in 523: when, at the end of his reign, Theoderic set about building a fleet, it was as much the Vandal as the eastern imperial threat that he feared. In Italy ecclesiastical allies like Ennodius bishop of Pavia and Pope Hormisdas died. Theoderic may have felt that the world was turning against him, and, in such circumstances, might have grown suspicious of anybody in his entourage, and ready to listen to malign gossip and insinuations about even such counsellors as Boethius. The charges against Albinus and Boethius of pro-Byzantine conspiracy, combined with Boethius' traditionalist defence of the senate, came at a disastrous moment in an ever more unstable and insecure court.

We cannot be certain whether there was any substance in the accusations of treason against Boethius. Many of his senatorial class were increasingly sympathetic to Constantinople. If John the deacon, the friend of Boethius, is identical with Pope John I, a pro-eastern cleric, then it is all the more likely that Boethius also looked to Constantinople. But that need not have meant anti-Gothic and pro-Byzantine political partisanship. John's predecessor Hormisdas had shown that theological reunification with the East and a co-operative attitude towards Theoderic were not incompatible. Yet the times were changing, and the traditionalist in Boethius may have longed for the re-establishment of the old relationship between the emperor and his Roman senate. But we cannot know how secret this longing was, or how apparent to interested observers, or even if there was such longing.

In a theological tractate probably written towards 520 Boethius

---

54 is too confident). On John I's mission to Justin and its aftermath (especially in relation to Boethius' trial and execution) see J. Richards, *The Popes and the Papacy in the Early Middle Ages, 476-752* (London 1979) 111ff.

[26] See Chadwick (1981) 62.

engages in a subtle analysis of the philosophical issues involved in the Christological controversy.[27] The stance which he adopts in this treatise, while it defends the Chalcedonian position, also assumes what was to become known as the Theopaschite formula (that in Christ God suffers in the flesh) proposed by Scythian monks about the same time as a means of preserving the diphysite doctrine without subscribing to Nestorianism (a radical diphysite position which seemed to compromise the unity of Christ's person). Boethius' conclusions anticipated the Christological doctrine which was ultimately favoured by Justinian. Although it is tempting to see in Boethius' arguments a political aim that might identify him as an explicitly pro-Byzantine partisan, this is unlikely.[28] His subtle analysis of the concepts of nature and person, and his careful use of Neoplatonic and Augustinian arguments, suggest that he was drawn to elucidate the terms of the controversy by a wish to bring clarity to an area where linguistic and logical confusion reigned; and his arguments have the force of conviction without manipulation. It would be untrue to assert that he is not personally engaged in what he writes in his tractate. But his engagement is that of the analytical philosopher, not that of the politically committed theologian. We certainly cannot assert that an obvious political tendency is apparent in this work, or that it contributed in any way to the downfall of Boethius. It was written before he was appointed Master of Offices by Theoderic. Boethius' fall was sudden, a symptom of the crisis mentality of the Ostrogothic court in the last years of Theoderic's reign.

(ii) Boethius the writer

The *Variae* of Cassiodorus present the image of a Theoderic concerned with the preservation of Roman culture in Italy.[29] This concern ranged over the arts and sciences, to philosophy and the restoration of civic buildings. In these spheres he found willing support among the senatorial families. The attitude to the past of the senatorial aristocracy was a generous one. Though Christianized, the Roman senatorial class was conscious of, and devoted to, its non-Christian past. This, at least, is true of those individual members of that class who occupied themselves with such matters. Large sums might be spent on the restoration of classical buildings, such as the theatre of Pompey in Rome. But the aristocrats were also builders of Christian

[27] Tractate 5 of *Op. sac.*, *Contra Eutychen et Nestorium* (pp. 72ff., Loeb edn.). Chadwick (1981) 180-202 gives a detailed analysis of the arguments and their significance. Schurr (1935) 108ff. remains indispensable. Cf. also Mair (1981) 208ff.

[28] Bark (1943/4), esp. 417ff., argues for the political tendency of Boethius' theological views: Matthews (1981) 43 n. 60 has reservations.

[29] See O'Donnell (1979) 55-102; Matthews (1981) 16ff.; Kirkby (1981); Chadwick (1981) 1ff.

churches. Nor was there felt to be any contradiction between these activities, any more than there was between being Christian and continuing to observe certain ancient pagan festivals, such as the Lupercalia.[30] This positive attitude to a non-Christian past extended to literature and philosophy. The scholarly preservation of classical literature through the editing of texts and the composition of commentaries is a feature both of the scholarship of members of the senatorial class and of the professional and institutionalized activity of the period. In the adoptive family of Boethius, this concern is exemplified in Symmachus' interest in Macrobius, whose writings evoke the Neoplatonic and antiquarian religious interests of a remarkable group of fourth-century pagan intellectuals, including Symmachus' great-grandfather, the leading senator of his day, Q. Aurelius Symmachus.[31] Around 500 a collection of the letters of this Symmachus was published: the defender of paganism against Ambrose and the emperor Valentinian II was recognized as a venerable ancestor by his pious Christian descendants.[32]

Boethius' literary activity reflects these attitudes. It is not surprising that, as a layman from a Christian intellectual family, he should compose theological treatises which address questions of Christology, the doctrine of the Trinity, the historical content of Christian faith, and the nature of goodness.[33] In doing so, he was preaching what he and other members of his class were practising in their involvement in the ecclesiastical life of Rome, whether in legal or organizational capacities. It is no exaggeration to say that the Church in Rome in his day was led by the aristocracy and clergy who either came from the great families, or were bound to them in the traditional Roman client-patron relationship. The two addressees of four of the five theological tractates – Symmachus and the deacon John, later to be Pope – characterize the circle from which these works emanate, and for which they are intended.

But it is no more surprising that much of Boethius' literary activity should have concerned itself with the non-Christian tradition.[34] It was not an activity motivated by any need to achieve a synthesis between secular and Christian literature and thought. The two elements – the Christian and the secular – were seen as complementary. The value of

[30] See Pope Gelasius' (492-6) *Tractate* 6 (pp. 598ff. Thiel ~ *Collectio Avellana, CSEL* 35.453ff.); cf. Chadwick (1981) 12ff.; *ODP* 48f.

[31] See n. 7 above. On Macrobius see J. Flamant, *Macrobe et le Néo-Platonisme latin, à la fin du IVe siècle* (Leiden 1977); Courcelle (1948) 3-36.

[32] See S. Roda, 'Alcune ipotesi sulla prima edizione dell' epistolario di Simmaco', *La Parola del Passato* 35 (1979) 31-54.

[33] On Boethius' theological works see Schurr (1935); Mair (1981); Chadwick (1981) 174-222. There is a new edition by M. Elsässer, *Boethius: Die Theologischen Traktate* (Hamburg 1988).

[34] See Courcelle (1948) 257-312; Kirkby (1981).

classical literature in the education of the Christian was perceived and accepted: it alone provided the training in eloquence and literary style which was prized and necessary for social and political success, as well as for a clerical career. Classical philosophy is the counterpart, not the rival, of Christian theology, and both cultivate spiritual liberation and intellectual illumination. Whether in Cassiodorus' educational plans for his monastic school at Vivarium, or in Boethius' concern with the philosophical tradition and the value of the liberal arts,[35] the same Christian cultural aims are found in alliance with an affirmative attitude to the classical heritage. These men are so self-assured in their Christianity (as well they might be in a Christianized society) that no need is perceived to make explicit reference to that Christianity when dealing with secular topics. It is important to bear this in mind when considering the absence of explicit Christian elements in the *Consolation*.[36]

Apart from the *Consolation*, the extant works of Boethius are technical in character. But we do know that he also wrote a pastoral poem, and this is likely to have been, not so much a poem in the Christian pastoral manner, as one in which the conventions familiar to Boethius from Virgil's *Eclogues* were employed: at all events, if the absence of Christian elements in the *Consolation* is anything to go by, we might expect Boethius' pastoral to be no less classical.[37] The poet of the *Consolation* refers to his earlier compositions (1 m. 1.1), and the skill and mastery of diverse metres in that work betray the experienced artist. Two poems – an epigram by Ennodius (*Carm.* 2,132) and an elegy by Maximianus Etruscus (*Eleg.* 3) – feature Boethius, in the first instance as addressee, in the second as a character. The themes of these poems are erotic, and conjure up the image of a Boethius who is an unscrupulous philanderer and even, in the second poem, a procurer. Boethian scholars have, for the most part, refused to believe that the sober and pious persona evoked in the *Consolation* is identical with the sexual adventurer of these verses. Shanzer is an exception, but she does not consider one possibility.[38] It may well be the case that the two poems describe an aspect of Boethius' behaviour of which we otherwise know nothing. But it is no less likely that they evoke a persona projected in erotic poems of Boethius, which themselves may or may not describe his actual behaviour. It would not

[35] See O'Donnell (1979) 177ff.; Chadwick (1981) 69ff.; Hadot (1984) 191ff.

[36] See pp. 24ff. below.

[37] Cassiodorus, *Ordo generis Cassiodororum*, ll. 17f. (*CCL* 96, p. v): *condidit et carmen bucolicum*; see W. Schmid, 'Tityrus Christianus', *Rheinisches Museum* 96 (1953) 101-65 (here 110).

[38] Shanzer (1983a). Barnish (1990) 20-8 develops the observations of F. Wilhelm ('Maximianus und Boethius', *Rheinisches Museum* 62 [1907] 601-14) on reminiscences of *Cons. phil.* in Maximianus' elegies, and sees in them an extended comic rehandling (with serious undertones) of themes of Boethius' work.

be surprising if Boethius, like his contemporary Ennodius, bishop of Pavia, occasionally turned his hand to bawdy verses. In a literary joke poetic persona and real character (or behaviour) are apt to be confused, and that is what may be happening in the verses of Ennodius and Maximianus.[39]

When we turn to the technical or scholarly writings of Boethius, we observe that their unifying factor is a concern with the educational disciplines known as the liberal arts. Boethius devoted his attention to the four mathematical disciplines (to which he was apparently the first to give the name of *quadruvium*)[40] of arithmetic, music, geometry, and astronomy, and to the study of logic. He may well have felt that the remaining disciplines of grammar (where Donatus was the authority, and where Priscian was active in Boethius' day and in contact with Symmachus, Boethius' father-in-law) and rhetoric (where Cicero, Quintilian, and Marius Victorinus were used) had been adequately covered. At all events, he betrays no plan of a comprehensive programme of writings on all the liberal arts.

In his works on mathematics and logic Boethius claims no originality.[41] He is a transmitter of scientific knowledge about whose survival and tendance he is concerned. The extant works on arithmetic and music are indebted to the Pythagorean-Platonic tradition, and owe most of their content to Nicomachus of Gerasa (the second-century Pythagorean) and, in the case of music, also to Ptolemy. Boethius' musical theory is less concerned with the actual art of music (the influence of Aristoxenus is negligible) than with the mathematical properties of musical structures, such as the proportionality of harmonic ratios. His work on music is in no sense a practitioner's handbook, but rather a guide to the pervasive presence of harmonious order in the universe. The influence of his musicology on the themes of the *Consolation* is discussed below.[42]

Boethius certainly intended to write on geometry and astronomy as well as on arithmetic and music, but the works are lost, and it is not even certain that he completed an astronomical work (the evidence for a geometrical treatise is clearer). His works on logic, on the other hand, form the most substantial part of his *oeuvre*.[43]

[39] On the creation of a (changing) poetic persona in Tibullus see F.-H. Mutschler, *Die poetische Kunst Tibulls* (Studien zur klassischen Philologie 18, Frankfurt 1985) 168ff., 294ff. See Williams (1968) 524ff.; Nisbet/Hubbard 1.xxvf. (Horace); J. Griffin, *Latin Poets and Roman Life* (London 1985) 48ff. (mainly on Propertius). Bawdy in Ennodius: *Carm.* 2.29, 30, 51-5, etc.; cf. Shanzer (1983a) 185 n. 1.

[40] *arith.* 1.1 (pp. 7.25; 9.28); see A. Kappelmacher, 'Der schriftstellerische Plan des Boethius', *Wiener Studien* 46 (1929) 215-25 (reprinted in Fuhrmann/Gruber [1984] 71-81) for a discussion of Boethius' possible programme of writings.

[41] On these writings see Chadwick (1981) 69-107; on *De institutione musica* see also Chamberlain (1970).

[42] See pp. 54ff.; 149f.

[43] See especially F. Solmsen, 'Boethius and the Organon', *American Journal of*

Logic fascinated Boethius, and he makes accurate and stringent use of it in his theological tractates, and in the last book of the *Consolation*, when he discusses the problem of divine foreknowledge and human free will. His ambitions in philosophy, however, were broader in scope than the discipline of logic. He had intended to translate all of Aristotle and of Plato into Latin, and furnish the translations with commentaries.[44] Of this grandiose plan only a part was achieved. Nothing of his Plato project survives: he may never have undertaken it. Of Aristotle he translated the major part of the so-called *Organon* (*Categories, De Interpretatione, Prior Analytics* and *Posterior Analytics, Topics*, and *Sophistici Elenchi*), to which may be added his translation of Porphyry's *Isagoge*, or introduction to Aristotelian logic.[45] We possess two commentaries of his on the *Isagoge*, and one on each book of the *Organon* except the *Topics* and the *Analytics*. We do not know if he ever wrote on these last two: a commentary on Cicero's *Topics* (which itself purports to be a translation of Aristotle) by Boethius is, however, also extant. There are, in addition, five extant treatises on logical topics, covering much of the ground of Aristotelian and later Peripatetic logic. This corpus is worthy of Barnes's description of it as 'a paradigm of sustained and systematic scholarship'.[46] Much of the content of the works is derivative, but the commentaries are not necessarily mere translations from Greek sources: Boethius is likely to have at least adapted and presented his material for his Latin audience as he thought most appropriate.[47]

Boethius is influenced by Porphyry's doctrine of the harmony of Plato and Aristotle, and Porphyry will have been the source of much of his knowledge of the exegetical Peripatetic tradition: his Aristotle is perceived within a Platonic metaphysical framework.[48] But the precise influence of the later Neoplatonic tradition upon his logic is difficult to prove; and this makes the hypothesis that Boethius studied under Ammonius the son of Hermeias at Alexandria as a young man

---

Philology 31 (1944) 69-74; J. Shiel, 'Boethius' Commentaries on Aristotle', *Mediaeval and Renaissance Studies* 4 (1958) 217-44 (reprinted with postscript in Fuhrmann/ Gruber [1984] 155-83); E. Stump, 'Boethius' works on the Topics', *Vivarium* 12 (1974) 77-93; Barnes (1981); Chadwick (1981) 108-73.

[44] *In Int.* II 2.3 (pp. 79f.): the passage is translated by Barnes (1981) 74.

[45] The best editions of the extant translations are in *Aristoteles Latinus* 1-3, 5, and 6 (1961-75): L. Minio-Paluello's Latin introductions are indispensable.

[46] Barnes (1981) 75; cf. ib. 85f. for details of editions of both translations and commentaries.

[47] For the argument that Boethius' Aristotle commentaries are, in essence, translations of Greek scholia see Shiel (n. 43 above); L. Minio-Paluello, 'Les traductions et les commentaires aristotéliciens de Boèce', *Studia Patristica* 2.2 (Berlin 1957) 358-65, agrees. But dissent is registered by, among others, Stump (n. 43 above); Barnes (1981) 79f.; Chadwick (1981) 129ff., 163.

[48] *In Int.* II 2.3 (pp. 79f.). Cf. Courcelle (1948) 264ff.; J. Bidez, 'Boèce et Porphyre', *Revue belge de philologie et d'histoire* 2 (1923) 189-201; Chadwick (1981) 120ff.

unconvincing.[49] In the *Consolation* the influence of Ammonius' Athenian teacher Proclus is more evident than that of Ammonius himself.[50] Boethius' contact with the later Neoplatonic schools is certainly demonstrable, and there is nothing inherently implausible in the view that Boethius spent some of his student days in Alexandria or (less likely) Athens, but we have no evidence which proves that this is so, and that Boethius was not merely familiar with some of the later Neoplatonists' writings, and also indirectly acquainted with their method.

Boethius' cultural programme is the culmination of a long Roman tradition of the transmission of Greek science and thought into Latin. Far from participating in a Hellenic renaissance, he developed and extended what others since Cicero's day had done.[51] In typically traditional manner he sees his writings as a counterpart and complement to his political activity.[52] Contemporaries like Cassiodorus appreciated the work of cultural transmission upon which he embarked.[53] In so doing, Boethius was affirming the continuity of a tradition, but he was also extending it, to embrace the latest developments in Greek Platonism, where this seemed to advance beyond what Porphyry and his immediate predecessors had achieved. This concern extends to the use of later Platonic sources in his theological tractates, though their influence there is counterbalanced by the powerful presence of Augustine.[54]

Boethius' technical writings are not embellished by literary ornament. He may allude to Latin poets like Virgil and Horace in the theological tractate *De fide catholica*, and write a rhetorically cadenced coda to the work;[55] and the introduction to the *Contra Eutychen et Nestorium* is a lively narrative of the circumstances which led him to write the work.[56] But these are isolated elements in works where rigour of argument and abundance of specialist detail predominate. The first commentary on Porphyry's *Isagoge* is written in dialogue

---

[49] Courcelle (1948) 268ff. (and elsewhere) is the proponent of this hypothesis. Chadwick (1981) 127ff. demonstrates the influence of Iamblichus and Syrianus upon Boethius' logic.

[50] See especially Klingner (1921) 43ff., 107ff.

[51] For the beginnings of this tradition see E. Rawson, *Intellectual Life in the Late Roman Republic* (London 1985). The notion of a 'Hellenic Renaissance' in Boethius' Italy is advocated by Courcelle (1948) 258f.; cf. Momigliano (1955). Kirkby (1981), esp. 55ff., provides a necessary corrective.

[52] Cf. esp. *In Cat.* 2 (*PL* 64.201B); *Cons. phil.* 1.4.5ff. See J. Shiel, 'Boethius the Hellenist', *History Today* 14 (1964) 678-86; Lerer (1985) 21f.

[53] *Ordo generis Cassiodororum*, ll. 18ff. (*CCL* 96, p. v); *Variae* 1.40; 1.45. Cf. Ennodius, *Ep.* 8.1 (§370, *MGH* 7.268).

[54] See Chadwick (1981) 203ff.

[55] *Op. sac.* 4, l. 78 (p. 58, Loeb edn.): *ima petierat*; cf. Virgil, *Georg.* 1.142; *Aen.* 8.67. Ib., l. 143 (p. 62): *numerosam annorum seriem*; cf. Horace, *Odes* 3.30.4f. Coda: ib., ll. 244ff. (pp. 68ff.). See Chadwick (1981) 176 and n. 1.

[56] *Op. sac.* 5, *praef.* (pp. 72ff., Loeb edn.).

form, with Boethius as the teacher and a character called Fabius as the
pupil. The opening of the work provides a succinct dramatic setting (a
winter retreat in the Aurelian mountains) reminiscent of the dialogues
of Cicero and Augustine, but with greater economy and less art.[57]
Fabius is likely to be a literary fiction: no attempt is made to
characterize him, and he is mainly a vehicle to recite Porphyry's text
and Marius Victorinus' commentary upon it. Lerer compares the
method adopted by Boethius with that of Fulgentius' *De Continentia*.[58]
Whether Boethius in this early dialogue foreshadows Philosophy in the
Consolation, and Fabius the prisoner, may be doubted.[59] The method of
the early dialogue is that of the traditional master-pupil exposé, as in
Cicero's *Tusculan Disputations*, and the tone is dictated by the needs of
exegesis, both of Porphyry's text and of Victorinus' treatment of it.
Boethius shows himself to be at home in the application of the literary
style apposite to his context. A similar fluency is apparent in the prose
prefaces to some of his theological tractates, with their traditional topoi
(appeals to the addressee's benevolence, presentation of works as
responses to requests from the dedicatee or others, self-depreciation,
and emphasis placed upon the labour involved), a phenomenon which
may also be observed in the prefatory letter to the *De institutione
arithmetica*.[60] All this suggests a conventional literary education
turned to practical effect, in the manner praised and practised by
Ennodius.[61] It is not, however, distinctive enough to amount to a
personal literary strategy culminating in the *Consolation*, as Lerer
argues.[62] Nothing in these earlier works really prepares us for the
surprise engendered by a reading of the *Consolation* and a consideration
of its complex literary form; and, while it is true that in some of the
earlier works, especially in the first commentary on the *Isagoge* and the
theological tractates, Boethius projects an authorial persona, there can
be no comparison between the conventional personae of teacher and
exponent in these works, and the figures of Philosophy and the prisoner
in the *Consolation*. That book, read against the background of Boethius'
other writings, is as startling and unpredictable as his terrible end.

(iii) The *Consolation*: genre and themes

Boethius has often been considered to be the last writer and thinker of
Latin antiquity and the first of the medieval period: writers as different

[57] *In Porph. Isag.* I 1.1 (*CSEL* 48.3f.).
[58] Lerer (1985) 69ff.
[59] Lerer (1985) 74f. argues for this foreshadowing.
[60] See Kirkby (1981) 57ff.; cf. T. Janson, *Latin Prose Prefaces: Studies in Literary Conventions* (Stockholm 1964).
[61] In e.g. his *Paraenesis didascalica* (*Opusc.* 6 = §452, *MGH* 7.310-15) and *Ep.* 8.1 (see n. 53 above).
[62] Lerer (1985) 69-93; cf. ib. 25ff.

as the fifteenth-century humanist Lorenzo Valla and the historian of Rome's decline and fall, Edward Gibbon, have voiced the view that he rightly belongs to the classical tradition, and yet that it is not merely his later influence and authority that makes him a 'founder of the Middle Ages'.[63] The influences upon the *Consolation* are many and varied, and they, too, point towards Boethius' debt to Greek and Roman antecedents. Indeed, perhaps more than in his writings on the liberal arts and on logic, the *Consolation* reveals a Boethius whose imaginative and intellectual worlds are firmly rooted in Latin literature from Cicero to Seneca.

But the *Consolation* is more than a late Latin work. It is part of a tradition of those writers who, in the words of Diogenes Laertius, 'philosophize in verse' (9.22). Diogenes names as representatives of this tradition Hesiod, Xenophanes, Parmenides, and Empedocles. To that list we would probably wish to add Lucretius, as well as the philosophically permeated didactic astronomical poems of Aratus and Manilius. What all these poets' works have in common is their form and their length. They are written in hexameters, the metre of epic; and they provide a comprehensive description of a world-picture.[64] Xenophanes is an exception: he wrote several short poems in a variety of metres. But the work later known as *peri phuseôs* was clearly written in hexameters, and its few surviving fragments are likely to have been parts of a greater whole.[65] It is this work that leads to Xenophanes' inclusion in the company of Hesiod and the other poets referred to by Diogenes Laertius.

There was no recognized genre of didactic poetry in antiquity.[66] Because they wrote hexameter verses (*epê*), Parmenides and Empedocles were included among the *epopoioi*, or epic poets. This

[63] See E.K. Rand, *The Founders of the Middle Ages* (Cambridge, Mass. 1928) 135-80. On Valla's and other humanists' views see A. Grafton, 'Epilogue: Boethius in the Renaissance', in Gibson (1981) 410-15. Gibbon's famous judgement on the *Consolation* – 'a golden volume not unworthy of the leisure of Plato or Tully, but which claims incomparable merit from the barbarism of the times and the situation of the author' (ed. Bury, 4.201) – need not have an ironical connotation, as Chadwick (1981) xv suggests, if leisure (*skholê, otium*) be the freedom from the need to work in order to secure a livelihood that Plato, Cicero, and Gibbon enjoyed, and 'not unworthy' a Latinizing emphatic affirmative.

[64] Manilius 2.1ff. acknowledges both the formal and the thematic aspects of the tradition: see pp. 57f. below. On the tradition of didactic poetry see B. Effe, *Dichtung und Lehre. Untersuchungen zur Typologie des antiken Lehrgedichts* (Zetemata 69, Munich 1977); E. Pöhlmann, 'Charakteristika des römischen Lehrgedichts', *ANRW* I 3 (1973) 813-901.

[65] See E. Heitsch (ed.), *Xenophanes* (Munich/Zürich 1983) 8f. A contrary view is given in G.S. Kirk/J.E. Raven/M. Schofield, *The Presocratic Philosophers*, 2nd edn. (Cambridge 1983) 166f.

[66] The category distinguished in the *Tractatus Coislinianus* (on which see Grube [1965] 144ff.) – theoretical (or practical) educational non-imitative poetry – is exceptional in ancient literary criticism. See Russell (1981) 204 for its division of kinds of poetry.

created problems for theoretical classifiers of kinds of poetry. In his
Poetics Aristotle remarks that Homer and Empedocles have nothing
but their metre in common, and that Empedocles is not a poet as
Homer is, but rather a scientific writer on nature *(phusiologos)*.[67]
Seen from the perspectives of this didactic philosophical poetry, the
Consolation is an exception in some respects. It is not written in
hexameters, but is rather a mixture of alternating prose and verse. It
contains 39 poems in a variety of metres, which can be seen as inserts
in a prose structure (though the opening elegy is also the work's
introduction). The poems are of various lengths: the shortest has 6
lines (3 m. 3), the longest 58 (3 m. 12). There is similar variety in the
lengths of the prose sections: the shortest takes up only 15 lines in a
standard modern edition (1.2), the longest 187 (4.6).[68] Modern scholars
who have considered the form and type of work of which the
Consolation is an example have related it to the so-called Menippean
satire, as well as to the prosimetric works of later antiquity. Its
possible relation to these literary types should be explored, before its
principal themes and the development of its argument are sketched.

The characteristics of Menippean satire are its mixture of prose and
verse (which may, but need not be, original), and a further thematic
mixture of the serious and the comic. Quintilian *(Inst. or.* 10.1.95)
treats it as a special kind of satire, and it has in common with other
types of satire the twofold purpose of entertaining and instructing. Of
Menippus of Gadara (first half of the third century BC), after whom the
literary form is named, nothing has survived, and the Menippean
satires of his Roman adaptor M. Terentius Varro (first century BC)
survive only in fragmentary form, in short extracts.[69] Many titles of
both Menippus' and Varro's works are known: through them, the genre
may be characterized.[70] Varro uses a wide variety of metres, and
appears to link prose and verse sections closely (with at least one
mid-sentence transition). His style is colloquial, full of energy, allusive
(literary, historical, and mythological references abound), and good-
humoured rather than sarcastic. He is a critic of social foibles, and
individual defects of character. He uses dialogue form in the satires.
Seneca's *Apocolocyntosis (Pumpkinification)* is a complete Menippean
satire. As with Varro, most of the verse is original rather than
quotations. It, too, uses a wide range of metres, and dialogue form, but
its tone is bitter and personal, a savage attack on the emperor
Claudius.[71] In this latter characteristic, it is quite different from the

[67] Aristotle, *Poetics* 1447b17ff.
[68] See Bieler's *CCL* edn.
[69] See J.-P. Cèbe, *Varron. Satires Ménippées*, 6 vols. (Rome 1972-83); L. Alfonsi, 'Le
Menippee di Varrone', *ANRW* I 3 (1973) 26-59; R. Astbury (ed.), *Varro: Saturae
Menippeae* (Leipzig 1985).
[70] See pp. 17, 19f. below for a summary view of the results.
[71] See P.T. Eden (ed.), *Seneca: Apocolocyntosis* (Cambridge 1984).

'diversified sermon'[72] of a typical Varronian Menippean. Other complete Menippea of the imperial period are found in the writings of Lucian (second century AD). Lucian's verses are mostly quotations, from Homer or tragedy (generally with a mock-heroic colouring). Lucian's style is urbane and witty, often with an element of the fantastic; it shows how the individual personality and concerns of the writer could characterize his approach to the tone of the work.[73] The emperor Julian (the so-called Apostate) wrote a Menippean satire, the *Kronia*, in the mid-fourth century AD, in which various Roman emperors are passed in review for divinization. The resemblance to the 'pumpkinification' of Claudius is evident, but superficial. In Julian's review, Caligula and Nero are stock tyrants, and fare particularly badly.[74]

One commonly found characteristic of Menippean satire is its link with popular moral philosophizing, in the tradition of the diatribe, but in a less systematic and more openly comic or serio-comic tone.[75] It is difficult to define formally, beyond the already mentioned features of mixture of prose and verse, diversity of metres, and dialogue. Shanzer, following Mras, suggests that thematic rather than formal similarities are crucial to its generic definition.[76] From the themes of extant satires, and from the titles of lost ones, a group of themes can be identified. These include: the heavenly voyage; the vision of the heavens; the council of the gods; parody of mystery religions; parody of legal motifs and language. The use of personifications is common. Journeys to the underworld are a further theme, as are parody of and polemic against philosophers, and parody of epic bombast.

In late antiquity the prosimetric form enjoyed a new lease of life. From the fourth century onwards, a variety of works, epistolary, encyclopaedic, and mythographical, are composed in a mixture of prose and verse. Boethius' *Consolation* is undoubtedly part of this 'boom in serious prosimetry'.[77] Two questions may be asked. Is the *Consolation*

---

[72] Parsons (1971) 64.

[73] See C. Robinson, *Lucian* (London 1979), esp. 9ff., who is cautious about attempts to define Menippean influence upon Lucian. Kirk (1982) tries to find links between Lucian and Boethius, but the alleged parallels which he adduces are no more than commonplaces of the diatribe tradition. Crabbe's (1981b, 268f. n. 71) comparison of Lucian's *Piscator* with the dramatic setting of *Cons. phil.* is, however, illuminating, even if she (quite rightly) does not attempt to prove that Lucian influences Boethius.

[74] See Eden (n. 71 above) 16.

[75] See Mras (1914), esp. 396ff. On diatribe Oltramare (1926) remains fundamental. Rutherford (1989) 21f. succinctly characterizes its salient features. Cf. N. Rudd, *The Satires of Horace* (Cambridge 1966, reprinted Bristol 1982) 1-35, 160-201; Gruber (1978) 27ff.

[76] Shanzer (1986a) 280; Shanzer (1986b) 31, 33ff.

[77] Parsons (1971) 65. Cf. A. Scherbantin, *Satura Menippea. Die Geschichte eines Genos* (Diss. Graz 1951); D. Bartonková, 'Prosimetrum, the Mixed Style, in Ancient Literature', *Eirene* 14 (1976) 65-92; Gruber (1978) 16ff.; Gruber (1981). For the medieval origins of the term *prosimetrum* see E. Norden, *Die antike Kunstprosa*, 2nd edn. (Leipzig/Berlin

an instance of a new kind of use of the prosimetric form, and what are its antecedents? And, secondly, what is the precise relation between the *Consolation* and the Menippean tradition?

Gruber has argued that, despite elements of continuity, a fundamentally new prosimetric movement originates (as far as our sources can tell us) in the fourth century.[78] What it has in common with the earlier Menippean tradition are such features as literary display, moral exhortation, and the use of dialogue. What is new about the later works is their concern with the display of rhetorical versatility as an end in itself, and the frequent thematic concern with educational themes. This new development may have originated in works of brief scope, such as some of the prosimetric letters of Ausonius, Paulinus of Nola, or – to give a later, fifth-century example – letters of Sidonius Apollinaris. The mixture of prose and verse is sometimes (in Gruber's phrase) of the 'preface-type', that is, a prose introduction to a poem with the same theme. The poem gives added emphasis to the theme, and provides a poetic signature or *sphragis* characteristic of the author (e.g. Ausonius, *Ep.* 26). This type is not, strictly speaking, prosimetric: it is, in fact, a version of the epistolary form of a letter introducing a poem.[79] This last kind, when the letter gives information about the origin, theme, title, and other prefatory details, is also found in Ausonius.[80] The one genuinely prosimetric form which Gruber identifies in Ausonius is *Ep.* 23, which begins with a full-blown poetic description of night, followed by a down-to-earth prose description of the time and date.[81] There is a deliberate change of tone in the transition from verse to prose, and yet there is, as later in the work, continuity and thematic progression. Furthermore, while the prefatory verses are Ausonius' own, the other verses in the letter are quotations from Paulinus' verse epitome of Suetonius' *De regibus*, whose receipt, with a letter of Paulinus, Ausonius is acknowledging. There is no satirical element in Ausonius' letter, however: it is a display of literary and stylistic competence. Paulinus' own *Ep.* 8 is prosimetric, and the verses have the function announced in the prose preface of leading the reader by their art to thoughts of the divine creator of all harmony: Paulinus characterizes them as a spiritual *remedium*. The introduction of verse here has an unmistakable

---

1909) 756 n. 4; Scherbantin, op. cit. 192f. The major late antique prosimetra are Martianus Capella's *De nuptiis Philologiae et Mercurii* (Shanzer [1986b] is an indispensable commentary on Book 1), Fulgentius' *Mitologiae*, and *Cons. phil.* Gruber (1981) gives references to several minor works.

[78] Gruber (1981).

[79] Cf. e.g. the introductory letter and epigram in Martial 8.

[80] For example, *Epicedion in patrem* (*Opusc.* 3.4); *Epitaphia heroum qui bello Troico interfuerunt* (*Opusc.* 6); prose and verse prefaces to *Parentalia* (*Opusc.* 4). Further examples are given by Gruber (1981) 216ff.

[81] Cf. the similar sequence in Seneca, *Apocol.* 2.

protreptic function characteristic of much later prosimetric literature, not least of the *Consolation*.

Gruber argues that Martianus Capella takes up the concerns of the later prosimetrum with rhetorical and educational matters and expands these in a work of encyclopaedic scope.[82] Martianus is aware of the Menippean tradition, but this takes little more than the form of acknowledging that the 'tediousness' (*taedium*) of his subject may be relieved by the 'pleasantness and wit' (*lepor, iocus*) of verse (8.809). The poems of Martianus' work, in fifteen different metres, break the monotony of the often bleak technical detail. They articulate the work structurally, as well as providing lyrical climaxes at key points. Gruber sees the presence of the personification Satura as a minimal aesthetic gesture in the direction of the Menippean tradition. For him, Martianus' work is formally similar to the short *Paraenesis didascalica* of Boethius' contemporary Ennodius, in which the author uses the prosimetric form to advocate the need for moral virtues as a prerequisite of education.[83] The several virtues, and then some of the liberal arts, are introduced in verse form; but the display of rhetoric's power in both prose and verse indicates that, for Ennodius, skill in the two mediums is essential for the educated person – a skill which he displays, virtuoso-fashion, in the little work itself. In Gruber's account, the Menippean elements in these later works are vestigial, and he emphasizes rather the new beginning which the prosimetric works of the fourth and fifth centuries represent.

Shanzer, on the other hand, takes Gruber to task for tending to blur the distinction between prosimetry and Menippean satire in this later tradition.[84] While she appears to misread Gruber's discussion of Ausonius *Ep.* 26, and his point about prose introductions to poetry – Gruber is not maintaining that all such forms are prosimetric, but only those where there is thematic progression or variety of tone and style, as with Ausonius, *Ep.* 23, discussed above – Shanzer may be right to suggest that, in the case of Martianus, Gruber is too ready to see his use of *satura* as nothing more than prosimetry. Shanzer argues that there are instances of the prosimetric form that are not *saturae* in any sense. But it is in the use of what she identifies as Menippean themes that she sees the essentially satirical form of Martianus' work. For her, it is Menippean because of the central metaphor of the *De nuptiis*, the heavenly voyage. The other themes – the council of the gods, the use of personifications, parody of legal motifs and language, use of material from mystery religious cults (though it is not easy to establish that Martianus uses it in parodistic manner), afterlife themes, a variation

---

[82] Gruber (1981) 221; cf. 210.
[83] See n. 61 above. Cf. R.A. Rallo Freni (ed.), *Magno Felice Ennodio. La Paraenesis didascalica* (Messina 1970).
[84] Shanzer (1986b) 30 n. 6, 42.

of the motif of the thirteenth labour of Hercules, erudite comedy about philosophers in the afterlife – are all adduced to corroborate her argument.[85] Shanzer stresses the comic elements in Martianus – he does undeniably have a learned, if heavy-handed, sense of humour – and, in particular, his acknowledgment of Varro as antecedent. This point, if accepted, would go far beyond Gruber's vestigial gesture towards the satiric element which is all that he finds Menippean about Martianus. Shanzer's main argument for Varronian influence upon Martianus is the latter's purported use of Varro's *Onos lyras*.[86] In Martianus (6.576f.; 8.806f.) the narrator is accused by Satura of not recognizing his true mother, Philosophy, of labouring to no avail, of being a donkey, and of having his sensibility dulled by his legal work: the influence of some Varronian themes from the *Onos lyras* satire may be reflected here, such as the plight of the 'uncultured man' (*amousos*) and the power of music, and the characterization of the *amousos* as advocate or politician. Moreover, as Shanzer further suggests, Varro's satire may have used the themes of the ascent of the soul and – linked to it – that of the Pythagorean celestial lyre of heavenly harmonic intervals: these themes can be found in Martianus' reference to Jupiter's celestial lyre (1.66), and to his description of Philologia's heavenly journey in terms of tonal intervals (*tonoi*) as well as distances (2.169ff.). Shanzer's account of the Varro satire is perforce speculative. But it raises the possibility that Martianus is using specific allusions to Varro to indicate programmatically that his work is a serio-comic Menippean satire.

Even if all of Shanzer's argument is not accepted, it undoubtedly remains the case that Martianus' work goes far beyond the prosimetra of late antiquity discussed by Gruber. The extravagant dramatic setting, the allegory, the colourful use of detail, the prevalence of Menippean themes and motifs – these are all reasons for admitting Martianus' debt to the earlier Menippean tradition. Martianus' use of that tradition is evolutionary, but also revolutionary in its inclusion of encyclopaedic material. His work is not merely a development of the didactic prosimetrum identified by Gruber (though it may owe something to it), but it is also and above all, as Shanzer, following and modifying Mras, argues, a reconciliation of Varro the scholar with Varro the poet.[87]

Let us now turn back to the *Consolation*, and to the two questions asked above. In answering them, it will be useful to begin with a brief

[85] Ib. 33ff.

[86] Ib. 38ff.; cf. Shanzer (1986a) 275ff.

[87] Mras (1914) 391; Shanzer (1986b) 42ff. See also L. Cristante, 'La *sphragis* di Marziano Capella (*spoudogeloion*: autobiografia e autoironia)', *Latomus* 37 (1978) 679-704 (the *sphragis* of Martianus' work alludes [9.998] to the Varronian etymology of *satura*). On poetic uses of the *sphragis* see Nisbet/Hubbard 2.335f. and index s.v.

account of the affinities between Boethius and Martianus. It now seems established beyond all doubt that the *Consolation* is influenced by Martianus, even if scholars disagree on the extent of that influence.[88] The scope of the works, the beginnings in the same elegiac metre, the regular succession of prose and verse parts (verse is, however, used more frequently in Boethius), the didactic purpose – all these point to the debt of the *Consolation* to the earlier work. Shanzer adduces further possible influences, some of which are metrical. She also draws attention to Boethius' use of the *Onos lyras* motif, and sees in Philosophy's rebukes to the prisoner, the dullness of the prisoner's wits at the beginning of the work, and the (at least partial) attribution of this to political and forensic activity, traces of the themes delineated in Martianus, and discussed above.[89] If Boethius owes these to Martianus, then other motifs – the heavenly journey, the descent of the soul, the descent into Hades – while they are all intrinsic elements of the philosophy of the *Consolation*, may have suggested to him the use and acknowledgment of the Menippean tradition in his work, and may have prompted his use of the mixed prosimetric form. While, as Gruber argues, the influence of Ennodius' *Paraenesis didascalica* upon Boethius cannot be discounted, and while Ennodius' justification for the use of poetry in that little work is echoed in Boethius' talk of the *dulcedo* of the poetry of the *Consolation*,[90] the fact remains that Martianus' use of personified and symbolic figures, the dramatic setting and development of themes, and the other features referred to above, all point to the *De nuptiis* as the true inspiration of the *Consolation*. However, not everything that, for Shanzer, constitutes Martianus' influence upon Boethius need be accepted as such. She is not convincing when she argues that the dismissal of the Muses at the beginning of the *Consolation* is mild polemic against Martianus' use of the Muses, Siren-like, as the voices of the heavenly spheres.[91] It is more likely that Boethius here is influenced by, and rejecting, Fulgentius' lascivious Muses.[92] Moreover, direct Varronian influence upon Boethius is impossible to determine.

[88] Barrett (1940) 76; Courcelle (1967) 17; Gruber (1978) 18f.; Chadwick (1981) 224; Shanzer (1986b) 38f. and commentary *passim*.

[89] Shanzer (1986a) 276ff., Shanzer (1986b) 38ff.

[90] Gruber (1978) 18; Gruber (1981) 211f. Ennodius, *Paraen. didasc.* 3: ... *pressis admonitione mentibus mollioris stili cura subvenitur*; for similar claims in *Cons. phil.* see pp. 32ff. below.

[91] Shanzer (1986b) 41.

[92] Fulgentius, *Mitologiae* pp. 8, 10. On the possible influence of this other late antique *prosimetrum* on *Cons. phil.* see Klingner (1921) 114ff.; Courcelle (1948) 279. Lerer (1985) 56ff. discusses the claims of another work by Fulgentius, *De continentia Vergiliana*, to have influenced *Cons. phil.* Cameron (1984) suggests that lost *Menippeae* of the fourth-century poet Tiberianus may have been the source of common elements (such as the function of the Muses) in Martianus, Fulgentius, and Boethius: for a sceptical reaction see Shanzer (1986b) 39 n. 70.

What is, of course, lacking in Boethius is an extensive use of satire, or comic language or situations, even to the limited extent to which these are a feature of Martianus' work. Lady Philosophy may drive away the 'whores of the stage' from the prisoner's side and fulminate against them in vigorous language, but that is a colourless passage compared with the fantasy even of Martianus. The exposure of the hollow nature of the gifts of Fortune and the apparent goods in Books 2 and 3 of the *Consolation* is more in the manner of the diatribe or of hortatory literature.[93] Try as we may, we cannot really ascribe a satirical strand to the *Consolation*. Influenced by Martianus it may be, but it is a case of an influence in which certain residual features of the Menippean genre, which have affected the manner in which Martianus conceived and presented his work, have also had an effect on the *Consolation*: polymetry, the dialogue and dramatic style, the themes of ascent and descent. But the resultant work is far less Menippean than the *De nuptiis*. What Gruber says of Martianus seems to be truer of Boethius: the latter's *Consolation* has only vestiges of the Menippean satire. Its debt to Martianus serves only to highlight the fact that, just as Martianus adopted but radically modified the Menippean form, so Boethius radically develops what Martianus has done.

But there are other influences upon the *Consolation*. Recent research has properly emphasized the influence of the dialogue form upon its structure, and the progression of its argument.[94] Boethius is familiar with the dialogues of Plato (whose presentation of Socrates' last days in the *Crito* and *Phaedo* has influenced him,[95] quite apart from the thematic influences of the *Gorgias, Republic*, and *Phaedrus*), Cicero, Seneca, and Augustine. The impression which Augustine's *Soliloquia*, in particular, left upon him has resulted in clear echoes in the *Consolation*. The most striking similarity between the two works is their form as inner dialogues – in Augustine, between his *ratio* and himself, in Boethius between Lady Philosophy and the prisoner. Whether this similarity betrays a 'characteristic Christian impulse' in a situation of personal crisis, as P.L. Schmidt suggests, must remain questionable.[96] But the authorial distinction which this particular choice of literary form implies is crucial for the interpretation of the *Consolation*, as Edward Gibbon, with brilliant insight, perceived: '... the sage who could artfully combine in the same work the various

[93] See pp. 23f. below.
[94] Gruber (1978) *passim*; Gruber (1981) 32; Lerer (1985) *passim*; Silk (1939), followed by Crabbe (1981b) 251ff., emphasizes the influence of Augustine's dialogues. For literature see n. 115 below.
[95] See pp. 53f., 97ff. below.
[96] Schmidt (1977) 126f. It is more plausible to see such 'inner dialogue' as a late development of the kind of self-address that is a feature of self-analysis in poetry (from Homer on) and philosophical literature (since Heraclitus): for the tradition of such self-scrutiny see Rutherford (1989) 14ff.

riches of philosophy, poetry, and eloquence, must already have
possessed the intrepid calmness which he affected to seek.'[97] For that
reason – because Boethius is both Philosophy and the prisoner – this
book adopts the terminological distinction of Lerer, and refers to
'Boethius' when the author of the *Consolation* is meant, and 'the
prisoner' when reference is made to that character in the dialogue.

The work's title indicates that it belongs to the consolation genre.
Gruber has ably summarized its debt to that genre, of which it should
be remembered that it includes consolations in the face of exile as well
as of death.[98] In Boethius the motif of banishment is transformed when
Philosophy demonstrates to the prisoner that he is not exiled but that
he has, rather, distanced himself from the true kingdom of philosophy.
A similar adaptation of other motifs is apparent: complaint about the
place to which one has been banished, coupled with the consolatory
theme that all places are somebody's home country; or the attack on
the informers who have caused the writer's exile. Boethius, like
philosophically displaced persons before him – Cicero and Seneca are
two obvious forerunners – consoles himself with philosophical
composition, and this real-life comparison is reflected in the theme
that philosophy provides the only true consolation. The treatment of
the passion of grief and of false assessment of goods is a further
consolatory element. Much of what Philosophy says is traditional in
consolation literature: the demonstration that lack of wealth is no evil;
the exhortation to be self-sufficient; the reference to the fortunate
condition of the family of the affected one; the demonstration that the
prisoner is – despite everything – not actually unhappy in any
essential sense; the argument that nothing out of the ordinary has
happened to him. The use of precepts and illustrative examples reflects
the rhetorical form of consolation literature, as does the occasional use
of medical metaphors. Finally, Boethius, like Cicero, Ovid, and Seneca,
consoles himself rather than others.[99] He develops the consolation-
topoi into something much more philosophically profound than his
predecessors: they are, in a sense, the springboard for the presentation
of full-blown positive Platonic doctrines in the latter half of the work.
But Gruber is undoubtedly right to see in the *Consolation* many
authentic elements of the consolation genre.

[97] Gibbon (ed. Bury) 4.202.

[98] Gruber (1978) 24ff. On consolation-literature in general see Kassel (1958); Courcelle
(1967); H.-Th. Johann, *Trauer und Trost* (Studia et Testimonia Antiqua 5, Munich
1968); P. von Moos, *Consolatio. Studien zur mittellateinischen Trostliteratur über den
Tod und zum Problem der christlichen Trauer* (Munich 1971); P. Meinel, *Seneca über
seine Verbannung* (Diss. Erlangen 1972).

[99] On Cicero's lost *Consolatio* to himself on the death of his daughter see *Att.* 12.20f.
and the fragments collected in C.F.W. Mueller's Teubner edn. of Cicero's works, 4.3
(Leipzig 1879) 332ff. Seneca: *Ad Helviam matrem de consolatione* (*Dial.* 12). Ovid:
Epistulae ex Ponto, Tristia.

The *Consolation* is also a protreptic work, an exhortation to philosophy, despite the important modification that it purports, not to win a newcomer to philosophy, but rather to portray the recapture of the prisoner, who once philosophized, but has strayed.[100] Like other examples of protreptic, the *Consolation* is an introduction to philosophy, demonstrating its value in the practical conduct of life, as well as in the treatment of fundamental intellectual problems.

It should be emphasized that it is beyond the scope of this discussion of influences to concern itself with the source of specific doctrines found in the *Consolation*.[101] It attempts rather to account for influences upon its structure and themes in a generic sense. As for its poetry, despite the occurrence of Platonic themes, it is not Neoplatonic verse in the sense that the poems of Synesius or Proclus are, even granted occasional traces of similar language or motifs. Thus, while the influence of Proclus' prose tractates upon the content of the *Consolation* is evident, Proclus the poet has either no influence at all, or only a minimal one, on Boethius' verses.[102] These are above all indebted to the Latin literary tradition, as will be seen in the other chapters of this book. Boethius is immersed in that tradition, and it is Virgil, Ovid, Horace, and Seneca who are the principal formative forces on his poetry. In his practice he reflects contemporary scholarly interest in the edition and study of classical rather than 'modern' literary texts.[103]

It has often been a matter for surprise that the Christian author of the *Consolation* did not turn for consolation to his Christianity in his hour of need. The notion that he deliberately turned away from his religion to pagan philosophy has been revived in some recent scholarship.[104] The only reasonably certain Biblical echo in the text of

[100] Gruber (1978) 29ff. On protreptic see I. Düring, *Aristotle's Protrepticus: A Reconstruction* (Göteborg 1961); S.R. Slings, *A Commentary on the Platonic Clitophon* (Amsterdam 1981); cf. Rutherford (1989) 23f. Cicero's *Hortensius* was an influential Latin protreptic, especially on Augustine (see *Confessions* 3.4.7f.): collections of the fragments and testimonia by A. Grilli (Milan 1962) and L. Straume-Zimmermann (Berne/Frankfurt 1976). On Horace, *Epist.* 1.1 and 1.6 as protreptics see Macleod (1979) 22f.

[101] On the sources of the *Consolation's* doctrines see especially Klingner (1921); Barrett (1940) 102ff.; Courcelle (1967); Gruber (1978); Chadwick (1981) 228ff.

[102] On possible influences of Proclus' *Hymns* see Klingner (1921) 41ff.; Theiler (1966) 321ff.

[103] See pp. 8ff. above.

[104] See especially Momigliano (1955) 212; Hagendahl (1983) 108f.; C.J. de Vogel, 'Boethiana II', *Vivarium* 10 (1972) 1-40, and 'The Problem of Philosophy and Christian Faith in Boethius' Consolatio', in *Romanitas et Christianitas. Studia J.H. Waszink ... oblata* (Amsterdam 1973) 357-70 (reprinted in Fuhrmann/Gruber [1984] 286-301), attempts, none too convincingly, to identify specifically Christian themes in *Cons. phil.* Cf. C. Mohrmann, 'Some Remarks on the Language of Boethius' "Consolatio Philosophiae" ', in *Latin Script and Letters AD 400-900. Festschrift ... L. Bieler* (Leiden 1976) 54-61 (reprinted in Fuhrmann/Gruber [1984] 302-10) claims to find traces of Christian liturgical language in the work. See also Obertello (1974) 1.746ff.

the *Consolation* is the apparent allusion to Wisdom 8:1 at 3.12.22f. where the prisoner expresses delight at the very words used by Philosophy, and not merely at the sentiment. But it is a case of a Biblical text used to reinforce a point of natural theology, not a specifically Christian tenet.[105] At the same time, the *Consolation* contains no philosophical doctrines incompatible with Christianity. But Boethius does not proclaim this fact: although he distinguishes in his theological tractates between faith and reason, and between revealed and natural religion,[106] that disjunction is implicit rather than explicit in the *Consolation*. Boethius' confidence in the right use of reason and philosophical argument – a confidence of which the theological tractates are also full – is developed in his last work to the limit. Chadwick's assessment is convincing: 'The book is an essay in natural theology apart from revelation; and the very possibility of that rests on Christian assumptions ... The *Consolation* is a work written by a Platonist who is also a Christian, but is not a Christian work.'[107] We must resist the temptation to read the work as documentary biography and nothing more, and to conclude that, because in it Boethius makes no mention of the consolations of Christianity, he was immune or indifferent or even hostile to these in his prison cell. The *Consolation* is a literary artefact. Its prisoner is consoled by philosophy, by reason and argument. It should not be allowed to become identical with the life which, inaccessible to us, was lived in the Pavia prison. What Boethius has chosen to show us is the extent to which philosophy can make his condition bearable and, even, blessed.

For that reason, one should not be over-impressed with arguments that seek to prove that, because the *Consolation* is influenced by a number of Augustine's overtly Christian writings, its own Christianity must somehow be there, just beneath the surface.[108] The comparison with Augustine merely emphasizes Chadwick's point that there is no philosophy that is incompatible with Christianity in the *Consolation*. Augustine is undoubtedly a formal influence on the *Consolation*. Crabbe has shown the importance of the *Confessions* in this respect. The two levels of narration in the *Confessions* – 'the straightforward recounting of events and rather unusual direct addresses to the deity' –

[105] See Chadwick (1981) 237f., 248ff.
[106] Ib. 248.
[107] Ib. 251f.; cf. 249. See also the judicious remarks of Liebeschütz (1967) 550ff.
[108] That is the tendency of G. Boissier's otherwise remarkable article 'Le Christianisme de Boèce', *Journal des Savants* (1889) 449-62. Cf. Silk (1939). Crabbe (1981b) 251ff. adopts a more subtle approach (see esp. 262f.), as does Schmidt (1977) 124ff. See also Mueller-Goldingen (1989) 391ff., who argues against the influence of Augustine's views on poetry upon Boethius, and Olmsted (1989), who stresses the traditional Graeco-Roman philosophical elements in *Cons. phil.*, showing that its generic purport (21f.) and tone make it a 'religious' inquiry in ways different from Augustine's *Confessions*.

may have influenced the prosimetric form of the *Consolation*. The poems of the *Consolation*, like the addresses in the *Confessions*, are 'outside and above the adjacent proses ... possess their own thematic design which spans the entire work ... the crucial issues are permanently before our eyes regardless of the immediate details discussed. There is an element of hindsight here that is comparable to Augustine's practice.'[109] There does appear to be an important similarity of method in the two works, despite great differences in themes and attitudes.

*

Before the detailed analysis of the poetry of the *Consolation* in the other chapters of this book, the principal themes and arguments of the work should be summarized, so that the context of the specialized discussions which follow may be clearer.[110]

Book 1 portrays the lethargy of the prisoner, and the beginnings of the cure proposed by the Lady Philosophy who appears to him in his prison, dismissing the Muses who have inspired the elegiac lament with which the work begins. He is alienated from the philosophy which once he professed, although that philosophy was one of the elements of the accusation brought – falsely, it is stressed – against him. As part of his therapy he voices his complaints against his accusers and betrayers in an elaborate self-defence. In his present state all that he has retained of philosophy is the knowledge that divine reason, and not chance, governs the universe, although such reason, apparent in natural processes, is impossible to discern in human behaviour, which appears to him lawless and disorderly. The prisoner has forgotten his true nature, and the design (or teleological function) inherent in things.

Book 2 begins with Philosophy's evocation of the nature of Fortune, which, in typically fickle fashion, has both given many apparently good things – family, honours, fame – to the prisoner, and also taken many of these things away. Having sketched this general picture of Fortune, Philosophy goes on to show that the so-called gifts of Fortune – wealth, honours and power, and fame – are not genuine goods. Yet Fortune's dealings with her victims can at least be put to good effect, if they lead to insight into what is good and bad for us.

In Book 3, themes of the preceding book are taken up again, but their

[109] Crabbe (1981b) 260. On the use of prosimetry in autobiography (possibly a conversion account) in a lost work of the fourth century by Acilius Severus see Jerome, *De viris illustribus* 111; cf. Gruber (1981) 219f.

[110] See the valuable analyses of the structure of each book of *Cons. phil.* in Gruber (1978); cf. Barrett (1940) 77ff. Rand (1904) was a pioneering article, and is still valuable. See also Gigon's introduction (xviii ff.) and nn. (279ff.) in the Gegenschatz/Gigon edn.

further treatment is no mere repetition: the argument is developed. The universal will to be happy is established, and it is shown that external goods like wealth, honours, power, fame, and pleasure are inadequate means to achieve the goal of happiness. True happiness is found only in becoming like the perfect being of the highest good which needs nothing: deification is the only appropriate goal for humans. God, the highest good, is a unity, and unity is the goal of all natural things, whether they are rational or not: self-preservation is a manifestation of the natural tendency to unity. Moreover, the universe is governed by divine providence, and from the perfectly good God only good can derive. Evil has no substantial reality, but is a misdirected tendency – towards false forms of unity, towards falsely perceived 'goods'.

At the end of the Book 3 the prisoner realizes that he has known all this, but forgotten it. He is now engaging in what Plato calls *anamnêsis* or recollection. Platonic themes – the fall of the soul and its ascent to the intelligible realm through philosophy, its 'return' to the truth from which it has declined, the structure of the World-Soul, and the dynamics of procession from, and conversion to, the divine source of all things – dominate the later poems of Book 3 and the earlier ones of Book 4. In Book 4, the theme is theodicy. Why in a world governed by a perfectly good God is there evil? Philosophy's answer begins by treating a preliminary point. The paradox that the evildoers are weak and powerless, and the good strong and powerful, is defended. From the proper perspective, it is argued, the good always get their reward, for goodness is a reward in itself. Likewise, the evildoers are always punished, for they, by their evil actions, corrupt their true nature. Evil is its own punishment, for the state of being evil is one of wretchedness. The sick moral state of the evildoers is an indication that they cannot be truly happy. Happiness is the reward of the morally good. Having established this, Philosophy goes on to consider the question of theodicy proper. In a world governed by providence, fate is the name given to the human perspective upon providential order, as observed in its historical progression. Providence is eternal and non-temporal; fate unfolds in time. The providential nature of fate cannot always be appreciated by the limited human mind and perspective, so that the good which, for example, God may derive from the evils of the world, is not always apparent. The gifts of Fortune, too, are subject to divine providence; what for us seems fated is for the best, and from a divine perspective the justification of all suffering and all well-being would necessarily be evident. The prisoner is invited to assent to the principle that all is for the best in a providentially governed world.

In the fifth and final Book the phenomenon of human free will is defended against the argument that, if all things are providentially governed, there can be no freedom for rational beings. Providence, it is argued, is not coterminous with the causes of future events. Furthermore, divine omniscience does not make what is foreknown by God necessary. God, in his timeless eternal present, knows all things as present. He does not know them through prior knowledge of the temporal sort. Divine knowledge is different in kind from human knowledge, and does not determine free human actions. The fact that there is no chance event in the universe does not entail that all things that happen do so necessarily. This explanation, it should be pointed out, does not explain how divine providence is related to free human actions.

The foregoing summary is merely intended to be a guide to the general progression of the work. It is deliberately uncritical of the arguments advanced by Boethius. A critical survey of those arguments is beyond the scope of the present book.[111]

*

It only remains to refer to one final point. Is the *Consolation* as we possess it complete, or is it unfinished? Gruber's analysis of the metrical symmetry of its poems suggests that the structure may be a complete one, or at least one to which little could be added without destroying that balanced structure.[112] On the other hand, Tränkle has pointed out that the treatment of the theme of the human soul and its immortality (or return to God) is strikingly missing, although it may be anticipated and deferred at 4.4.22f.[113] Similarly, the programmatic questions at the end of Book 1 seem to promise an anthropological part to follow the theological one, but which never materializes. The absence of a concluding poem may also indicate an unfinished work, as may the fade-out of the prisoner as interlocutor. And what are the 'other questions to be dealt with' (*alia quaedam tractanda*, 5.1.1) from which Philosophy is diverted by the prisoner's question about chance and providence at the beginning of Book 5? Tränkle's arguments must be taken seriously. In attempting to counter them, Gruber points to the somewhat abrupt endings of Plato's *Republic* and Cicero's *De re publica*.[114] That is perhaps a feature of the dramatic mimesis of the dialogue. Promises of later treatment of topics that are not treated, apparent diversions of the argument from its course, replacement of dialogue by uninterrupted speeches from the chief interlocutor: these

---

[111] For discussions of the philosophically most interesting argument, that divine foreknowledge does not preclude free human actions (*Cons. phil.* 5.3ff.), see E. Gegenschatz, 'Die Gefährdung des Möglichen durch das Vorauswissen Gottes in der Sicht des Boethius', *Wiener Studien* 79 (1966) 517-30; R. Sorabji, *Time, Creation and the Continuum* (London 1983) 253ff.

[112] Gruber (1978) 21ff., with the fold-out between pp. 16 and 17.   [113] Tränkle (1977).

[114] Gruber (1978) 415.

are touches that – in Plato's, Cicero's, and Augustine's dialogues – are often added to give vivid colouring to the conversation that is being represented.[115] Boethius could easily have introduced them with a similar purpose in mind. Once again, we should not be misled by too strict an equation of literary fiction with the author's real situation and predicament, inferring, without real evidence, that death or other circumstances prevented the work's completion. On balance, Gruber's arguments for the symmetrical structure of the work suggest completeness rather than, as Tränkle would have it, a missing sixth book. It may also be the case that Boethius feels that he has suggested enough about the essential goodness and freedom of the human mind-soul in the work to make an anthropology unnecessary.

---

[115] For the typology of the dialogue in Greek and Roman literature see R. Hirzel, *Der Dialog. Ein literarhistorischer Versuch* (Leipzig 1895); J. Andrieu, *Le dialogue antique. Structure et présentation* (Paris 1954); A. Hermann/G. Bardy, art Dialog, *RAC* 3 (1957) 928-55; M. Hoffmann, *Der Dialog bei den christlichen Schriftstellern der ersten vier Jahrhunderte* (Texte und Untersuchungen 96, Berlin 1966); B.R. Voss, *Der Dialog in der frühchristlichen Literatur* (Studia et Testimonia Antiqua 9, Munich 1970); Schmidt (1977). Though focusing on Plato's dialogues, there is much of general interest on the genre's philosophical dimensions in the essays in C.L. Griswold, Jr. (ed.), *Platonic Writings, Platonic Readings* (New York/London 1988).

CHAPTER TWO

The Poetics of the *Consolation*

A recent writer on Greek tragedy asserts that

> a modern reader who wants to find his way into the individual plays
> must attempt to reconstruct the presuppositions and expectations which
> made tragedy possible in its native context; that is to say, he is
> committed first of all to the discipline which I shall call *poetics*.[1]

The discussion goes on to specify that such a study is a historical
enquiry into aspects of a particular cultural context, that it is a study
of a genre, which in turn is study of 'a set of possible meanings', of 'the
typical range of meaning definitive of the genre'.[2]

In this chapter 'poetics' has a range of reference comparable with
that intended by Malcolm Heath. There are, of course, difficulties in
applying such a concept to the study of the *Consolation*. For one thing,
Greek tragedies are a readily recognizable body of plays composed for
performance at dramatic festivals in one city in a limited historical
period, whereas the *Consolation* is a unique work whose genre, itself a
problem, is in no sense as clearly definable as that of tragedy.
Moreover, though not 'mere' autobiography, it has personal and
confessional elements that contrast with the ostensibly impersonal
nature of tragedy. But these factors make no essential difference to the
undertaking. The reader of the *Consolation* must, like the reader of
tragedy, engage in a historical enquiry into the 'presuppositions and
expectations' that make such a work possible. We cannot define the
contemporary audience of the *Consolation*, its addressee, as we can
that of Attic tragedy: that is to say, we can only describe it in broader
terms of a likely class of reader for whom it is intended (it is assumed
here that it is a 'public' utterance, a highly polished and artistically
subtle work of art intended to be read and admired by others). Nor can
we study the immediate and near-contemporary cultural reception of

[1] M. Heath, *The Poetics of Greek Tragedy* (London 1987) 1.
[2] op. cit. 1f.

the work, as we can that of Greek tragedy through Attic comedy, the philosophical writers, vase-painting, and the scholia. On the other hand, the *Consolation* is self-conscious about the effects and role of poetry in a way that tragedy is not. In addition, its use of poetry in a philosophical work can be examined against the clearly definable attitudes to poetry in that specific tradition. It will become apparent that a generic study will not be the result of this investigation. Though genre has been and will be invoked and considered in defining the aims and artistry of the *Consolation*, its affiliation with other works characterized as belonging to particular genres is too varied and too loose for it to be itself an example of any one genre. Finally, in this study the poetics of the *Consolation* is the poetics of its poetry. It will be obvious that this cannot be studied in separation from the prose sections, or rather that any study of the poetics must be in the context of the complete work. But in this chapter the poems are the centre of attention, and the remainder of the work is adduced only in so far as it is relevant to the understanding of the functions of the poetry.

To define the task of this chapter more precisely, then: poetics in this context implies an investigation of the presuppositions and expectations that make the poetry of the *Consolation* possible. It is an enquiry into the views on the function, status, and effect of poetry that either emerge from the text of the *Consolation* itself, or constitute its context.

Now it is obvious that we do not find, and should not expect to find, a fully-fledged poetics in a literary work like the *Consolation*. Yet what Helene Foley writes of another literary tradition is no less true of Boethius' work: 'in a tradition so unbroken, in which the response of one poet to another remained continuous ... literary and aesthetic views logically remain embedded in the shape of the poetic works themselves.'[3] Like Hellenistic and Roman writers before him, Boethius distinguishes in the course of the work between different kinds of poetic enterprise, form, and subject matter. He refers to the effect of particular poems, and he suggests, through mythical examples and metaphor, what he conceives the status of poetry to be. Such references within the work have the cumulative force of a poetics, or a part thereof, in a manner comparable with equivalent references in Homer or Hesiod,[4] or in the way in which Horace's assertions about poetry in the *Odes* and the *Epistles* constitute a poetics, or part of one.[5] I should

---

[3] H.P. Foley, Review of Russell (1981), *American Journal of Philology* 103 (1982) 466-9 (here 469).

[4] See Grube (1965) 1ff.; G. Lanata, *Poetica pre-Platonica* (Florence 1963) – a valuable collection of texts with comm.; H. Maehler, *Die Auffassung des Dichterberufs im frühen Griechentum* (Hypomnemata 3, Göttingen 1963) 9ff.

[5] *Odes*: see Nisbet/Hubbard 1.xixf.; Fraenkel (1957) 432ff. (on 4.2). *Epistles* I: see Macleod (1979). *Epistles* 2.1: see Fraenkel (1957) 383ff.; Grube (1965) 253ff. Cf. *Serm.* 1.4 (on which see Fraenkel [1957] 124ff.). On *Ars poetica* and in general see C.O. Brink, *Horace on Poetry*, 3 vols. (Cambridge 1963-82).

like to call this kind of poetics based on the internal evidence of the work itself the *immanent poetics* of the work. It is distinguishable from, but cannot ultimately be considered separately from, the *external* evidence for the work's poetics, in the sense of views about poetry, or a particular literary theory, that might have had a decisive influence upon Boethius' choice of the prosimetric form, or specific literary works or types of literary activity, or attitudes to poetry in a philosophical context, that might have provided the range of possibilities out of which this particular work developed.

The first task of this chapter, then, is to examine the evidence in the *Consolation* itself for its immanent poetics. It will become at once obvious that this examination will not begin to make proper sense until it is understood against its traditional background. But it is none the less instructive to begin with what Boethius actually says about poetry in the work. The next sections of this chapter must, of course, be complemented by the detailed discussions of the functions of poetry in the thematic context of Chapters 3-5: Boethius' actual poetic practice is the most conclusive evidence for his views on the role of poetry in his work.

(i) Poetics in the *Consolation*

The prisoner occasionally refers to the effects of certain poems in the *Consolation* on his sensibility. After 2 m. 8, spoken by Philosophy, he says:

> She had just finished her singing, and the agreeableness (*mulcedo*) of her song bewitched me, eager as I was to hear more, and amazed, my ears still pricked (3.1.1).

And after a particularly long disquisition on the notions of providence and fate, Philosophy says to him:

> But I see that you have been burdened for a long time now by the weight of the enquiry and tired by the length of the discussion, and are waiting for some sweetness (*dulcedinem*) in song. Have something to drink, then, that you may be refreshed by it and strive more strongly on to further matters (4.6.57).

The context of the first of these two passages might initially seem to suggest that there is a clear distinction between the effects of the prose sections and those of the poems:

> How well you have revived me, both (*vel*) with the weight of your ideas and (*vel*) with the pleasantness (*iucunditate*) of your singing! (3.1.2).

However, *vel ... vel* is not disjunctive, but a late Latin equivalent of *et ... et* (as in the translation just given).[6] And the rhetorical effects of both prose and verse are, in fact, considered together by Boethius. What is here distinguished is, on the one hand, the serious intent of the ideas expressed, and, on the other, the pleasing aesthetic form of the poems. Boethius is not implying that the poems do not express serious thoughts. Moreover, at this stage of the *Consolation*, Philosophy the singer's principal effect upon the prisoner is described in the medical, therapeutic terms characteristic of the early part of the work.[7] She is the 'greatest solace of weary hearts' (3.1.2) whose words revive and refresh (*refovisti*, ib.) the prisoner in his lethargy, so that he is ready to move from the milder remedies to the 'more bitter' ones (*acriora*, ib., cf. 1.5.11f.) promised by his mentor. In 3.1.1 it is the attractive power of poetry that is evoked, its power to 'bewitch' (*defixerat*) the prisoner. An aspect of poetry's protreptic function is thus highlighted. In the second passage quoted above it is the refreshing nature of the poetry that is stressed, its function as a restful interlude in the argumentative sequence. Philosophy anticipates the delights of song:

> But if the pleasures (*oblectamenta*) of poetic song delight (*delectant*) you, you must postpone for a little while this enjoyment (*voluptatem*), while I weave arguments fastened together in sequence (4.6.6).

This characterization of poetry is typical for the work. Elsewhere, Philosophy's song is described in similar terms:

> When Philosophy had finished softly and sweetly singing these words, while maintaining the dignity of her expression and the gravity of her countenance ... (4.1.1).

Sweet, soft song and grave seriousness of purpose are thus not incompatible: the words comment on the antecedent Orpheus poem, one of the most subtle statements of the work.[8] A similar notion of the serious purport of poetry is suggested by the following passage:

> But since it is not yet time for stronger remedies, and it is a well-known fact that minds are such that, as often as they lose true beliefs they cover themselves in false ones, from which an impassioned blindness arises and disturbs the true vision – I shall attempt for a while with gentle and mild poultices to lighten this blindness, so that when the darkness of

---

[6] See Gruber (1978) 233.

[7] On the medical themes and motifs of *Cons. phil.* see Schmid (1956). Wolf (1964) adds some interesting observations on the symbolism of Book 1, but her attempt to counter Schmid's arguments is unsuccessful. On the metaphor of medical therapy in philosophical contexts see Rutherford (1989) 19 with n. 54: a key text is Cicero, *Tusc. disp.* 3.1.1-3.6.

[8] See pp. 188-207 below.

deceptive passions is removed, you may be able to perceive the brightness
of true light (1.6.21).

It will be shown below that the medical metaphors in this passage
clearly refer to poetry as much as prose, when they are read in the
context of Book 1. As Thomas Curley has pointed out, the passage
suggests a philosophical function of verse: 'its ability to induce clarity
of vision is emphasized.'[9] That is to say, it has an important
propaedeutic function in the philosopher's progress towards understanding.

Just as poetry is a serious part of the philosophical enterprise, so too
the effects ascribed to poetry can be paralleled by those induced by
prose. A prose diatribe passage about Fortune is introduced thus:

> So let the persuasiveness of rhetoric's sweetness appear, which only
> advances on the right path when it does not abandon our teaching, and
> let it sing now lighter, now graver measures, with that poetic art
> (*musica*) that is a servant in our home (2.1.8).[10]

Significantly, it is not merely the sweet persuasiveness of rhetorical
prose that is here stressed – its similar effect upon the hearer as that of
verse – but also the variation possible in its moods and levels ('now
lighter, now graver measures'), a variation that corresponds to the
degrees of intensity of treatment prescribed by Philosophy for her
patient.[11] Moreover, it is suggested that rhetoric can be philosophically
respectable in so far as it 'advances on the right path', and is consonant
with true philosophical principles. A moral dimension is thereby
introduced: rhetoric (like poetry) is susceptible of corruption. We shall
return to the rhetoric and the *musica* that are consonant with
philosophy later. First of all, however, a further passage should be
quoted, on the effect of the passages in both prose and verse where
Fortune's attitude to the prisoner is evoked (2.1) and where Fortune
speaks to him in prosopopoeia (2.2 and 2 m. 2):

> 'These words of yours,' I said, 'are indeed splendid, and smeared as they
> are with the sweet honey of rhetoric and poetic art (*rhetoricae ac musicae
> melle dulcedinis*), they delight (*oblectant*) only as long as they are heard.
> But those who are unhappy have a more profound sense of their
> misfortunes, and so when these words have ceased to resound in their
> ears, deep-seated sadness presses heavily upon the heart' (2.3.2).

[9] Curley (1987) 359.

[10] This sentence is mistranslated by Büchner, Gigon/Gegenschatz, Tester, and Lerer
(1985) 112, all of whom fail to observe that *succinat* ('let it sing'), like *adsit* ('let ...
appear'), is a jussive subjunctive. O'Donnell (1984) 155 analyses the sentence, and Watts
translates it, correctly. On *musica* meaning 'poetry' Mueller-Goldingen (1989) 375 n. 17
refers to Venantius Fortunatus, *Carm.* 3.18.16 and Ausonius, *Ep.* 6.38.

[11] Cf. 1.5.11f. See Gruber (1978) 167.

Even rhetoric and poetry consonant with philosophy may have no more than a temporary efficacy. Philosophy's reply to the prisoner's complaint here is that these parts of the 'cure' have been merely a 'poultice' (*fomenta*), and not yet the fully-fledged remedies (*remedia*) which are to follow (2.3.3). At one level, this is an indication, by means of dramatic dialogue, of the persistence of the prisoner's sick condition. But at the same time the passage seems to corroborate and develop what the earlier 2.1.8 (quoted above) says: there is a hierarchy of kinds of appropriate rhetoric which can be applied to the condition of the prisoner and the stage of the cure reached. Some kinds of rhetoric may be stronger medicine than others, to adopt Boethius' metaphor. This passage anticipates a development in the degree to which the artistry of the work, whether in prose or in poetry, will be philosophically 'concentrated'.

Despite this notion of levels of appropriate rhetoric, however, the prisoner's reservations at 2.3.2 express an unease with the artistry of rhetoric and *musica* that is found elsewhere in the work. The image of art as honey coating (*oblita*) arguments is an unmistakable echo of Lucretius' famous justification of his poetry:

> *volui tibi suaviloquenti*
> *carmine Pierio rationem exponere nostram*
> *et quasi musaeo dulci contingere melle* ... (1.945ff.).

I have chosen to set forth my doctrine to you in sweet-speaking Pierian song, and as it were to touch it with the Muses' delicious honey ... (tr. Rouse/Smith).

Lucretius also uses the medication metaphor in the same context. The sick child drinks the bitter wormwood juice from the cup whose rim is besmeared with honey, so that it is 'beguiled ... not betrayed' (*deceptaque non capiatur*, 1.941). And Lucretius' art has the same kind of effect: it makes his 'somewhat harsh ... doctrine' (*ratio ... tristior*, 1.943f.) more palatable.[12] This Lucretian passage is closer to 2.3.2 than 1.5.11f., with which Curley compares it, but Curley is right to point out that for Boethius 'verse is not, as in Lucretius, merely something sweet to disguise the bitter taste of truth, but a milder form of the truth itself, a kind of pabulum from which the invalid may draw sustenance until fit for solid food'.[13] Epicurus' much-attested hostility to poetry renders a justification of it, such as Lucretius provides, necessary.[14]

---

[12] Lucretius 1.926-50 = 4.1-25.
[13] Curley (1987) 359. In 1.5.11f. the motif is, rather, the Stoic image of *tumor* ('swelling') as a metaphor for the passions (cf. Cicero, *Tusc. disp.* 4.29.63): see Schmid (1956) 133f. with n. 3; Gruber (1978) 148f.
[14] On Epicurus' attitude to poetry see C. Diano, 'La poetica di Epicuro', *Revista di*

One may ask whether the Platonist Boethius had not to face the same artistic and philosophical problem. For Boethius will have been unable to ignore Plato's banishment of the poets from his ideal state because, as Cicero puts it, 'they make our minds soft ... [and] are charming (*dulces*)' (*Tusc. disp.* 2.11.27).[15] In his *De re publica* Cicero himself engages in a critique of the poets and makes suggestions about them that reflect Plato's:

> Indeed, I [would send them] to that same place where he expels Homer, crowned with garlands and besmeared with unguents, from that imaginary city of his (*Rep.* 4.5.5).[16]

Was poetry a problem for the Platonist Boethius? In attempting to answer this question we must turn to the opening of the *Consolation*. In the first two poems of Book 1 of the work the question of the appropriateness of poetry (which is a theme also of the first prose section) is introduced programmatically by means of the topos of the choice of genre. The first distich of the introductory elegy –

> *Carmina qui quondam studio florente peregi,*
> *flebilis, heu, maestos cogor inire modos* (1 m. 1.1f.)

> I who once in the full flower of studious enjoyment brought songs to completion, tearful, ah, am compelled to begin sad measures

– is a daring combination, in the form of reminiscence, of two Virgilian

---

Estetica 7.3 (1962). On Lucretius see J.H. Waszink, 'Lucretius and Poetry', *Mededelingen der koninklijke Nederlandse Akademie van Wetenschapen*, Afd. Letterkunde N.S. 17 (1954) 243-57; C.J. Classen, 'Poetry and Rhetoric in Lucretius', *Transactions and Proceedings of the American Philological Association* 99 (1968) 77-118; P.H. Schrijvers, *Horror ac divina voluptas. Etudes sur la poétique et la poésie de Lucrèce* (Amsterdam 1970). On Philodemus' poetics see C. Jensen, *Philodemos über die Gedichte: Fünftes Buch* (Berlin 1923); Grube (1965) 193ff. But reconstruction of Philodemus' arguments is problematic (see Russell [1981] 43f.), and his influence upon Roman poetry difficult to establish (see Brink [n. 5 above] 1 *passim*). Philodemus also wrote verse epigrams without philosophical content: see A.S.F. Gow/D.L. Page (edd.), *The Greek Anthology: The Garland of Philip and Some Contemporary Epigrams* (Cambridge 1968) 1, ll. 3160-3345; 2, pp. 371-400 (nn.); the text also in D.L. Page (ed.), *Epigrammata Graeca* (Oxford 1975) ll. 4794-4979.

[15] See Boethius' comment on Plato's views in *mus.* 1.1 (p. 181.20ff.), quoted below, pp. 54f. Cf. Crabbe (1981b) 250. Mueller-Goldingen (1989) 372 n. 10 rightly criticizes Courcelle (1970) 235 for asserting that Boethius knows Plato's views via Cicero; he will have known both Plato's *Republic* and Cicero's use of it.

[16] Cf. Cicero's dismissive remarks on lyric poetry in Seneca, *Ep.* 49.5. These Ciceronian views have to be counterbalanced by the high moral and political value placed upon poetry in the speech *Pro Archia*, and by his sense of the importance of his own poetic efforts: see Williams (1968) 31f., 39f. See further p. 52 below on Cicero's use of poetic quotations in his philosophical writings.

passages.[17] One is the finale of the *Georgics*, especially the lines

> *illo Vergilium me tempore dulcis alebat*
> *Parthenope studiis florentem ignobilis oti* ... (*Georg.4*.563f.).

> I, Virgil, at that time lay in the lap
> Of sweet Parthenope, enjoying there
> The studies of inglorious ease ... (tr. Wilkinson).

The other passage is the purported (but probably not Virgilian) opening of the *Aeneid* quoted by Donatus and Servius:

> *Ille ego* qui quondam *gracili modulatus avena*
> carmen ... ([Virgil] *Aen.* 1.1a-b).

> I am he who once tuned my song on a slender pipe ... (tr. R.D. Williams).[18]

The contexts of these two passages are similar. In each, poetic progress is being stressed. In the *Georgics* Virgil, having delivered his envoi to his theme with the lines quoted above, recalls, with a reminiscence of *Eclogues* 1.1, his previous incursion into pastoral poetry (*Georg.* 4.565f.). In the lines prefixed to the *Aeneid* the writer's intention is similar: following the reference to the *Eclogues* in the quoted verses, the progress towards *Georgics* and *Aeneid* is evoked:

> ... *et egressus silvis vicina coegi*
> *ut quamvis avido parerent arva colono,*
> *gratum opus agricolis, at nunc horrentia Martis*
> *arma virumque cano* ... (1b-d, 1).

> ... and then leaving the woods made the nearby fields obey the husbandman however greedy, a work to win favour with farmers; but now I sing the bristling arms of Mars and the man ... (tr. R.D. Williams).

Thus the sequence (i) pastoral – (ii) didactic poetry (*Georgics*) is here imitated and extended to (iii) epic. Boethius wishes his readers to recall this sequence. He too has written pastoral poetry – we know that

[17] See Alfonsi (1942/3) 723, developed by Crabbe (1981b) 247f., to whom much of the following is indebted.

[18] See R.D. Williams (ed.), *The Aeneid of Virgil*, 2 vols. (London 1972) 1.156f., from which this and the next translation are taken. On *Aen.* 1.1a-d see R.G. Austin, '*Ille ego qui quondam ...*', *Classical Quarterly* N.S. 18 (1968) 107-15; P.A. Hansen, '*Ille ego qui quondam ... once again*', *Classical Quarterly* N.S. 22 (1972) 139-49. For the poetic form of the type 'I wrote X in the past; now it is more appropriate that I write Y' see Gruber (1978) 51, who refers to Catullus 68.15ff. and Ovid, *Tristia* 5.1.7f. Cf. [Virgil] *Elegiae in Maecenatem* 1.1ff. for a variation on the theme (poems in youth and in age). Crabbe (1981b) 246ff. links *Cons. phil.* 1 m. 1.1ff. to Ovid's poems of exile, and demonstrates Boethius' use of the topoi of change of genre and *recusatio* (on the latter topos see

from Cassiodorus – and that he will have taken the *Eclogues* as a
model is evident.[19] He may also have read Theocritus.[20] It is likely that
the reference to *carmina* in 1 m. 1.1 refers to that poetry, though the
metre of the poem may indicate that Boethius also wrote elegy.[21] But
the poem's opening distich does not introduce a progression on the
artist's part comparable with the *rota Vergilii*. On the contrary,
Boethius presents the persona of the prisoner in a state of artistic and
personal collapse. He is compelled (*cogor*) to take up the sad measures
of elegy (*maestos ... modos*).[22] His statement is an apology for his
theme, and is expressed in the terms traditional in such avowals of
choice. It is reminiscent of Ovid:

> *hic quoque talis erit, qualis fortuna poetae*:
>   *invenies toto carmine dulce nihil.*
> *flebilis ut noster status est, ita flebile carmen,*
>   *materiae scripto conveniente suae* (*Trist.* 5.1.3ff.).

This [book] will also be like its poet's fortune: you will find nothing
pleasant in the whole poem. My condition is tearful, and so is my poem:
the writing is adapted to its subject.[23]

And it echoes Propertius:

> *et mihi iam toto furor hic non deficit anno,*
>   *cum tamen adversos cogor habere deos* (1.1.7f.).

And now this madness does not let me be after a whole year, even though
I am compelled to have the gods against me.

Here, the second part of the pentameter (*cogor habere deos*) influences
Boethius' *cogor inire modos* both formally and thematically.

The prisoner's condition at the outset of the *Consolation* may seem to
justify an elegy, as does Ovid's in his Black Sea exile, when he writes
the *Tristia* and *Epistulae ex Ponto*.[24] But lament provides no
consolation. This is not evident from the poem itself, whose themes –

Nisbet/Hubbard 1.81ff., 2.179ff.).

[19] See p. 10 with n. 37 above.

[20] *In Int.* II 3.9 (p. 234.12f.), where 'reading Theocritus' is the example used in a
discussion of propositions about future contingents.

[21] For Boethius in a elegiac context see Shanzer (1983a); cf. pp. 10f. above.

[22] The themes of sadness and weeping run through the entire poem: 2 *flebilis*, 4
fletibus, 8 *maesti*, 14 *maestis*, 16 *flentes*. Reichenberger (1954) 9f. observes the
concentrated elegiac vocabulary of 5-18.

[23] Cf. Ovid, *Amores* 1.1; 1.3.19ff.

[24] See n. 18 above. Ovidian echoes in 1 m. 1 include especially the motif of the Muses
faithful to the troubled poet (*Trist.* 4.1.19ff.; 4.10.115ff.) and the death-wish (e.g. *Trist.*
3.2.23ff.); for further examples see Gruber (1978) 51ff. On the motif of the Muses' fidelity
see W. Stroh, 'Tröstende Musen: Zur literarhistorischen Stellung und Bedeutung von
Ovids Exilgedichten', *ANRW* II 31.4 (1981) 2638-84.

Boethius' changed state and the fickle nature of Fortune – introduce
motifs which will be taken up and developed in the course of the work:
to that extent, the opening elegy is an essential thematic prelude to the
work. But if it is thematically apt, its expression ín poetry of the kind
used is immediately criticized and devalued by Boethius in the
following prose section, where it is described, critically, as a 'tearful
complaint' (*querimoniam ... lacrimabilem*, 1.1.1). It has been observed
above that the prisoner, in the poem, describes himself as being
compelled (*cogor*, line 2) to compose it. It is composed under dictation
from the Muses (line 3) – a traditional motif in poetic composition, but
here emphasized by the prisoner to bring out his sense of the
involuntary nature of the whole undertaking. [25] That becomes clear in
the following prose section. The theme of the dictating Muses is taken
up and they are identified as one kind of Muse:

> The Muses of poetry ... standing by my couch and dictating words to my
> tears (1.1.7).

These Muses of poetry are castigated by Philosophy as lethal Sirens,
'sweet to the point of destruction' (*usque in exitium dulces*, 1.1.11), as
'whores of the stage' (*scenicas meretriculas*, 1.1.8), to be contrasted
unfavourably with Philosophy's own Muses, who will cure the poet's
ills (1.1.11). Boethius is here invoking the contrast between the 'Muse
of pleasure' of Plato's *Republic* (607a) and the 'Muse of truth' of the same
work (548b), who has to do with philosophical arguments (*meta
logôn te kai philosophias*).[26] Later in the *Consolation* he will refer to
Plato's Muse:

> *quodsi Platonis Musa personat verum,*
> *quod quisque discit immemor recordatur* (3 m. 11.15f.).

> But if Plato's Muse sings out the truth, what each one learns, forgetting
> he remembers.

We shall return to the motif of Muses and Sirens later.[27] For the time
being it is sufficient to note that Boethius, through Philosophy's
dismissal of the Sirens, dismisses poetry of the type of elegy found in 1
m. 1. Note that elegy, as a metrical and poetic form, is not thereby
dismissed. Philosophy herself delivers an elegy at 5 m. 1, on the Tigris
and Euphrates as images of a natural law. There are, therefore,
themes appropriate to this metre and type of poem.[28] It is above all

---

[25] A further important theme of *Cons. phil.* is thereby introduced, the condition of
enslavement to the passions (see pp. 97ff. below).

[26] Cf. *Timaeus* 47d on Muses and the perception of harmony.

[27] See pp. 59f. below.

[28] 5 m. 1 has, however, affinities with epigram: see Scheible (1972) 157 n. 2; Gruber

subject-matter and emotional tone that Boethius criticizes in 1 m. 1 and 1.1.

It is, moreover, not merely a certain kind of elegy that is being dismissed here: to some extent, Boethius is starting to reject poetry spoken in the *persona* of the prisoner. For after this opening poem the prisoner delivers only three poems in the entire work. One is descriptive and transitional, 1 m. 3, the other two probe complex problems, and ask concerned questions, one about the power of evil (1 m. 5), the other about problems of providence (5 m. 3). They cannot, either in theme or in tone, be put on a level with the opening elegy. Yet both are, so to speak, devalued in the prose sections which follow them. The first poem, the prisoner says, has been howled, dog-like, by him in his pain (*haec ubi continuato dolore delatravi*, 1.5.1). Of the second poem Philosophy says, rather wearily, that it is an old complaint, a *vetus ... querela* (5.4.1). In this latter case the devaluation of the poem is more subtle. For Philosophy has herself engaged in a complaint of her own at 1 m. 2,[29] and has called it a *querela* (1.2.1), thus granting lament of the right kind and about the right subjects a positive literary status.[30] Moreover, as Curley has perceptively pointed out, there is a shift in emphasis from 1 m. 5 to 5 m. 3.[31] In the earlier poem the prisoner can merely ask the questions about purported providence and slippery fortune (1 m. 5.28f.); in the later poem, which begins with a series of questions (5 m. 3.1-24), the prisoner can himself, such is his progress under Philosophy's guidance, reason out an answer (ib. lines 25ff.). Curley argues that the prisoner has now learned 'the proper use of verse', and so may use it again for the first time *in propria persona* since Book 1. But it is important to understand that the answer in the poem 5 m. 3 is only a small part of the answer to the overriding problem of 5.2, the problem which underlies the questions of the poem which succeeds it, namely, the apparently irreconcilable nature of the notions of divine foreknowledge and human free will. The 'answer' of lines 25ff. merely accounts, by reference to the Platonic *anamnêsis* doctrine, for the in-between stage of half understanding, and half not knowing, the truth. What is not answered is precisely the object of the *querela* referred to in 5.4.1, and although the rest of that prose section, together with 5.5 and 5.6, attempts to give an answer to the question of foreknowledge and free will, it is stressed from the outset that a full

---

(1978) 382. On 5 m. 1 see pp. 173ff. below.

[29] On 1 m. 2 see pp. 41ff., 109ff. below.

[30] See Curley (1987) 357. Glei (1985) 227, by lumping the laments together, sees Philosophy's as no different from the prisoner's, and regards 1.2.1 as a case of Philosophy 'calling herself to order'. But in saying 'It is the time for cure rather than lament' at 1.2.1 Philosophy is simply announcing the need for therapy and the therapeutic sequence; and it will be therapy for precisely those ailments diagnosed in 1 m. 2, namely, the prisoner's loss of rational control, and domination by anxiety and the passions.

[31] Curley (1987) 364f.

understanding of the complexities of that answer is beyond the capabilities of human reason (5.4.2). In fact, it can only be understood if the human mind somehow transcends itself and is raised to the level of divine intelligence (5.5.11f., 5.6.1).[32] So there is undoubtedly progress in the *querela* of 5 m. 3, but the prisoner still needs the guidance of Philosophy. His anguished questions are all too human and expose a blindness that is in no sense culpable, but none the less must be transcended and overcome. To that extent the use of the term *querela* at 5.4.1 points to continuing deficiencies in the prisoner's condition, but now they have become deficiencies inherent in the human condition, even when the mind has been strengthened by philosophical insight. It is important not to lose sight of the hint of criticism that attaches to the poetic questionings (and partial answer) of 5 m. 3.

The prisoner is thus made to appear like the work's symbol of the degradation of poetry, Orpheus. For the Orpheus of 3 m. 12, whose songs, delivered 'in tearful measures' (*flebilibus modis*, line 7), should recall the 'sad measures' (*maestos modos*) delivered by the 'tearful' (*flebilis*) prisoner in 1 m. 1.1f., cannot thereby assuage his grief and passion:

> *nec qui cuncta subegerant*
> *mulcerent dominum modi* (16f.).[33]

> Nor could the measures which had subdued all else soothe their master.

And he becomes the very type of the earth-bound, passion-bound human who cannot ascend to the vision of light and truth (lines 55ff.).

In 1 m. 2 Philosophy complains that the prisoner's mind is dulled (*mens hebet*, 2), and she compares his present state with that of his former dealings with astronomy and natural philosophy. The scheme outlined in lines 1-21 of the poem and summarized in 22f. as

> *rimari solitus atque latentis*
> *naturae varias reddere causas*

> accustomed to search out and report the many varied causes in secret nature

corresponds, as has long been observed, to the traditional programmatic content of a didactic poem treating themes in natural philosophy (including meteorology and the climatic causes of agricultural

---

[32] Cf. 1.4.39 on deification and Gruber (1978) 130f., who traces the motif from Pythagoras to late antiquity.

[33] Orpheus' failure is presented in the very terminology – *mulcerent* – used by Boethius to evoke the characteristic power of poetry at 3.1.1. (*mulcedo*) and elsewhere:

productivity).[34] What has not been seen is that the list of former achievements of the prisoner given in the poem is an inversion of the achievement of Epicurus, as described by Lucretius (1.62f., 72ff.). There, the depressed condition of humanity in the past, before Epicurus,

> *humana ante oculos foede cum vita iaceret*
> *in terris oppressa gravi sub religione* (1.62f.),

when man's life lay for all to see foully grovelling upon the ground, crushed beneath the weight of Superstition (tr. Rouse/Smith),

corresponds to the prisoner's present condition.[35] In both poets the theme of the liberating journey to and through the heavens is evoked:

> *hic quondam caelo liber aperto*
> *suetus in aetherios ire meatus* ... (1 m. 2.6f.)

This man, once accustomed to move freely under open skies along the paths of the starry ether ...

> ... *et extra*
> *processit longe flammantia moenia mundi*
> *atque omne immensum peragravit mente animoque* ... (Lucret. 1.72ff.).

And forth he marched beyond the flaming walls of the world, as he traversed the immeasurable universe in thought and imagination ... (tr. Rouse/Smith)

His dealings with the scientific themes mentioned are described by Lucretius as a victory for Epicurus (*pervicit*, 72; *victor*, 75), which redounds to the benefit of all mankind (*nos exaequat victoria caelo*, 79). But the prisoner had his victory in the past (*victor habebat*, 12) and is now a victim, and no victor (1ff., 24ff.).[36]

---

see pp. 32ff. above (I owe this observation to Anna Wilson). On 3 m. 12 see pp. 188-207 below.

[34] See Reichenberger (1954) 13ff.; Gruber (1978) 80f.

[35] Cf. *Cons. phil.* 1 m. 2.24f. '*nunc* iacet .../ ... pressus gravibus *colla catenis*'; 27 '*cogitur ... cernere* terram'. The Lucretius passage is brilliantly analysed by E.J. Kenney, '*Vivida vis*: Polemic and Pathos in Lucretius 1.62-101', in T. Woodman/D. West (edd.), *Quality and Pleasure in Latin Poetry* (Cambridge 1974) 18-30.

[36] For the heavenly journey in similar contexts in Manilius see 1.13ff., 2.58f., 2.139ff., 5.1ff. In a passage remotely reminiscent of 1 m. 2, Manilius (1.13ff.) distinguishes between astronomical knowledge (evoked through the topos of the heavenly journey) and the higher, astrological themes of his work. Like Boethius, Manilius here presents a rejected or superseded programme, and a higher, more comprehensively philosophical one. See further pp. 57f. and n. 96 below. On the motif of the heavenly journey see R.M. Jones, 'Posidonius and the Flight of the Mind', *Classical Philology* 21 (1926) 97-113; A.-J. Festugière, *La Révélation d'Hermès Trismégiste* 2 (Paris 1949) 441ff. (the latter on Cicero's *Somnium Scipionis*). Reichenberger (1954) 12 n. 2 observes the relevance of

Scholars have long since identified the passages, particularly those in the Augustan poets, which list themes in natural philosophy.[37] But their function in Boethius has not always, it would seem, been properly appreciated. Commentators usually talk of a retrospective survey of activities that should now, under Philosophy's guidance, be revived by Boethius. As Gruber writes, Philosophy 'introduces the change to ascent'.[38] But it is characteristic of the development of the *Consolation* that, apart from the theme of the cyclical and recurrent processes in nature (which, as will be shown in Chapter 4, are set in quite a different context that is not primarily scientific), the themes listed in 1 m. 2 are not treated at all in the work. What is being named here is not a programme for the *Consolation*. But what is the purpose of its detailed enumeration?

Boethius' poetic intention may be better appreciated by comparison with an enumeration of natural philosophical topoi in Propertius 3.5.23ff. There the motif functions as a *recusatio*.[39] Love elegy is defended as the appropriate artistic medium of the young poet. In his old age, loveless and grey-haired, he *could* turn to the themes of natural philosophy. But such assertions only serve as a prelude to fend off expectations that he might compose epic on military themes (cf. lines 47f.). It is implied that this is *a fortiori* out of the question. The list of natural philosophical and supernatural themes given in over 22 lines (25ff.) is a *reductio ad absurdum* of the traditional lists, and it becomes evident that, here as elsewhere, Propertius has no intention whatsoever of writing poetry on such topics. He simply wishes to continue writing love elegies.

Boethius stands this motif, so to speak, on its head. Rather than considering themes in natural philosophy as a possible future preoccupation, he makes Philosophy situate that occupation unequivocally in the past. The resultant *recusatio* is less direct, but no less emphatic. And the effect of the *recusatio* is attained. The poet clears the way for his current task. This task is not depicted as the more modest, or easier, one (a recurrent theme in *recusationes*), but as the creation of an entirely different kind of poetry about more important themes, to be delivered in the work in the persona of Philosophy.

Manilius 1.13ff. to 1 m. 2.

[37] Gruber (1978) 80; Innes (1979) 168f.

[38] Gruber (1978) 76; cf. Scheible (1972) 24f. for a more cautious approach.

[39] See Innes (1979) 170. The enumeration of such topoi in Virgil, *Georgics* 2.477ff. is first and foremost an evocation of the themes and concerns of the poem itself, representing the scientific ambition summarized ib. 490-2. It situates *Georg.* in the (not exclusively Lucretian: see D.O. Ross, *Backgrounds to Augustan Poetry. Gallus, Elegy and Rome* [Cambridge 1975] 29ff.) tradition of philosophical-scientific nature poetry. No *recusatio* in favour of the alternative of pastoral contentment (ib. 483-9, 493f.; cf. 458ff.: the lines may refer to the *Eclogues*) is intended by Virgil, nor does he dismiss the alternative: it is a foil to what he has hoped to achieve in *Georg.* Cf. Thomas (1988) 1.249ff., whose interpretation is here adopted. On the *recusatio* motif see n. 18 above.

The naming of elevated themes in Augustan poetry corresponds to statements in rhetorical theorists about sublime themes, as D.C. Innes has shown.[40] Such sublime themes are listed in writers such as Demetrius, the author of *On Style*, 'Longinus', the author of *On the Sublime*, and Hermogenes: they treat, above all, of *ta theia*, where besides the gods themselves, *ta phusika*, natural phenomena, have priority. Themes in natural philosophy also have priority in general over ethical topics. This attitude is reflected, for example, in Cicero, where 'things great by nature' (which include *divina*, things whose causes are unclear, and marvels on earth and in the heavens) are listed before 'things great by convention (*usu*)', like love of gods or native country, or fame, as subjects appropriate for rhetorical amplification, even if the precedence of themes treating natural phenomena is not stressed by him (Cicero, *Partitiones oratoriae* 16.56). One can, therefore, say that Boethius' *recusatio* is situated in the context of ancient reflections about what constitutes a sublime theme in verse, and that it can only be understood against that background. There may be no explicit mention of the poetic treatment of the themes in question in 1 m. 2. But Boethius, in juxtaposing the mention of such themes and the sample of elegy given in 1 m. 1, is stressing both what kind of poetry is to be unequivocally rejected, and what kind of sublime theme he is none the less going to avoid. That is, didactic poetry in hexameters, like the poetry of Lucretius and of Manilius.

To sum up: poetry in the *Consolation* is said to provide refreshment, pleasure, delight, yet such functions of poetry are not necessarily inconsistent with its serious purpose, which, at the very least, can be propaedeutic to philosophy. Poetry and rhetorical prose can function on various levels of seriousness and intensity. Some types of poetry and some kinds of poetic inspiration are rejected out of hand: for example, personal elegy, whether lament or love poetry. The poems spoken by Philosophy remain the proper paradigm of verse, but even poetry of a serious philosophical kind spoken by the prisoner is subject to adverse criticism. Finally, one generally recognized form of sublime philosophical poetry, the treatment of themes of natural philosophy, is rejected, not because of any inherent defects in it *qua* type, but because its subject-matter does not represent the highest reaches of philosophical endeavour.

(ii) Background to the *Consolation*'s poetics

Boethius' remarks about the effects of poetry are part of a Greek and Roman tradition of aesthetic or critical theory, and they may be clarified by being seen against that traditional background. The degree

----

[40] Innes (1979).

of emphasis that Boethius places upon certain aspects of his views may also be explained with reference to their background, to which I now turn. The several aspects to be considered will be treated in the order in which they were noted in the previous section.

One preliminary remark is, however, apposite. Boethius' originality should not be denied. But that originality, for a Latin author of the early sixth century, can only be achieved against the background of an acknowledged tradition. A Boethian poetics is not self-generated. So, to the question 'Why poetry?', one kind of answer will inevitably derive from what may be called the external poetics of the *Consolation*. Positive models, which may include a poetic exemplar, a tradition of exegesis, or a rhetorical theory, can legitimize the poetry of the work and give it its particular coherence. This section of the chapter is in large part a search for external influences that generate a positive model for our work.

Boethius' references to the effect of poetry are both very general and quite traditional. The key words used in such references are, as has been seen, terms for 'sweetness', 'pleasantness', 'agreeableness', etc. (*dulcedo, mulcedo, voluptas, oblectamenta, iucunditas*). That poetry is 'sweet' (*hêdus*) is commonplace in Homer, and that this includes its sounds, the 'desirable words' (*epe' himeroenta*), is repeatedly said. Significantly, the effects of speeches in assembly are described in similar terms: Nestor is 'sweetly speakng' (*hêduepês*), and his words are sweeter than honey (*Il.* 1.247ff.).[41] Gorgias the Sophist regards it as evident that songs 'bring pleasure (*epagôgoi hêdonês*) and divert pain' (DK 82B 11.10). Enjoyment is a criterion applied by Dionysos in Aristophanes' *Frogs* to the judgement of tragic poetry (*tôi d'hêdomai*, 1413).

This hedonistic view of poetry is also found in Plato. He argues in the *Gorgias* that pleasure (*hêdonê*) is the aim of all poetry, including tragedy, and that in its aim to please it is a species of rhetoric, a contemptible art, morally dangerous and pandering to man's lower instincts (*Gorgias* 501e ff.). In the *Phaedrus* rhetoric is said to be 'a kind of beguiling (*psukhagôgia*) of the mind through words' (261a). The term *psukhagôgia* here may be neutral in sense,[42] but there can be no doubt that Plato considers the poets to engage in emotional onslaughts upon the sensibilities of their audiences (*Ion* 535a ff.). It is poetry's appeal to the emotions, and the apparent surrender of rational control by its recipients, that is part of Plato's attack on poetry in the *Republic*

---

[41] See Grube (1965) 3. Heath (n. 1 above) 5ff. gives a wide range of references in Homer, Hesiod, and the Homeric Hymns; cf. n. 4 above. For Boethius Homer himself is a 'voice flowing with honey (*melliflui ... oris Homerus*)', 5 m. 2.3. The survey on the following pages of attitudes to poetry in ancient critical theory was unable to take account of G.A. Kennedy (ed.), *The Cambridge History of Literary Criticism. Volume 1: Classical Criticism* (Cambridge 1989), which appeared after it was written.

[42] See R. Hackforth, *Plato's Phaedrus* (Cambridge 1952) 123 n. 1.

(605c ff.). Poetry is dangerous enchantment (*Rep.* 606c). Plato cannot
escape from the fact that poetry, even poetry of which he may approve,
gives enjoyment and pleasure. In the *Laws* pleasure given is one of the
criteria of good art, along with mimetic correctness or accuracy, and
moral usefulness (*kharis, orthotês, ôphelia*). But the pleasure of good
art has to be pleasure of the right kind, consistent with the principle
that what is morally best is also the most pleasurable (*Laws* 658ff.).[43]

Plato's views on the emotional aspects of poetry are not inconsistent
with earlier and contemporary views. That language in general, and
poetry in particular, 'beguiles' is a common view from Homer
onwards.[44] The notion of poetry's magical power is found in Gorgias'
Helen (DK 82B 11.10ff.) and, as has been noted above, is an extension
of the Homeric view of poetry as enchantment. Aristotle, like Plato, is
concerned with the 'proper kind of pleasure' (*oikeia hêdonê*) effected by
poetic forms, especially tragedy, in his *Poetics*: it is the pleasure that
accompanies the emotions of pity and fear. 'Imitation' (*mimêsis*) is the
means whereby artistic pleasure is provided, and Aristotle seems to be
arguing that the proper pleasure of good art is the cognitive experience
of imitation, that is to say, it is not an autonomous or self-contained
emotion, but involves intellectual understanding: it 'assumes an
interplay and integration of the intellect and the emotions'.[45]

Plato's views on the perils of poetry are not the first of their kind in
the Greek tradition. That poetry may not be 'true' is expressed as early
as Hesiod's *Theogony*, when the Muses say

> we know to tell many lies that sound like truth,
> but we know to sing reality, when we will (27f., tr. West).[46]

It should be noted that, on this view, not all poetry is 'lies'. Indeed,
Greek poets are insistent that they are telling the truth.[47] Such
insistence is not incompatible with the view that there is occasional
untruth in poetry (e.g. Pindar, *Ol.* 1.28ff.; *Nem.* 7.20ff.). But the

[43] In the *Republic* Plato allows hymns and eulogies in his just city (607a; cf. 372b,
459e, 468d), but still regards them as mimetic (604e): see Halliwell (1988) 153. On the
limitations of the good poet of *Laws* 829c-d see Russell (1981) 104. Discussions of Plato's
views are legion: see e.g. Grube (1965) 46ff.; R. Harriott, *Poetry and Criticism before
Plato* (London 1969) 78ff.; Halliwell (1986) 1ff.; Halliwell (1988) 3ff. and comm. *passim*;
G.F. Else, *Plato and Aristotle on Poetry* (Chapel Hill, NC 1987); P. Vicaire, *Platon:
Critique littéraire* (Paris 1960).

[44] See *Odyssey* 1.337, 11.333ff. = 13.1ff., etc.; cf. Harriott (n. 43) 123ff.; Halliwell (1986)
64 n. 24, 188f.

[45] Halliwell (1986) 77; see in general ib. 62ff. Commentaries on Aristotle's *Poetics*:
D.W. Lucas (Oxford 1968), with important appendixes in essay form; Halliwell (1987).
See also Grube (1965) 70ff.; Else (n. 43); I. Bywater, *Aristotle on the Art of Poetry* (Oxford
1909) is still valuable.

[46] Cf. *Odyssey* 19.203.

[47] See e.g. Hesiod, *Works and Days* 10; Pindar, *Ol.* 13.52, etc.; cf. M.L. West (ed.),
Hesiod: Theogony (Oxford 1966) 162.

systematic attack on the untruthfulness of poetry, and its assumed consequent harmfulness, comes from theorists and intellectuals, and is found as early as the sixth century in Xenophanes, and later in Heraclitus.[48] When a fifth-century author of Sophistic background asserts that 'poets compose for pleasure, not for truth', we must assume a polemical background to the assertion. But the same author echoes Hesiod, and may or may not introduce greater complexity into the discussion, by also saying that the best artists 'deceive the most by producing things that resemble the truth' (3.10).[49] Even before Plato and Aristotle, then, the inadequacy of the antithesis truth-falsehood (or pleasure) is felt by Greek critics, and the genesis of the notion of the artefact as fictional construct, 'deliberately' deceiving its addressee, may be observed.

When we turn to rhetorical theory, we find that it recognizes the elements of pleasure and emotional manipulation in oratory. In the Roman tradition this is most apparent in Cicero's view on the tasks of oratory, which he formulates as: to teach and instruct (*docere*), to please or entertain (*delectare*), and to influence emotionally (*movere*) (*Brutus* 185f.).[50] These rhetorical tasks are reflected in Horace's views in the *Ars poetica*:

> *aut prodesse volunt aut delectare poetae*
> *aut simul et iucunda et idonea dicere vitae* (333f.).

> Poets aim either to do good or to give pleasure – or, thirdly, to say things which are both pleasing and serviceable for life (tr. Russell).

> *omne tulit punctum, qui miscuit utile dulci*
> *lectorem delectando pariterque monendo* (343f.).

> the man who combines pleasure with usefulness wins every suffrage, delighting the reader and also giving him advice (tr. Russell).

As Grube points out, the elements of *docere* and *delectare* are here, just as the art of *movere* was discussed by Horace in *Ars poetica* 88ff.[51] The interaction of rhetorical and poetic theory is complemented by cross-fertilization in the practice of the two arts. That study of the poets and adaptation of poetic artistry to rhetorical purposes enhances oratory is attested both by oratorical practice and assertions about the practice. In Tacitus' *Dialogue on Orators* this is strikingly expressed by Marcus Aper, speaking of passages 'resplendent with out-of-the-way poetic colouring' in orators:

[48] Xenophanes: DK 21 B 11. Heraclitus: DK 22 B 40, 42.
[49] The source is *Dissoi Logoi*: the first quotation comes from 3.17 (DK, vol. 2, pp. 410f.). See Russell (1981) 85f.; Halliwell (1986) 14f.
[50] On the variants in Cicero see Grube (1965) 178.
[51] Grube (1965) 252 n. 1.

Yes, an orator now has to provide poetic beauty as well, not the Accius or
Pacuvius variety, mildewed with age, but drawn from the shrines of
Horace, Virgil, and Lucan. These are the ears and these the judgements
that contemporary orators have to pander to – and it is for this reason
that they have become more pretty and more ornate in style. And if our
speeches do bring pleasure to their hearers, that doesn't make them any
less effective (*Dial.* 20.5f., tr. Winterbottom).

Quintilian also recognizes the importance of the study and imitation of
poetry in the training of the orator (*Inst. or.* 10.1.27ff.). Poets may
provide instances and examples of 'sublimity of language, range of
emotion, appropriateness in depiction of character ... [and] pleasure'
(ib. tr. Winterbottom). But Quintilian warns against incautious
adaptation of poetic practices by the orator: poetry may induce
pleasure and delight in ways inappropriate to oratory, which should
instruct as well as move.[52] It is a question of identifying and being
influenced by the right poetic exemplars, for example, Homer (10.1.46),
Virgil (10.1.85f.), or Horace (10.1.96). In Quintilian's views tensions
are expressed that also occupy philosophical theorists. How legitimate
is the pleasure felt in poetry, and how 'useful' in a moral sense (or how
morally damaging) is it?

These last-mentioned questions are part of a problem referred to
above, namely, whether there is a type of *musica* that is consonant
with philosophy, both in the sense that it may be practised by the
philosopher, and in that it may constitute a legitimate subject of
philosophical concern. It will be appropriate to begin detailed
discussion of this topic by considering some further examples of its
treatment in the rhetorical and literary critical tradition.

In the *Poetics* Aristotle appears to counter Plato's attack on the poets
by the consideration that poetry contributes to philosophical
understanding in that it generalizes: '... poetry is both more
philosophical and more serious than history, since poetry speaks more
of universals, history of particulars' (9,1451b5ff., tr. Halliwell). The
mimetic function of poetry, for Aristotle, exposes and expresses an
insight into 'the universal conditions and determinants of human
existence'.[53] This is indeed a doctrine of poetic universality, but it is
important to understand that Aristotle is not saying that the poet and
the philosopher are dealing with universals in the same manner and
with the same purposes. The philosopher deals with universals in
analysis whose aim is the attainment of truth. But the poet exploits
universals in a fictional context: '[the poet] speaks of the sort of events
which could occur' (9,1451b5, tr. Halliwell). That is to say, the status of

[52] See Leeman (1963) 311ff.
[53] Halliwell (1987) 108.

poetic universals 'is intrinsically that of the possible not the actual'.[54] At the same time, poetry, in enlightening the reader's or audience's understanding, 'does a service for the life of contemplation'.[55] Aristotle is certainly saying that poetry is an appropriate objèct of study for the philosophically inclined reader. Its relation to truth, though complex, is none the less positive.[56]

Aristotle's positive view of poetry is reflected in later theory, though never with the subtlety which he displays. Whereas there is always evidence of the old pre-philosophical view that poetry aims at pleasure and 'beguilement' *(psukhagôgia)* – for example, in Alexandrian theory[57] – rhetorical and philosophical theory, concentrating on subject-matter rather than technique, reflects aspects of Aristotle's position in partial forms. Theophrastus links poetry and oratory in an influential manner, if the history of that link in Hellenistic and Roman rhetorical and poetic theory is considered. Aristotle had distinguished between the audience of oratory and that of poetry, and had aligned the latter more with the activity of philosophy. But Theophrastus links poetry and oratory as both oriented towards audiences and persuasion, by contrast with philosophy, which is oriented towards facts and the demonstration of truth (fr. 65 Wimmer).[58] This contrast has the effect of driving a wedge between poetry and philosophy and confining discourse about the former to matters of composition and technique. Yet other approaches are not lacking. One tradition is reflected in Horace's *Ars poetica*, where moral understanding is posited as a prerequisite of good poetry:

> *scribendi recte sapere est et principium et fons.*
> *rem tibi Socraticae poterunt ostendere chartae*
> *verbaque provisam rem non invita sequentur* (309ff.).

> Wisdom is the starting-point and source of correct writing. Socratic books will be able to point out to you your material, and once the material is provided the words will follow willingly enough (tr. Russell).

And Horace adds a list of ethical topics, whose principles will provide the author with the material for appropriate characterization. Poetry has a magical taming or civilizing power, as well as being the vehicle of legal wisdom (391ff.). Here philosophy informs the subject-matter and, in a sense, even generates the form of poetry.[59] The theory espoused by

---

[54] Halliwell (1987) 110.

[55] Russell (1981) 92.

[56] See Russell (1981) 93. Glei (1985) 236 sees in Boethius' poetic undertaking in *Cons. phil.* a reflection of his wish to reconcile the doctrines of Plato and Aristotle (*In Int.* II 2.3 [pp. 79f.]), extended to their views on poetry.

[57] See Russell (1981) 94.

[58] On Theophrastus' literary criticism see Grube (1965) 103ff. Fr. 65 is translated in Russell (1981) 203f.

[59] Cf. Horace, *Epist.* 1.2.1ff. The moral defence of poetry's sublimity, contrasted with

Horace is consciously didactic: poetry is the appropriate vehicle of moral principles. It is important not to lose sight of this attitude in assessing the presence of philosophical themes in later Roman poetry, including that of Boethius.

It has been noted above that rhetoric, or the study of oratory, may appropriate poetry in a way that tends to separate it from philosophy. But the rhetorical tradition may also facilitate the *rapprochement* of poetry and philosophy, especially when both are considered from the viewpoint of level of style. Quintilian, once again, provides an illuminating example of this. When he considers the uses of poetry in the service of rhetoric, it is above all its *sublimitas* that he stresses.[60] And it is by implication the sublimity of Plato's style that he praises at *Inst. or.* 10.1.81, as he does that of Aristotle and Theophrastus (10.1.83). The rhetorical excellence of some philosophical writing provides a basis for the linking of verbal artistry and argumentative brilliance: the purported etymology of Theophrastus' name typifies the function of artistically contrived expression in philosophical discourse (ib.), recalling the similar point made by Cicero (*Orator* 19.62), in a context where, among other matters, Plato's 'pleasantness' (*suavitas*) as well as his 'seriousness' (*gravitas*) is praised.[61]

Texts such as those just adduced show that the notion of highly contrived and sophisticated style is not found alien by writers on rhetoric to the composition of works of philosophy. Cicero is conscious that Plato's attack on oratory is belied by his oratorial skills and predilections: 'In ridiculing orators he seemed to me to be himself the greatest of orators' (*De oratore* 1.11.47). Indeed, there seems to be a contradiction in Plato between precept and practice, a contradiction that is at the heart of Platonist problems about the value of poetry. And not just Platonist problems: it is Aristotle who, in a sense, remains a philosophical exception in his positive views about poetry's intellectual content. Epicurean hostility to poetry is well attested, and Lucretius is a surprising exception to that school's tendency. The Stoics, for their part, adopt an attitude that is, on the whole, constructive towards poetry: their attitudes are revealing and should be considered briefly.[62] They are less complex, and more clearly classifiable, than Aristotle's views, and their enormous influence in later antiquity, whether directly or indirectly via the Neoplatonists, makes them more important for Boethius than is often realized. With the Stoics also the philosophical poem re-emerges for the first time

---

corrupt, aggressive eloquence, is found in Maternus' first speech in Tacitus' *Dialogue* 12.

[60] See Leeman (1963) 314.

[61] Theophrastus' name can be taken to mean 'of divine speech'. See also Cicero, *Brutus* 31.120f.; Leeman (1963) 203, 361f.

[62] See De Lacy (1948).

since Presocratic philosophy as a vehicle of communication: Cleanthes' *Hymn to Zeus* is the most celebrated example.

Although the Stoics condemn the passions and urge their eradication, they appear to have allowed the pleasure felt in poetry to be legitimate. Such pleasure, however, is not the irrational passion that is either identical or coincident with a false judgement of the mind, but rather a form of 'good passion' (*eupatheia*), that is, it is the emotion appropriate to the philosopher. It is thus not so much 'pleasure' (*hêdonê*) as 'joy' (*khara*) or 'delight' (*terpsis*).[63] It is a rational pleasure, and so beneficial, a means to the end of the good life: the Stoics adopt a utilitarian attitude to poetry. But only poetry which provokes the right kind of emotional response in the right kind of recipient is unequivocally approved: poetry that arouses the passions is condemned, although the notion of benefit may have allowed even such poetry to have its function, and even the non-philosopher may benefit from it.[64] In educational contexts, poetry may be a preparation for philosophy, a means of attracting and so instructing the pupil, and also, more generally, a means of providing good and evil examples of behaviour, to be imitated or rejected.[65] Most interestingly of all, Cleanthes asserts that certain philosophical themes require poetic form if they are to be appropriately expressed (*SVF* 1.486): he may have felt that way about his *Hymn to Zeus*. Thus poetry has a function both for the uneducated and the educated, for the non-philosopher as well as for the sage. The Stoics also appear to have confronted the problem of fiction, or the 'untruth' of poetry, and to have argued that fictional aspects are (or at least can be) an essential element in the total aesthetic effect that the poem has on the audience.[66] The Stoics were especially interested in the linguistic form and structure of poetry, and exploit the allegorical interpretation of the poem's meaning. Poetry can embody truth, and so Homer in particular, but also other poets, are sources of knowledge and wisdom: Chrysippus quoted poets as evidence in support of the arguments in his writings (*SVF* 2.904ff.).[67] The practice spread: in Cicero's day not merely the Stoics, but also Philo of Larissa in the Platonic Academy, peppered their lectures with poetic quotations (Cicero, *Tusc. disp.* 2.11.26). No doubt the use of poetry in this way goes hand in hand with the

---

[63] On the 'good passions' in Stoicism see Inwood (1985) 173ff.

[64] De Lacy (1948) 249ff. Posidonius, however, appears to have argued in favour of an irrational faculty of soul, and hence for a function of music and poetry through which the emotions experience irrational pleasure. But such experiences may cure emotional disturbances, and so be philosophically beneficial: see F168 Kidd/Edelstein ~ F417 Theiler (from Galen, *De placitis Hippocratis et Platonis* 448ff.); cf. I.G. Kidd, 'Posidonius on Emotions', in A.A. Long (ed.), *Problems in Stoicism* (London 1971) 200-15 (here 205f.).

[65] De Lacy (1948) 270.

[66] De Lacy (1948) 267ff.

[67] De Lacy (1948) 243ff., 259ff., 264.

rehabilitation of rhetoric in the Academy from Philo (at least) onwards.[68]

Cicero follows the practice of including poetic quotations in his philosophical writings, and he adapts the use of poetic quotation to the philosophical allegiance of the interlocutors.[69] Thus the sparse and superficial use of verse quotations in passages where he, the professed Academic, speaks in his own person, or has others expound Academic or Peripatetic[70] views, contrasts with the extensive and frequent quotations, justifiying and underlining the arguments, of his Stoic characters. Epicurean interlocutors are, as might be expected, given practically no quotations from the poets. His teacher Philo's practice may be followed in the use of poetry as embellishment and elegant decoration in Academic passages of the philosophical writings.

Later discussions of poetry in philosophical contexts, especially in the Neoplatonists, will be considered in the next section of this chapter. It is now time to turn to another kind of possible external influence on, or external model for, Boethius' poetic practice, one that may be described as the influence of practitioners rather than of theoreticians.[71] That is to say, what poetic models may have determined his use of poetry in the *Consolation*, and also, what literary and related practices might have formed his positive poetics?

One relevant consideration is the fact that in late antiquity the teaching of philosophy was practised by those who also taught rhetoric. The example of Philo of Larissa has been referred to above, of whom Cicero relates that he taught both philosophy and rhetoric in alternate cycles (*Tusc. disp.* 2.3.9). One may also mention, for example, Favorinus, Longinus the contemporary of Plotinus, and Themistius.[72] The terms *philosophus* and *sophus* can denote the orator, versifier, grammarian, and textual critic: in the epitaph for the city prefect Vettius Agorius Praetextatus, who died in 384, the works of the *sofi* include prose and verse literature in Greek and Latin, its interpretation and textual emendation, but also by implication higher philosophical activities (evoked in the metaphor of the mysteries). In Martianus Capella, Simonides, Archimedes, and Euclid alike are called *philosophi* (5.538, 6.587); in Diocletian's day the term can be applied to mining engineers.[73] From the time of the Sophists of the

---

[68] Cf. *Tusc. disp.* 2.3.9. See Hadot (1984) 45ff.

[69] See Jocelyn (1973) 67ff.

[70] On a critical attitude towards poetry in Aristotle, *Rhetoric* 3.1 (1404a) and 3.5 (1407a) see Jocelyn (1973) 68, who points out (n. 59) that Cicero approved of Peripatetic views on literature: the influence of the *Poetics* upon him appears negligible.

[71] The distinction should not be allowed to obscure the fact that the statements of Lucretius or Horace, discussed above (pp. 35, 47, 49f.), are as relevant to what follows as are those of Manilius (pp. 57f. below) to the preceding discussion.

[72] See Hadot (1984) 228f.

[73] For these meanings of *philosophus* and *sophus* see Curtius (1954) 216f.

Roman empire in the second century AD onwards[74] the terms *sophistês, rhêtôr,* and *philosophos* have equivalent meanings, and can certainly include rhetorical and literary activities as well as philosophy. These tendencies, which, it cannot be denied, imply a trivialization of the words for 'philosopher' to include all skilled avocations, at the same time demonstrate that it might be considered normal for a philosopher in late antiquity to have at least rhetorical and literary interests, and to write poetry.[75]

Thus it can be observed that Boethius is influenced by poetic as much as prose antecedents in the rhetorical and argumentational elaboration of the prose sections of his work. This is particularly the case with Virgil, whose poetry influences his prose no less than his verse.[76] But it is also true of Lucretius, as Milanese has shown in his discussion of the influence of the prooemium of Book 2 of *De rerum natura* on 1.3, and in other instances.[77] The case of Virgil is perhaps unremarkable, given his pervasive influence in all kinds of later Latin literature, but the example of Lucretius indicates that the prose writer Boethius feels no inhibitions about submitting to the influence of the Epicurean poet, even in a passage like 1.3, which castigates the 'Epicurean crowd' (1.3.7). Poetry, as well as prose, can contribute to the articulation of philosophical truth, and through the medium of prose as well as verse.

It will be shown in Chapter 3 that the setting and some of the detail of Plato's *Phaedo* influence aspects of the *Consolation*.[78] A further likely influence is to be noted here. In Plato's dialogue Socrates is said to be composing poetry (versifying Aesop, and writing a hymn to Apollo) in prison, and he explains this, for him, novel activity as a reaction to dreams which he has often had, urging him to 'make art (*mousikên*) and practise it' (60e, tr. Gallop). In the past he has understood these dream-injunctions metaphorically, as encouraging him to philosophize, but now, on the verge of death, he practises poetry and so obeys the dream commands literally (60e ff.). Socrates is repeatedly portrayed by Plato as calling himself the servant of, or dedicated to, Apollo (*Apology* 23c, 33c; *Phaedo* 85b), though in the *Apology* this is a reference to his obedience to the Delphic oracle rather

---

Praetextatus' epitaph: *ILS* 1259.

[74] See in general G.W. Bowersock, *Greek Sophists in the Roman Empire* (Oxford 1969); on terminology see J.L. Moles, 'The Career and Conversion of Dio Chrysostom', *Journal of Hellenic Studies* 98 (1978) 79-100 (here 88-93). Cf. Rutherford (1989) 80ff.

[75] The counter-tendency, giving a specialized meaning to the term 'philosopher', is found in Plotinus' description of Longinus as a *philologos*, but not a *philosophos* (Porphyry, *Vita Plotini* 14).

[76] One particularly clear instance is the influence of *Eclogue* 10.46 at 1.5.3, noted by Gruber (1978) 142.

[77] Milanese (1983) 137-48.

[78] See pp. 97ff. below.

than to the practice of any literary art. Later in the *Phaedo* Socrates is
made to combine the two pursuits in a striking metaphor. He describes
his philosophical discourse in prison as a swan-song, but departs from
the traditional explanation of the fable, that the swan sings a lament for
its imminent death:[79]

... the swans [do not] sing in distress, but rather, I believe, because,
belonging as they do to Apollo, they are prophetic birds with
foreknowledge of the blessings of Hades, and therefore sing and rejoice
more greatly on that day than ever before (*Phaedo* 85a-b, tr. Gallop).

A philosopher writes poetry on the eve of his death in prison, and in
obedience to a divine command, and he also sees his philosophizing as
a form of song: the potency of this Platonic metaphorical and literal
complex for Boethius cannot be overestimated, especially when the
influence of the *Phaedo* is discernible elsewhere in his work. Curley
has drawn attention to these passages, and seen in them the notion of
a transformation of traditional attitudes to poetry analogous to that
accomplished in the case of Boethius:

As Socrates reinterprets the swan song as a paean of joy, so does
Boethius transform his song from elegiac lament, by way of philosophic
remedium and *refrigerium*, into an intellectually sophisticated expression of the human condition.[80]

Boethius' practice of musicology influences certain themes of the
Consolation, as Chamberlain in particular has shown.[81] An influence
of his theory, as set out in *De institutione musica*, may also be
discerned in the poetics of the *Consolation*. Boethius' 'instrumental
music' includes that of the human voice in song, and so the poems in
the *Consolation* may be accounted types of that kind of music. It is
significant that Boethius addresses himself in his work on music to
Plato's attacks on poetry and music in the *Republic*, and in so doing

[79] On the motif see W.G. Arnott, 'Swan Songs', *Greece and Rome* 34 (1977) 149-53.
[80] Curley (1987) 366. Shanzer (1984) 365 n. 60 refers to the generic form identified by
Alan Cameron ('The Date and Identity of Macrobius', *Journal of Roman Studies* 56
[1966] 25-38 [here 28f.]) of a dialogue set immediately prior to the death of the main
interlocutor (such as *Phaedo* or Cicero's *De re publica*), and argues that this form may
also typically involve a change of literary genre for the interlocutor. The examples which
she gives are *Phaedo* and Tacitus' *Dialogus*. The latter is, however, not a convincing
instance. Maternus is not so much shown as turning to dramatic poetry from legal
oratory, as arguing for his continued preference for, and proposing exclusive future
practice of, poetry (*Dial.* 4, 11, 13). Moreover, even if the *Dialogus* has influenced this
aspect of *Cons. phil.*, the latter's uniqueness should not be forgotten: in it the prisoner is
an interlocutor before 'his' (the author's) own death. In that respect, it may be compared
with poems in which a person gives instructions before death (e.g. Horace, *Odes* 2.20;
Propertius 1.21; 2.13), to which the generic name *mandata morituri* has been given by F.
Cairns, *Generic Composition in Greek and Roman Poetry* (Edinburgh 1972) 90f.
[81] Chamberlain (1970) 84ff.

distinguishes between good and bad types of music:

> Plato believes that that music is a great sentinel of the state which is of
> the best moral kind and composed with a sense of propriety, such that it
> is modest, simple, and masculine, and not effeminate, fierce, or complex
> (*mus.* 1.1, p. 181.20ff.).

For Boethius music is the only one of the four arts of the *quadruv̄ium*
that is related to ethics as well as to the investigation of truth (*mus.*
1.1, p. 179.20ff.). Musical melodies and rhythms actually have an
influence on the moral disposition, for good or evil (*mus.* 1.1, p.
181.1ff.). They can cure emotional disorders (*mus.* 1.1, p. 184.7ff.).
Crabbe is surely right to link such notions to Philosophy's attack on,
and dismissal of, the Muses of elegy at the opening of the
Consolation.[82] The distinction between morally sound and unsound
music, moreover, legitimizes the use of poetry in the expository
development of the work. As Chamberlain suggests, the opening elegy
is an example of *musica effeminata.* Philosophy, by contrast, is 'the
complete *musicus*',[83] not merely because of the wholesome effect of her
music, but also because she fulfils the criteria set down by Boethius as
characterising the perfect practitioner of the art: she has instrumental
skills (including vocal ones), she is creative, and she (it must be
assumed) exercises the judgement of rhythms, melodies, etc. that the
rational musician does (cf. *mus.* 1.34, p. 224.25ff.). The links between
music and reason, the investigation of truth, and moral improvement,
elevate poetry to a level that makes it unproblematic for the Platonist
Boethius to include it in his philosophical enterprise.

Chamberlain's claim that cosmic music is implicitly contained in the
nature imagery and subject-matter of the *Consolation* will be discussed
in Chapter 4.[84] Attention should, however, be given here to his claim
that Boethius' third kind of music, human music, can be implicitly read
into the work. Human music is, first, the harmonization (*coaptatio,
consonantia, temperatio*) of body and soul, and, secondly, the harmony
of the different parts of the body (*mus.* 1.2, p. 188.26ff.). Chamberlain
argues that 'it is simply an implicit physical structuring that causes
the soul to respond to instrumental music'.[85] The form or harmony
within the human person responds to, and so can judge, external
forms: Chamberlain refers to 5 m. 4.30ff. The reference to the soul's
'joining' (*compages*) at 2.5.9 echoes the use of the term *compago* to refer
to the unity of body and soul at *mus.* 1.1 (p. 186.3).[86] The 'motions' of

[82] Crabbe (1981b) 250.
[83] Chamberlain (1970) 85.
[84] See pp. 148ff.
[85] Chamberlain (1970) 91.
[86] Chamberlain (1970) 91f. For the following see ib. 92f. The term used by Boethius at
Cons. phil. 2.5.9 is, however, not *compago*, as Chamberlain assumes, but *compages* (the

the soul referred to in 3 m. 11.4 and elsewhere have musical dimensions, especially when the background of the *Timaeus* is considered. Finally, the notion of the soul as a 'harmonious tempering' (*temperies*, 4.6.26; *temperamentum*, 4.6.28) has not merely medical connotations but also musical ones. This would not be surprising in a Platonist who is also an expert in the Pythagorean sciences of music and mathematics. We may not, however, agree with Chamberlain that Boethius wishes the reader explicitly to recall his threefold division of music when responding to such themes in the *Consolation*. For one thing, they appear to function in quite different ways in the work. Human music, since it is no more than a metaphor for the body-soul structure, will inevitably be reflected in the psychological assumptions of the work, without any need to appeal to its 'musical' character. Cosmic music, on the other hand, as will be seen in Chapter 4, informs and sustains themes and images crucial to the work's meaning. And instrumental music is part of its very structure: here the theory of the work on music can be adduced to justify the presence and particular function of the poems in the work. Rather than responding to the musical elements in the *Consolation* as an elaboration of what the theory of music propounds, then, that theory should be adduced with discrimination and appropriate restraint. Only then can its contribution to the understanding of the work be properly appreciated. That it informs the work's poetics should be evident from the foregoing.

Possible influences on the prosimetric form of the *Consolation* have been discussed in Chapter 1.[87] The enterprise of undertaking to treat philosophical themes in verse will also have been influenced by Roman poetic antecedents in the broader sense. One such antecedent will have been Lucretius, writing in verse in a school tradition that is unequivocally hostile to poetry. His influence upon Boethius has already been observed above.[88] It has long been recognized that Senecan choral lyric is a model for several poems in the *Consolation*, both for its use of mythical exempla and for its generic moralizing. Chapters 3-5 explore several aspects of the presence of Seneca's poetry in Boethius.[89] Some of Boethius' poems may be read as dialogues with their Senecan model, in which he not merely echoes Seneca, but also modifies and challenges him. That Seneca was, in addition, a martyr for philosophy's sake in Boethius' eyes will have enhanced his value as an exemplar for his art.[90]

To this category belongs also the treatment of Stoic cosmological

---

detail does not affect his argument).

[87] See pp. 15ff. above.

[88] See p. 35.

[89] See e.g. pp. 78f., 128ff., 193ff.

[90] Boethian dialogues with Seneca: see pp. 193ff. Seneca the martyr: *Cons. phil.* 1.3.9; 3.5.10.

themes identified by Lapidge in Lucan, Manilius, Paulinus of Nola, and others, and discussed in Chapter 4.[91] Boethius is, in Lapidge's words, 'the culmination of the earlier Latin tradition of cosmological imagery',[92] and it is significant that it is a tradition found in poems which are not always predominantly philosophical in tenor.

Horace, too, will have been a potentially influential forerunner, whether in the precepts of a work such as the *Ars poetica* or in the practice of his *Epistles*, different as in the tone and import of the philosophical message of the latter from that of Boethius.[93]

A model of quite a different kind will have been Virgil. The difference is mainly due to the importance which Virgil acquires in the exegetical, especially the Neoplatonic, tradition. Virgil, described by Macrobius as the poet who writes 'not with human but with divine genius' (*Sat.* 5.1.18), and whose work, in following nature, also reflects (as does music for Boethius) the harmony imposed on nature by its divine creator – 'and so, following no other guide than nature itself, the mother of all things, he wove this, so to speak, musical concord of dissonant elements' (ib.) – this Virgil is an example to Boethius of what poetry can achieve at the sublimest level.[94] For Alexander Severus in the Neoplatonically influenced life in the *Historia Augusta*, Virgil is 'Plato among the poets' (*Alex. Sev.* 31.4), and Virgil's *Aeneid* was the subject of Neoplatonic commentaries.[95] Over and above the specific influence of Virgil on the language and themes of the *Consolation*, the authority of the poet canonized by Roman Neoplatonic tradition must be remembered when Boethius' undertaking is considered.

Manilius' *Astronomica* is likely to have been known to Boethius, but a specific explicit debt cannot be established. Manilius' programmatic statements are none the less of interest, as they establish the elements of a poetics in a work which avowedly has both a scientific and a philosophical purport.[96] In the proem to Book 1 Manilius describes himself as worshipping at two altars and in two shrines. By implication, these are philosophy and poetry:

> *bina mihi positis lucent altaria flammis,*
> *ad duo templa precor duplici circumdatus aestu*
> *carminis et rerum* ... (1.20ff).

[91] Lapidge (1980); see pp. 125ff. below.
[92] Lapidge (1980) 834.
[93] See n. 5 above. Boethius quotes *Serm.* 2.5.59 at *Cons. phil.* 5.3.25.
[94] See Curtius (1954) 441f.
[95] See Courcelle (1984); Hadot (1984) 242f. Cf. P. Hadot, *Marius Victorinus: Recherches sur sa vie et ses oeuvres* (Paris 1971) 215ff.
[96] For the proem to Manilius 1 see Wilson (1985). W. Hübner, 'Manilius als Astrologe und Dichter', *ANRW* II 32.1 (1984) 126-320, is an indispensable general survey of the entire work; cf. also (for the work's philosophical content) A. Reeh, *Interpretationen zu den Astronomica des Manilius, mit besonderer Berücksichtigung der philosophischen Partien* (Diss. Marburg 1973).

Two altars with flame kindled upon them shine before me; at two shrines I make my prayer, beset with a twofold passion, for my song and for its theme (tr. Goold).

In the previous lines, using the motif of the journey through the universe, he has distinguished between astronomical knowledge, 'but this knowledge alone is not enough' (*quod solum novisse parum est*, 16), and the greater themes of astrology, which knows the 'very heart of the sky' (*praecordia mundi*, 17) and the ways in which the lives of living beings are controlled (18). Manilius is conscious of writing in a tradition whose patron is Homer, even if Homer provides only the form, hexametric verse, and the cosmological themes are found only in Hesiod and later poets (2.1ff.). It is interesting to observe that the external form of Homeric verse establishes the genre, and also that the cosmological category is generous, including pastoral (Theocritus is referred to at 2.39ff.). Such deliberate acknowledgment of a tradition does not preclude the usual claims of originality (2.57ff., cf. 1.4ff., 1.113ff.).

If Wilson is right to see in 1.16ff. a distinction by Manilius between *novisse* (referring to astronomical knowledge) and *scire* and *cernere* (referring to higher astronomical and philosophical understanding), then a passage in Book 3 may make more sense than it might otherwise appear to do.[97] There (3.34) Manilius speaks of his astrological theme as *nosse nimis* ('what passes understanding', tr. Goold). But Manilius' terminology does not appear to be fully consistent in this respect: at 4.893 *noscere* is used of the higher understanding.

The proem of Book 3 is interesting in another respect. Manilius there, while making the unsurprising claim to deliver 'true utterances' (*veras ... voces*, 3.37), interestingly disclaims any intention to write 'beguiling songs' (*dulcia carmina*, 3.38), for *ornari res ipsa negat contenta doceri* ('my theme of itself precludes adornment, content but to be taught', 3.39, tr. Goold). This may be one of those occasions in the poem when Manilius disassociates himself from Lucretius (here he may be alluding to the passage in which Lucretius describes his art as the honey smearing the rim of the cup which makes his bitter doctrine more palatable, 1.936ff.).[98] But the passage is not just establishing a contrast with Lucretius: Manilius' apology confronts the whole tradition of the justification of poetry and rhetoric in a didactic context as a pleasant adornment that helps the persuasiveness of the argument. It is a claim that the artistry of his poem belies, but that is not the important thing. Unlike Boethius, Manilius sees no particular merit in, no special need to justify, the pleasure-giving aspect of poetry.

[97] Wilson (1985) 289.
[98] See p. 35 above.

Although no specific Christian background need be adduced to account for the form or contents of the *Consolation*, Christian attitudes to poetry may none the less have fuelled Boethius' undertaking: they certainly do not call it into question. For Jerome the pagan poets are useful means, if properly used, in the defence of Christian truths in a rhetorically sophisticated way, and poetry is found in some books of the Bible, pre-eminently the Psalms.[99] Here, then, are positive models, even if they are ones that Boethius does not opt to follow directly or explicitly. Again, though not invoking their methods, he need not have been uninfluenced by Christian attitudes to poetic inspiration, such as those found in Juvencus, Prudentius, or Paulinus of Nola, where the Holy Spirit, or Christ, or the Christian God, are invoked rather than the Muses as inspirers of a Christian poetry consistent with truth and faith, or where the Muses are invited to become Christians.[100] If Boethius opts for Plato's Muse, he none the less does so against the background of a favourable Christian attitude to poetic artistry.

The rejection of the Muses of poetry in favour of other sources of inspiration, referred to in the preceding paragraph, has a rich and varied background. Its genesis is undoubtedly in Plato, in the invocation of the philosophical Muse in *Republic* 548b, *Timaeus* 47d and 48d, and *Phaedo* 61a, and the contrast between poetical and philosophical Muses is common in later antiquity.[101] When the prisoner's poetical Muses are called Sirens by Philosophy (1.1.11) the appellation is also traditional: the Sirens are throughout antiquity symbols, not merely of the magic power of human song, but also of the persuasiveness of oratory, including its power to deceive and 'lie', a feature it shares with poetry in such contexts.[102] In Philosophy's contrast between poetry's Sirens and her Muses (1.1.11) a further motif is exploited. The rivalry between Muses and Sirens and their contest was a feature of certain myths, and philosophical exegesis of such stories considered the Sirens to be a type of inferior Muse. The divine Muses, on the other hand, are linked with philosophy itself:[103] Proclus' distinction between the noetic or intelligible harmony typified by the Muses, and the cosmic, material harmony represented by the Sirens, is the climax of such interpretations (*In. remp.* 2.237.16ff.).

A related, and contemporary, contrast will have been familiar to Boethius. When in 507 Theoderic requests him to find a lyre-player for the Frankish court, Cassiodorus, who writes the request on his king's

[99] Jerome, *Ep.* 70. See H. Hagendahl, *Latin Fathers and the Classics* (Göteborg 1958) 312ff.; Curtius (1954) 444.
[100] e.g. Prudentius, *Cathemerinon* 3.26ff.; Juvencus, *Evangeliorum libri* 1.60ff.; Paulinus of Nola, *Carm.* 10.21f., 15.30. Cf. Curtius (1954) 242.
[101] See above all P. Boyancé, *Le culte des Muses chez les philosophes grecs* (Paris 1937); cf. Gruber (1978) 71f.
[102] See Kaiser (1964) 111ff.
[103] Kaiser (1964) 118.

behalf, includes in it an excursus on the power of song, and contrasts the 'harmful sweetness' (*noxia dulcedo*) of the Sirens' song with the miraculous effects of the Psalms of David (*Variae* 2.40.10f.). Boethius may have been attracted by Sirens, but he had no excuse for not knowing how dangerous they were, and what healthy alternatives were available to him.

This section has shown that Boethius stands in a rich and varied tradition. It is one that reflects his concern that there is, on the one hand, a potential contrast between the art of poetry, which deals in fictions and is an instrument of emotional manipulation, and the science of philosophy, which uses arguments and appeals to reason, but that, on the other hand, philosophy needs to attract its addressee, to persuade and satisfy. Argument presupposes use of the devices which oratory and poetry employ. In the background against which the *Consolation* was written, there were many elements, some of which will have influenced Boethius more than others, to legitimize his undertaking and provide him with a positive model for it.

(iii) A positive theoretical model for the poetry of the *Consolation*?

Neoplatonic philosophers from Porphyry to Proclus elaborate a poetic theory whose chief aim is to reconcile the thought of Plato with interpretations of the poetry of Homer, Hesiod, and others. Ilsetraut Hadot may be right in seeing a reference in a text of Apuleius (*Florida* 20) to Platonic school concern with interpretation of poetry in Athens in the middle of the second century AD, where, along with geometry, music, and dialectic, poetry forms part of the advanced syllabus.[104] The nature of such interpretation cannot be ascertained, but that there is Platonic exegesis of poetry before Porphyry seems undeniable.[105] A figure like Numenius, a Neopythagorean of the second century AD with strong Middle Platonic affiliations, is known to have elaborated an allegory of the *Odyssey*, whether personally or through his influence upon his circle, as an account of soul's progress (fr. 33 des Places), and such allegorical accounts seem to lie behind Plotinus' reference to the *Odyssey* as a symbol or parable of moral struggle in *Enneads* 1.6.8. Although Plotinus can arguably be said to have an aesthetics,[106] there is no trace of a poetics in his writings. He does, however, have something to say about the process of artistic creativity, and he modifies the notion of art as imitation or *mimêsis* in the following passage:

---

[104] Hadot (1984) 93.

[105] Plato's dialogues themselves provide a starting-point, e.g. Pindar (fr. 169 Snell/Maehler) in *Gorgias* 484b-c; Simonides (542, *Poetae Melici Graeci*, ed. D.L. Page) in *Protagoras* 339b ff.

[106] See E. de Keyser, *La signification de l'art dans les Ennéades de Plotin* (Louvain 1955); A.N.M. Rich, 'Plotinus and the Theory of Artistic Imitation', *Mnemosyne* 13 (1960) 233-9.

But if anyone despises the arts because they produce their works by imitating nature, we must tell him, first, that natural things are imitations too. Then he must know that the arts do not simply imitate what they see, but they run back up to the forming principles (*logoi*) from which nature derives; then also that they do a great deal by themselves, and, since they possess beauty, they make up what is defective in things. For Pheidias too did not make his Zeus from any model perceived by the senses, but understood what Zeus would look like if he wanted to make himself visible (5.8.1.33ff., tr. Armstrong).

The example of Pheidias appears to be traditional. It is found in Cicero, *Orator* 2.9:

Surely that sculptor, when he made the image of Jupiter or Minerva, did not look at anyone from whom he might derive a likeness, but in his own mind there dwelt some supreme form of beauty, looking at and concentrated upon which he guided his skilled hand to produce the likeness of the divinity.

The central idea here, as in the Plotinus passage, is that the artist engages in introspective activity when creating his artefact. His model is within him, in his mind (though in Plotinus' case the forming principles or *logoi* also transcend the mind). This idea derives from an analogy with the activity of the Demiurge of the universe, as that was understood in Middle Platonic thinkers for whom the Platonic Forms have become the thoughts of God.[107] That the application of this theory to artistic activity enhances and elevates the role of the artist from that of a mere imitator of sensible reality seems undeniable, whether Plotinus is disagreeing with Plato deliberately or not.[108] Certainly Plotinus provides later Neoplatonists with a good pretext (if they needed one) for a more positive evaluation of art, including poetry.

Porphyry devoted more than one work to Homeric criticism: in his *De antro nympharum* he interprets the account of the nymphs' grotto in Book 13 of the *Odyssey* in figurative terms.[109] If Porphyry is the source of the notions expressed in Macrobius, *In somn. Scip.* 1.2.6ff.,[110] then the division of literary fictions (*fabulae*) given there indicates that he allowed for a useful form of literature, one that exhorted its audience to virtue, and could legitimately be used by philosophers:

---

[107] See W. Theiler, *Die Vorbereitung des Neuplatonismus* (Berlin 1930 = Berlin/Zürich 1964) 15ff.; J. Dillon, *The Middle Platonists* (London 1977) 93ff., 137f.; Russell (1981) 104ff.

[108] See Armstrong's note, Loeb edn. 5.240f.

[109] See Porphyry, *The Cave of the Nymphs in the Odyssey* (a revised text with translation by Classics Seminar 609, SUNY Buffalo = Arethusa Monographs 1, Buffalo, NY 1969).

[110] See Hadot (1984) 113ff.

In other fictions the contents are indeed based on the solidity of truth,
but this very truth is expressed through invented and fictional means, and
hence this is called an imaginative (*fabulosa*) narrative, and not a fiction
(*fabula*). Of such a kind are the mystery-rites, or what a Hesiod or an
Orpheus relates concerning the genealogies and actions of the gods, or the
reported secret sayings of the Pythagoreans (*In somn. Scip.* 1.2.9).

This list of approved literature interestingly omits Homer. Yet Homer,
if he is not the only concern of later Neoplatonic interpretation, is
never absent from the centre of the stage in the elaborate and
systematic exegesis of Syrianus and Proclus. It is the latter's
classification of poetry in the 6th Essay of his so-called *Commentary on
the Republic* (*In remp.* 1.177.4ff. Kroll) that is the most detailed
discussion we have of later Neoplatonic views. Developing his teacher's
(Syrianus) distinction, itself traditional, between inspired and
uninspired poetry, Proclus further divides the inspired type of poetry
into inspired and didactic, the latter sharing some of the
characteristics of the inspired poetry of Syrianus; and to the
uninspired kind corresponds what may be called mimetic or
imaginative poetry.[111] Each of these kinds of poetry corresponds in
turn to a degree or kind of the soul's life, and the description which
Proclus gives of the three lives in the soul elucidates and complements
what he says about the three kinds of poetry. The first, or inspired
kind, corresponds to the life of the soul at the highest, when it is united
with the transcendent divine principles of the universe:

> The best and most perfect life is that in which the soul is linked with the
> gods and lives the life most closely akin to them and united with them in
> extreme similarity, belonging not to herself but to them, rising above her
> own intellect, and awaking in herself the ineffable symbol (*sunthêma*) of
> the unitary existence of the gods, joining like with like, her light to the
> light yonder, the most unitary element of her own substance and life to
> the One that surpasses all substance and life (1.177.15ff., tr. Russell).[112]

The related inspired type of poetry is

> full of divine goods, setting the soul amid the principles that are the
> causes of existing things, and bringing together that which fills and that
> which is filled in an ineffable unity, laying out the former for
> illumination immaterially and nontactually, and at the same time
> summoning the latter to share its light (1.178.11ff.).

This poetry is a form of madness which

---

[111] Sheppard (1980) is fundamental: for the foregoing see 95ff., 182. Lamberton (1986)
188ff. summarizes and discusses Proclus' views. See also J.A. Coulter, *The Literary
Microcosm. Theories of Interpretation in the later Neoplatonists* (Leiden 1976).
[112] This and the following translations are taken from Russell (1981) 199f.

fills the inspired soul with due measure; and therefore it adorns its last activities with metre and rhythm (ib. 27ff.).

The second type of life is

that in which the soul turns to herself ... makes intellect and knowledge the principles of her activity; she unrolls multitudes of arguments, contemplates all kind of changes of the forms ... and makes an image of the intelligible substance by comprehending the nature of the Intelligibles in one single unity (1.177.25ff.).

To it corresponds didactic poetry, which

has its being by reference to the actual intelligent and scientific disposition of the soul. It knows the substance of real things, contemplates noble and good deeds and words, and brings everything to metrical and rhythmical expression (1.179.4ff.).

The works of such poets are

full of admonition and good advice, and laden with intelligent moderation; they enable those who have a good natural endowment to share wisdom and other virtue, and they afford means of recalling to mind (*anamnêsin*) the periods of the soul and the eternal principles and various powers contained in these (ib. 10ff.).

Finally, the third kind of life is that which employs

visions (*phantasiai*) and sensations ... entirely filling itself with inferior realities (1.178.4f.).

To it corresponds the mimetic type of poetry, which is

mixed with opinions and imaginings ... Sometimes this makes use merely of copying (*eikasia*), sometimes it puts forward an apparent but not real resemblance ... It is a shadow-drawing of reality, not exact knowledge. The goal it sets itself is the beguilement (*psukhagôgian*) of the hearers, and it looks especially to the element of the soul which is emotional and given to joy and sorrow (1.179.15ff., 25ff.).

What kinds of poetry does Proclus include in his three classes? The first kind, inspired poetry, on the evidence of the *Commentary* includes most of Homer, understood allegorically.[113] Among the examples of such inspired poetry given by Proclus (1.193.10ff.) is the deception of Zeus by Hera and their subsequent lovemaking on Mount Ida (*Iliad* 14.153ff.), which Proclus himself has treated earlier in the work (*In*

[113] See Sheppard (1980) 163.

remp. 1.132ff.), seeing it in terms of Neoplatonic metaphysical processes. Likewise interpreted is the binding of Ares and Aphrodite by Hephaestus (*Od.* 8.266ff.), treated by Proclus at *In remp.* 1.141ff.[114] Even the most shocking Homeric passages to a Platonic sensibility, of the kinds explicitly censured by Plato in the *Republic* (the Ida episode comes in for such criticism in *Rep.* 390b-c), are thus shown by Proclus to contain profound truths, and so are found acceptable by him.

The second kind of poetry, didactic verse, appears to eschew allegory, and expresses ethical and other truths in a direct fashion. The poetry of Tyrtaeus and Theognis falls into this category, and possibly the poetry of the Presocratic philosophers.[115] But didactic poetry is also found in Homer. Homer conveys knowledge of the soul's parts and the soul's relation to body, and of the order and sequence of the elements that constitute the universe (1.193.4ff.). Finally, mimetic poetry can also be found in Homer. Proclus' surprising example is *Odyssey* 3.1f., which describes the sun rising out of a lake, an example presumably chosen because it represents an optical illusion (1.192.21ff.). This is the lower kind of mimetic poetry. The higher kind represents the sensible world as it is, by the process called *eikasia* or 'copying' in Proclus' account. His example is the Homeric representations of the various kinds of heroic behaviour (1.192.28ff.) Sheppard has shown that Proclus' use of examples and distinctions based on Homer reflects earlier Homeric interpretation, even if the meaning and value of the Homeric passages urged by Proclus are novel, inasmuch as they reflect his philosophical views.[116] In the case of mimetic poetry Proclus' assertions are evidently a response to Plato's views on poetry in Book 10 of the *Republic*. By using the discussion of mimesis in the *Sophist* (235d ff.) to draw the distinction between eikastic and phantastic poetry, Proclus concludes that Plato's critique is directed only against the lower kind, phantastic poetry (1.188.28ff.).[117] Proclus is not interested in saving eikastic poetry from Plato's strictures, but both inspired and didactic poetry are intended to escape condemnation, and be seen as vehicles of philosophical communication.

Inspired poetry is on a lower level than the inspiration of a philosopher like Plato, but it is higher than the inspired activity of an exegete like Proclus' teacher Syrianus.[118] A problem in applying Proclus' theory to any poetry besides that explicitly mentioned in the *Commentary* cannot be avoided. Proclus names only Homer as an inspired poet. From other Procline texts we could add Orphic poetry and the verses of the so-called *Chaldaean Oracles* as further types of

[114] Sheppard (1980) 62ff., 68, 80f.
[115] *In remp.* 1.186.22ff.
[116] See Sheppard (1980) 162ff.
[117] Sheppard (1980) 187ff.
[118] Sheppard (1980) 174ff.

verse that he would consider inspired. Is inspired poetry confined to these canonical texts, the scriptures, as it were, of later Neoplatonism? Can inspired poetry still be written? Given the description of it by Proclus quoted above, it would not seem impossible that it could. Sheppard speculates whether Proclus might have regarded his own *Hymns* as inspired poetry.[119] Their subject-matter – the gods, their attributes, and prayers for their gifts – might seem to comprise the dealings with metaphysical first principles and the human mind's aspiration to union with them that Proclus considers to be essentials of inspired poetry. But he gives us no clue as to his own estimation of his poetry.[120] We shall have to bear this in mind when, at a later stage of this section, we turn to consider a possible application of Proclus' theory to Boethius' poetry.

Before we do so, one further aspect of Proclus' theory should be considered. It has been noted above that Proclus appears to assume that didactic poetry avoids allegory. But does it eschew myth also? Proclus, at an earlier stage of the *Commentary* (1.76.24ff.), distinguishes between two kinds of myth, the inspired and the educational. The subsequent description of the two types of educational myth, dealing with physics and ethics respectively (1.86.19ff.), seems to indicate that they treat the same kinds of theme as didactic poetry, and Sheppard is surely right to conclude that educational myths may feature in didactic poetry, even if Proclus does not explicitly say so.[121] Furthermore, Proclus appears to distinguish three modes of representation in the *Commentary*: symbolism, analogy, and imitation. The last-mentioned is unproblematic: it is mimesis in the pejorative, Platonic sense. The distinction between the first two is best expressed in Sheppard's words:

> *Analogia* ... is a matter of representing something on a higher level of reality by something on a lower level which is like it. This is to be distinguished from symbolism where there is no resemblance between symbol and object symbolised.[122]

To give examples: the union of Zeus and Hera on Mount Ida, the Homeric example of inspired poetry referred to above, bears no intrinsic likeness to the interaction of metaphysical principles which is

---

[119] Sheppard (1980) 176f.

[120] This may be due to scholarly modesty. Just as Syrianus is an inspired exegete for Proclus, so Proclus is for Marinus, *Vita Procli* 23. But one does not make such a claim for oneself.

[121] Sheppard (1980) 193.

[122] Sheppard (1980) 199; cf. W. Beierwaltes, *Proklos. Grundzüge seiner Metaphysik* (Frankfurt 1965) 171 n. 23; J. Dillon, 'Image, Symbol and Allegory: Three Basic Concepts of Neoplatonic Allegorical Exegesis', in R. Baine Harris (ed.), *The Significance of Neoplatonism* (Norfolk, Va. 1976) 247-62.

represented by it. But when Homer describes the relation of the *eidôlon* of Heracles to his soul (a plausible example of didactic poetry in Homer) his description is analogous to the psychological realities thus evoked: it is a mythical representation of these that is 'like' them in the sense meant, just as (to use another Procline example of *analogia*) mathematical figures are analogous representations of the higher realities of the intelligible world.[123]

It is now time to return to Boethius, and to ask whether the theory described on the foregoing pages can with any plausibility be applied to the poetry of the *Consolation*. It is certainly plausible that Boethius knows the theory: his acquaintance with Proclus, if not specifically with the *Commentary on the Republic*, has long since been demonstrated. But does it make any sense to adduce Proclus' theory of poetry in explanation of Boethius' poetic practice?

Let us suppose, as a working hypothesis, that Boethius was influenced by Proclus' theory. What are the consequences of this hypothesis? One consequence surely is that the poems spoken by Philosophy in the *Consolation* must fall into one of the two categories of inspired or didactic poetry. What poems might be candidates for the former category? One possibility is 4 m. 1, which, as will be shown below, is essentially a reworking of a part of Plato's *Phaedrus*. In his *Platonic Theology* Proclus considers this dialogue of Plato's to be an example of his inspired (*entheastikôs*) manner (1.4, pp. 17ff. Saffrey/Westerink).[124] It might, then, follow that Boethius' reworking is no less inspired, or at least it is inspired as poetry, as distinct from philosophy, can be. But does 4 m. 1 represent philosophical truth symbolically, in the sense referred to above? Here we come up against the obstacle of Proclus' lack of detailed exposition and examples of his types of poetry. It is undoubtedly true to say that the soul does not have wings, does not go on a journey through the heavens, does not attain to the borders of the supracelestial sphere, as the poem's metaphors describe it. The philosophical core of the poem (and its original in the *Phaedrus*) is that the soul may recover its true identity and that this will give it authentic moral insight (4 m. 1.23ff.). Now if we take the allegorical examples of Proclus' *Commentary on the Republic* as criteria of what the inspired poem should be, 4 m. 1, while in one sense not using a symbol that is like that which it represents, is not, strictly speaking, symbolic in Proclus' special sense of the term. It is more like an analogy, as that is explained above. For there is an affinity between the metaphor of flight and the notion of psychological reform, or between the image of return and the idea of rediscovery of true identity. This is, in Sheppard's words, 'allegory on the level of

---

[123] See S.E. Gersh, *Kinêsis Akinêtos. A Study of Spiritual Motion in the Philosophy of Proclus* (Philosophia Antiqua 26, Leiden 1973) 83ff.
[124] See Sheppard (1980) 174f.

Soul', and it is plausible to conclude that the metaphor of 4 m. 1, like the example she gives, is didactic rather than inspired, and is different in kind from the notion that Zeus and Hera represent the metaphysical principles of the Monad and the Dyad.[125]

What of the other poems in the *Consolation* that might count as inspired? From the foregoing discussion it would seem to follow that we must look to poems to which the term 'allegorical' might plausibly be applied. But the likely candidates here, the Orpheus (3 m. 12) and Circe (4 m. 3) poems, while arguably allegorical at least in part,[126] are, once again, not about the first or highest Hypostasis, the One of Neoplatonism, but rather about the vicissitudes and 'movements' of the human soul. They might be classifiable as allegory at the level of Mind or *nous* (or of Soul): they certainly correspond more to Proclus' account of his second-level poetry, the didactic, 'recalling to mind the periods of the soul'.[127]

It seems to be the case that when Proclus calls the *Phaedrus* 'inspired' he uses the term in a sense different from that of the 6th Essay of his *Commentary on the Republic*. Indeed, even within the 5th and 6th Essays of the *Commentary* there is a difference in what he appears to mean by inspired poetry. The poetry so referred to in the 5th Essay (1.57.23ff.) is overtly educational and didactic, and is much more like the didactic poetry of the later discussion.[128] Proclus' notion of the inspired in poetry changes and develops. Mostly it appears against the background of a twofold division (inspired/uninspired) which, Sheppard argues, Proclus inherits from Syrianus,[129] but in the 6th Essay of the *Commentary* the inspired is subdivided to create the new concept of the didactic poem. The very novelty, not of the idea of the didactic as such, but of the distinction between metaphysical allegory at the level of the 'One in the soul' in the developed way in which Proclus elaborates it, and the didactic at the level of mind or *nous*, leads to the notorious obscurities of Proclus' doctrine mentioned above.

One such obscurity is directly relevant to Boethius. It has been seen that didactic poetry is distinguished from the other two kinds in that it is not representational, neither allegorical nor mimetic. But this seems to be qualified by the notion that it can employ myth for its educational purposes, and by the suggestion that it may operate by analogy.[130] If we are to apply the term 'didactic' to the three Boethius poems

---

[125] Sheppard (1980) 47: the example is that of Numenius' use of Odysseus' wanderings as a representation of the soul's attempt to escape the material world (fr. 33 des Places: see p. 60 above).

[126] But they are not all allegory: see pp. 188-220 below.

[127] The Orpheus poem is explicitly didactic: 3 m. 12.52.

[128] See Sheppard (1980) 19.

[129] Sheppard (1980) 95ff.

[130] Sheppard (1980) 193ff.

mentioned above, then we must allow the representational elements of myth and metaphor a place in the didactic repertoire. We cannot, of course, use Boethius to prove that Proclus does, after all, allow didactic poetry to be representational, but we can conclude that the poetry of the *Consolation* is only didactic in Proclus' developed sense if that type of poetry includes the kind of mythical representation found in the Boethius poems under consideration.

Much of the other poetry of the *Consolation* is readily classifiable as didactic: the poems on the tyrant-theme, those with an explicitly ethical colouring, the poems which link themes about the physical structure of the universe to ethical concerns. A non-representational poem *par excellence* is the central poem of the work, 3 m. 9, which, while based on the *Timaeus* of Plato, can be read as an evocation of principles of physics and ethics in a distinctive Neoplatonic manner.

Yet, when all is said and done, Boethius' use of myth and imagery in poetry recalls uses of such means in a phase of Platonism earlier than Syrianus or Proclus. We are reminded more of the Numenius example, or of Plotinus' use of the *Odyssey*, both referred to above.[131] Boethius, very much the late Neoplatonist in other respects, seems to be less so when we turn to his philosophical poetry, again with the exception of 3 m. 9, where the influence of the Neoplatonic hymnology of Proclus (and possibly also Synesius) is apparent.[132]

What, then, has been the point of the hypothetical application of Proclus' theory to Boethius' poems, and what are the results of this discussion? Dependence of Boethius upon Proclus cannot be proved. Much of Boethius' poetry, indeed almost all of it, is didactic in the pre-Proclus sense, and does not require the Procline definition or distinctions to make sense. But the discussion has been worthwhile for a number of reasons. One consequence of it is the greater conceptual clarity gained. By matching the poems of Boethius against the claims of Proclus' theory, we have seen what those poems are not. They are not Neoplatonic inspired poetry in the Procline sense. They are didactic in a more general sense than that allowed by Proclus, unless we understand the imprecise assertions of the 6th Essay of the *Commentary* about didactic poetry to accommodate what we find in Boethius. But, above all, this discussion has shown how varied the influences upon Boethius were. Not uninfluenced by Neoplatonic poetry (3 m. 9), but not confining himself to that kind of verse; informed about the details of later Neoplatonic philosophy (and so possibly familiar with Proclus' theory), but not writing to any programme; a Roman poet, drawing on the elements in his tradition which legitimize, and are creatively fecund for, his enterprise, so that

[131] See p. 60 above.
[132] See Klingner (1921) 41ff.; Theiler (1966) 321ff.

the unmistakably Neoplatonic elements in a piece like the Orpheus poem are neither overtechnical nor, ultimately, the only way of reading the poem comprehensibly (even if its meaning is incomplete without them): Boethius is not reducible to any formula, or any one-dimensional description of his achievement. Finally, even if the poems are spoken by the Lady Philosophy, Boethius is evidently not using this fiction to give them a privileged, inspired status. Inspired they may be, in the didactic sense advocated in Proclus' 5th Essay, and Boethius' Philosophy may be Neoplatonic: but she is also Roman, and the expression of his own poetic persona. The poems are not so much revelation as self-discovery: Boethius' Philosophy is, after all, not divine (cf. 4.6.53f.).[133]

(iv) Quotations from other poets in the *Consolation*

The *Consolation*, in a manner reminiscent of Menippean satire, quotes from other authors, chiefly poets, in ways that add colour and resonance to the text, as well as being signposts to its meaning. Boethius thus gratifies his reader, who is expected to recognize the quotation and, sometimes, its context and hence its relevance. Do these quotations reveal any attitude or attitudes to poetry that are relevant for the understanding of Boethius' poetics?

It is not surprising to find Homer, the greatest of poets for a Neoplatonist (and not merely for a Neoplatonist), quoted no less than five times in the *Consolation*, and evoked as *melliflui ... oris Homerus* ('Homer of the voice flowing with honey' 5m. 2.3). The Homer texts, on three occasions, are ones often quoted in ancient literature, and so they have acquired a kind of independent life. Only one, the adapted quotation of *Iliad* 3.277 (etc.) at 5 m. 2.1 ('[the sun] sees all things and hears all things'), seems to have an undeniably specific Neoplatonic pedigree.[134] But it does not have its technical Neoplatonic reference or meaning in Boethius, where there is no sense that it refers to the notion that the celestial bodies possess only sight and hearing. Boethius is simply using it to express vividly (and in a learned way) the popular notion that the sun sees and hears everything. Boethius may have been made more aware of the Homeric verse from its use by later Neoplatonists, but he is not using it to show us that Homer is philosophizing Neoplatonically. Similarly, the adapted quotation of *Iliad* 2.204f. at 1.5.4 ('there is one ruler, one king') may equally be sparked off by its use in Alexandrian Neoplatonists, but it also features in a long tradition of philosophical monotheism.[135] Homer, an example of eloquence at 5 m.

---

[133] See Shanzer (1983b) 282.

[134] Courcelle (1948) 286f. argues for a specific debt to the later Neoplatonists in this and the following Homer quotations in *Cons. phil.* Cf. Courcelle (1967) 106 n. 2, 145 n. 6, 166, 281.

[135] See Gruber (1978) 143f. (criticizing Courcelle: see previous note). For the other

2.1, is here, by implication, an example of authority, but Boethius is not making for him any claim that has not been made by the many predecessors who quote the line. The third quotation of this kind, the free quotation of *Iliad* 24.527f. at 2.2.13 ('two jars, one of evils, the other of blessings'), is one often found in consolation literature, so that, once again, its occurrence in the later Neoplatonists may not carry any particular significance for Boethius.[136] It is significant that its context in the *Consolation* is the diatribe-style address of Fortune to Boethius, that is to say, a context of popular moralizing.

The other two Homeric quotations in the *Consolation* seem to be chosen by Boethius for their literary aptness, rather than because they are familiar tags found in philosophical literature. They depend for their effectiveness on knowledge of the Homeric context. When at 1.4.1 Philosophy quotes *Iliad* 1.363 ('Speak out, do not hide it in your mind') she addresses the grieving prisoner in the words Thetis uses in her consolation of Achilleus, her son. None of the other Homeric passages discussed above depends in such a way on its original context when quoted by Boethius, and only the quotation from *Iliad* 24 comes from a passage which is thematically comparable with its Boethian context of consolation. When *Iliad* 12.176 is quoted at 4.6.53 ('It would be too much effort for me to recount all this, as if I were a god') the purpose is again, in part, literary aptness and embellishment, to underline the impossibility of human comprehension of divine providence. But Glei may be right when he suggests that Philosophy is identifying herself with Homer *qua* poet here, and that his difficulty in describing the fighting (the *Iliad* context) is somehow parallel to Philosophy's in elaborating the doctrine of providence.[137] The two situations are similar. Only the inspiration granted to the poet will allow him to describe complicated battle scenes, and human reason will never fully comprehend divine laws. To that extent, Homer is here again quoted with a relevant context. The quote is a learned and resonant embellishment of the narrative.

The image of Homer which emerges from these quotations is not a distinctive one. Homer reflects monotheism, he teaches of the good and evil gifts of Fortune, he is eloquent and may be used for literary embellishment. There is nothing either distinctively Boethian or characteristically Neoplatonic about the quotations and their use.[138]

Homer quotations see Gruber's comments ad loc.

[136] Its context in Achilleus' speech in the *Iliad* is itself consolatory: see C. Macleod (ed.), *Homer: Iliad, Book XXIV* (Cambridge 1982) 131f. To the passages cited by Gruber (1978) 177 add those from Plutarch referred to by Mueller-Goldingen (1989) 383 n. 41.

[137] Glei (1985) 229; cf. Mueller-Goldingen (1989) 384.

[138] Lamberton (1986) 274ff. attempts to find a Neoplatonic tendency in Boethius' Homer quotations. His most interesting observations are on *Il.* 12.176 at 4.6.53 (where he sees a reference to negative theology) and *Il.* 3.277 at 5 m. 2.1 (compared with Plotinian 'correction' of traditional theology: see ib. 90ff. for a discussion of this and other

What is apparent is that Boethius uses Homer as he is used in philosophcal literature of a rhetorically intense kind, whether to express a notion or adorn an argument.

The other poetic quotations do not add to this overall impression or seriously modify it. Euripides' *Andromache* is quoted twice, at 3.6.1 on the hollowness of glory or fame (*Andr.* 319f.), and at 3.7.6 (a paraphrase rather than a quote) on the theme of childlessness and good or bad fortune (*Andr.* 418ff.). In both cases a moralizing point is reinforced, without reference to the original context: this is the typical ancient practice of quoting Euripidean *sententiae* divorced from their place of origin.[139] At 3.7.6 Philosophy speaks of 'my Euripides': the phrase does not amount to any explicit legitimization of tragedy by Boethius, and may merely reflect the popularity of Euripides in Stoic literature, which is particularly influential in this part of the *Consolation*.

Embellishment and reinforcement of argument are the apparent purpose of three further poetic quotations, that of Juvenal 10.20ff. at 2.5.34 (on the risks of wealth), Catullus 52.2 at 3.4.2 (on the hollowness of honours and political office), and of Horace (*serm.* 2.5.59) at 5.3.25 (on foreknowledge). It may be wrong to accuse Boethius of misunderstanding Lucan 1.128 ('the conqueror's cause pleased the gods, that of the conquered, Cato') at 4.6.33.[140] Of course he is not using the terms *victrix/victa causa* in Lucan's sense, in which Cato is the better party in defeat. Rather he is stressing that divine providence and human judgement often diverge, and implying that the providential disposition is the better. Either he is abstracting the striking phrases from their context in Lucan and using them freely, or he is deliberately playing on the paradox of Lucan's lines and correcting them: if Cato is indeed the good and just man, it is providential that he should die, even if human judgement cannot fathom the appropriateness of such a course of events.

The quotation from Parmenides at 3.12.37 ('on all sides, like the bulk of a well-rounded ball', tr. Barnes)[141] reinforces the notion of the divine nature as self-contained, perfect, the centre of the universe. It is

---

kinds of Homer allusion in Plotinus). The observation (ib. 279) that 5 m. 2.11 also uses Homeric material, namely *Il.* 1.70, is anticipated by Gruber (1978) 387; cf. also Virgil, *Georg.* 4.392f. In general, Lamberton's attempt to find Neoplatonic elements in Boethius' Homeric allusions is strained. Mueller-Goldingen (1989) 382ff. offers a more nuanced interpretation, but he, too, is inclined to over-systematize, seeing in the allusions Boethius' recognition of Homer's authority as a moral teacher.

[139] See H. Funke, art. Euripides, *Jahrbuch für Antike und Christentum* 8/9 (1965/6) 233-79; cf. Mueller-Goldingen (1989) 387f.

[140] Gruber (1978) 361; Glei (1985) 232, rightly criticized by Mueller-Goldingen (1989) 386, who, however, interprets the allusion in a restricted cognitive sense. The theme is, rather, theodicy.

[141] Parmenides: DK B 8.43. The translation is taken from J. Barnes, *Early Greek Philosophy* (Harmondsworth 1987) 135.

quoted also by Plato (*Sophist* 244e) and frequently by the Neoplatonists:[142] no specific attitude to Parmenides is thereby conveyed by
Boethius.

Although there may be objections to the emendation by Shanzer of the
Greek quotation at 4.6.38 to give a hexameter which she attributes to a
Hermetic source, her emendation, if correct, would provide a perfectly
acceptable kind of quotation in the context of the *Consolation*: divine
providence can so protect the holy man that he is not affected even by
bodily pain.[143] The lines could describe the *apatheia* of the Stoic sage,
that is to say, they could be understood out of their esoteric context.[144]
That a writer of late antiquity should express such reverence as
Philosophy does ('somebody more excellent even than me') for a
Hermetic source need come as no surprise.

Virgilian lines are quoted in adapted form or paraphrased on several
occasions, but it is not always demonstrable that they are quoted with
explicit reference to their original context: they mould Boethius'
phrasing, because he is so imbued with the Latin of their source. Glei's
attempt to relate all the Virgil passages to their sources is brave but
misguided:[145] he succeeds only once in demonstrating that the context is
implied by Boethius, at 4.6.32, where *Aeneid* 2.426f. ('most just and the
greatest maintainer of right') is quoted. The Virgilian sequence to the
quotation, *dis aliter visum* ('the gods thought otherwise', 428), is not
quoted by Boethius, but is clearly alluded to by him. Glei, however,
misreads Boethius' intentions here. Boethius does not misunderstand
Virgil. Virgil in *Aeneid* 2.428 writes elliptically. R.D. Williams para-
phrases thus: 'you might have thought he would therefore have been

---

[142] See Courcelle (1948) 287; Courcelle (1967) 166. It is, however, questionable
whether its quotation by Boethius indicates explicit approval for philosophical poetry, as
Mueller-Goldingen (1989) 387 suggests.

[143] Shanzer (1983b), who provides (279) a fuller conspectus of MSS variants for the
line than the critical editions. Those editions print an emendation of M. Haupt's (*Hermes*
3 [1869] 146), *andros dê hierou demas aitheres oikodomêsan*, meaning 'the heavens built
the body of the holy man' (for attempts to ascribe the line to its possible source see
Shanzer, art. cit. 277f.). Shanzer uses a common early Latin translation of the line (*viri
autem sacri corpus virtutes edificaverunt*), which may derive from an interlinear gloss, to
emend *demas aitheres* to *dunameis demas*, giving a meaning 'the virtues built the body
of the holy man'. She relates the line to Hermetic doctrines of spiritual and moral rebirth
and the acquisition of a new body (art. cit. 281ff.). G. Fowden, *The Egyptian Hermes*
(Cambridge 1986) 211 n. 88, objects to the attribution of the line to a Hermetic source on
the grounds that *demas* is not a Hermetic term (the term used with reference to the new
immortal body is *sôma*: see e.g. *Corp. Herm.* 13.3) and *hieros* is never applied to persons
in the extant Hermetic corpus. Unfortunately, Fowden appears to be commenting on the
line as emended by Haupt, and not on Shanzer's version of it. That does not affect his
remarks on *demas* and *hieros*, but it means that he does not deal with the strongest part
of Shanzer's argument, based on the reading *dunameis* (which is a Hermetic term: e.g.
Corp. Herm. 13.9).

[144] See Gruber (1978) 361 (on 4.6.37).

[145] Glei (1985) 230ff.

spared, but the gods willed otherwise.'[146] That is exactly what Boethius is also saying: 'all-knowing providence thinks differently.'[147] It is interesting that Boethius conflates this example with the Lucan quote just discussed, which immediately follows it. In Virgil's case the true attitude to providence emerges: Boethius needs to correct Lucan. If that is so, then neither here nor elsewhere is Boethius critical of Virgil or dismissive of him, as Glei argues.

To conclude: the uses of quotations from poetry are primarily rhetorical in the *Consolation*. A specific Neoplatonic role is not evident.[148] At the same time, poetry can contain and express philosophical truths, either unequivocally (Homer on monotheism, the Hermetic quote, Virgil as just discussed) or if properly explored (Lucan), and it is always a potential vehicle of sound ethical sense. This is a varied use of poetry, which clearly accommodates it in the philosophical enterprise. It does not amount to a poetics, but is something at once more diverse and more practical, a complex familiarity with the possibilities of an art form.

---

[146] R.D. Williams (ed.), *The Aeneid of Virgil* (London 1972) 1.234. If there is an 'accusing note' in Virgil's words, as R.G. Austin ad loc. suggests, there is no evidence (despite Mueller-Goldingen [1989] 386) that Boethius registers that note and deliberately uses the idea differently from Virgil.

[147] See Alfonsi (1979/80) 367. It should be noted that Boethius uses the same construction (*videri* + dative) as Virgil.

[148] But see Gruber (1978) 99 on the use of Virgil, *Aeneid* 10.898f. at 1.3.1.

CHAPTER THREE

The Motif of the Tyrant

Political themes are important in the *Consolation*. It is a work written by an ex-consul, a man who has held the prestigious and influential post of Master of the Offices, and worked closely with Theoderic in the administration of government. Boethius' career was splendid, and it is now in ruins. This political fall is not the least of the likely reasons for the prisoner's depression and distress at the work's outset. His lethargy need not be a contrivance, the fictional prelude to a philosophical tractate. In the first four books of the *Consolation* political themes are interwoven with the very fabric of the work's structure, and linked to its overriding themes: the role of Fortune in human affairs, the nature of true goodness, the diagnosis of evil and its place in the economy of things, the nature of happiness. The prisoner provides a detailed apologia for his political activity (1.4), and Philosophy analyses that apologia and puts it in a philosophical context (1.5; 2.3). In the parallel discussions of the gifts of Fortune in Book 2, and the external 'goods' in Book 3, the nature of power and political office is examined, along with wealth and fame; and it is the perversion of power, tyranny, that gets almost all the attention (2.6 and 2 m. 6; 3.4; 3 m. 4 and 3.5). Finally, when Boethius discusses the paradox that evil men are weak rather than powerful, it is again to the example of tyranny that he returns (4.2 and 4 m. 2).

It will be shown in the following pages that, even if Boethius' concern with these political themes may have grown out of his own experience, in both its positive and its negative aspects, he understands his political fate in traditional Roman terms, in the light of historical antecedents and values. Theoderic may be the tyrant he knows, but it is to the example of Nero that he turns; and the reasons for this, as will be seen, are not just caution and possible concern for the safety of his family and friends. Reference to tradition is the means whereby he can articulate his understanding of what has happened to him. The exploration of historical *exempla* and their relevance parallels the exploitation of myths in the work, and, like the myths, the historical examples are interpreted against a philosophical background.

Tyranny, in particular, is understood to be a form of passion (in the philosophical sense),[1] and analysis of tyranny is analysis of the guises adopted by behaviour dominated by the passions. In addition, tyranny as metaphor is a striking traditional expression for the power of passion over the soul, a power that, once it is understood, is seen to be hollow. Thus Boethius in prison can console himself by understanding and living the life of authentic freedom, and by 'demythologizing' the notion of Theoderic's power.

This chapter will focus on three poems which elaborate the tyrant motif: 2 m. 6, 3 m. 4, and 4 m. 2. It will be necessary to devote considerable attention to the context of these poems, and to the elaboration and echoes of the theme throughout the work. It will, however, be seen that, as so often in the *Consolation*, themes and images are crystallized in the poems, which make the main concerns of the work more specific, and at the same time enable Boethius to generalize with a new profoundity and vividness. But before discussion of Boethius' tyrant poems, some aspects of the antecedent tradition of the tyrant motif should be considered.

(i) The tyrant-motif: the background to Boethius

When the chorus in Aeschylus' *Agamemnon* react to the sounds of the assassination of Agamemnon they twice (1355, 1365) use the word *turannis* in a pejorative sense, just as Solon had done.[2] In post-Aeschylean tragedy the theme of tyranny is variously exploited, whether in the behaviour of Creon in Sophocles' *Antigone* or the depiction of Zeus in the *Prometheus Bound*, frequently and explicitly described as a tyrant or one whose rule is tyranny.[3] To the reader of the *Consolation* it is particularly interesting that Zeus' tyranny is evoked in medical terms, described as sickness, and that the theme of its future cure recurs in the *Prometheus Bound*.[4] Tragedy also deals with tyranny as a theme within scenes of a play (as opposed to the actual behaviour of characters): this is especially characteristic of Euripides.[5] The tyranny of Zeus (but Pericles may be meant) is a theme of Cratinus' comedy *Ploutoi* (fr. 73 Austin). The topic of tyranny

---

[1] The literature on the passions is vast: a starting point is provided by A.A. Long, *Hellenistic Philosophy* (London 1974), index s.v. 'passions (emotions)'. Early Stoic views and some criticisms of them are discussed in detail by Inwood (1985) 127ff. Stoic texts are translated in Long/Sedley 1.410ff. (comm. 419ff.).

[2] Solon, fr. 32.2 West; cf. fr. 33.6: *turanneusas*. See (on unjust kings) Hesiod, *Works and Days* 202ff., 248ff.

[3] Creon: *Antigone* 730ff.; cf. Sophocles, *Oedipus Tyrannus* 628ff. Zeus: *Prometheus Bound* 222ff., 305, 310, 736f., etc. See M. Griffith (ed.) *Aeschylus: Prometheus Bound* (Cambridge 1983) 7, 84, 220. Cf. the characterization of the bad tyrant in Herodotus 3.80.3ff.

[4] See Griffith (n. 3) 20f.

[5] Euripides, *Suppliant Women* 429ff.; *Phoenissae* 503ff.; *Ion* 626ff.; fr. 605.

is exploited in Greek declamation, and its use in this rhetorical-educational context has influenced both the Roman declamatory tradition[6] and the development of the theme in Roman historiography and literature. But before we can turn our attention to that development, reference must be made to one further Greek element that undoubtedly contributes to the complex of which Boethius is an heir. That is the use of the theme in Plato.

The discussion of tyranny and the tyrannical man in *Republic* 562a ff. is a primary influence upon Boethius.[7] In particular, the description of the rule of the desires (*epithumiai*) in the soul of the tyrannical man (571ff.), and especially the dominance of the 'master passion' *erôs*, 'a tyrant dwelling within who steers all affairs of the soul' (573d), sets up an image which Boethius repeatedly reflects: that of the tyrant who, though apparently free, is dominated by passions, and whose passions tyrannize his soul.[8] It is a passage from the *Republic* (329c) that Cicero quotes in *De senectute* when he compares the power of sexual passion with that emanating 'from a savage and raging master' (*domino, sen.* 14.47). The theme is a popular one in the philosophical tradition.[9] It is found in aphoristic form in the Pythagorean-influenced *Sentences* of Sextus:

> It is most terrible to be a slave to passions. [One has] as many masters as there are passions of the soul (*Sentences* nos. 75 a+b, p. 20 Chadwick).

The influence upon Boethius 4 m. 2 is patent.[10]

A passage in Seneca brings out the contrast between *rex* and *tyrannus* as metaphors for states of the soul:

> Our soul is now a king (*rex*), now a tyrant (*tyrannus*): a king, when it keeps its gaze upon the good, cares for the well-being of the body entrusted to it, and does not give it any shameful or base commands; but when it is uncontrolled, desiring, indulgent, it changes to an abominated and terrible state of ill repute and becomes a tyrant. The uncontrolled

---

[6] See S.F. Bonner, *Roman Declamation* (Liverpool 1949); G.A. Kennedy, *The Art of Rhetoric in the Roman World* (Princeton, NJ 1972) 91ff.; id., 'The Sophists as Declaimers', in G.W. Bowersock (ed.), *Approaches to the Second Sophistic* (University Park, Pa. 1974) 17ff.

[7] See also Plato, *Gorgias* 510aff. Cf. Scheible (1972) 135f.; G. Heintzeler, *Das Bild des Tyrannen bei Platon* (Stuttgart 1927). See also Aristotle, *Politics* 5, 1310bff., where, however, good and bad tyrannies are distinguished.

[8] Enslavement to passions: see already Euripides, *Hecuba* 864ff.

[9] Especially in diatribe (for which see Ch. 1, n. 75): see Epictetus 1.9.15. On the tyrant-theme in Epictetus see C.G. Starr, 'Epictetus and the Tyrant', *Classical Philology* 44 (1949) 20-9; cf. Rutherford (1989) 66 n. 58, who also (65f.) comments perceptively on Marcus Aurelius' difficulties, as emperor, in utilizing the sage-tyrant motif. Cf. Bion of Borysthenes, fr. 11 and Kindstrand ad loc.; Oltramare (1926), index s.v. 'Passions asservissantes'.

[10] See pp. 94ff. below.

passions capture and importune it ... (*Ep.* 114.24).

Another Seneca text exploits the contrast *rex-tyrannus* in ethical terms whose influence on the characterization of the tyrant in Boethius is (at least as far as this type of contrast is concerned) obvious:

> What is the difference between a tyrant and a king ... except that tyrants are cruel for their pleasure, kings only for good reasons and by necessity? ... Tyrants take delight in cruelty ... for since [the tyrant] is hated because he is feared, so he wishes to be feared because he is hated ... He does not know what frenzy is engendered when hatred increases beyond measure (*De clementia* 1.11.4-12.4, tr. Battles/Hugo).[11]

So far two strands of tradition have been identified: the poetic and literary exploitation in Greek literature of the tyrant-theme, influencing in turn the declamatory tradition; and the philosophical theme of passion *qua* tyranny, and of tyrants as dominated by passion, originating in Plato, but widespread in philosophical moralizing contexts where the influence of diatribe is apparent. To these should be added a further strand of the Roman tradition, the motif of tyranny in poetry where the influence of philosophy, usually Stoicism, is patent.[12] This strand, unwisely neglected in Boethian scholarship, is of considerable interest when the formation of the *Consolation* is considered.

In *Odes* 2.16 Horace, evoking the ideal of *otium*, remarks that it is *non gemmis neque purpura venale nec auro* ('not to be bought with gems or purple or gold', 7f.). And in the following lines he contrasts the man of wealth and power with the wise man or sage (*sapiens*): the latter is free from the fear (*timor*) and desire (*cupido*) which plague the former:

> *non enim gazae neque consularis*
> *submovet lictor miseros tumultus*
> *mentis et curas laqueata circum*
>   *tecta volantis.*
> *vivitur parvo bene, cui paternum*
> *splendet in mensa tenui salinum*
> *nec levis somnos timor aut cupido*
>   *sordidus aufert* (9ff.).

For neither riches nor the consul's lictor can move on wretched disturbances of the mind and cares that flit around panelled ceilings. He

---

[11] Such contrasts were elaborated rhetorically in popular philosophical literature on kingship, of which *De clementia* itself is a prime example. Cf. Dio Chrysostom, *Orations* 1-4. See P. Hadot, art. Fürstenspiegel, *RAC* 8 (1972) 555-632; Rutherford (1989) 54f.

[12] Another distinctively Roman development is the polemical biographical tradition of Stoic opposition to imperial 'tyranny': see p. 86 with n. 34 below for its influence on *Cons. phil.* 1.3 and 4.

lives well on little, whose ancestral salt-cellar shines spotlessly on his humble table, whose easy sleep neither fear nor base greed steals.[13]

The just and upright man

> *non voltus instantis tyranni*
>   *mente quatit solida neque Auster (Odes* 3.3.3f.).

the face of a threatening tyrant does not shake from his firm resolve, nor the south wind.

What Horace expresses in the condensed and cryptic style of his lyric poetry is developed in expansive manner in Seneca's tragedies, where tyrannical characters, such as Lycus in *Hercules furens*, Aegisthus in *Agamemnon*, and Atreus in *Thyestes*, are of considerable importance.

Atreus may serve as an example of Seneca's method. He unashamedly describes himself as a *tyrannus* (*Thy.* 177) – and the context leaves one in no doubt that the pejorative sense is intended. In the dialogue with a servant (204ff.) the servant warns: *quos cogit metus / laudare, eosdem reddit inimicos metus* ('those whom fear compels to praise, fear makes into enemies', 207f.).[14] But Seneca's Atreus welcomes false praise that is feigned, as it confirms his power: *quod nolunt velint* ('Let them will what they do not want', 212). The servant contrasts the good king with this grim alternative: *rex velit honesta: nemo non eadem volet* ('A king should will what is good: everybody would wish the same', 213). But Atreus will have nothing to do with 'decency, concern for right, integrity, piety, trust' (*pudor ... cura iuris sanctitas pietas fides*, 215f.), and demands total licence (214f.).[15] Atreus considers death to be, not a punishment, but a favour which his victims may supplicate: *perimat tyrannus lenis: in regno meo / mors impetratur* ('A gentle tyrant might kill: in my kingdom death is begged for', 247f.). The view is shared by other Senecan tyrants.[16] Finally, when the servant tries to dissuade Atreus from violence that may recoil on him, possibly through the bad example which his actions give his children, Atreus' reply reveals a cynical pessimism that undermines all values:

> *ut nemo doceat fraudis et sceleris vias,*
> *regnum docebit. ne mali fiant times?*
> *nascuntur. istud quod vocas saevum asperum,*
> *agique dure credis et nimium impie,*
> *fortasse et illic agitur* (312ff.).

---

[13] See Nisbet/Hubbard ad loc. for a discussion of the individual motifs.

[14] A typical Senecan theme: Tarrant (1985) 121 refers to *Oed.* 705f.; *Ag.* 72; *Ep.* 105.4. To these *clem.* 1.12.4 should be added.

[15] Typically: see *Troad.* 335; *clem.* 1.8.2; Tarrant (1985) 121f.

[16] e.g. *Ag.* 994f. (and Tarrant ad loc.); *Herc. fur.* 511ff.

Even if nobody should teach the ways of deceit and crime, kingly power will do so. Are you afraid they [the children] will become wicked? They are born like that. What you call fierce and harsh, what you believe is cruel and most impious behaviour, is perhaps being plotted by the other side, too.

In the choral ode which follows this scene (336ff.) a picture of true kingship is given that, by contrast, highlights and defines the evils of tyranny. Building on the Stoic idea that the sage (*sapiens*) is the only true king,[17] the chorus evokes an image of a ruler who despises wealth and extravagant luxury (344ff.), is free of fears and of the need to court popular opinion (348ff.), is not tempted by the earth's riches (353ff.), unaffected by the violence of nature and of war (358ff.), and goes forward to meet his fate deliberately and uncomplainingly (367f.). The true king is controlled by his 'good sense' (*mens ... bona*, 380) and this protects him against all external threats (369ff.). This king will be free from the destructive passions of fear and desire, and becomes thereby a symbol of the control of reason in the individual (so that the *sapiens* = *rex* equation is the moral of this depiction, which is thus a depiction of any individual as much as of a ruler):

> *rex est qui metuet nihil;*
> *rex est qui cupiet nihil:*
> *hoc regnum sibi quisque dat* (388ff.).[18]

He is a king who fears nothing, he is a king who desires nothing: this kingdom each individual grants himself.

The details of this ode, which, as Tarrant has shown, owes much both to Horace and to Virgil's *Georgics* 2.490ff., correspond to motifs, emblems, and evaluations which colour Boethius' tyrant poems. He is undoubtedly an heir to this tradition, and, here as elsewhere, Seneca will have influenced him.

The theme of the tyrant – with the contrast between him and the just ruler or politician – is important in later Latin epic.[19] In Lucan's *Pharsalia* Julius Caesar is portrayed as a tyrant subverting Roman *libertas*, whose real defender against him, but also against *fatum* and *fortuna*, is Cato (rather than Pompey). Caesar's motivation and behaviour are characterized by Lucan thus:

---

[17] Cf. Horace, *Epist.* 1.1.106f.; 1.10.8. See Tarrant (1985) 140 for further instances. Cf. *SVF* 1.216; 3.617.

[18] On the textual difficulties of 388f. see Tarrant (1985) 146, who follows F. Leo in deleting them as an interpolation. O. Zwierlein's 1986 Oxford edn. accepts them as genuine. For the gnomic futures *metuet* and *cupiet* cf. Horace, *Epist.* 1.16.65f.

[19] See G. Williams, *Change and Decline. Roman Literature in the Early Empire* (Berkeley/Los Angeles, CA 1978) 205 n. 31.

> sed non in Caesare tantum
> nomen erat fama ducis, sed nescia virtus
> stare loco, solusque pudor non vincere bello;
> acer et indomitus, quo spes quoque ira vocasset,
> ferre manum et numquam temerando parcere ferro,
> successus urguere suos, instare favori
> numinis, inpellens, quidquid sibi summa petenti
> obstaret, gaudensque viam fecisse ruina (1.143ff.).

But Caesar had more than a mere name and military reputation: his energy could never rest, and his one disgrace was to conquer without war. He was alert and headstrong; his arms answered every summons of ambition or resentment; he never shrank from using the sword lightly; he followed up each success and snatched at the favour of Fortune, overthrowing every obstacle on his path to supreme power, and rejoicing to clear the way before him by destruction (tr. Duff).[20]

Caesar (and in a sense also Pompey) aims at 'harsh tyranny' (saeva ... regna, 2.314f.). Caesar's conduct of war in Italy betrays a gratuitous violence and lust for destruction (2.650ff.), even if he is not always portrayed as a monster.[21] Cato's eulogy of Pompey (9.190ff.) mingles faint praise with a vision of what the ideal politician should be: in some respects, such as in his death and its circumstances, Pompey reveals what the good ruler of Seneca's Thyestes 337ff. does:

> forsitan in soceri potuisses vivere regno.
> scire mori sors prima viris, sed proxima cogi (Lucan, 9.210f.).

You might perhaps have stooped to go on living under the tyranny of your kinsman. Happiest of all men are those who know when to die; and next come those upon whom death is forced (tr. Duff, amended).

In Statius' Thebaid[22] Adrastus, the king of Argos, is the benevolent ruler, model of the Stoic sapiens, and contrasted with the grim tyrant Eteocles, king of Thebes. Adrastus is 'mild' (mitis, 1.467), and the peace of his kingdom (1.390ff.) is broken by the arrival of Polynices and Tydeus, bringing frenzy and madness (rabies, furor: 1.408,438). Polynices, in particular, epitomizes arrogant pride (superbia) and its concomitant anxieties and ambitions (1.320ff.). The arrival of Polynices and Tydeus undermines the idyllic peace of Argos, which, though ruled justly, enjoys prosperity to excess (luxus, 1.517ff.). At Thebes the tyrant Eteocles sits on the throne which he has usurped, anxious for opportunities to commit crime:

---

[20] Cf. 2.439ff.

[21] The contrast of libertas and regna (freedom/tyranny): 3.145. Caesar's clemency: 4.363ff.

[22] For the following see D. Vessey, Statius and the Thebaid (Cambridge 1973) 92ff.

ibi durum Eteoclea cernit
sublimem solio saeptumque horrentibus armis.
iura ferus populo trans legem ac tempora regni
iam fratris de parte dabat; sedet omne paratus
in facinus queriturque fidem tam sero reposci (2.384ff.).

Then he [Tydeus] beholds the cruel Eteocles high upon a throne and girt round with bristling spears. The appointed seasons of his reign already past, he was holding the people under savage rule in his brother's stead; prepared for every crime he sits, and complains of so late a claiming of his promise (tr. Mozley, adapted).

Eteocles feels the fear that haunts a tyrant (3.1ff.). His mind is convulsed with passion, and confused feelings of regret, particularly regret at not having committed greater crimes, course through his thoughts (3.18ff.). Maeon, by contrast, exemplifies dutifulness (*pietas*) and readiness to confront death and resist tyranny (3.59ff.). Eteocles is motivated by anger (*irae*, 3.77) to greater violence against Maeon, whose Stoic suicide only drives the tyrant to raging frenzy (*rabies*, 3.96ff.), in which he desecrates Maeon's corpse. But that corpse remains untouchable, a symbol of the powerlessness of the tyrant in the face of virtue (3.99ff.). In Book 10 it is Menoeceus who is the example of virtue, by contrast with the *furor* of Capaneus.[23]

The influence of the tyrant-type is also discernible in Tacitus' portrayal of Augustus and his successors, especially Tiberius, though the extent to which his account of Tiberius is a depiction of a type-character is a matter of scholarly controversy, as is the degree to which Germanicus is an idealized foil to his uncle, exemplifying the qualities of 'ancient virtue' (*prisca virtus*) and *pietas*.[24] In Suetonius, the Caesars and their reigns are judged by the criterion of moral restraint, and imperial vices are described in terms of the misuse of power by autocrats who abandon themselves to luxury and lust. The influence of imperial panegyric and Hellenistic (philosophically influenced) kingship literature is evident in Suetonius' analysis of

[23] In the *Argonautica* of Valerius Flaccus both Pelias (1.22ff.; 1.700ff.) and Aeetes (5.519ff.; 7.32ff.) are characterized as tyrants.
[24] On the tyrant-type in Tacitus, especially in the *Annals*, see B. Walker, *The Annals of Tacitus. A Study in the Writing of History* (Manchester 1952) 78ff., 204ff., 240ff. (204ff. also provides a discussion of antitypes). On Tiberius: ib. 217f.; cf. 82ff. On Germanicus as foil: ib. 232ff.; cf. 118ff. For reservations about this approach, and arguments that Tacitus is, on the contrary, giving a historically reliable account of the atmosphere of mistrust and conflict in the relations between Tiberius and Germanicus, as well as of the complexities of Tiberius' character, see D.C.A. Shotter, 'Tacitus, Tiberius and Germanicus', *Historia* 17 (1968) 194-214; id., 'Tacitus and Tiberius', *Ancient Society* 19 (1988) 225-36. Cf. D.O. Ross, 'The Tacitean Germanicus', *Yale Classical Studies* 23 (1973) 209-27. On stereotyping of tyrants in Roman historiography see J.R. Dunkle, 'The Rhetorical Tyrant in Roman Historiography: Sallust, Livy and Tacitus', *Classical World* 65 (1971/2) 12-20.

imperial vices and virtues.[25]

Such is the rich background against which the tyrant motif in Boethius should be considered. This survey has, of necessity, been brief: an adequate discussion of the texts referred to is beyond the scope of this book. The following passages will add further details, revealing influences upon the thought and language of individual passages in the poems or in the *Consolation* as a whole (for example, tyrannical persecution of philosophers, and philosophers' defiance of tyrants). As is the case with other instances of his confrontation with traditional motifs, Boethius modifies and adapts aspects of the tyrant motif. His tyrant poems are no mere patchwork of topics. They are fully and convincingly integrated into the overall structure of the work, as detailed analysis will demonstrate.

(ii) The first Nero poem (2 m. 6)

Novimus quantas dederit ruinas
urbe flammata patribusque caesis
fratre qui quondam ferus interempto
matris effuso maduit cruore
corpus et visu gelidum pererrans   5
ora non tinxit lacrimis, sed esse
censor exstincti potuit decoris.
hic tamen sceptro populos regebat
quos videt condens radios sub undas
Phoebus, extremo veniens ab ortu,   10
quos premunt septem gelidi triones,
quos Notus sicco violentus aestu
torret ardentes recoquens harenas.
celsa num tandem valuit potestas
vertere pravi rabiem Neronis?   15
heu gravem sortem, quotiens iniquus
additur saevo gladius veneno!

We know how much destruction he once caused, with the city ablaze and its senators slaughtered, that savage man who murdered his brother and was drenched with his mother's gushing blood, who ran his eye over her cold body (5), and did not wet his face with tears, but could evaluate her

---

[25] See A. Wallace-Hadrill, *Suetonius: The Scholar and his Caesars* (London 1983) 142ff.; cf. n. 11 above. On the theme in Claudian (where Theodosius' achievements are contrasted with the behaviour of the usurpers [called *tyranni*, as often in fourth-century texts: see Courcelle (1980) 205ff.]) see W. Taegert (ed.), *Claudius Claudianus: Panegyricus dictus Olybrio et Probino consulibus* (Zetemata 85, Munich 1988) 131, 151 (on ll. 75ff., 107f.). Cf. A. Cameron, *Claudian: Poetry and Propaganda at the Court of Honorius* (Oxford 1970) 35f.; Matthews (1975) 257; cf. ib. 228f., 247ff. for eulogies of Theodosius by other authors, esp. Pacatus, *Panegyr.* 2 (*XII Panegyrici Latini*, ed. R.A.B. Mynors [Oxford 1964]); Ambrose, *De obitu Theodosii* (*CSEL* 73); Augustine, *De civitate dei* 5.26. See also in general F. Christ, *Die römische Weltherrschaft in der antiken Dichtung* (Tübinger Beiträge zur Altertumswissenschaft 31, Stuttgart/Berlin 1938).

destroyed beauty. Yet this man ruled with kingly sceptre the peoples that Phoebus sees as he hides his rays under the waves, or comes from the farthest east (10), those overpowered by the icy grip of the north, and those burnt by the dry heat of the fierce sirocco as it scorches the hot sands once again. Was lofty power ineffectual to alter evil Nero's madness? (15) O harsh destiny, when the sword of injustice is joined to the poison of rage!

One of the most striking anecdotes employed by Boethius to illustrate philosophical defiance of tyranny is recounted at 2.6.8:

> When a tyrant thought that he would compel a free man to betray those conspiring against him, the man bit off his tongue and spat it in the raging tyrant's face. So the torture which the tyrant thought was the means of his cruelty, the sage made the occasion of his virtue.

It matters little whether the philosopher was Zeno of Elea or Anaxarchos of Abdera: the anecdote is related of both philosophers, and is evidently part and parcel of philosophical martyrological hagiography.[26] It is the example that interests Boethius, and the moral which it illustrates. The confrontation is emblematic for the *Consolation*. On the one hand, the philosopher, a free man, a sage, whose defiance exhibits his courageous goodness; on the other, the tyrant, by implication neither free, nor wise, nor good, but 'raging' (*saevientis*) in his cruelty. So much is explicitly expressed in the text. But the emblematic nature of the anecdote may be explored further. The tyrant is a travesty of the ideal Roman emperor, whose virtues are celebrated in literature (notably panegyric), on the coinage, and on inscriptions from the first century AD on: the ruler who possesses and exercises *clementia, iustitia, civilitas, pietas, liberalitas, continentia*, and other qualities.[27] The philosopher, on the contrary, expresses his virtue paradoxically by the action of biting off the tongue which is the normal instrument of his actvity in debate and argument: his action speaks louder than any words, and, in making himself apparently powerless, he is not merely anticipating defiantly, and so devaluing, the tyrant's punishment, but is also expressing the true power of enlightened behaviour. These themes, and the issues which they raise, will be further explored in the following pages.

The tyrant defied in the anecdote of 2.6.8 is said to 'rage' (*tyranni saevientis*). The description is almost a cliché in contexts where the

---

[26] Diog. Laert. 9.27, 59. Zeno and Anaxarchos appear to be mentioned together in lists of philosophical martyrs, which may have led to some contamination of their life histories: see Cicero, *Tusc. disp.* 2.22.52; *nat. deor.* 3.33.82.

[27] See L. Wickert, art. Princeps, *RE* 22 (1954) 1998-2296 (here 2231ff.); Wallace-Hadrill (n. 25 above) 145ff.; A. Dihle, *Die Entstehung der historischen Biographie*, Sitzungsberichte der Heidelberger Akademie der Wissenschaften, Phil.-hist. Klasse 3/1986 (1987) 61ff.

tyrant-motif occurs (1 m. 4.11; 2 m. 6.17) or the wicked are being described (4.3.5; 4.4.1); what is significant, however, is the fact that Boethius is adapting to the tyrant a common description in Latin literature of the cruel and relentless aspects of Fortune.[28] It is when he considers his political downfall that the prisoner finds Fortune cruel. His apologia begins with an evocation of *fortunae in nos saevientis asperitas* ('the harshness of fortune raging against us', 1.4.2). The same Fortune ... *tremendos* saeva *proterit reges / humilemque victi sublevat fallax vultum* ('fiercely tramples down kings who were just now dreaded, and deceitfully raises up the downcast face of the conquered', 2 m. 1.3f.). The effect of this equation tyrant = Fortune is above all to allow each element to correct superficial understandings of the other. Thus, for example, the prisoner mistakenly considers evil men (such as tyrants) to be not merely happy but also powerful, and Fortune by analogy to be 'without a master' (*sine rectore*, 1.6.19).[29] But Fortune, upon reflection, can be considered a teacher: when adverse, Fortune reveals the fragility of human happiness, and so draws its victims towards the good, and reveals loyal and honest friends (2.8). This Fortune, the argument of the *Consolation* demonstrates, is reducible to an instrument of divine providence (3.12.17ff.; 4.6): God can make evils and evil men a means of impelling others towards goodness (4.6.50ff.). God, then, is Fortune's master. That is why every kind of fortune is good (4.7). Likewise, the seeming power of the tyrant is revealed as powerlessness. The tyrant is vulnerable and can be overthrown, even by evil men (1 m. 5.39ff.). All power is precarious and limited (2 m. 1; 2.2.11f.; 2.6.10f.; 3.5.1ff.). And power, like Fortune, is ultimately an instrument of providence (4.6.33ff.). Thus the equation tyrant = Fortune is seen to be right, but in a more profound, more complex sense. It is not their power, but their function in a providentially ordered universe, that links the tyrant and Fortune (4.6.10,53).

At the stage of the work marked by the poem 2 m. 6 this line of argument has not been fully developed; but certain crucial elements of the argument have already been explored. The traditional conflicts between philosophers, Greek and Roman, and tyrannical rulers, have been sketched (1.3.9ff.), and the inability of the latter to inflict any real harm on the former suggested (1.3.12ff.). The vulnerability of rulers has been established (1 m. 5.39ff.; 2 m. 1; 2.2; 2.6), and the related paradox of the powerlessness of tyrants evoked (1 m. 4.11ff.; 2.2; 2.6). In addition, two further themes have been developed. One is the autobiographical one, the specific fate of Boethius in the state ruled by

[28] See pp. 216f.
[29] Compare the description of the wicked who prey upon philosophers, 'without a leader (*nullo duce*), but driven only by delusion ...' (1.3.12). Fortune, too, is apparently 'uncontrolled' (1.6.19: here the reference is to the delusion of those who, like the prisoner, imagine (a) Fortune's power to be absolute, (b) being without a master to be a good thing).

Theoderic, and the prisoner's incipient understanding of that fate. The other is the distinction drawn by Boethius between authentic goodness and power. These two themes, the apologetic and the philosophical, must be explored briefly before 2 m. 6 can be analysed.

In his apologia Boethius begins by offering a Platonic, philosophical reason for entering politics. He refers to the much-quoted sentiment of the *Republic*, that the best states would be those where philosophers were rulers, or whose rulers were philosophers, and makes it clear that he understands this to be an imperative for a philosopher, who undertakes political office for the common good (1.4.5ff.).[30] But once he develops the argument of his apologia, it becomes evident that Boethius understands it in traditional Roman terms. He took the political risks which led to his arrest in order to defend and preserve the Roman senate (1.4.20ff.). His reported statement when accused is protective of the senate's collective identity:

> Then Boethius the patrician, who was Master of the Offices, said in the king's presence: 'Cyprianus' charge is false. But if Albinus [so] acted, then I and the whole senate acted [thus] with one mind. It is false, my lord king' (*Anonymus Valesianus* 85).

Even the senate's 'self-deluding folly' (1.4.24) in failing to save him, and in actually passing decrees against him, cannot change that loyalty.[31] Forged documents had alleged that he had striven for liberty (*libertas*, 1.4.26), and Boethius, though emphasizing that they were forgeries, admits the will to *libertas* and regrets its absence in the current situation (1.4.27). He recalls that consular power had once been the foundation of *libertas* against the arrogance (*superbia*) of kings (2.6.2). *Libertas* and the consulship (*consulatus*): it is a self-dramatization utterly unreal in the world of Theoderic's rule. Boethius is projecting himself by implication as a second Brutus.[32]

Moreover, Boethius sees his opposition to Theoderic in traditional terms of opposition to a tyrannical ruler. Theoderic is not named in the *Consolation*, but referred to (1.4.17,32) as *rex* (the title is not pejorative): his tyrannical nature is, however, brought out by the description 'king eager for destruction', *rex avidus exitii* (1.4.32), and his desire to implicate the whole senatorial order in the charge of

[30] Plato, *Republic* 473cff., 487e, etc.; *Letter* 7, 326b, etc. Shanzer (1984) 364ff. notes the additional influence of the *Apology* and *Phaedo* on Boethius' apologia.

[31] Cf. 1.4.32, 36. See pp. 3ff. above.

[32] For the earlier ideological background see C. Wirszubski, *Libertas as a Political Idea at Rome* (Cambridge 1950), esp. 143ff. J. Moorehead, '*Libertas* and *nomen Romanum* in Ostrogothic Italy', *Latomus* 46 (1987) 161-8, shows how Theoderic sought to associate himself with the idea of *libertas* (cf. e.g. Cassiodorus, *Variae* 3.11.1; 3.12.1; 3.43.2; 5.16.5; 10.4.7; Ennodius, Ep. 4.26.1) as part of the attempt to legitimize his rule, whereas Boethius (art. cit. 165f.) uses (or is alleged to use [*Cons. phil.* 1.4.26]) the term *libertas* in a traditional sense that could not be applied to Gothic rule.

treason (ib.).[33] In addition, Boethius, by his choice of antecedent *exempla*, sets his actions in the context of philosophical opposition, until death, to tyrannical rulers of the Roman world: Soranus against Nero (1.3.9), Canius against Caligula (1.3.9; 1.4.27), Seneca against Nero (1.3.9; 3.5.10), and Papinianus against Caracalla (3.5.10).[34] Philosophy, in a first reaction to the apologia, sees it as a legitimate stance, even if it is dangerously under the influence of emotions like grief and anger (1.5.7ff.). And in the later, more detailed reaction at 2.3, Philosophy balances the prisoner's complaint at his bad fortune with a counter-catalogue of his good fortune (2.3.4ff.). In other words, it is no part of Philosophy's reply to Boethius' complaints that his attitudes and assumptions are those of a lost world and hence illusory. There is indeed reference to historical change in the *Consolation*, to the institution of the tribunate to counter the same abuses of power by the consuls which had led in the first place to the establishment of the consulate (2.6.2), and to the decline of the offices of praetor and *praefectus annonae* (3.4.15).[35] But in both cases it is not the phenomenon of change as such that is the object of the reference. The decline of the consulship illustrates rather the truth that political office does not itself confer goodness on its holders (2.6.3); the decline of other offices in the post-Constantinian period demonstrates that they possess no intrinsic power, but that their prestige depends upon fickle opinion (3.4.13ff.). Nor should these lessons surprise us, for they are of the traditional kind encountered in moralizing diatribe, which seeks to draw a universally valid moral from contingent historical experience. Consideration of this leads to two conclusions in the case of Boethius. First, Boethius' understanding of his political career and downfall does not remain an autobiographical excursus in the work as a whole, but links directly to its central ethical themes because of the way in which it is interpreted. Secondly, the Roman colouring is aptly traditionalist because it is authentic, a reflection of Boethius' 'mental and emotional

[33] Barnish (1983) 583ff. discusses the portrayal of Theoderic as tyrant in *Anon. Vales*. (94: *non rege sed tyranno*), noting further similarities between the accounts of the events leading to the death-sentence on Boethius in that work (whose date of composition he proposes as about 550 [art. cit. 577f.]) and in *Cons. phil.* (ib. 590). See also Ch. 1, n. 17. On *tyrannus* in *Anon. Vales*. see Courcelle (1980) 195, 202ff. Boethius' self-dramatization in *Cons. phil.* does not, however, devalue it as a historical document, as E. Reiss (displaying complete unawareness of the conventions of ancient historiography and biography) argues ('The Fall of Boethius and the Fiction of the *Consolatio Philosophiae*', *Classical Journal* 77 [1981] 37-47 ~ id., *Boethius* [Boston, Mass. 1982] 80-102). Shanzer (1984) 353ff. disposes of Reiss's arguments.

[34] For the Roman tradition of Stoic martyr-literature see R. MacMullan, *Enemies of the Roman Order* (Cambridge, Mass. 1966) 1-94; H. Musurillo, *The Acts of the Pagan Martyrs* (Oxford 1954), esp. 236ff.; Wirszubski (n. 32 above) 136ff.; Rutherford (1989) 59ff.

[35] See W. Ensslin, art. praefectus, *RE* 22 (1954) 1272ff.; G. Wesenberg, art. praetor, ib. 1602ff.

horizons' in the senatorial tradition that persisted in late Roman politics.[36] Both these conclusions illustrate the fact that the *Consolation* is 'internalized' biography of a morally interpretative kind.

When Boethius argues that power is not intrinsically good, he adduces two grounds: power can be held by the wicked (but if it were intrinsically good it could not be conjoined with its opposite), and power not merely does not make its possessor good, but may assist his corruption (2.5.32f.; 2.6.13,20). Behind those arguments lies the Stoic doctrine of 'indifferent' things, which do not, of themselves, either harm or benefit, and can be used both well and badly.[37] Boethius implies that power, like wealth and other external goods, is no more intrinsically evil than it is good. His formulations echo those found in Seneca:

What is good makes people good (*Ep.* 87.12).

What can happen to the most contemptible and evil people, is not good (ib. 15).

When what we want to attain makes us meet with many calamities, it is not good (ib. 28).

Seneca indicates that, in orthodox Stoic manner, wealth is not good, but, by implication, indifferent (*Ep.* 87.15,22,28ff.), whereas greed (*avaritia*), the moral failing, is evil (ib. 22). Boethius says the same of wealth and power in relation to *avaritia* or 'lust' (*libidines*, 2.6.18). This is the immediate ideological background against which the poem 2 m. 6 is set: it is time to turn to the detail of that poem.

In the first Nero poem two images or sets of images are juxtaposed (1-7; 8-13) and then (14-17) a moralizing conclusion is drawn.[38] The first part is a catalogue of the evils perpetrated by Nero: the burning of Rome, the killing of senators, the murders of Britannicus and Nero's own mother, Agrippina, and his cold-blooded and cynical attitude to her dead body. The matricide and its aftermath are the most detailed and the climactic items of this catalogue (4-7). Nero is the type of the ruthless and unemotional destroyer. The incidents and their interpretation are traditional, and indebted to the picture of Nero portrayed by Tacitus, Suetonius, and Dio Cassius.[39] In the Agrippina detail, Boethius chooses to echo the most gruesome version. Whereas

[36] See Matthews (1981) 38 and in general 25ff., to which this paragraph is greatly indebted.
[37] Cf. e.g. Diog. Laert. 7.101ff. (see Long/Sedley 1.354ff.).
[38] See Scheible (1972) 64ff.
[39] See J. Rougé, 'Néron à la fin du IVe et au début du Ve siècle', *Latomus* 37 (1978) 73-87; Scheible (1972) 64f.

Tacitus regards it as a matter of dispute that Nero assessed the beauty of his mother's body (*Ann.* 14.9) and Suetonius is inclined to believe such reports (*Nero* 34.6), Dio Cassius is actually able to quote his words on the occasion (61.14.2: 'I did not know that I had such a beautiful mother'). Such elaboration of a motif for emotional effect is extended by Boethius (5ff.). The Nero example makes specific the general remarks about power and political office of the preceding 2.6,[40] but it does so in a way that links explicitly to the double image of the destructiveness of power abused in 2.6.1. There Boethius says of power and offices:

> If these things have fallen to the lot of the most evil men, what Etnas belching flames, or what deluge, have caused as much destruction?

The image of the fires of Etna[41] is echoed in the fire that destroys Rome (*urbe flammata*, 2 m. 6.2). The image of the flood is reflected in Agrippina's blood 'drenching' (4) Nero, and it may recall the attempted assassination by shipwreck (to which Boethius does not explicitly refer) of Agrippina by Nero (Tacitus, *Ann.* 14.3ff.). Thus the images of the prose section are given concrete vividness in the description of Nero's atrocities. This is a frequent but not universal pattern. Earlier in Book 2 the opposite process has occurred. The general assertions of 2 m. 1 about the ways in which Fortune can overthrow great rulers *una hora* (9) are illustrated by the specific examples of Croesus and Perseus of Macedon in the following prose section (2.2.11f.).

The second part of the Nero poem (8-13) is introduced as a contrast (*tamen*, 8) to the sequence of his atrocities. It employs the motif of the world-wide extent of his rule, which extends to the four corners of the earth. The motif is ancient, and in its simplest form, 'from sunrise to sunset', occurs in Mesopotamian inscriptions, in Greek texts relating to the Persian empire, and in celebrations of the extent of Roman rule from Cicero and Sallust onwards.[42] The inclusion of north and south is found in Horace's eulogies of Augustan rule (*Odes* 3.4.29ff.; 3.8.18ff.; 4.14.41ff.), and once in praise of his own poetic fame (*Odes* 2.20.13ff.), but he also employs the east-west formula (*Odes* 1.35.29ff.; 3.5.1ff.; 4.15.14ff.): it is clearly a favourite motif, which he varies by reference to places, peoples, climates, or rivers.[43] The motif is common in Augustan and post-Augustan literature.[44] It is not always applied to

[40] See Gruber (1978) 210.

[41] Cf. 1 m. 4.7f.; 2 m. 5.25f.

[42] For some references see Fraenkel (1957) 451 n. 4.

[43] See W. Theiler, *Untersuchungen zur antiken Literatur* (Berlin 1970) 404ff.; Nisbet/Hubbard 2.344ff.

[44] Cf. e.g. Virgil, *Aen.* 8.726ff.; Tibullus 2.5.58ff.; Crinagoras, *Epigrammata Graeca* (ed. D.L. Page) 5136ff., of Tiberius, there (5136) called Nero – but that does not make the epigram a source for Boethius, as Scheible (1972) 66 claims; Velleius Paterculus 2.126.3

the extent of empire. In Sophocles' *Oedipus at Colonus* the chorus imagines disasters (*atai*) lashing the aged Oedipus from the four corners of the globe (1245ff.). Pindar thinks of the fame of the Aiakides extending from the north to beyond the sources of the Nile (*Isthm.* 1.6.22ff.). In Senecan tragedy the motif can express the way in which love ranges universally (*Phaedra* 285ff.), or the extent of the peace wrought by Hercules (*Hercules furens* 882ff.).

Boethius' use of this motif is ironical.[45] What is a motif of praise, or at the very least of impressive power, is juxtaposed to a catalogue of the emperor's atrocities. The contrast of sordid arson and killings and of great geographical spaces is striking. But even nature is so described by Boethius that it reflects the grimness of a tyrant's rule. Thus the peoples of the frozen North are overwhelmed (11)[46] by their environment, while those of the South are described as tortured by the heat and drought in the climactic two lines of the section (12f.). Boethius takes up a tendency inherent in the motif – the vivid description of the extremes of north and south; but where, for example, it is exploited by Horace to evoke the savagery of distant peoples like the Britanni (*Odes* 3.4.33), in Boethius the motif is extended, so that nature reflects the horrors of tyrannical rule. This use of nature imagery to express the nature of human emotions, desires, and actions is reminiscent of Seneca's poetic technique.[47]

The poem speaks of the 'lofty (*celsa*) power' (14) of Nero. The use of the adjective *celsus* links to other instances in the *Consolation*. In 1 m. 5 the prisoner complains of the evils of injustice: *at perversi resident* celso / *mores solio* ... ('But evil behaviour is entrenched on a high throne ...', 31f.). In the poem following the one under discussion, death's impartiality is stressed:

> *mors spernit altam gloriam,*
> *involvit humile pariter et* celsum *caput*
> *aequatque summis infima* (2 m. 7.12ff.).

Death despises lofty glory, envelops alike the humble and the eminent, makes the lowest and the highest equal.

In the next tyrant poem, 4 m. 2, the picture of rulers on their high thrones is an image once again of perverse rule: *Quos vides sedere* celsos *solii culmine reges* ... ('The kings you see seated high on

---

(see Woodman ad loc.); Rutilius Namatianus, *De reditu* 1.57ff.

[45] Contrast his use of the same motif at 3 m. 5.5ff.

[46] For the use of *premere* in the sense of being overwhelmed politically by a superior power see Virgil, *Aen.* 10.53f.; cf. 7.737f.

[47] See C. Segal, 'Boundary Violation and the Landscape of the Self in Senecan Tragedy', *Antike und Abendland* 29 (1983) 172-87 (reprinted in id., *Interpreting Greek Tragedy* [Ithaca, NY 1986] 315-36).

towering thrones ...', 1). But the poem which precedes that one has
indicated that it is only the philosophical ascent of the mind that
achieves true eminence:

> *Sunt etenim pennae volucres mihi*
> *quae* celsa *conscendant poli* ... (4 m. 1.1f.).

For I have swift wings with which to rise to the heights of heaven ...

Boethius is concerned in the tyrant poems to show that tyrants are the
opposite to what they seem to be (weak not strong, captive not free,
etc.). Here he skilfully uses the same epithet to suggest both what
tyrants are not, and what philosophers, on the contrary, are.

The poem calls Nero 'savage' (*ferus*, 3) and speaks of his madness
(15). The insanity of the tyrant is a traditional motif. In the concluding
four lines (14-17) Boethius generalizes, drawing a conclusion from the
two juxtaposed sections that have preceded. On the one side of the
picture is the insane tyrant; on the other, his immense power. The
individual case of Nero proves the general point of the preceding prose
argument: power does not make the powerful any better, but, if they
are bad, highlights and exposes their badness (2.6.18,20). Power and
evil are also the keynotes of the last two lines, symbolized by the sword
and poison respectively. The reference to the sword in the context of
the insane rule of Nero is an elliptic allusion to the Roman proverb
employed, for example, by Seneca: 'It is wrong to entrust a sword to one
who is insane' (*De ira* 1.19.8).[48] The poison of evil, here aptly
characterized by a key word of the tyrant-motif, 'raging' (*saevus*, 17),
may have been chosen by Boethius not merely because of its general
connotations, but also because it is particularly suited to the theme of
the tyrant *qua* poisoner.[49] In addition, the image of poison will assume
a special importance in the *Consolation*: applied to Circe's potions and
to the exegesis of these as the passions, it can stand for the moral
corruption that distorts human nature (4 m. 3.35ff.). The dehumanizing effects of evil are apparent in one of its most compelling
incarnations, the bestial (*ferus*, 3) tyrant. As often in the *Consolation*, a
key term introduced here, at this stage of the work, foreshadows its

---

[48] See Scheible (1972) 66. For the proverb see A. Otto, *Die Sprichwörter und
sprichwörtlichen Redensarten der Römer* (Leipzig 1890, reprinted Hildesheim 1962)
153f.

[49] Cf. Pliny the Elder, *Nat. hist.* 22.46.92 (Nero as *venenum*). On *saevus*, etc. see pp.
83f. above. In Virgil, *Aen.* 7.19 Circe the poisoner is called *dea saeva*: in Boethius' Circe
poem mental poisons 'rage' (*venena ... saeviunt*, 4 m. 3.35, 39) in their victims. The
thematic links between poison, passions, 'rage', tyranny, and bestialization form a subtle
pattern in *Cons. phil.* Further instances of the poison motif: 2 m. 5.9, the dye used to
colour luxury silks is called *venenum*; 4 m. 2.6, the term is applied to the effects of lust.
Cf. Persius, *Sat.* 3.35-7.

fully-fledged use in 4 m. 3, and also links the tyrant-motif to the larger context of the destructive power of the passions.

(iii) The second Nero poem (3 m. 4)

Quamvis se Tyrio superbus ostro
  comeret et niveis lapillis,
invisus tamen omnibus vigebat
  luxuriae Nero saevientis;
sed quondam dabat improbus verendis   5
  patribus indecores curules.
quis illos igitur putet beatos
  quos miseri tribuunt honores?

Much as he might deck himself proudly in Tyrian purple and snow-white pearls, Nero was still hated by everybody, rank in his raging excess. Yet the monster used to confer on revered (5) senators curule offices – but ones that brought no glory. Who, then, would consider those men blessed to whom the wretched grant honours?

After the sequence on the illusory nature of power and the distinction between power and goodness, which reached its climax in 2 m. 6, Boethius turns to the more subtle temptations of glory and reputation. The longing for these latter is not quite so despicable as that for power, it seems:

> And yet this is the one thing that could attract minds outstanding by nature, but who have not yet achieved the finishing touches by the perfecting of their virtues – namely, desire for glory and a reputation for having performed the greatest services to the state (2.7.2).

But glory and fame are soon seen to be no less insubstantial than power itself. Boethius employs the topoi of the insignificance of Roman achievement in the context of the vast cosmos (2.7.3ff.), and of the minimal nature of any historical period in comparison with the infinity of time (2.7.13ff.) – both evidently influenced by Cicero's *Somnium Scipionis* and Macrobius' commentary on it – to stress the contemptible nature of fame.

In reading such passages, we feel that we are closer to the vulnerable features of Boethius' own character than when he discourses on the tyranny of rulers as such. For the opportunities to achieve distinction through offices conferred by imperial or kingly gift offer the greatest – strictly speaking, the only real – scope for ambitious members of Boethius' senatorial class at this time. It is revealing that Boethius recalls in such detail the occasion of his son's consulships in 522, the panegyric which he then delivered, the largesse distributed to popular satisfaction on the occasion (2.3.8). For it is by such means that fame and pre-eminence were preserved, and the vicarious winning of fame epitomized by the consulships of his sons is no less valued than his own distinctions – and is indeed a reflection and extension of these.[50]

There is, therefore, a shift from the theme of power to that of conferred titles and offices, and the distinction, pomp, and glory attaching to these. That is apparent in the next poem:

> quid o superbi colla mortali iugo
>   frustra levare gestiunt?
> licet remotos fama per populos means
>   diffusa linguas explicet
> et magna titulis fulgeat claris domus,
>   mors spernit altam gloriam ... (2 m. 7.7ff).[51]

O why do the proud long – pointlessly – to relieve their necks of the yoke of mortality? Though fame spread through distant peoples, and be talked about far and wide, and though a great house glitter with brilliant titles of honour, death despises lofty glory ...

These lines anticipate the second Nero poem, 3 m. 4. That poem is itself preceded by a prose section in which the theme of magistracies is dominant. In it Boethius makes Philosophy recall Catullus' vilification of magistrates and those who aspire to office:

And indeed they [offices] do not usually put wickedness to flight, but rather make it famous. And so it happns that we are angry that they have often fallen to the lot of the most wicked of men. That is why Catullus calls Nonius, even though he was sitting in a curule chair, 'the wart' (3.4.2).

This is a strikingly precise reminiscence of Catullus: sella in curuli struma Nonius sedet ('There's Nonius the wart sitting in a curule chair', 52.2, tr. Goold). The contemporary Decoratus (3.4.4) is to Boethius what Nonius represented to Catullus. Boethius, in the same section, returns to the topos of 2.7, the irrelevance of Roman political office in the non-Roman world (3.4.11ff.).[52] Corresponding to the historical considerations of 2.7.13ff. is the reflection on the decline of certain Roman offices, such as the praetorship (3.4.15). These thematic

---

[50] See Matthews (1981) 21.

[51] The punctuation of line 7 deviates from that of the CCL edn., which takes o superbi to be a vocative. Tränkle (1968) 280 attempts to remove the apparent solecism (third person gestiunt is odd with the vocative: O'Donnell [1984] 177 is confusing) by emending levare (8) to passive levari, making colla ('your necks') the subject. But Gruber (1978) 221 is surely right to take quid o as an exclamation ('O why') and superbi as subject (as does Tester, Loeb edn.).

[52] Gruber (1978) 252f. argues correctly against Courcelle (1967) 348 that this cannot be a reference to purported Ostrogothic contempt for Roman magistracies. The reference to the barbarian world is rather part of the traditional topos on the limitations of fame and power: cf. 2.7.7; 3.5.4; 3.6.5.

similarities link 2.7 and its poetic sequel to 3.4 and the following Nero poem.

Scheible has suggested that, whereas 2 m. 6 concentrated on Nero's cruelty, 3 m. 4 focusses upon his *luxuria* (4).[53] That, however, is true only of the first part (1-4) of this short, bipartite poem. Its second part (5-8) turns to the chief theme of the antecedent section – magistracies. As will be seen, these lines are climactic, and the memorable part of the poem. But something must first be said about the first section. The theme of luxury and extravagance is introduced by traditional references, familiar to readers of Horace, Virgil, and Seneca, to such items of luxury as rich dyed clothes and pearls (1f.). The references are emblematic in Boethius, pointers which he does not need to elaborate. It was characteristic of the men of the Golden Age that they did not know how ... *lucida vellera Serum / Tyrio miscere veneno* ('to dip shining silken cloth in Tyrian dye', 2 m. 5.8f.). The kings of 4 m. 2 are 'brilliant in bright purple' (2). In 3 m. 8 the two motifs are combined again. Men in their perversity know *quae gemmis niveis unda feracior / vel quae rubentis purpurae* ... 'which sea is more fertile in snow-white pearls, which in the red murex ...', (11f.). The allurements of precious stones and pearls are recalled in 3 m. 10: ... *Indus calido propinquus orbi / candidis miscens virides lapillos* ... ('Indus, close to the torrid zone, mingling its emeralds and its bright pearls ...', 9f.). By using these images as ciphers Boethius links themes and passages significantly, so that the reference is not confined to Nero, or, rather, Nero becomes typical of moral blindness to what is authentic, and what false, goodness.

Boethius' use of the verb *comere*, 'to deck' (3 m. 4.2), may be intended to recall the bitter image *fraus mendaci* compta *colore* ('deceit decked in lying colours') in 1 m. 5.38. But there is a more striking use of language in 3 m. 4.3, where the words *invisus* ... *vigebat* both frame the verse, and by their linked use express the paradox of the lines: that the splendour of Nero's appearance and wealth – his apparently flourishing state (*vigebat*) – none the less provokes hatred (*invisus*) rather than admiration. It is this contrast that the poem turns on, and that clarifies the *quamvis* of line 1 and *tamen* of 3. The *tamen* of 2 m. 6.8 announces a parallel contrast, there between cruelty and extent of power that cannot affect that cruelty. The use of *vigere* to connote perverse, rank 'flourishing' is similar to Sallust's ... *pro pudore, pro abstinentia, pro virtute audacia, largitio, avaritia vigebant* ('in place of decency, self-restraint, and virtue there flourished insolence, corruption, and greed', *Cat.* 3.3). Finally, Boethius displays his verbal dexterity in framing the tyrant's name in two key words evocative of his state: *luxuriae Nero saevientis* (4).

[53] Scheible (1972) 87.

To turn to the second part of the poem. Its meaning is clear. Although those given offices are worthy people (*verendis/patribus*, 5f.), senators, since the donor of offices is evil (*improbus*, 5), the offices themselves become unseemly,[54] and convey no true glory (7f.). The reference to *curules* in 6 is typical of Boethius' subtle use of a word to link with other passages, so that the context is enriched by the reminiscence. When Philosophy recalls the great moment of his sons' installation as consuls she thinks of them 'sitting in the curule chairs in the senate' (2.3.8), and, as has been seen, when considering unworthy holders of offices, she evokes Catullus' 'Nonius ... sitting in a curule chair' (3.4.2). Nonius typifies the unproblematic blackguard in office, but the *curulis* link and the related development of Boethius' argument cast the shadow of Nonius, so to speak, over the innocent sons of Boethius, as over all holders of office (Boethius himself included) from the hands of tyrants, whether these be called Nero or, by implication, Theoderic. The persona of Philosophy is used by Boethius to express condemnation of his sense of achievement, and to expose the hollow nature of such achievement.

Finally, the poem's concluding couplet, by a skilful juxtaposition of three terms, two positive, one negative (framed by the other two), brilliantly conveys the paradox of Boethius' theme (7f.). The tyrants are the *miseri*, and from that fact, as from a rotten core, the infection of what should be positive (*honores*) spreads, so that those who should be fortunate holders of offices cannot, in fact, be considered *beati*: they are contaminated by the *miseria* of the donors. Verbal artistry reflects the apparent contradictions, and the true diagnosis, of the nature of glory in a tyrannical state. And with the concluding word *honores* Boethius emphasizes the climax of the theme which he has developed since 2.7, the effects of tyranny upon those who hold political office and other distinctions under that tyranny.

(iv) The tyrant's masters (4 m. 2)

Quos vides sedere celsos solii culmine reges,
purpura claros nitente, saeptos tristibus armis,
ore torvo comminantes, rabie cordis anhelos,
detrahat si quis superbis vani tegmina cultus,
iam videbit intus artas dominos ferre catenas;   5
hinc enim libido versat avidis corda venenis,
hinc flagellat ira mentem fluctus turbida tollens,
maeror aut captos fatigat aut spes lubrica torquet.
ergo cum caput tot unum cernas ferre tyrannos,
non facit quod optat ipse, dominis pressus iniquis.

Those kings you see seated high on towering thrones, brilliant in bright purple, hemmed in by grim arms, threatening wild-eyed, gasping in their

---

[54] *indecores*, 6, used predicatively: see O'Donnell (1984) 190.

hearts' madness – if anybody should pull away from those proud men the cover of their futile trappings, he will at once see that the masters wear constricting chains within (5). For hence lust disturbs their hearts with the greedy poison of desire, hence anger lashes the mind, violently stirring up storm-waves, or sorrow exhausts or slippery hope torments the captives. So, since, as you see, one head contains so many tyrants, he does not do what he himself wants, oppressed by evil masters.

The final tyrant poem does not exploit the name or theme of Nero, but it is none the less linked both verbally and thematically to the two earlier poems. Over and above the specific tyrant motif, however, this poem, more explicitly than its predecessors, situates the motif in its broader ethical context; and that in itself is an indication of the development of the work as a whole at this stage.

The poem begins with what appears at first sight to be a description of kings (*reges*, 1) and their power rather than an evocation of tyranny: the word *tyrannos* does not occur until line 9. The first two lines evoke the familiar emblems of the throne and purple robes, and add to them the armed bodyguard (*tristibus*, 2, introduces a dark touch). There may, however, be a deliberate echo in line 1 of the detail of Boethius' anguished vision of injustice in 1 m. 5: *at perversi resident celso / mores solio* ... ('But evil behaviour is entrenched on a high throne', 31f.); and line 3 of our poem leaves the reader in no doubt that it is kingship's perversion, tyranny, that is the poem's focus. The tyrant's wild and terrible appearance, *ore torvo*, was evoked in 4 m. 1.29f., the concluding lines of the preceding poem: ... *quos miseri torvos populi timent / cernes tyrannos exsules* ('the tyrants whose ferocity wretched peoples fear you will see as exiles'). But again this feature, on its own, need not suggest tyranny. When Philosophy displays her anger at the Muses who provide the prisoner with false consolation at the beginning of the work, her verbal outburst is visually paralleled by her appearance, 'with wild blazing eyes' (*torvis inflammata luminibus*, 1.1.7), and there can be no doubt that this is righteous anger, such as a good ruler might also express. It is only the complementary part of the line, *rabie cordis anhelos*, that turns the reader's attention unequivocally towards the tyrant-image, and recalls the *pravi rabiem Neronis* of the first tyrant poem (2 m. 6.15). It may be that Boethius intends the boundaries between kingship and tyranny to be indeterminate in this poem because the argument of the work has, since the middle part of Book 3, become more Platonic in character. The preceding prose section 4.2 has, as commentators have long observed, developed arguments of Plato's *Gorgias*, in particular the argument that the wicked are weak and not powerful because they cannot obtain what they seek, namely the good. What is important to note, however, is that Boethius' argument is an extension and modification of Plato's. Plato speaks in *Gorgias* 466a ff. as much of politicians in general (*rhêtores*) as of *turannoi* (466d1ff.), though he does not speak specifically of the 'wicked' (or of the good), but rather of those who do not know what the good really is. The rhetorically trained politician does not possess insight into what constitutes the good life. That is the point of the paradox that apparently powerful politicians do not have power, because they do not do 'whatever they want', but only 'whatever seems good to them' (466d8ff.). When Boethius adapts this part of the argument he hardens the distinction into the Stoic one between the sage and the wicked man:

> From all this the power of good men, and the indubitable weakness of the bad, are indeed evident, as is the clear truth of Plato's view that only the wise can do what they want, but that the wicked can perform what seems good to them, yet cannot achieve what they want (4.2.45).

And that sentiment inhabits the following poem, whose tyrant-ruler *non facit quod optat ipse* ... ('does not do what he himself wants ...', 4 m. 2.10). Now from a Platonic point of view, and especially from one that has been modified Stoically, as Boethius has been observed to do, all non-philosophical politicians fail to do 'whatever they want' when they perform actions which result in harm for them, for they, like all human agents, aim at a presumed good. In other words, the philosophical context of the poem makes it appropriate for Boethius to play down the difference between the tyrant and other rulers, and stress rather the common delusion and weakness of all non-philosophical rulers.

The paradox of the tyrant's weakness is intensified in the next lines. Boethius exploits the appearance-reality contrast, as he has done in the two Nero poems.[55] The *superbia* of rulers is superficial, their external splendour (*cultus*, 4) hollow: within, they are bound fast in the chains of their passions (5ff.). The image of chains is recurrent in the *Consolation*. In the description by Philosophy of Boethius' abject state, he is said to lie ... *pressus gravibus colla catenis* ('... his neck pressed down with heavy chains', 1 m. 2.25) and in that context the influence of the Cave imagery of Plato's *Republic* (especially 514a) is most evident. The chains metaphor can be used to evoke the power of Fortune, where it sometimes merges with the metaphor of the yoke (2.1.16; 2 m. 7.7f.; 2.8.4). The man who is swayed by mutable things *nectit qua valeat trahi catenam* ('links the chain by which he may be led', 1 m. 4.18). But most often it is the passions that enchain the mind of man (1 m. 7.29ff., 3 m. 1.12 (again the yoke metaphor), 3 m. 5.1ff. (reins), 3 m. 10.1ff., 3 m. 12.3f.).[56]

---

[55] See pp. 93f. above.
[56] See Gruber (1978) 86f. For the metaphor 'chains of desire' see Cicero, *De senectute* 3.7.

In Seneca the chains metaphor can be used to evoke the retarding influence of the body upon the soul, in Platonic manner:

> For this body is the burden and punishment of the soul; it [soul] is oppressed by the body's weight, it is in chains unless philosophy has come to it, and bid it be refreshed by the spectacle of nature, and released it from the earthly to the heavenly sphere (*Ep.* 65.16).

There is an extended use of the metaphor in *De vita beata*, where Seneca, having explained the Stoic doctrine that virtue is sufficient for happiness, turns to talk to those progressing towards virtue:

> But the man who is still on the road to virtue, who, even though he has proceeded far, is still struggling in the toils of human affairs, does have need of some indulgence from Fortune until he has loosed that knot and every mortal bond. Where then lies the difference? In that some are closely bound, others fettered – even hand and foot (*adstricti alii, districti quoque*). He who has advanced toward the higher realm and has lifted himself to higher levels drags a loosened chain; he is not yet free, but still is as good as free (*De vita beata* 16.3, tr. Basore).

These and similar passages[57] derive ultimately from Plato's image in the *Phaedo* (62b, 82e) of life as a form of imprisonment. The image is a favourite of Cicero's, who links it explicitly to the 'chains' image.[58] Its tradition shows that it is susceptible to a variety of philosophical usages, from the popular Platonic to Stoic (as in the example from Seneca's *De vita beata*); and it lends itself to vivid, diatribe style. Boethius can use it in Stoic contexts, where the command to eradicate the passions is urged:

> *gaudia pelle,*
> *pelle timorem*
> *spemque fugato*
> *nec dolor adsit.*
> *nubila mens est*
> *vinctaque frenis*
> *haec ubi regnant* (1 m. 7.25ff.).

> Banish joy, banish fear, put hope to flight, don't let grief be present. The mind is clouded and bound and bridled, where these rule.

But it can also occur where he is urging dominance, rather than eradication, of the passions, in accordance with Platonic and Aristotelian tenets:

---

[57] See P. Courcelle, 'L'âme en cage', in K. Flasch (ed.), *Parusia. Festgabe für Johannes Hirschberger* (Frankfurt 1965) 103-16.
[58] Cf. Cicero, *Tusc. disp.* 1.30.74; *rep.* 6.14.14, etc. See O'Daly (1987) 71 with n. 101.

Qui se volet esse potentem,
animos domet ille feroces
nec victa libidine colla
foedis summittat habenis (3 m. 5.1ff.).

Whoever wants to be powerful, he must tame his fierce spirits, and must
not place his neck, defeated by lust, under loathsome reins.

And it can also contribute to a more purely Neoplatonic vision:

Felix, qui potuit boni
fontem visere lucidum,
felix, qui potuit gravis
terrae solvere vincula (3 m. 12.1ff.).

Blessed is he who can look upon the clear source of goodness, blessed he
who can loose the chains of heavy earth.

In the poem under discussion, finally, it reinforces the vivid images of
the devastating effect of the passions (6-8), but does not give a specific
philosophical colouring to the passage, which is in diatribe style, and
could be part of a Stoic as much as a Cynic or Platonic context.

The influence of the image of the prisoners in the Cave of Plato's
Republic has been noted above. That powerful image, echoed in 3.1.5
('true happiness, of which your mind dreams, but cannot really see it
because its sight is engrossed with images'), is liable to influence
Boethius, given its importance in the Neoplatonic tradition, where it
assumes the role of a symbol for this world and human involvement in
it.[59] But it is striking that for Boethius the themes associated with the
Cave image are not so much concerned with the picture of the world as
a cave or a prison, as with the notion that the human being who is
dominated by his passions is imprisoned in his corporeal nature: and
that Philosophy, which can provide the prisoner with insight into his
condition by showing him the lack of value that external 'goods'
possess, can free him from that prison. Now this notion is found in
another Platonic work, referred to above also, the *Phaedo*, where the
cage or prison simile of 82e ff. has clearly influenced Boethius in a way
that commentators do not always acknowledge. Yet much that is found
in the *Phaedo* passage is echoed in Boethius. There is the soul which
can only 'view the things that are as if through a prison' (tr. Gallop),
that 'is wallowing in utter ignorance', whose prison is 'effected through
desire, so that the captive himself may co-operate most of all in his
imprisonment'. And there, too, is personified Philosophy, which 'takes

[59] Plotinus 4.8.1; Porphyry, *De antro nympharum* 8f.; Proclus, *In remp.* 2.31 Kroll; cf.
Cons. phil. 3 m. 10.1ff.

it in hand, gently reassures it and tries to release it'.[60] The resemblances to the *Consolation* are striking: there one finds the 'gentler remedies' (*leniora remedia*) referred to frequently in the earlier part of the work; and what else is the *Consolation* but a *paramuthêtikos logos*[61] of Philosophy who 'gently reassures' (*êrema paramutheitai, Phaedo* 83a3)? The process described in the Cave image of the *Republic* is quite different. There the prisoners are first compelled (515c) to turn round and look into the light. Moreover, the content of the philosophy brought by Philosophy to the soul in the *Phaedo* corresponds to the themes of the *Consolation*: turning away from the world of the senses and inquiry pursued through them, 'urging it to collect and gather itself together, and to trust none other but itself, whenever, alone by itself, it thinks of any of the things that are, alone by *itself*; and not to regard as real what it observes by other means, and what varies in various things', so that 'the soul of the true philosopher abstains from pleasures and desires and pains, so far as it can' (83a–b). Now these themes are of course frequent in Platonic literature and, from Aristotle onwards, a staple element of protreptic. What is striking about the *Phaedo* text, however, is the fact that they occur in one short passage in the context of the prison simile and in conjunction with the personification of Philosophy. There can be no doubt that we have here to do with a chief source of the *Consolation* that is often neglected. It is likely that a confluence of two Platonic texts – the *Phaedo* passage and the Cave passage from the *Republic* – has been effected by Boethius, as it has by Plotinus (4.8.1).[62] To Boethius in his captivity the *Phaedo* will have had a special attraction. It is not merely the picture of the imprisoned soul freed by philosophy that will have suggested the symbolism of his situation to him, but he will also have identified with the imprisoned and condemned Socrates of Plato's dialogue. The influence of the *Phaedo* is not lessened by the consideration that the *Consolation* goes another way than, and develops in a different manner from, Plato's work.

With the theme of the passions that enchain the ruler Boethius introduces specific evocations of the effects of four of those passions: lust, anger, sorrow, hope (*libido, ira, maeror, spes*). To understand this sequence properly one must not be misled by the fact that four passions are mentioned, for the sequence selected by Boethius is not that of the four primary passions, appetite (*epithumia*), fear (*phobos*), distress (*lupê*), and pleasure (*hêdonê*), of Stoic ethics.[63] The Latin term

[60] R. Hackforth, *Plato's Phaedo* (Cambridge 1955) 95 observes the parallel with *Cons. phil.*

[61] On the connotations of this term (Latin *consolatio*) see Kassel (1958) 3f.

[62] In Plotinus 4.8.1 other Platonic texts – from *Cratylus, Phaedrus*, and *Timaeus* – are also quoted or alluded to: see Armstrong's Loeb edn. 4.400 n. 1.

[63] *SVF* 3.377ff.; see also Long/Sedley 1.410ff. for Eng. tr. of selected texts and brief but illuminating commentary. Inwood (1985) 127ff. provides a detailed and perceptive

libido is from Cicero onwards a common translation of *epithumia*. In Stoic school definitions of *orgê* (translated *iracundia* or *ira*) it is understood to be a subdivision of *epithumia qua* 'desire for revenge': it should not, therefore, be seen as a separate primary passion here.[64] Scheible's assertion that Cicero in *De officiis* 1.20.69 elevates anger to the status of a fifth primary passion is unwarranted on such slender evidence.[65] *Maeror* is identifiable with *klausis*, which in Stoic terms is a subdivision of *lupê*.[66] It may, therefore, be taken to represent the passion of distress here: its use by Boethius is appropriate, for it is a key term in the *Consolation*. The opening elegy speaks of 'sad measures' (*maestos ... modos*) sung by the 'tearful' (*flebilis*) prisoner (1 m. 1.2) whose condition is one of *dolor* (10). The prisoner's face is downcast with sorrow (*in humum maerore deiectum*, 1.1.14). *Maeror* and related terms recur throughout the first four books of the *Consolation* (1.4.28; 1.5.2; 1.5.11; 1.6.10; 2.1.9; 2.1.12; 2.3.2; 3.12.1; 4.1.1; 4.1.3): as the patient responds to the healing care of Philosophy the references decrease and eventually cease.[67]

Thus far the sequence is evidently one either of primary passions or of recognizable subdivisions of these, if one follows the Stoic scheme (as Cicero, for example, does in Book 3 of the *Tusculans*). With it we may compare the sequence in 1.5.11: *dolor ira maeror*. There a primary passion, *dolor*, and one of its subdivisions, *maeror*, parallel *libido* and *ira* in our poem. In 1 m. 7.25ff. we find the sequence *gaudia, timor, spes, dolor*. Here *gaudia* is presumably Stoic *hêdonê* (whose commonest translations are *voluptas* and *laetitia*),[68] for, even in a context where the Stoic doctrine may be being adapted to his purposes, Boethius can hardly be advocating eradication of the Stoic 'good passion' (*eupatheia*) of joy (*khara*), translated by Cicero as *gaudium*, a term which the Latin tradition adopted.[69] *Timor* and *dolor* are readily identifiable as primary passions. But what of *spes*? It also features in our poem, and its occurrence in the catalogues of passions in both places has been found

---

discussion of early Stoic doctrines. For Panaetius and Posidonius see L. Edelstein, *The Meaning of Stoicism* (Cambridge, Mass. 1966) 52ff.; I.G. Kidd (Ch. 2, n. 64 above). For the Latin tradition Cicero, *Tusc. disp.* 3.10.23-11.25; 4.6.11-9.21 is of prime importance, terminologically as well as thematically: there *epithumia* = *libido*; *phobos* = *metus*; *lupê* = *aegritudo*; *hêdonê* = *laetitia*, *voluptas*. Elsewhere (in Cicero and later writers) *cupiditas* is a variant of *libido*, *timor* of *metus*, *tristitia* of *aegritudo*: equivalent verbal forms are also used frequently. Cf. O'Daly (1987) 46 (there 46-54 on emotions in Augustine's thought).

[64] See *SVF* 3.394ff.; Cicero, *Tusc. disp.* 3.5.11.

[65] Scheible (1972) 135.

[66] *SVF* 3.414; cf. Cicero, *Tusc. disp.* 4.8.18.

[67] See Gruber (1978) 51.

[68] In the enumeration of the four primary passions in Virgil, *Aen.* 6.733 (*hinc metuunt cupiuntque, dolent gaudentque*) *gaudere* = *hêdonê*. On Neoplatonic and patristic (esp. Augustine's) exegesis of the verse see Courcelle (1984) 486ff.

[69] Cf. *SVF* 3.435, 437.

problematic.

A clue to the significance of the inclusion of *spes* may be provided by 1 m. 4.13ff.:

> *nec speres aliquid nec extimescas,*
> *exarmaveris impotentis iram;*
> *at quisquis trepidus pavet vel optat,*
> *quod non sit stabilis suique iuris,*
> *abiecit clipeum locoque motus*
> *nectit qua valeat trahi catenam.*

> Do not hope for anything or fear anything, and you will have disarmed the uncontrolled [tyrant's] anger. But whoever anxiously fears or desires, because he is not stable or his own master, has thrown away his shield, and, his position abandoned, links the chain by which he may be led.

Misplaced hope, like fear, when the objects of hope and fear are inconstant and not stable, is a form of enchainment of the self, and avoiding such hope or fear disarms the despot's anger: the context (tyrant, chains, anger) is clearly relevant to the interpretation of our passage. One should not try to link *spes* explicitly to the four primary passions.[70] The link of hope and fear is best understood against the background of the discussion in Seneca, *Ep.* 5.7ff.[71] There, quoting the Middle Stoic Hecaton (a pupil of Panaetius), 'you will cease to fear, if you cease to hope', Seneca explains that fear (the recognizable passion) is a consequence of hope, when that hope is an anxious concern about the uncertain future, a perversion of the good quality of foresight (*providentia*). The notion is found elsewhere in Seneca. In an extended quotation from the Cynic Demetrius, the mind is said to have attained calm and stability if, among other things,

> it has come to despise what is a product of chance, if it has elevated itself beyond fear and does not embrace the boundlessness of greedy hope (*De beneficiis* 7.1.7).

The *sapiens* lives a life that is not controlled by either hope or fear. This insight, that hope can be a product of, and itself produce, anxiety, is so evidently true that it needs no Stoic pedigree to commend it. And its occurrence in Demetrius as well as Hecaton, in addition to its adoption by Seneca, testifies to its broad acceptability in ethical contexts where contentment is being discussed. This is apparent from a passage in Horace:

---

[70] As do Gruber (1978) 161 and, to a lesser extent, Scheible (1972) 45.

[71] Cf. *torquemur* (Seneca, *Ep.* 5.9) with *torquet* (*Cons. phil.* 4 m. 2.8); *catena* (*Ep.* 5.7) with *catenas* (4 m. 2.5).

> *inter spem curamque, timores inter et iras*
> *omnem crede diem tibi diluxisse supremum;*
> *grata superveniet quae non sperabitur hora (Epist.* 1.4.12ff.).

> Amid hopes and cares, attacks of fear and anger,
> think of each dawn as lighting your last day:
> an hour not counted on will be a gift (tr. Macleod).

The notion 'live for the present' is also the moral of Seneca's discussion in *Ep.* 5.7ff. We should not, therefore, look for a specific school substitution (in Epicureanism, for example) of hope for the passion of appetite or desire,[72] although the Stoics would presumably consider the hope here discussed to be covered by their definition of appetite as 'an irrational desire, or pursuit of an expected good'.[73] The notion is a moral maxim that would be acceptable to a 'pig from Epicurus' herd' (Horace, *Epist.* 1.4.16), but not merely to such a one. A further passage in Horace illustrates the notion perfectly:

> *qui timet his adversa, fere miratur eodem*
> *quo cupiens pacto; pavor est utrubique molestus,*
> *inprovisa simul species exterret utrumque.*
> *gaudeat an doleat, cupiat metuatne, quid ad rem,*
> *si, quidquid vidit melius peiusve sua spe,*
> *defixis oculis animoque et corpore torpet? (Epist.* 1.6.9ff.).

> And if you fear their opposites, you're impressed
> much as you are if you want those things. Both ways,
> something strikes and flusters the mind that sees it.
> Happy or sad, eager or anxious, what
> does it matter, if every pleasant or painful shock
> turns down your eyes and numbs your mind and body? (tr. Macleod).

It is particularly instructive to compare the two Horace extracts just quoted with Boethius. In both, Horace, like Boethius, includes some or all of the primary passions, but also such passions as *ira* and *spes*, in his catalogues. Neither poet is concerned with a list of cardinal passions. Both are concerned with highlighting certain passions particularly relevant to the moral point that they are making, and with the observation that hope can be destructive. What Boethius says in the two poetic passages under discussion (1 m. 7.25ff. and 4 m. 2.6ff.) is also said by him in more elaborate terms at 2.1.15:

> For it will not be enough to consider what is before one's eyes, but prudence reckons how things are going to turn out; and the

---

[72] As does Gruber (1978) 161.
[73] Cf. *SVF* 3.391; Long/Sedley 1.411. There is no reference to *elpis* (hope) in Stoic divisions of *epithumia* (appetite): cf. e.g. *SVF* 3.397.

changeableness found in good fortune and in bad makes Fortune's threats unfeared and her flattery undesired.[74]

The language used in lines 6-8 of the individual passions links those lines to terms and themes of the work as a whole. When Boethius refers to the 'greedy poisons' of desire (6), the theme of the tyrant-poisoner of 2 m. 6.17 is echoed, and the poem is linked to the other instances of the poison-motif in the *Consolation*.[75] The comparison of anger with the winds whipping up the waves (7) reinforces the theme of passions as storms (1 m. 2.4f.; 1 m. 3; 1 m. 7) and the related motif of life as a sea journey in a storm.[76] Line 8 echoes Martianus Capella's *... indiga veri / cura facit dubium vel spes incerta fatigat* ('[Humanity] which anxiety lacking in true knowledge makes doubtful and uncertain hope exhausts', 1.21.3f., tr. Shanzer). But it also functions within the context of the *Consolation*: *captos* ('captives')[77] recalls the prisoner theme which, as the preceding pages have shown, typifies both the notion of life as imprisonment and, more particularly, of the passions as gaolers. Finally, the use of the adjective *lubrica* with reference to *spes*, while it echoes Statius – *sed me spes lubrica tardat* ('but slippery hope impedes me', *Achil.* 1.547) – links this dominant passion in the ruler to Fortune, itself 'slippery'[78] and liable to make its victims its slaves.

In these ways principal themes and concerns of the work as a whole are reinforced and their ramifications and connections suggested. The final two lines of the poem reiterate the general point of lines 4f.: the ruler/tyrant is powerless, his passions are his tyrannical masters. Thus the poem has an a–b–a–b structure: two descriptive sections with vivid pictorial detail (a), each followed by a generalizing assertion (b) which puts the descriptions in context. The symmetry of this structure is reflected in the fact that the (a) sections are of 3 lines each, and the (b) sections each of 2 lines. While the two other poems discussed in this chapter do not display such symmetry, they too are clearly articulated, 2 m. 6 in an a–aa–b structure, and 3 m. 4 in an a–b form.[79] All three poems are masterly in their condensed, epigrammatic expression.

---

[74] Here prudence (*prudentia*) is contrasted with anxious hope or fear in a manner strongly reminiscent of Seneca, *Ep.* 5.7ff. (see pp. 101f. above).

[75] See p. 90 above.

[76] 1.3.11, etc. (Gruber [1978] 107 lists further instances). See pp. 121ff. below.

[77] *captos* is the reading of some MSS: it is the reading chosen by Büchner and Gruber, and is adopted here in preference to the alternative *captus* (chosen by Weinberger and Bieler), the acc. pl. of *captus, –us*, 'power of comprehension' (cf. O'Donnell [1984] 221).

[78] See 1 m. 5.28f.

[79] See pp. 87, 93 above.

CHAPTER FOUR

Nature in the Poetry of the *Consolation*

E se il mondo là giù ponesse mente
  al fondamento che natura pone,
  seguendo lui avria buona la gente (Dante, *Paradiso* 8.142ff.).

And if the world down there paid due regard
to the foundation Nature lays, content
to build on that, the race were nobly rear'd.

The advice to humanity to model life upon nature, proffered to Dante
in the sphere of Venus, is a reverberation of a central theme in the
Consolation:

O felix hominum genus,
si vestros animos amor
quo caelum regitur regat! (2 m. 8.28ff.)

O blessed human race, if the love by which the heavens are ruled should
rule your hearts![1]

In an ordered and hierarchical universe the mind can turn to patterns
that provide paradigms for behaviour: the natural world informs the
moral sphere. But there is discord in nature, too. Storms, earthquakes,
floods disturb the ordered patterns; man's physical life, with its
manifestations of illness, ageing, and death, seems prone to the same
chaotic and annihilating forces. Boethius has the sense of nature's
violence that Keats's friend, the painter Benjamin Robert Haydon,
expressed in his criticism of Shelley's nature worship:

Yes, I go out on the mountains, full of holy feeling – & then an Eagle
darts on a lamb, or a Hawk on a lark – & pick [*sic*] it before my eyes![2]

---

[1] Cf. Dante, *Inferno* 1.37ff.; *Paradiso* 1.73ff.; 33.145 ('l'amor che move il Sole e l'altre
stelle'). On cosmic *amor* in Dante's *Commedia* see Dronke (1965) 389. The translation of
Paradiso 8.142ff. is by G.L. Bickersteth, *Dante Alighieri: The Divine Comedy* (new edn.,
Oxford 1981) 577.

[2] Quoted from R. Gittings, *John Keats* (London 1968) 112.

But this insight of Boethius' does not, as one might imagine, lead him to reject the order in nature. On the contrary, his vision of that order must subsume the experience of nature's violence and destructiveness. This is the tension that gives life to Boethius' nature motifs in the *Consolation*.

The themes of nature and order (or disorder) pervade the *Consolation*. In this chapter they will be considered book by book, as they occur in the work. Although certain themes – the succession of the seasons, stormy weather, the perpetual harmonies of the heavens – recur regularly throughout the work, they do so in changing, developing contexts, and they cannot be understood divorced from their contexts. That in itself is the justification for a book by book approach to the motifs to be considered. But there is a further, related reason for this approach. The nature motifs, because of their frequency and centrality, provide the perfect example of the function of poetry in the *Consolation*. Always related to their context, but at the same time announcing, anticipating or foreshadowing certain topics, or recalling and reflecting topics already treated, the nature themes connect, bridge, and highlight the focal points of the work. Involved though Boethius is with argument and analysis, with the life of the mind in its introspective abstraction, the poet in him never loses the links with the world which he inhabits. He appropriates that world, and reads in it the great themes of mental and moral anguish and stability, reflected and symbolized in the change and variety of the natural universe.

*

The natural world which is the source of so many pictures and images in Boethius' poetry is, to a large extent, filtered through the Greek and Roman literary traditions of which he is the heir. As Dryden observed of Milton, Boethius 'saw Nature ... through the spectacles of books',[3] and, while no doubt he observed the natural world and could on occasion draw upon his own direct experience of it, his nature themes are not in the first place visual impressions of precisely noted details. His poetic art, like that of Lucretius and the Augustan poets in this respect, consists rather in the exploitation of traditional descriptive elements for particular thematic effects. Thus stylistic sound-effects and other linguistic techniques will be at least as important as visual depictions. More importantly, the nature themes, like the mythological motifs, are in the service of the ideas which the poetry seeks to express, or rather, as Gordon Williams writes of Augustan poetry, there is an

---

[3] See Samuel Johnson, *Lives of the English Poets* 1.123 (World's Classics edn.).

'imaginative world of ideas in which poetical concepts exist in a continuum with the real objects of nature'.[4] A consequence of this tendency is that the natural world is constantly related to human concerns, whether of the prisoner as participant in the dramatic dialogue, or of Boethius as author, or of the reader as addressee. The poetry of the *Consolation* has in common with much poetry in the Latin tradition (and with Greek poetry also) the aim of communicating emotional intensity (*pathos*) convincingly, and of endowing such thought as it contains with pathos. To that end, the nature themes are a recognized and adaptable means.[5]

(i) Book 1

There are two nature metaphors in the opening elegy of the work. One is traditional, and no doubt a dead metaphor, almost a cliché: the prisoner refers to his 'green youth' (*viridisque iuventae*, 1 m. 1.7), happy and blessed, with which his present state, distraught, prematurely aged, emaciated, is contrasted (7ff.). But the associations with the natural world suggested by the epithet 'green' are heightened by the description of the prisoner's greying hair: *intempestivi funduntur vertice cani* ('Before their time, white hairs spread over my head', 11). *Intempestivi* introduces the notion of unseasonal change or deterioration, and the white hairs spread (*funduntur*) ominously, like a fall of snow in summer, before their time: one is reminded of Horace's 'snow on the head' (*capitis nives, Odes* 4.13.12). At the outset of the work, Boethius identifies in the persona of the prisoner grave dislocation of nature, the physical symptom and counterpart of the mental and moral lethargy that Philosophy will diagnose.

The second nature metaphor of 1 m. 1 occurs in line 19, where Fortune's face is called 'clouded' (*nubila*). The adjective often carries

---

[4] Williams (1968) 637.

[5] See Williams (1968) 634-81. Much has been written on the representation of landscape, and its implications for attitudes to nature, in Roman poetry: see esp. (on Virgil) V. Pöschl, *Die Dichtkunst Virgils* (Heidelberg 1957); H.D. Reeker, *Die Landschaft in der Aeneis* (Spudasmata 27, Hildesheim 1971); (on Horace) S. Commager, *The Odes of Horace: A Critical Study* (New Haven, Conn. 1962) 235-306; C. Segal, *Landscape in Ovid's Metamorphoses: A Study in the Transformations of a Literary Symbol* (Hermes Einzelschriften 23, Wiesbaden 1969). A study that examines the topic in several Augustan poets and in the art of the period is E.W. Leach, *The Rhetoric of Space: Literary and Artistic Representations of Landscape in Republican and Augustan Rome* (Princeton, NJ 1988). Although landscape motifs are not a feature of the poems of *Cons. phil.*, there is much to be learnt by the reader of Boethius from these studies. Cf. also the notes in Thomas (1988). D.O. Ross, *Virgil's Elements. Physics and Poetry in the Georgics* (Princeton, NJ 1987), attempts to uncover the scientific and philosophical presuppositions of Virgil's poem, and their artistic elaboration: *mutatis mutandis* the present chapter pursues a similar goal in the case of Boethius. Baltes (1980) is fundamental on Boethius' 'world-picture'. For nature symbolism in Boethius see further Alfonsi (1955); Salemme (1970/1).

the connotation of 'gloomy' or 'melancholy', but in this context it is more likely to express the unclear, changing, even fickle aspects of Fortune: *nunc ... fallacem mutavit nubila vultum* ... ('Now ... clouded, she has changed her deceptive looks', 19). In a similar image Ovid laments the loss of friends which follows upon a fall in fortunes: '

> *utque.comes radios per solis euntibus umbra est,*
>   *cum latet hic pressus nubibus, illa fugit,*
> *mobile sic sequitur Fortunae lumina vulgus:*
>   *quae simul inducta nube teguntur, abit* (*Tristia* 1.9.11ff.).

As a shadow accompanies those who pass through the rays of the sun, but when the sun is hidden, hemmed in by clouds, the shadow vanishes, so the fickle crowd follows the light of good fortune, but, when once the veil of darkness covers it, the crowd is gone (tr. Wheeler).[6]

Fortune can suddenly 'cloud over': that is precisely the image which Boethius also evokes. Ovid's brilliant merging of this image with that of the crowd of friends that dogs the footsteps of the fortunate man, like his shadow in the sunlight, but then disappears when the sunshine of his good fortune is overcast, is less directly reflected in Boethius, but it is none the less suggested in the friends apostrophized in line 21, who bragged about his good fortune in times past. Like Ovid in his exile, the prisoner is alone in his prison.

There is a further dimension to the notion of clouded Fortune. The epithet foreshadows the theme of light and dark in the work, as well as suggesting the earthly character of all fortune. But there is more to it than that. Clouded Fortune reflects the prisoner's unperceiving, befogged mental state: when that state begins to alter for the better, it will be described in the image of winds blowing away storm-clouds and letting the sun shine through (1 m. 3).

However, before such a development takes place, there is Philosophy's assessment of Boethius' condition in 1 m. 2. The opening lines of that poem take up and expand the images of 1 m. 1:

> *Heu, quam praecipiti mersa profundo*
> *mens hebet et proprie luce relicta*
> *tendit in externas ire tenebras*
> *terrenis quotiens flatibus aucta*
> *crescit in immensum noxia cura!* (1 m. 2.1ff.)

Ah, how sheer is the depth in which the mind is drowned! It is dulled and, its own light gone, it strives to go into the outer dark, whenever poisonous anxiety, swollen by earthly gales, grows boundlessly.

---

[6] Gruber (1978) 56 refers to this Ovid passage, but does not exploit its possibilities in relation to 1 m. 1.

108   4. *Nature in the Poetry of the* Consolation

The central picture here is of the stormy sea or 'deep' (*profundo*, 1) in which the mind, like a boat or a drowning man, is submerged, and all but unconscious (*hebet*, 2). *Praecipiti* may describe the violent tossing of the waves; but it also suggests the steep fall of boat or man from the crest of one wave to the depth below it. The drowning mind is caught between great walls of lashed-up sea: the word-order of line 1 represents the mind's encirclement.

What does the sea represent? The key-word *praecipiti* suggests the theme of the fall of the soul from a 'higher' or celestial dimension into the material world.[7] It would be inaccurate to call this idea Neoplatonic: it is found in Cicero and Seneca, in contexts where Stoic elements have acquired a strong Platonic colouring. One striking passage in Cicero must suffice as an example:

> For the heavenly soul has sunk deep from its lofty dwelling place and is, so to speak, submerged in the earth, a place that is opposed to the divine nature and eternity (*De senectute* 21.77).

Yet when we consider that the sea symbolises the material world in Neoplatonic allegory, it is difficult not to see the characteristic Neoplatonic notion of the soul's descent alluded to here.[8] But what is striking is that Boethius maintains the metaphor within the bounds of Latin literary tradition. This is apparent in 3f. also. The thematic complex dark – earth – 'outer', contrasting with light – heaven(s) – 'inner', is expressed there in *in externas ire tenebras / terrenis ... flatibus*. At one level these images convey no more than mental confusion and bewilderment. In Manilius, the reader is made to object to the poet's demands upon him:

---

[7] For *praeceps, praecipitare* in such contexts see Gruber (1978) 76.

[8] Cf. Porphyry, *De antro nympharum* 34; Proclus, *In Crat.* p. 88 Pistelli; Proclus, *In Parmenidem* 5.1025. On the interpretation of the 'place of Unlikeness' (*anomoiotêtos topos*, Latin *regio dissimilitudinis*) in Plato, *Politicus* 273d-e in relation both to the material world in general and the sea in particular see J. Pépin, 'A propos du symbolisme de la mer chez Platon et dans le néoplatonisme', *Association Guillaume Budé. Actes du Congrès de Tours et de Poitiers* (3-9 septembre 1953), Paris 1954. 257-9; G. Dumeige, art. Dissemblance, *Dictionnaire de Spiritualité*, fasc. 22-3 (1956) 1330-46; on the tradition in general see P. Courcelle, 'La "région de dissemblance" dans la tradition néo-platonisante', *Recherches sur les Confessions de saint Augustin*, 2nd edn. (Paris 1968) 405-40 and the earlier studies by Courcelle and others referred to there 405 n. 1, esp. P. Courcelle, 'Tradition néo-platonicienne et traditions chrétiennes de la "région de dissemblance" (Platon, *Politique* 273d)', *Archives d'histoire doctrinale et littéraire du Moyen Age* 24 (1957) 5-33. For the symbolism of the sea in the patristic tradition see H. Rondet, 'Le symbolisme de la mer chez saint Augustin', *Augustinus Magister* (Paris 1954) 2.691-711; H. Rahner, *Symbole der Kirche. Die Ekklesiologie der Väter* (Salzburg 1964) 239-564. For Boethius cf. Viarre (1975) for one aspect of the theme. For its treatment in Latin poetry see E. de Saint-Denis, *Le rôle de la mer dans la poésie latine* (Lyons 1935).

rursus et in magna mergis caligine mentem,
cernere cum facili lucem ratione viderer (4.388f.).

and you are plunging my mind back into deep darkness just when I
thought a simple principle was enabling me to see light (tr. Goold).

And the poet must remind him of his aim:

    ... conaris scandere caelum

   ...

    et transire tuum pectus mundoque potiri (4.390,392).

    you are seeking to scale the skies ... to pass beyond your understanding
and make yourself master of the universe (tr. Goold).

Here the images of dark and 'fall' contrast with those of light and
ascent. The inner-outer contrast is found frequently in Seneca,[9] and is
a recurring motif of the *Consolation*, with its repeated insistence that
genuine goodness and happiness is to be found within us, and not in
external things (2.4.22; 2.5.14,24, etc.). These sentiments are Stoic, but
a Neoplatonist would also subscribe to them. The point, however, is
that to read the themes of 1 m. 2.1ff. in exclusively Neoplatonic terms
is to read the lines too narrowly. Thus, the image of darkness, which
for the Neoplatonists is both a metaphysical symbol of matter and a
metaphor for the moral perversity that is opposed to the light of
goodness, has, in the *Consolation*, a primarily moral, rather than
metaphysical, significance.[10] At 1 m. 3.1 *tenebrae* represent mental
confusion caused by moral blindness; at 1 m. 5.35, the dark is human
evil, contrasted with *virtus*; in 3 m. 10.12 earthly wealth and treasures
cast their dark shadow on the greedy and desiring mind.

A similar moral intent informs the final part of the opening complex
of 1 m. 2. The great storm-wave blown up by the 'earthly gales' (4) is
'poisonous anxiety' (*noxia cura*, 5): we are in the world of Roman
moralizing, and recognize a theme familiar in Epicurean and Stoic
contexts, and in poetry, such as that of Horace, influenced by such
contexts.[11]

The 'sea', therefore, of these lines, while it may be influenced by
Neoplatonic symbolism, is a metaphor at the moral, rather than the
metaphysical end of the spectrum, as is the image of darkness referred
to above. The sea which engulfs the mind is here not so much the
material universe in itself, as the anxiety that derives from
preoccupation with material concerns. In a similar way, Boethius, in 3

[9] e.g. *De providentia* 6.5; *De vita beata* 16.3: see further Gruber (1978) 191.
[10] This is also true of the uses of the dark-light motif in 3 m. 12 and 4 m. 1: see pp.
190ff. below.
[11] e.g. Horace, *Odes* 3.1.25ff., 37ff. (there 40 *atra Cura*); *Serm.* 2.7.114f. Gruber (1978)
80 also refers to Lucretius 1.50f.; 2.16ff.

m. 10, introduces the themes of the soul's fall and of dark and light in an overtly moral context of greed, wealth, and pleasure (3,7ff.):

> *splendor quo regitur vigetque caelum*
> *vitat obscuras animae ruinas* (15f.).

The brightness by which the heavens are ruled and flourish flies from the soul's dark fall.

Thus, the balance between the moral and the metaphysical meanings of these metaphors, crucial to Neoplatonism, is here upset, so that the moral meaning may predominate. And this (from a Neoplatonist perspective) 'untechnical' use of images is precisely what links the verses to the moralizing imagery, derived from Platonism, of the Roman poetic and philosophical tradition.

What applies to the images of darkness and the sea applies also to the image of earth. The prisoner, in his demoralized, lethargic state, is 'earthbound' (1.1.13, 1 m. 2.27). Later in the *Consolation* the image acquires a more specifically Platonic colouring:

> *sed quonam lateat quod cupiunt bonum*
>   *nescire caeci sustinent*
> *et quod stelliferum transabiit polum*
>   *tellure demersi petunt* (3 m. 8.15ff.).

But in their blindness they put up with not knowing where the good they desire lies hidden, and, sunk in the earth, they look for what is beyond the starry sky.

Here the allusion (17) to *Phaedrus* 247c (anticipating 4 m. 1) seems unmistakable,[12] as does the Neoplatonic colouring of:

> *dissice terrenae nebulas et pondera molis*
> *atque tuo splendore mica* (3 m. 9.25f.).

Scatter the weight and fogs of heavy earth, and shine in your own brilliance!

But even as late as 5.2.9f. a similar cluster of images is employed in a manner that, again, is not exclusive to Neoplatonists.[13] What appears to happen in this case is that an image gains in complexity and so keeps pace with the development of the work as a whole: inevitably, in the middle of the work in Book 3, that means that images acquire unmistakable Neoplatonic overtones. But that is no justification for reading such explicit overtones into them at an earlier stage of the

---

[12] See Gruber (1978) 272.
[13] See pp. 190f. below.

work. To do so is to miss the work's vital development. In 1 m. 2 the connotations of 'earthbound' are, as yet, no more complex than they are in Manilius 4.387ff., where preoccupation with gold, jewels, farming, sailing, and war is *tanto bona velle caduca* ('[to be] willing to pay so high a price for perishable goods!', 403, tr. Goold), whereas the astronomer should aim for knowledge, which is equated with the heavens, and with deification or transcendence of the merely human (406f.). Of course the images of 1 m. 2.24-7 have the Neoplatonic potentiality that Boethius exploits later in the work, and that is the reason why they are introduced here. But that Neoplatonic dimension is not yet part of their explicit meaning. We should not read the potential of an image, its future development, as its primary meaning at an earlier stage of the work.

The contrast in the Manilius passage just referred to, between the earthbound pursuits of miners, farmers, and others, and the sky-scanning activity of the astronomer, is relevant to 1 m. 2. For, following the lines which I have just been discussing, Philosophy describes the prisoner's earlier astronomical pursuits (6ff.). Not merely that, but he is also portrayed as the sometime philosopher-scientist, the spectator of nature's operations and laws:

> *rimari solitus atque latentis*
> *naturae varias reddere causas* (22f.).

> accustomed to search out and report the many varied causes in secret nature.

These laws include the causes of the winds and of seasonal change. In other words, earthly processes are also a fit object of study for the philosopher: what is essential is that one understands, and so in a sense dominates, the subject matter: knowledge is a form of conquest (*victor*, 12). It is this sense of intellectual triumph, rather than the mental tranquillity which study of the heavens, for example, is traditionally supposed to convey, that is stressed here.[14] By contrast, the prisoner's present condition is that of a defeated man, whose incarceration also characterizes his mental state:

> *nunc iacet effeto lumine mentis*
> *et pressus gravibus colla catenis*
> *declivemque gerens pondere vultum*
> *cogitur, heu, stolidam cernere terram* (24ff.).

> Now he lies, the light of his mind extinguished, his neck weighed down with heavy chains, and, his gaze sunk under the burden, he is forced, ah, to look upon the mindless earth.

[14] Cf. e.g. Cicero, *Tusc. disp.* 5.25.71. See Gruber (1978) 80f.

Here again, the associations of darkness and earth predominate: the poem concludes with the images of its beginning. *Stolidam* in the last line is a word usually applied to persons or personal qualities:[15] the metaphor suggests that the earth reflects the dullness of the befogged mind. At 3 m. 8.19 *stolidis mentibus* both echoes this line, and corresponds to more normal usage.

In 1 m. 2.18ff. the motif of the seasons is introduced, with allusions to spring and autumn: it is the first of a number of seasonal references in the work. Here the notion of causality predominates, but Boethius none the less elaborates a double vignette of the two seasons:

> *quid veris placidas temperet horas*
> *ut terram roseis floribus ornet,*
> *quis dedit ut pleno fertilis anno*
> *autumnus gravidis influat uvis* ... (18ff.).

What modulates the spring's calm hours, so that it adorns the earth with blossoming roses, and who gave fruitfulness to autumn in the fullness of the year, when teeming ripe grapes hang heavily ...

The motif of the seasons is traditional, and Boethius' primary debt is to its prior occurrences in the poetic tradition, even if it should not be forgotten that it is a stock topic of rhetoric.[16] It will be appropriate to consider some poetic treatments of the topic here, prior to discussions of its function in this and later poems in the *Consolation*.

There are two notable instances in Lucretius. The first stresses the notion of ordered causation in nature:

> *praeterea cur vere rosam, frumenta calore,*
> *vites autumno fundi suadente videmus,*
> *si non, certa suo quia tempore semina rerum*
> *cum confluxerunt, patefit quodcumque creatur,*
> *dum tempestates adsunt et vivida tellus*
> *tuto res teneras effert in luminis oras?* (1.174ff.).

Besides, why do we see the roses put forth in spring, corn in the heat, grapes under persuasion of autumn, unless because each created thing discloses itself when at their own time the fixed seeds of things have

[15] It is applied to *audacia* in Tacitus, *Histories* 4.15, as Salemme (1970/1) 86 observes. Plautus, however, uses it in a similar manner to Boethius: '*nullumst hoc stolidiu' saxum*', *Miles gloriosus* 4.2.35.

[16] On the seasons-motif in Greek and Roman literature see G.M.A. Hanfmann, *The Season Sarcophagus in Dumbarton Oaks*, 2 vols. = *Dumbarton Oaks Studies* 2 (1951) 1.87ff.; F. Bömer, *P. Ovidius Naso: Metamorphosen, Buch I-III* (Heidelberg 1969) 246ff. (on *Met.* 2.26ff.). Both scholars also give attention to the artistic tradition: see further n. 224 below. As a rhetorical topic: see Pseudo?-Hermogenes' reference to the *ekphrasis khronôn*, p. 22 Rabe. For the comparison of the four stages of human life with the four seasons see Ovid, *Met.* 15.209ff.; Cicero, *De senectute* 19.70 with J.G.F. Powell's comm. (Cambridge 1988) ad loc.

streamed together, and the lively earth safely brings out things young and tender into the borders of light? (tr. Rouse/Smith).

Besides the notion of causation, 1 m. 2.18ff. shares with this Lucretius passage its emblematic use of roses as a symbol of spring, and grapes of autumn. The second Lucretius passage is more elaborate, and highlights the ordered succession of the seasons:

> *it Ver et Venus, et Veneris praenuntius ante*
> *pennatus graditur, Zephyri vestigia propter*
> *Flora quibus mater praespargens ante viai*
> *cuncta coloribus egregiis et odoribus opplet;*
> *inde loci sequitur Calor aridus et comes una*
> *pulverulenta Ceres et etesia flabra Aquilonum;*
> *inde Autumnus adit, graditur simul Euhius Euan;*
> *inde aliae tempestates ventique sequuntur,*
> *altitonans Volturnus et Auster fulmine pollens;*
> *tandem Bruma nives adfert pigrumque rigorem*
> *reddit; Hiemps sequitur crepitans hanc dentibus algu* (5.737ff.).

On come Spring and Venus, and Venus' winged harbinger marching before, with Zephyr and mother Flora a pace behind him strewing the whole path in front and filling it with brilliant colours and scents. Next in place follows parching Heat, along with Ceres his dusty comrade and the Etesian Winds that blow from the north. Next comes Autumn, and marching with him Euhius Euan [Bacchus]. Then follow other seasons and winds, Volturnus thundering on high and Auster lord of lightning; at length Shortest Day brings the snow and restores the numbing frost; after it comes Winter, its teeth chattering with cold (tr. Rouse/Smith).

At this stage it will suffice to note the linking of winds and seasons in this brilliant passage.

Horace's use of the motif in the ode *Diffugere nives* is no less striking. The poem's opening evokes the transition from winter to spring:

> *Diffugere nives, redeunt iam gramina campis*
> *arboribusque comae;*
> *mutat terra vices, et decrescentia ripas*
> *flumina praetereunt* (*Odes* 4.7.1ff.).

The snows are fled away, leaves on the shaws
    And grasses in the mead renew their birth,
The river to the river-bed withdraws,
    And altered is the fashion of the earth (tr. Housman).

But in the course of the poem the theme of seasonal change and succession becomes a symbol of the mutability and instability of human life:

frigora mitescunt Zephyris, ver proterit aestas,
    interitura, simul
pomifer autumnus fruges effuderit, et mox
    bruma recurrit iners (9ff.).

Thaw follows frost; hard on the heel of spring
    Treads summer sure to die, for hard on hers
Comes autumn with his apples scattering;
    Then back to wintertide, when nothing stirs (tr. Housman).

The almost indecent haste of change in these lines is compounded by the thought that nature at least gives compensation for loss (13), whereas human life knows no such renewal (14ff.).[17] The tone of the poem gradually darkens. Here, then, seasonal change leads to thoughts of dissolution and death (which dominates the poem's last fifteen lines).[18] In the counterpart ode to this in *Odes* 1,[19] *Solvitur acris hiems*, death is also the foil to spring, and is a theme of the poem (1.4.13ff.), but it is more than counterbalanced by the delights of spring and youth. The opening verses of that earlier ode also contrast spring with antecedent winter and mark the transition from one to the other season, and they are a fine example of Horace's pictorial vividness:

Solvitur acris hiems grata vice veris et Favoni
    trahuntque siccas machinae carinas,
ac neque iam stabulis gaudet pecus aut arator igni
    nec prata canis albicant pruinis (1.4.1ff.).

Biting winter melts, and spring follows pleasantly, with the west wind; the sleds drag the dry keels down to the sea; the flocks do not find joy now in their stables, nor the ploughman at the fire, and the fields are no longer white with frost.

As might be expected, Virgil's *Georgics* is a source of some significant samples of the seasons motif. The economy of mentioning all four seasons in four or five lines is a *tour de force* that attracts Virgil as much as Horace or Ovid:

optima vinetis satio, cum vere rubenti
candida venit avis longis invisa colubris,
prima vel autumni sub frigora, cum rapidus Sol
nondum hiemem contingit equis, iam praeterit aestas (*Georgics* 2.319ff.).

Best time for planting is the flush of spring
When the white bird, the bane of trailing snakes,

---

[17] See Fraenkel (1957) 420. A.E. Housman's translation of *Odes* 4.7, quoted here, is found in his *More Poems* (London 1936) 21f.
[18] Cf. Seneca, *Phaedra* 764ff.
[19] Fraenkel (1957) 419 discusses the linking mechanisms.

Appears; or close upon the frosts of autumn,
When summer's waning but the fiery steeds
Of the sun have yet to reach the Signs of winter (tr. Wilkinson).

Or:

primus vere rosam atque autumno carpere poma,
et cum tristis hiems etiamnum frigore saxa
rumperet et glacie cursus frenaret aquarum,
ille comam mollis iam tondebat hyacinthi
aestatem increpitans seram Zephyrosque morantis (ib. 4.134ff.).

He was the first in spring to gather roses,
In autumn, to pick apples; and when winter
Was gloomily still cracking rocks with cold
And choking streams with ice, he was already
Shearing the locks of the tender hyacinth
While grumbling at the lateness of the summer
And absence of west winds (tr. Wilkinson).

In these passages of Virgil the degree of descriptive vividness is related, as it is in Boethius, to the context. In the first text, where the topic is the suitable time for sowing, the two favoured times, spring or late autumn, are described, while the other two seasons are merely mentioned. In the second text, the old man of Tarentum works hard in all seasons, but especially in harsh winter, whose grim weather is highlighted. So that season is the one described, but all are mentioned, because Virgil is intent upon having him work in a real seasonal year, in contrast to the Saturnian farmer of the end of Book 2.[20]

Seasonal sequences are also found in Ovid, and two, in particular, are worth quoting here.[21] The first comes from the *Metamorphoses*, and it is a remarkable personification of the four seasons, seen by Phaethon in the house of his father Phoebus:

Verque novum stabat cinctum florente corona,
stabat nuda Aestas et spicea serta gerebat,
stabat et Autumnus, calcatis sordidus uvis,
et glacialis Hiems, canos hirsuta capillos (*Met.* 2.27ff.).

Young Spring was there, wreathed with a floral crown; Summer, all unclad with garland of ripe grain; Autumn was there, stained with the trodden grape, and icy Winter with white and bristly locks (tr. Miller).

---

[20] See Thomas (1988) 2.172ff. The praises of spring in *Georg.* 2.323ff., and the account of spring and autumn storms in 1.311ff., also contain motifs found in treatments of seasonal change, although their function in their contexts is different from the functions discussed in this section. See Thomas (1988) 1.215 on the ambivalent status of spring in *Georg*.

[21] Cf. Ovid, *Met.* 15.199ff.; *Remedia amoris* 187f.

In a second passage Ovid, in exile at Tomi, considers his unfortunate state:

> *vere prius flores, aestu numerabis aristas,*
>   *poma per autumnum, frigoribusque nives,*
> *quam mala, quae toto patior iactatus in orbe* ... (*Tristia* 4.1.57ff.).

Sooner will you count the flowers of spring, the grain-ears of summer, the fruits of autumn, or the snowflakes in time of cold than the ills which I suffered driven all over the world ... (tr. Wheeler).

In this passage the thematic sequence is applied to convey the notion of quantity. Description of the seasons' characteristics is thus avoided, and one emblematic characteristic of each is merely mentioned.

In Manilius the winter-summer contrast is brought out in the following passage:

> *hinc rigor et glacies nivibusque albentia rura,*
> *hinc sitis et sudor nudusque in collibus orbis,*
> *aestivosque dies aequat nox frigida brumae.*
> *sic bellum natura gerit, discordat et annus* (2.419ff.).

The one season brings frost and ice and a countryside white with snow, the other thirst and sweat and an earth with hillside parched; and the chill wintry night rivals in length the summer's day. Thus nature wages warfare and the year is split in faction (tr. Goold).

This opposition is reflected in opposing zodiacal signs (2.414ff.): the notion of natural conflict is important in Boethius, as will be seen. But for Manilius this conflict is not absolute, and is balanced by natural harmony:

> ... *quia ver autumno tempore differt*
> *(fructibus hoc implet maturis, floribus illud)*
> *sed rationi pari est, aequatis nocte diebus,*
> *temporaque efficiunt simili concordia textu*
> *permixtosque dies mediis hiemem inter et aestum*
> *articulis uno servantia utrimque tenore*
> *quo minus infesto decertent sidera bello* (2.425ff.).

... For though in point of season spring differs from autumn (the one fills the earth with fruit, the other with flowers), yet it enjoys a like principle, seeing that day is levelled with night in each. And the seasons, which are harmonious in their likeness of texture and, as links joining winter and summer, maintain with the same tenor on either side days of identical blend, bring it about that the constellations refrain from clashing in violent warfare (tr. Goold).

Here the extremes are mediated by the means: spring and autumn bridging winter and summer. And the whole is an exemplar of cosmic *concordia discors*. One notes that only the two extremes are described in any detail (419f.).

A further passage in Manilius provides a lengthy description of the four seasons (3.625ff.). I quote only the pictorial details of each seasonal evocation. Summer:

> *tum Cererem fragili properant destringere culmo*
> ...
> *et tepidas pelagus iactatum languet in undas* (3.629,631).

Then men make haste to strip the grain from the brittle stalk ... and after its storms the sea sinks back to rest upon warm waters.[22]

Winter:

> *tunc riget omnis ager, clausum mare, condita castra,*
> *nec tolerant medias hiemes sudantia saxa,*
> *statque uno natura loco paulumque quiescit* (641ff.).

Then every field is frostbound; the sea is closed to ships; the camp is stationary; rocks covered with rime are unable to endure midwinter's cold: nature stands motionless and for a while is still.

Spring:

> *tum primum miti pelagus consternitur unda*
> *et varios audet flores emittere tellus;*
> *tum pecudum volucrumque genus per pabula laeta*
> *in Venerem partumque ruit, totumque canora*
> *voce nemus loquitur frondemque virescit in omnem* (652ff.).

Then first the sea is calmed with tranquil wave, and the earth dares to send forth flowers in all their variety; then amid happy pastures the tribes of bird and beast hasten to meet and breed, and the whole woodland speaks with melodious voice and grows green to full foliage.

Autumn:

> *tum Liber gravida descendit plenus ab ulmo*
> *pinguiaque impressis despumant musta racemis;*
> *mandant et sulcis Cererem, dum terra tepore*
> *autumni resoluta patet, dum semina ducit* (662ff.).

This is the season when the Wine-god comes down in full strength from the laden elm, and the rich must pours foaming from pressed bunches of grapes; and this the season when men commit the corn to the furrows,

---

[22] This and the following translations are by Goold.

whilst the soil, relaxed by autumn's warmth, opens to clasp the seed (tr.
Goold).

The background to these descriptions is a discussion of the so-called
tropic signs, but the descriptions do not add to that discussion. They
are pictorial elaborations befitting the conclusion of the book. For our
purposes, therefore, the context of these descriptions is, for once,
irrelevant.

A further text may be adduced from the *Hercules Oetaeus*, a play
which is known to, and influences, Boethius:[23]

> *vere dum flores venient tepenti*
> *et comam silvis revocabit aestas*
> *pomaque autumno fugiente cedent*
> *et comam silvis hiemes recident,*
> *tu comes Phoebo, comes ibis astris* (*HO* 1576ff.).

As long as the flowers will bloom in mild spring, and summer will
summon back the leaves to the woods, and the fruit falls ripely as
autumn vanishes, and winter stripes away the foliage from the trees, you
will always be a companion to Phoebus and to the stars.

The nice balance of these lines, their symmetry (foliage on trees in
summer, trees bare of foliage in winter; blossom in spring, fruit in
autumn), is again apt to the context. Hercules' fame will be
everlasting, it will remain constant, as his immortality in heaven will:
appropriately, the notion of 'all time' is conveyed by the succession of
lines, one per season, suggesting regularly paced change.

It has already been noted above that the details of Boethius'
description of spring and autumn in 1 m. 2 are traditional. Roses and
grapes feature in the first Lucretius passage quoted, roses in the first
Virgil passage, and grapes again in Ovid and in the second Manilius
passage, and it would be tedious to list other texts where these typical
and obvious seasonal characteristics occur. The use of *temperare* in 1
m. 2.18 suggests a passage in Seneca's *Phaedra*[24] which will be
referred to again in the discussion of 1 m. 5:

> *cur tanta tibi* [*sc. Naturae*] *cura perennes*
> *agitare vices aetheris alti,*
> *ut nunc canae frigora brumae*
>   *nudent silvas,*
> *nunc arbustis redeant umbrae,*
> *nunc aestivi colla leonis*

---

[23] *Hercules Oetaeus* is generally regarded as not by Seneca, though it is included in the
MSS and editions of his tragedies: for a possible dating in the mid-second century see O.
Zwierlein, *Kritischer Kommentar zu den Tragödien Senecas* (Stuttgart 1986) 313-43.
[24] See Salemme (1970/1) 75.

Cererem magno fervore coquant
viresque suas temperet annus? (Phae. 964ff.).

Why do you [Nature] take such care to maintain the everlasting
succession of the vast sky's movements, that now white winter's frosts
strip the forest, now shade returns to the orchards, now Leo's mane
ablaze burns the crops with raging summer heat, and [now] the year
modulates its strength?

But *temperare* in a spring context is also common in Latin poetry, in
Horace[25] and elsewhere. Likewise, *gravidus*, of ripe fruit, is
traditional,[26] and found, for example, in Manilius' description (3.662f.)
of the elm branches weighed down with the ripe grapes grafted on to
them, quoted above, a passage in which *plenus* also denotes autumnal
abundance, as it does in Boethius' *pleno fertilis anno* (1 m. 2.20). In this
passage, then, Boethius stays within secure and conventional limits. It
is not the fact of change as such, as the laws governing seasonal
differences, that he wishes to stress. He focuses on two of the seasons,
because this part of the poem is, in a sense, a sequence of paired
phenomena: sun and moon, morning and evening star, spring and
autumn.[27] Moreover, because the seasons are part of a list of natural
phenomena mastered by the philosopher, Boethius will not want to
give them undue emphasis, either by listing all four, or by spectacular
descriptions which will distract the reader from his overall purpose. So
the extremes of summer and winter are avoided, and the language
which describes spring and autumn is subdued and conventional.

It is now time to turn away from the motif of the seasons and from 1
m. 2, to consider further poems in Book 1 of the *Consolation*.

In 1.2 Philosophy diagnoses the prisoner's state as one of lethargy,[28]
leading to self-forgetfulness (1.2.6), and she begins the process of his
cure by cleaning his eyes of that which is obscuring their sight: 'Let us
cleanse his eyes for a while of the dark cloud of mortal things' (1.2.6).[29]
Boethius is merging here the notion of mental darkness with the
prisoner's tears, as at 1.1.13: 'But I, whose sight, drowned in tears, had
grown dim, and who could not make out who this woman was of such
commanding authority, was amazed into silence.' Thus immediately
after Philosophy has said that she will clear the prisoner's eyes: '...
drawing her dress into a fold, she dried my eyes, which flowed with
tears' (1.2.7). The total picture – tears, stupefied silence, downcast
visage – typifies his mental darkness throughout this sequence, so that

[25] Cf. Horace, *Odes* 4.12.1; *Epist.* 1.12.16.

[26] See Virgil, *Georgics* 1.111, 319; 2.5, 143, 424.

[27] See Scheible (1972) 20.

[28] Schmid (1956) discusses the theme of lethargy and its cure in *Cons. phil.*, with rich
documentation of the ancient medical material (see esp. 115 n. 1). Cf. Ch. 2, n. 7 above.

[29] Gruber (1978) 93 stresses the allusion to the mental darkness of 1.1.13 and 1 m.
2.1ff., at the expense of Boethius' tears.

at 1.1.13 tears and darkness combine with dumbness and the downcast stance (*visu ... in terram defixo*), just as at 1 m. 1.24ff. darkness and the downcast stance are combined, and in 1.2.6f. darkness and tears. The prisoner's tears have become part of the image of mental obfuscation. So, when they are dried by Philosophy, his mental vision[30] returns:

> *Tunc me discussa liquerunt nocte tenebrae*
> *luminibusque prior rediit vigor ...* (1 m. 3.1f.).

Then the night was scattered and darkness departed from me, and their former strength returned to my eyes ...

The influence of a memorable image in Virgil's *Aeneid* has rightly been observed here.[31] Turnus, told of the siege of the capital city of the Latins and Amata's suicide, is described in the following terms:

> *obstipuit varia confusus imagine rerum*
> *Turnus et obtutu tacito stetit; aestuat ingens*
> *uno in corde pudor mixtoque insania luctu*
> *et furiis agitatus amor et conscia virtus.*
> *ut primum discussae umbrae et lux reddita menti,*
> *ardentis oculorum orbis ad moenia torsit*
> *turbidus eque rotis magnam respexit ad urbem* (*Aen.* 12.665ff.).

The picture of their changed fortunes struck Turnus dumb, bewildered
      him.
Speechless and staring, he stood there, his heart in a violent conflict,
Torn by humiliation, by grief shot through with madness,
By love's tormenting jealousy and a sense of his own true courage.
As soon as the mists parted and he could think again clearly,
He turned his blazing eyes upon the walls, in great
Distress of mind, looked back at the city there from his chariot.
                    (tr. Day Lewis)

What distinguishes this passage from its Homeric models, where a hero's vision is restored and the restoration is described in terms of clouds or mist giving way to light (*Iliad* 15.667ff.; 20.341f.), is the state of emotional turmoil from which Turnus awakes, and that is what links it to the Boethius passage, over and above the verbal reminiscence of line 669. For it will become increasingly clear in the course of Book 1 that it is conflicting passions that are causing Boethius' blindness and sickness, and those passions will be compared

---

[30] On the concept of the 'eyes of the mind' see Plato, *Republic* 533d; in the New Testament see Ephesians 1:18 (cf. *ThWNT* 5.378.22ff.). See further O'Daly (1987) 90. The whole tradition is massively documented and studied by G. Schleusener-Eichholz, *Das Auge im Mittelalter*, 2 vols. (Munich 1985).
[31] By Scheible (1972) 31.

with clouds and the storm-tossed sea in 1 m. 7.1ff. In the Virgil passage the storm and cloud metaphors are predominant (*aestuat, agitatus, discussae umbrae, turbidus*). It is Virgil's application of such metaphors to a mental state,[32] combined with the description of recovery as the clearing of clouds and light returning, that influences Boethius.

It has been noted how the language of the opening lines of 1 m. 3 reflects both the mental state of the prisoner and the metaphor of the storm-cloud, so that the two terms of the comparison develop along parallel lines, so to speak, even before the simile of 3ff. makes the metaphor explicit.[33] There may be a model for the storm-description of 3f. –

> *ut cum praecipiti glomerantur sidera Coro*
> *nimbosisque polus stetit imbribus* ...

Just as when the headlong Corus gathers up the heavens into a mass, and the sky is veiled in rain-clouds ...

– in a passage from Seneca:[34]

> *Fugit insanae similis procellae,*
> *ocior nubes glomerante Coro* ... (*Phae.* 736f.).

She's gone like a mad storm, faster than Corus gathers up the clouds ...

But a storm-description in the *Georgics* may also have influenced Boethius here:

> *saepe etiam immensum caelo venit agmen aquarum*
> *et foedam glomerant tempestatem imbribus atris*
> *collectae ex alto nubes* (1.322ff.).

And often too a mighty host of waters
Invades the sky, and gathering from the deep
Clouds roll and roll together an ugly storm
Of murky rain (tr. Wilkinson).

The somewhat unusual use of *glomerare* in this last passage – the clouds 'gather the storm into a mass' – is closer to Boethius' *glomerantur sidera* than the more conventional description of the wind gathering clouds into a mass in the Seneca passage.[35]

[32] Cf. already Homer, *Il.* 9.4ff.; 10.5ff.; 14.16ff.

[33] See Salemme (1970/1) 81.

[34] See Salemme (1970/1) 70f.

[35] See Thomas (1988) 1.213. In Boethius 1 m. 3.3 *sidera* cannot mean 'stars' (so Salemme [1970/1] 71), for a daytime scene is being described (line 5). For *sidus* as 'heavens' or 'sky' where a storm is evoked see Virgil, *Aen.* 12.451 and (with reference to a

In v. 7 clouds give way suddenly (*subito*, 9) to brilliant sunshine. The suddenness is emphasized by anacoluthon:[36] *hanc si Threicio Boreas ab antro / verberet...* ('If Boreas, released from his Thracian cave, whips this [night] away ...', 7f.). A similar device describes the sudden recovery of Turnus in the *Aeneid* passage quoted above (*ut primum ...*, 669). But this similarity may be due less to the influence of the Virgilian passage upon Boethius than to both poets' rhetorical use of a mode of expression that perfectly conveys sudden change.

At the end of 1 m. 3 the light-metaphor, which has hitherto featured in the *Consolation* only in the negative sense of clouded or extinguished light, is used to affirm the dawning insight of the prisoner:

> *emicat et subito vibratus lumine Phoebus*
> *mirantes oculos radiis ferit* (9f.).

> Phoebus shines with sudden sparkling light, and strikes eyes full of wonder with his rays.

To find here a reference to the sun-like nature of the perceiving eye, in the manner of a famous passage in Plotinus (*Enn.* 1.6.9.30ff.), is to read too much into these lines.[37] In Plotinus, the inherent affinity of the eyes and the sun is emphasized: 'To any vision must be brought an eye adapted to what is to be seen, and having some likeness to it. Never did eye see the sun unless it had first become sunlike' (tr. MacKenna). Boethius is not saying that much, but merely evoking the brilliant sunlight striking the eyes. Indeed it is the difference between the sun, and the eyes that are struck by its light, that he stresses, for what the prisoner now sees and, for the first time, recognizes, is Philosophy herself (1.3.1). Note how the poem is linked to the following prose passage by a sustained use of its metaphors: 'In just the same way the clouds of sadness dissipated, and I drank in the sky's brightness' (1.3.1). This link, and the continuation and development of the themes and, above all, the metaphors and images of earlier passages in the work make 1 m. 3 more than a mere interlude or transitional poem. It is unique in the work in that it is a poem neither spoken by Philosophy nor, strictly speaking, by the prisoner, but one that is, rather, part of the narrative. Yet it is a typical poem in its use of key images and motifs.

If the two preceding poems have evoked images of a man drowning, lost in clouds and darkness, overwhelmed, the next poem, 1 m. 4, uses

---

specific constellation) ib. 11.259f. In all three cases adjacent words (*abrupto* and *triste* in the Virgil passages, *glomerantur* in Boethius) facilitate the storm-connotation (I owe this point to Anna Wilson).

[36] See Salemme (1970/1) 81.

[37] As does Gruber (1978) 98.

nature-metaphors to construct a counter-image, the positive model of the philosopher-sage impervious to whatever fate and fortune may bring:

> *non illum rabies minaeque ponti*
> *versum funditus exagitantis aestum*
> *nec ruptis quotiens vagus caminis*
> *torquet fumificos Vesaevus ignes*
> *aut celsas soliti ferire turres*
> *ardentis via fulminis movebit* (5ff.).

The rage and threats of the sea, rousing and tossing up the swell from the depths, will not move him; nor will Vesuvius, whenever it erupts, and, furnances belching, flings out its fires; nor will the blazing lightning's path, which often strikes high towers.

The man who is unshaken by either stormy seas or lightning recalls Horace, *Odes* 3.3, on the *iustum et tenacem propositi virum* ('man who is just and tenacious of his purpose', 1, tr. Williams) whom

> *neque Auster,*
> *dux inquieti turbidus Hadriae,*
> *nec fulminantis magna manus Iovis* (4ff.)

[neither] the south wind, wild emperor of the restless Adriatic, nor the mighty hand of thundering Jupiter (tr. Williams)

can shake. But Boethius' lines also recall Seneca's king-sage,

> *quem non concutiet cadens*
> *obliqui via fulminis,*
> *non Eurus rapiens mare*
> *aut saevo rabidus freto*
> *ventosi tumor Hadriae* (*Thyest*. 358ff.).

whom the lightning's zigzag path will not strike as it comes down, nor the storm-wind seizing the sea, nor the swelling wind-tossed Adriatic, its waves fiercely raging.[38]

Seneca's *via fulminis* appears to be a direct influence upon Boethius.

Between these two metaphors Boethius inserts that of erupting Vesuvius. The novelty of Vesuvius as a volcanic *exemplum* distracts Scheible from Boethius' careful adaptation of traditional Virgilian language here.[39] It may well be that the eruption of the year 511 impressed Boethius and makes the reference apt, but rather than

---

[38] For the wise man who is unafraid of sea-storms see also Horace, *Odes* 3.1.25ff. (cf. n. 11 above). Tarrant (1985) 142 notes the Horatian colouring of *Thyest*. 358ff.

[39] Scheible (1972) 34.

looking to that or to relatively colourless references to the volcano in Statius,[40] it is above all Virgil's evocations of Etna that should be recalled by the reader. One passage is the *Georgics*:

> *quotiens Cyclopum effervere in agros*
> *vidimus undantem ruptis fornacibus Aetnam ...* (1.471f.).

> How often we saw
> Etna, asurge with cracking furnaces ...
> Boil over onto the fields of the Cyclopses (tr. Wilkinson).

The picture of the furnaces of Etna which Virgil conjures up here[41] is subsequently developed in the *Aeneid*, where the lines that evidently influence Boethius occur:

> *ingentemque insuper Aetnam*
> *impositam* ruptis *flammam exspirare* caminis (*Aen*. 3.579f.).

> Aetna was dumped down bodily upon him
> And like a leaky furnace jets out the fire (tr. Day Lewis).

Elsewhere in the *Consolation*, when Boethius thinks of volcanoes as terrifying natural forces, it is Etna that he names (2 m. 5.25; 2.6.1).

Boethius' description of Vesuvius may derive from Virgil's description of Etna, but he gives it his own distinctive colouring. Thus the volcano is *vagus* because its apparently irregular and unpredictable behaviour is symptomatic of unreliable, fickle fortune.[42] The sage is indifferent to it, not so much because such an attitude is equivalent to the philosopher-scientist's understanding and hence control of nature, as in 1 m. 2,[43] but rather because he has learnt to practise freedom from the passions (*apatheia*). There is no indication that Boethius wishes to see a parallel between understanding natural processes and being absolved of fear of them: that is too Epicurean a reading of 1 m. 3, which is essentially a Stoic poem.[44]

The term *fumificos* in line 8 is sufficiently unusual to be worthy of remark. It is used by Ovid to describe fire-breathing bulls (*Met*. 7.114), and by Prudentius to evoke the torches that can be an instrument of the martyr's torture (*Peristef*. 3.118): it will have sounded novel and striking in the ears of Boethius' readers. Finally, the verb *torquere*, used of the fires of the volcano tossed up in whirls, may echo a storm-description in Virgil:

[40] Statius, *Silvae* 3.5.72f.; 5.3.205ff.: see Scheible (1972) 34.
[41] Probably influenced by Lucretius 6.681: *flamma foras vastis Aetnae fornacibus efflet*.
[42] See Gruber (1978) 111.
[43] So Scheible (1972) 34.
[44] Cf. lines 13ff.: see pp. 101f. above.

cum Iuppiter horridus Austris
torquet aquosam hiemem et caelo cava nubila rumpit (Aen. 9.670f.).[45]

when Jupiter, terrible in the South wind,
Bursting the clouds above us, unleashes tornadoes of water.

(tr. Day Lewis)

The volcano motif is incorporated into a sequence whose other members are part of the *apatheia* motif. It attains moralizing force with Boethius, so to speak. The lightning motif, on the other hand, is part of the *apatheia* tradition. But Boethius' use of it extends beyond its immediate function (to provide an instance of a terrifying natural force) to recall its use in a quite different moralizing context, that of the vulnerability of the high and mighty. That Boethius models his lines on Horace seems obvious:

... celsae graviore casu
decidunt turres feriuntque summos
fulgura montis (Odes 2.10.10ff.).

High towers collapse with a greater fall, and lightning strikes the mountain peaks.

And Seneca's line, *feriunt celsos fulmina colles* ('lightning strikes the hilltops', *Ag.* 96), itself modelled on Horace, anticipates the terse briskness of Boethius (line 9).

The next poem, 1 m. 5, follows upon the prisoner's extended apologia for his behaviour and bitter complaints about his political downfall. He sees himself as guiltless, an innocent victim of intrigue and conspiracy. He finds in his fate an example of the triumph of evil and vulnerability of the good, summed up in the vivid image of 'criminal workshops' (*nefarias sceleratorum officinas*) at 1.4.46. This theme will dominate the second part of the following poem (25ff.). But in the first part Boethius unfolds an extended picture of cosmic order maintained by a divine creator-ruler (*conditor*, 1; *rector*, 27.46): the poem speaks of astronomical laws (4), of an 'ancient law' (23) that extends to seasonal change, of a universe operating with secure limits (25), or held together by bonds (*foedera*, 43) which the poet would wish to see governing men's affairs (*firma stabiles foedere terras*, 48). Lapidge has shown that the theme of cosmic bonds is Stoic in origin and is widespread in Latin poetry.[46] Its source is in Stoic cosmology, in the notion of the universe permeated by *pneuma*, whose creation of tension (*pneumatikos tonos*) maintains the world in existence. Chrysippus, in particular, speaks of the stable coherence (*sunekheia*) of the cosmos, of

---

[45] Cf. *rumpit* with *ruptis* in line 7 of Boethius' poem.
[46] Lapidge (1980).

the natural joining (*sumphuia*) or sympathy (*sumpatheia*) of its parts. He employs the metaphor of the *desmos pneumatos* or fiery breath-bond to express the notion of cosmic coherence. In the Latin tradition, Cicero takes up this Stoic language in *De natura deorum*.[47] As Lapidge has shown, it is not only in the poetry of Lucan and Manilius, influenced as that poetry is by Stoic doctrines and images, that such metaphorical language is found. It features in Christian Latin poetry (Paulinus of Nola, Orientius, Marius Victor, Dracontius) and prose (Minucius Felix) as a metaphor for cosmic harmony, in contexts where the Stoic world-picture is rejected, implicitly or explicitly. Key terms of this tradition can be identified.[48] Some of these, e.g. 'bonds' (*foedera*), occur already in Lucretius and Virgil, that is to say, they also have a Latin poetic pedigree that is not Stoic. Common to occurrences of this motif is the concept of an active immanent force in nature, in virtue of which nature coheres. Boethius is part of this tradition, and, whatever the influence of the geometric cosmology of the *Timaeus* and related Neoplatonic concepts[49] upon his thought and language, it is clear that the primary influence is that of his Latin poetic predecessors. What is particularly interesting is that he reflects a tradition of Christian poetry here, even if the themes and idioms of his poetry in the *Consolation* are not explicitly Christian. Thus the theme of cosmic *amor* in 2 m. 8 is not exclusively Neoplatonic:[50] it has an antecedent in Lucan's 'holy cosmic love' (*sacer orbis amor*, 4.191). The motifs of *foedera* and 'laws' (*leges*)[51] in 1 m. 5 are thus part of a poetic tradition that begins with Lucan (1.80; 4.189ff., etc.) and Manilius (1.252; 2.62). Boethius' *foedera nectis* (1 m. 5.43) shows that he is thinking of the theme of cosmic bonds, as he is elsewhere in the *Consolation*:

> *Quod mundus stabili fide*
> *concordes variat vices,*
> *quod pugnantia semina*
> *foedus perpetuum tenent* ... (2 m. 8.1ff.).

That the universe brings about harmonious change with unwavering fidelity, the warring elements keep perpetual truce ...

> *Quantas rerum flectat habenas*
> *natura potens, quibus immensum*

---

[47] His Stoic interlocutor Balbus speaks of the *continuatus spiritus*, of the *consentiens conspirans ... cognatio rerum*, and of the universe held together *quodam vinculo circumdato* (*nat. deor.* 2.7.19; 2.45.115).

[48] Such as: *foedera, conpages, nexus, nectere, iungere, cingere, ligare, pugnantia semina, amor, leges*.

[49] Like the *taxis* or *suntaxis* of the universe: see Theiler (1966) 175f., 180ff.

[50] See Lapidge (1980) 835, criticizing C. De Vogel, 'Amor quo caelum regitur', *Vivarium* 1 (1963) 2-34.

[51] For the two terms together see Virgil, *Georgics* 1.60; Lucan 2.2.

legibus orbem provida servet
stringatque ligans inresoluto
singula nexu ... (3 m. 2.1ff.).

With what powerful reins strong Nature guides all things, with what laws she in her foresight maintains the vast universe, and, binding them in a band that cannot be dissolved, draws every single thing together ...

tu numeris elementa ligas, ut frigora flammis,
arida conveniant liquidis, ne purior ignis
evolet aut mersas deducant pondera terras (3 m. 9.10ff.).

You bind the elements with numbers, so that cold and flames, dry and liquid, are counterbalanced, that fire, too pure, may not fly up and away, or heavy masses sink the earth.

This does not mean that Boethius does not blend this theme (and so develop it) with specifically Neoplatonic motifs, such as that of conversion (*epistrophê*) in 3 m. 2.34ff.[52]

The examples of cosmic harmony given in 1 m. 5.5ff. correspond to those which describe the prisoner's scientific activities in 1 m. 2.9ff. They are: the waxing and waning of the moon in relation to the sun's influence (corresponding to sun and moon in the earlier poem), evening and morning star, and seasonal change. In this way a significant bridge is established between the activities of the scientist-philosopher and the prime examples of cosmic harmony, so that it becomes apparent that the prisoner has not entirely forgotten (or has begun to recall) the results of his former inquiries. But we should not read the elaboration of these motifs naturalistically, as if the prisoner were being shown to have made so much progress in so little time. The poetry of the *Consolation* bridges the different times of the work's dramatic progress, so that motifs anticipate their full development, and, in particular, cardinal themes are expressed but only fully appropriated in the detailed argument of subsequent prose sections.[53] That is certainly happening in 1 m. 5. But it is also important to see that the ideas of that poem about cosmic harmony are presented as incomplete and hence deficient. The prisoner cannot see the extension of divine providence to human affairs: he can only see injustice and the triumph of the wrongdoer in a world where 'slippery Fortune' (28f.) rules. The deficiencies of his vision are brought out by his description of his 'howling' them in grief (1.5.1), and by Philosophy's understanding of them as a symptom of his alienation from his true identity (1.5.2ff.). The influence of Seneca's *Phaedra* 959ff. upon 1 m. 5 may highlight the fact that the prisoner 'is being theatrical in the worst sense'[54] and still

[52] See further pp. 146ff. below, on 2 m. 8.
[53] See Crabbe (1981b) 260.
[54] Lerer (1985) 223, and, in general, 221ff. See further pp. 129ff. below.

under the baneful influence of the Muses: certainly the tone of his lament in the poem is akin to the *clamor* of tragedy, as Fortune describes it later in the work: 'For what else does tragedy's cry (*clamor*) weep but Fortune overthrowing happy kingdoms with an indiscriminate blow?' (2.2.12).[55]

Of the three paradigms of change in the poem, that of seasonal change is the one that will recur most often in the work, and to it some attention should be given. In 1 m. 5 it is the contrasts that are exploited: in 1 m. 2 it was rather the parallel phenomena (produce of spring and autumn) that were isolated. So Boethius begins with the extremes of winter and summer:

> *tu frondifluae frigore brumae*
> *stringis lucem breviore mora,*
> *tu cum fervida venerit aestas*
> *agiles nocti dividis horas* (14ff.).

You cut back the daylight, and its hours grow briefer when winter cold brings the leaves flowing down; you, when burning summer comes, apportion the quick night hours.

The element of order stressed here is the balancing contrast of winter's short days and long nights, and the long days and short nights of summer. But the reader's attention is focused more on two pictures, the burning heat of summer and winter's icy cold, with the result that the jarring contrast almost overrides the theme of order or harmony. And of these two pictures, it is that of winter that is the more detailed and vivid. The parallel with Seneca has often been observed:

> *ut nunc canae frigore brumae*
> *nudent silvas ...*
> *nunc aestivi colla leonis*
> *Cererem magno fervore coquant ...* (*Phae.* 966ff., 969f.).

that now white winter's frosts strip the forests ... now Leo's mane ablaze burns the crops with raging summer heat.

But Boethius modifies and adapts Seneca.[56] By the use of *frondifluus*, a *hapax legomenon*, Boethius summons up a landscape, not merely, as in Seneca, the fact of trees losing their leaves: it is a picture of 'an autumn that is already winter', tinged with melancholy. The mood is that of Virgil's

---

[55] Cf. Lerer (1985) 223 n. 53, who refers to Cassiodorus, *Variae* 4.51.7, where the loud sounds of tragedy are stressed; cf. Marcus Aurelius 11.6 on tragic 'screamers' (*kekragotes*).

[56] See Salemme (1970/1) 70. The dark mood is emphasized by the verb *stringis* in line 15 ('cut back, prune, strip'); cf. 1 m. 6.12 (see pp. 134f. below). On Senecan influences in 2 m. 5 see the perceptive commentary of Traina (1980).

quam multa in silvis autumni frigore primo
lapsa cadunt folia ... (*Aen.* 6.309f.).

Multitudinous as the leaves that fall in a forest
At the first frost of autumn ... (tr. Day Lewis).

Virgil thereby suggests the pathetic crowd of dead souls in the underworld. Thus the prisoner's pessimism of the moment permeates his account of the wonderful harmony of nature, so that it almost seems to lack that harmony, and in this way the dissonances of the poem's second half are foreshadowed.

Variation is also a feature of Boethius' use of seasonal motifs. If the earlier 1 m. 2 had featured spring and autumn, it is winter and summer that feature in 1 m. 5. The other two seasons are then referred to by the names of characteristic winds, Boreas (autumn) and Zephyrus (spring). But variation is achieved in a setting of symmetry. The two names of winds are paralleled by the naming of two stars, Arcturus, representing the September sowing season, and Sirius, the Dog Days in July/August. The overall seasonal pattern is stressed: lines 14-22 emphasize both nature's destructive power (leaves stripped from trees by winds and icy weather, crops burnt dry by the sun) and its no less great power of renewal (seeds, foliage). The oneness of nature is achieved against the setting of its negative violence and its variety: *tua vis varium temperat annum* ('your power modulates the changing year', 18).[57]

Reference has already been made to the choral ode in Seneca's *Phaedra* which has clearly been a model for Boethius. The overall progression of Seneca's ode, as well as some of its individual lines, are undoubtedly reflected in Boethius' poem.[58] Even where their language is not the same or similar, both poems progress in similar fashion, and by use of related examples. Seneca, like Boethius, turns from the invocation of the divine ruler to examples of cosmic order, and the examples given are those also found in Boethius: the order of the heavenly bodies, the sequence of the seasons. Both poems turn from reflections on heavenly harmony and nature's laws to the apparent indifference of nature or God to human affairs,[59] where good men suffer and the wicked prosper:

[*cur*] *hominum nimium securus abes,*
non sollicitus prodesse bonis,
nocuisse malis? (*Phae.* 975ff.)

---

[57] *Vis* here is to be linked to the *vis animae divina* of Manilius 1.250 (the equivalent of Stoic *pneuma*: see Lapidge [1980] 820).
[58] See further Lerer (1985) 222f.
[59] Cf. the similar juxtaposition in Claudian, *In Rufin.* 1.1ff.

[Why] do you stand indifferently so far from men, not eager to benefit the good or harm the wicked?

hominum solos respuis actus
... cohibere ... (Boethius 26)

Men's actions alone you scorn to hold in check ...

castos sequitur mala paupertas
vitioque potens regnat adulter ... (*Phae.* 987f.)

Evil poverty dogs the pure; powerful in his vice, the adulterer rules ...

... premit insontes
debita sceleri noxia poena,
at perversi resident celso
mores solio ... (Boethius 29ff.).

The punishment due to crime is visited on the innocent, and evil behaviour is entrenched on a high throne ...

But Seneca's ode ends despairingly, with a sense of the futility of virtue:

o vane pudor falsumque decus (989).

O pointless modesty and false honour!

Boethius, however, ends his poem with a supplication which emphasizes its prayer-form:[60]

o iam miseras respice terras,
quisquis rerum foedera nectis!
...
rapidos, rector, comprime fluctus
et quo caelum regis immensum
firma stabiles foedere terras (42f., 46ff.).

O look now on the unhappy earth, whoever you are who binds the world's bonds ... Master, restrain the rapid surgings of the sea [of fortune], and make the earth stable in its bonds, the laws by which you rule the vast skies.[61]

Yet once again, this concluding prayer is anticipatory. Although the dark overtones of the poem are not dispelled by it, and despite the fact

---

[60] See Gruber (1978) 133.
[61] On *foedus* and *foedera*, translated 'bonds' then 'laws' in this extract, see p. 126 and n. 51 above.

that the prisoner cannot see providence at work in human affairs, the future development of the *Consolation* is here adumbrated, and the understanding of divine involvement in human actions, here wished for, is anticipated: the poem's conclusion – an unconvinced wish – is seen in a later poem, 2 m. 8, to be possible of fulfilment, and the conclusion of that later poem reflects, in its language as well as in its thought, the end of the earlier one:

> *o felix hominum genus,*
> *si vestros animos amor*
> *quo caelum regitur regat!* (2 m. 8.28ff.)

> O blessed human race, if the love by which the heavens are ruled should rule your hearts!

The optimism of the later parts of the *Consolation* is latent in 1 m. 5. This can be seen by comparing the accounts of *virtus*, quoted above, in Seneca and Boethius. Seneca writes of 'grim' (*tristis*) *virtus* gaining perverse rewards for goodness (*Phae.* 985f.), while in Boethius *virtus*, though obscured by darkness, is none the less *clara* (34f.), that is to say, its intrinsic brightness persists and is not annihilated by the fate of the virtuous. At this stage of the work, the prisoner has certainly not assimilated that teaching, and so this must rank as yet another anticipated development of the argument, what one might call the proleptic function of the poems.

Virtue obscured by darkness: the light-dark imagery of the opening poems is sustained, if briefly, in 1 m. 5. But it has been modified, in keeping with the development of the work. Whereas, in the earlier poems, it functioned as an image of the prisoner's mental and moral state, now it is used to reflect his sense of his unjust downfall, imprisonment, and condemnation. He is the good man, languishing in darkness: the prison-metaphor is also latent in these lines.

There is a final nature image in the poem's last section:

> *homines quatimur fortunae salo.*
> *rapidos, rector, comprime fluctus* ... (45f.).

> We humans are tossed on the sea of fortune. Master, restrain the rapid surgings of that sea ...

On examination, two strands are discernible in this image. One is the metaphor of life as a sea journey. Interestingly, it seems to be of philosophical origin. That is to say, it occurs first in Plato's *Phaedo* (85d) and *Laws* (803b), and is popular with the Neoplatonists.[62] Its use

[62] Cf. Gruber (1978) 107. See G. Pfligersdorffer, 'Bemerkungen zu den Proömien von

in 1 m. 5 is anticipated in an earlier prose section of Book 1: 'And so there is nothing to be amazed at if we are tossed about by the storms which blow from all sides on this sea of life' (1.3.11). In both passages, the metaphor of the sea journey is linked to another, that of the stormy sea of life, and in both the poem and a later prose passage (2.2.8) the image is further linked to the workings of fortune. The metaphor of the stormy sea is also found frequently in philosophical contexts.[63] Boethius makes this network of images into one of the cardinal motifs of his work, as Viarre has shown.[64] Viarre's discussion highlights the 'destabilizing' elements in this thematic complex: turbulent Fortune, unstable wealth or power, the drowning mind, the instability of material creation, the relation of the theme to the notion of elements in conflict. The use of these images here, and their repeated use in later parts of the work, to be discussed below,[65] should remind us that there is much disorder in the prisoner's vision of nature, even in those contexts where he simultaneously exalts the order and harmony of the natural world. To the thesis of order the antithesis of disorder is repeatedly appended: the reader must await the final synthesis.

From 1 m. 6 on, Philosophy is for an extended sequence the speaker of the poems. The consequence is that the perspectives from which nature is viewed alter subtly. 1 m. 6 is a good initial example of this. It takes up the theme of the preceding poem. There is order in nature. As in the previous poem, there is a movement from the world of nature to that of man. But whereas in 1 m. 5 order in human affairs was wished for, but not apparent, in the later poem Philosophy suggests that there is, by implication, such order in human affairs, or that there must be. The greater part of the poem (1-15) is a further reworking of the seasonal motif (that also links it to 1 m. 5); the poem's 'moral' is explicated in seven concluding lines (16ff.). An interesting structural feature is that each season of the sequence in the poem's first part is given a smaller number of lines than its antecedent: thus summer is given six lines (1-6), winter four (7-10), spring three (11-13), and autumn two (14f.).[66] The generalizations of the poem's second part are thus longer (seven lines) than any individual section of the first part, and so the second part, though shorter, seems, when the poem is read, to counterbalance the first. Moreover, the fact that successively fewer

---

Augustins Contra Academicos I und De beata vita', in K. Forstner/M. Fussl (edd.), *Augustino Praeceptori. Gesammelte Aufsätze zu Augustinus* (Salzburg 1987) 33-58 (here 37-46); C. Bonner, 'Desired Haven', *Harvard Theological Review* 34 (1941) 49-67. See n. 8 above.

[63] See Gruber (1978) 107. Cicero, *Tusc. disp.* 5.2.5 combines the metaphors of sea-journey, storm, and safe return to harbour. For the related image of the road of life see 1 m. 7.23ff., and cf. Courcelle (1970) 243 n. 179.

[64] Viarre (1975).

[65] See e.g. pp. 135ff., 139ff., 170ff. below.

[66] See Gruber (1978) 149.

lines are devoted to each season means that the transition to pithy generalizations is not as abrupt as it might otherwise have been. That is undoubtedly the main reason for the poem's structure.[67]

Some details of the evocations of the individual seasons call for comment. Each seasonal example makes the same point, which is the poem's moral: there is a right time for everything. One does not sow seed in high summer (1-6). The influence of Virgil's *Georgics*, with its guidance to seasonable times for ploughing and sowing (1.43ff., 204ff.), is evident in these opening lines.[68] Even the fate of the farmer who sows out of season – *quernas pergat ad arbores* ('let him resort to oak trees [acorns]', 6) – is akin to that of the failed farmer of the *Georgics* (1.155ff.). And, just as Virgil links the diet of acorns to an unfortunate reversion to the pre-agricultural life of the Golden Age by making a reference to that diet introduce the sequence (1.148ff.), and the diet of failure conclude it (1.155ff.), so too Boethius evokes failure in the terms used to describe the Golden Age diet in 2 m. 5.4f.[69] What is appropriate in one age is not so in another: thus the theme of seasonable nature is reinforced.

There is a further Virgilian echo in the phrase *negantibus / sulcis* (3f.), the furrows which 'say no' to the seed. The notion of the soil refusing to produce or co-operate is found, with use of the same verb *negare*, in the *Georgics* (2.215, 234): it is a form of personification[70] that is consonant with the evocation of Ceres in line 5: *elusus Cereris fide* ('cheated of the trust placed in Ceres'). The fields which, in the Golden Age, were *fidelia* (2 m. 5.2) now prove treacherous. A similar point is made in 2.1.18, where nature's unreliability is seen as a sign of the rule of Fortune: but the poem 1 m. 6 does not encourage us to think about Fortune. Its suggestion is that one should not do certain things at certain times, or success is precluded: it is not suggesting that if things are done at the right time, success must follow. Thus the perspectives of the poem are deliberately narrower than they might be. Boethius does not make Philosophy take up the challenge which 1 m. 5 threw down and explain the workings of Fortune in human affairs. The assertion of human order in 1 m. 6 is general and dogmatic: it is only the starting-point of Philosophy's reply. Yet the nature of that reply is intended, among other things, to exemplify the idea of the appropriate time or moment. The poem follows a prose sequence in which Philosophy argues that the medicines must match the patient's ailment and be administered in the appropriate sequence which

---

[67] Gruber (1978) 149 adduces a further possible reason: the decreasing numbers of lines per section in the first part increase the pace of the poem, so that it corresponds to the *praeceps via* condemned in line 20.

[68] See Scheible (1972) 40.

[69] On 2 m. 5 in general see pp. 179ff. below.

[70] See Thomas (1988) 1.196f.

proceeds from milder to stronger doses (1.5.11f.).[71]

In another way, too, the notion of human order is subtly introduced in the poem. The seasonal sequence focuses on human activities of the farmer or country person: sowing, plucking flowers, picking fruit. Thus the idea of human co-operation with nature is suggested, and with it the image of a patterned life in conformity with nature's laws. Once again, Boethius shows himself to be a careful reader of Virgil's *Georgics*.

But it is not only Virgil who has influenced this poem. The theme of the appropriate produce of each season which runs through these lines is part of the stock of seasonal motifs in general: an obvious forerunner is Lucretius (1.174ff.). And Horace is behind the picture of the unripe grape unseasonably picked:[72]

> *tolle cupidinem*
> *inmitis uvae: iam tibi lividos*
>   *distinguet autumnus racemos*
>   *purpureo varius colore* (*Odes* 2.5.9ff.).

Stamp out desire for the unripe grape! Soon many-coloured autumn will decorate for you the dark clusters in a ripe shade of blue.

> *nec quaeras avida manu*
> *vernos stringere palmites*
> *uvis si libeat frui;*
> *autumno potius sua*
> *Bacchus munera contulit* (1 m. 6.11ff.).

And you would not try to prune vines in spring with greedy grasping hand if you want to enjoy the grapes; Bacchus has bestowed his gifts rather upon autumn.

Boethius succeeds in the first part of the poem in presenting a picture of nature which is both negative and positive. Nature is inhospitable and destructive if one does not co-operate with her laws: the key words punctuating the sequence 1-11 emphasize this.[73] But the positive side of nature is suggested, even when the other aspect is stressed, in a kind of counterpoint. Thus the reference to the sun's rays (*Phoebi radiis*) in line 1, in the context of summer heat, nevertheless suggests the bright light of the sun that is such a positive image elsewhere in the work, and recalls 'the sun glittering with light' (*vibratus lumine Phoebus*) that breaks through the clouds at 1 m. 3.9, or the 'light of the rosy sun' (*rosei lumina solis*) of 1 m. 2.8. And the

---

[71] See Scheible (1972) 42.
[72] See Scheible (1972) 41.
[73] 1 *grave*; 3 *negantibus*; 5 *elusus*; 7 *numquam*; 9 *saevis*; 10 *stridens ... inhorruit*; 11 *avida manu*.

'abundant seeds' (*larga ... semina*) of 3f., while stressing the foolish generosity of the sower of a doomed crop, also hints at the rich potential of the seed, if properly sown. The theme of the absence of flowers in winter is evoked in lush language that depicts those absent flowers in all their spring glory (7f.). And the promise of the grape is likewise suggested (13ff.). In this way images of light, colour, rich fertility and ripeness pervade even the negative part of the poem. The concentration of such positive images in lines 3-13, moreover, facilitates the transition to the poem's second, generalizing part, for behind both the prohibitions and their positive counterparts is the deity:

signat tempora propriis
aptans officiis deus (16f.).

God distinguishes the seasons with functions given to each one.

The deity's disposition of nature maintains a distinct, articulated sequence of change: the ordered succession (*vices*, 19) of that sequence is in deliberate contrast to the *vices* of slippery Fortune complained about by the prisoner (1 m. 5.28f.).[74]

The 'fixed order' (21) propounded in 1 m. 6 will culminate in the image of the universe in the Platonic poem 3 m. 9. But the world-view of the earlier poem has not attained the complexities of the later one. It corresponds to a Stoic view of providence and order in nature, and Scheible is right to draw attention to a passage in Epictetus (1.12.15f.) which argues that it is not freedom that is the goal of our wishes, but rather to 'wish each thing in the way it happens' in accordance with the divine disposition of things.[75] In that passage Epictetus refers to the contrasts of the seasons as an example of divinely ordained order ('summer and winter, and abundance and dearth ...') and adds that such contraries (*enantiotêtas*) are not inconsistent with the harmony of the whole (*sumphônias tôn holôn*). The whole passage could stand as an epigraph to 1 m. 6.

Like the two preceding poems, 1 m. 7 moves from nature images to moral concerns. Furthermore, its structure reflects that of the immediately preceding 1 m. 6.[76] Three nature images (1-19) – the spring-autumn sequence in 1 m. 6.11ff., with its focus on the grape, can be read as a single motif – are followed by a shorter, generalizing, and moralizing conclusion (20ff.). The evocation of nature's violence is a further link with the antecedent poems. But what is interesting about 1 m. 7 is that there is no attempt to situate the nature images in a

---

[74] See Gruber (1978) 152.
[75] Scheible (1972) 41.
[76] See Scheible (1972) 43.

context of order or cosmic harmony. The sequence of images – starlight obscured by clouds, sea water muddied by sand, a river dammed by rocks – of the first part of the poem conjures up a picture of nature contaminated, obstructed, and restricted by forces within itself. The aptness of the images, and the reason for Boethius' avoidance of any suggestion of harmony, become apparent in the second part, when it is established that they are images of the distortion wrought by the passions. The second part of the poem takes up and reflects the images of the first part (a feature that distinguishes it from 1 m. 6, where there is no such correspondence).[77] The following thematic links may be observed:

light	1-4 ~ 21-2
storm/passions	5-13 ~ 25-9
path	14-19 ~ 23-4[78]

But the link between the two evocations of light and path show that this poem is using images in a distinctive and novel way. Only in the four lines (25ff.) that enumerate the four passions is the poem free of imagery. The language of images has, in other words, become a greater part of the statement of this poem than has been the case hitherto in the work. That is undoubtedly because the poem aspires to do no more than enumerate the passions, evoke their destructive power, and urge their eradication. The detailed analysis and criticism of the passions will occupy Books 2 and 3. By echoing the images of the first part of the poem in the second (and by the ring-composition technique whereby 'cloudy mind' [*nubila mens*, 29] reflects 'black clouds' [*nubibus atris*, 1]) Boethius evokes the sensation of a mind that is enclosed in the confines of itself, of a world in which distortion is present everywhere, and from which, without radical change, there can be no escape.

Some observations on the individual images are called for. The image of clouds obscuring light has already occurred at 1 m. 3.2ff., and is implicit in 1 m. 5.34f. (cf. also 1 m. 2.24). Boethius subtly links 1ff. to 21f. not merely by the image of light, but by the use of the word *lumen*, meaning 'light' in 4 and 'eye' in 21. But it is the limpidity of the opening lines which is the most striking aspect of the image:[79]

[77] Scheible (1972) 44.

[78] Scheible (1972) 44 understands the link between 5ff. and 25ff. to be implicit: it is the only unconvincing part of her set of correspondences. Her reference to Horace, *Odes* 3.9.22ff., while it shows that the 'sea of passion' image is established in Latin poetry (cf. Virgil, *Aen.* 12.665ff.), cannot be used to demonstrate a link that is not made explicit by Boethius.

[79] Scheible (1972) 43 finds them 'commonplace and unpoetic', and concludes that it is the influence of prose diatribe, rather than of poetry, that is felt here: Gruber (1978) 159 agrees. Surely a misjudgement, both about the language of poetry and the style of diatribe.

Nubibus atris
condita nullum
fundere possunt
sidera lumen (1 m. 7.1ff.).

Hidden by black clouds the stars can cast no light.

A passage in Horace uses the same words and images in language that is no less lacking in elaboration:

... *simul atra nubes*
condidit lunam neque certa fulgent
sidera nautis (*Odes* 2.16.2ff.).

... as soon as a black cloud has hidden the moon and the stars do not shine steadily for sailors.

Only the detail of the sailor is missing in Boethius.[80] It is misleading to call such clear and limpid language 'unpoetic', for it has its place even in the highly-wrought language of ancient poetry, and often acts as a foil to more extravagant language.[81]

The second image, of the sea-storm, is traditional and, as the commentaries point out, frequent in both Greek and Roman poetry since Homer (*Od.* 5.291ff.; *Il.* 2.144ff.), whose influence on the tradition is decisive. Boethius' language betrays Virgilian echoes,[82] but the image of a sea 'clear as a calm day' muddied by churned-up sand is novel, and Boethius' poetic originality may be at work here.[83]

Homeric, Virgilian, and other echoes are found in the third image, of the river's course. The dual picture of the river's movement and the obstacles which check its flow, essential to Boethius' employment of the image in this context, is found in one Homeric simile, when a river is said to rush downhill, sweeping all before it, until it reaches the level plain (*Il.* 13.137ff.). The Homeric comparison is with Hektor rushing down upon the Achaeans until their serried ranks check him. Even if Boethius is not influenced directly by this Homeric passage, it is none the less strikingly like his image.

The poem's final double image of the mind beclouded and 'fettered by the bridle' (*vinctaque frenis*, 30) of the passions echoes the closing picture of the first poem spoken by Philosophy, 1 m. 2.24ff.:

[80] Scheible alludes to this Horace passage, but rejects it as an influence on Boethius for the reason referred to in the previous note.

[81] Compare lines 5ff. of Boethius' poem with lines 1f. and 5ff. in Horace: in each case the colourful language of these lines is a foil to the plain terms of the passages quoted above.

[82] Compare 5 *mare volvens* with *Aen.* 3.196 *volvunt mare*, and 8ff. *vitrea ... unda* with *Aen.* 7.759 (same phrase).

[83] So Scheible (1972) 43f.

nunc iacet effeto lumine mentis
et pressus gravibus colla catenis ...

Now he lies, the light of his mind extinguished, his neck weighed down
with heavy chains ...

There are antecedents in the Platonic tradition for such a link of two
such characteristic Platonic images.[84] But the passage which is likely
to have influenced Boethius most is one from the *Aeneid* that
Augustine quotes on several occasions:

hinc metuunt cupiuntque, dolent gaudentque, neque auras
dispiciunt clausae tenebris et carcere caeco (*Aen.* 6.733f.).

Whence these souls of ours feel fear, desire, grief, joy,
But encased in their blind, dark prison discern not the heaven-light
above (tr. Day Lewis).

The 'Orphic', Platonic and Pythagorean inspiration of these lines has
long been recognized by Virgilian scholars, and Neoplatonic
commentators on the *Aeneid* in late antiquity were alive to the lines'
symbolic potential.[85] Their combination of the enumeration of the four
cardinal passions, and the images of darkness, confinement, and
imprisonment, reverberates in the similarly related motifs of the
Consolation, just as their transmigration context in the *Aeneid* is
reflected in the interpretation given by Boethius to the Homeric
account of the transformation into animals of Odysseus' companions.
We are dealing here less with a specific Virgilian influence on a single
text of Boethius, however, than with the pervasive influence of a
complex of images and ideas on the *Consolation* as a whole. This motif
closes the sequel of poems (excluding the opening elegy) that began
with 1 m. 2 in a kind of ring-composition marking the conclusion of
Book 1 of the work. But it also echoes 1 m. 4.[86] It is a development of
that earlier poem inasmuch as it explicates the image of the Stoic sage,
who is indifferent to fortune (1 m. 4), but only because he has
eradicated the passions (1 m. 7).

(ii) Book 2

It is a feature of the *Consolation* that themes of the first book are taken
up and elaborated in the subsequent books. The themes of the first four
poems of Book 2 are a case in point. The sequence 2.1 – 2 m. 4 is a

[84] See Scheible (1972) 27, who refers to Clement of Alexandria, *Paedagogus* 1.29 and
Plotinus 6.9.9.46ff.
[85] See Courcelle (1984) 480ff.
[86] See Scheible (1972) 46.

clearly demarcated section of the work. It is (despite 1.5.11f.) the beginning proper of Philosophy's treatment of the prisoner's lethargy, using gentle medicines: 'But it is time for you to taste and swallow something gentle and pleasant, which, once ingested, will pave the way for stronger draughts' (2.1.7). This stage of the treatment lasts until 2 m. 4, to be replaced by the 'stronger medicines' of 2.5.1 and the following section. What the gentler treatment consists in is an exposé of the mutable and unreliable nature of Fortune, of the transient nature of Fortune's gifts; and Boethius' own career is the chief example of what Fortune has given and taken away (2.3.4ff.), as well as of what she has left (2.4.3ff.). Consideration of the particular gifts of Fortune, such as wealth and power, follows in 2.5ff. So the themes of change and instability, of vulnerability and anxiety, that were encountered in the first book, are now developed in the first part of Book 2. We may expect, and we find, that the related nature metaphors and images recur and are expanded.

Gruber observes that 'the actual *Consolation* begins only in the second book'.[87] The themes of humanity's common subjection to fickle Fortune, and of the necessity to endure what Fortune brings, are common in consolatory literature.[88] Precisely such themes run through the cluster of nature images in the first four poems of Book 2. When, in the opening lines of 2 m. 1, Fortune is compared to the variable tidal currents of the Euripus, Boethius is taking over a motif that expresses the instability of bodily health and the external gifts of Fortune in Hipparchus,[89] and of all phenomena in Plato (*Phaedo* 90c). The word *poikilos* ('changeable') in Hipparchus, applied to the Euripus currents, recurs as a description of Fortune in Ps.-Plutarch's *Conslatio ad Apollonium*, as part of a comparison of human life with the sea, and influences uses of *varietas* and *varius* in Latin writers.[90] The motif is found not merely in 2 m. 1.2, but also in a later poem of the sequence, where the related verbal form *variare* occurs:

rara si constat sua forma mundo,
  si tantas variat vices,
crede fortunis hominum caducis,
  bonis crede fugacibus! (2 m. 3.13ff.).

If the world hardly ever keeps its form, if it goes through great changes, have trust in passing human fortunes, have trust in fleeting good things!

The 'changes' of Fortune here and in 2 m. 1.1 echo verses of the first book:

[87] Gruber (1978) 162.
[88] See Kassel (1958) 54ff.
[89] DK 68 C 7 (5).
[90] See Kassel (1958) 63f. Cf. Plutarch, *Cons. Apoll.* p. 211.1ff. Pohlenz.

nam cur tantas lubrica versat
Fortuna vices? (1 m. 5.28f.)

For why does slippery Fortune go through so many changes?

And such themes are announced in the work's opening elegy, with its theme of untrustworthy 'clouded' (*nubila*) Fortune (1 m. 1.17ff.). Fortune's 'changes' have crystallized in the image of the wheel of Fortune in 2.1.19 (cf. 2.2.9), so that the use of the term in the immediately following 2 m. 1.1 both refers to the wheel and subsumes the broader connotations of 'changes' (*vices*) – vicissitude – in the other passages. Through the term and its related images Boethius suggests that Fortune and nature, the theatre of change, may have elements in common, may even, perhaps, be identical: only in the course of the argument do the differences between the two become clear. Thus the images and metaphors of the work serve its progressive, pedagogical purpose.

In 2 m. 2 the image of the cornucopia is adduced. It is at once a symbol of nature's fruitfulness, and of Fortune's beneficence.[91] Boethius' *pleno Copia cornu* ('Plenty with full horn', 6) echoes Horace's *adparetque beata pleno Copia cornu* ('Blessed Plenty with full horn appears', *Carm. saec.* 59f.). In neither poet is the cornucopia explicitly related to Fortune, but in Boethius the link is evident, for Fortune's prosopopoeia in the preceding prose section has stressed the same themes as the poem (cf. especially 2.2.14). And the link is not difficult to make, for it is a common iconographical motif in Roman art, from the frescoes in the house of Verecundus in Pompeii to the sculptured friezes of sarcophagi, where Fortune with the horn of plenty appears among other celestial and cosmic phenomena.[92] In this implicit sense Boethius links the nature metaphors of 2 m. 2 to the Fortune complex of the poetic sequence.[93]

In the prose section 2.2 Fortune dwells on the phenomenon of change in nature, giving examples:

> Although the sky may produce clear days, and, again, hide them in dark night; although the year may at one time crown the earth's face with flowers and fruits, at another time obscure it with clouds and chilly

[91] See Nisbet/Hubbard 1.223; Gruber (1978) 179.

[92] See F. Cumont, *Recherches sur le symbolisme funéraire des Romains* (Paris 1942) 80 and Pl. 3.

[93] The proverbial references in 2 m. 2.1ff. to quantities that cannot be reckoned – sands and stars – are not, strictly speaking, nature metaphors, although their antecedents are, in Boethius' case, almost certainly literary: cf. Homer, *Il.* 2.800f.; Catullus 7.3ff. (for further instances see Kroll ad loc.). Scheible (1972) 51 n. 2 observes that the examples of sand and stars occur also in Scriptural contexts, such as Genesis 22:17 and Hebrews 11:12, but (unlike the images of 2 m. 4, discussed pp. 143f. below) Boethius' source here is probably not Biblical.

weather; though the sea may rightly beckon with smooth calm, and then foam with storms and floods ... (2.2.8).

Precisely these three examples of natural phenomena were given in 1 m. 2.6ff., in the catalogue of the prisoner's erstwhile achievements as an investigator of nature's laws. And the same set of examples is used in 2 m. 3 to exemplify the succession of natural events in an ever-changing world: day succeeds night (1-4), autumn spring (5-8), calm is followed by the storm (9-12). The last motif, that of the sea's changeability, is one found in consolatory contexts,[94] and a range of examples like those of Boethius is to be observed in a consolatory letter of Seneca's, where acceptance of chance occurrences and acquiescence in nature's laws are urged:

> Nature, however, regulates this kingdom that you see through successive changes: cloudy weather is followed by clear skies, calm seas are churned up, the winds blow changeably, day follows night, there are risings and settings in the heavens ... (*Ep.* 107.8).

Boethius thus moves within the ambit of traditional examples for a traditional theme, and, once again, betrays his awareness of the links between the Fortune motif and consolatory literature.[95]

In 2 m. 3 the instances of change in nature are used to illustrate the observation that

> *constat aeterna positumque lege est,*
>   *ut constet genitum nihil* (17f.).

it is fixed by everlasting law and unchanging that nothing that comes into being is unchanging.

Seneca, in the letter quoted above, makes a strikingly similar point (both in purport – which is not surprising – and in language): 'The everlastingness of things persists through contraries. Our soul must be adapted to this law ...' (*Ep.* 107.8f.). There are, after all, two (not unrelated) ways of looking at nature's mutability. If one is stressing the disturbing aspect of the transience of all things, of their mutability as a law in itself, then one will present change as Boethius does in 2 m. 3 and Seneca does to some extent in the quoted letter. A similar

---

[94] See Kassel (1958) 63.

[95] It is not the case, as Curley (1987) 352 asserts, that the 'concern that the remedy be appropriate to the condition of the patient is the one and only motif that Boethius borrows from the conventions of the *Consolatio* as a genre'. Curley is referring to 1.5.11 and related passages. The Fortune theme of the first part of Book 2 is, of course, part of the appropriate process of cure, but in its details it shows the influence of consolatory themes. On the other hand, Curley is right (ib.) to stress that *Cons. phil.* transcends the genre's conventional limits in so far as it is a comprehensive consolation *of philosophy*.

approach, and one closer in mood to Boethius than to Seneca, is adopted by Horace in *Odes* 4.7.[96] But one can also stress the durable aspect that underlies change and see either order in change or identity underlying change. The last approach is found in Pythagoras' speech in Ovid's *Metamorphoses*. There, despite the fact that the traditional examples of day and night and other instances of celestial change (*Met.* 15.186ff.), as well as of the seasons are given (199ff.), the thematic emphasis is on the generation of the new from the old, and the underlying identity of the *spiritus* or *anima* throughout all change (165ff.).[97]

Similarly, just as the phrase 'eternal law' (*aeterna lex*) in 2 m. 3.17 refers to the fact that all Fortune's gifts are, like nature itself, 'fleeting' (16), so too Boethius can employ the second approach referred to above in speaking of the 'ancient law' (*antiqua lex*) of orderly change at 1 m. 5.23.[98] And, just as the thought of winter giving way to spring can, in Horace, *Odes* 4.7, lead to pessimistic thoughts, so too can it lead to the bright optimism of *Odes* 1.4.[99] Boethius reflects both approaches found in the tradition. When, as in 2 m. 3, he wishes to stress the sad inevitability of change, the key words used stress that aspect: *rara ... constat, variat vices, fortunis ... caducis, bonis ... fugacibus*. These phrases come from the second, generalizing part of the poem (13ff.), but the nature images of the first part are correspondingly grim, with such words as *pallet, hebetata, prementibus, insanum, spinis, ferventes, concitat*, emphasizing the less pleasant features of change. Seneca adopts a similar technique to make a similar point:

> *non sic prata novo vere decentia*
> *aestatis calidae despoliat vapor*
> (*saevit solstitio cum medius dies*
> *et noctes brevibus praecipitat rotis*),
> *languescunt folio lilia pallido*
> *et gratiae capiti deficiunt rosae,*
> *ut fulgor teneris qui radiat genis*
> *momento rapitur nullaque non dies*
> *formosi spolium corporis abstulit* (*Phae.* 764ff.).

> Not so swiftly young spring's fair meadows
> Are despoiled by burning summer's heat
> When at the solstice midday rages
> And the night-times sweep their shortened course.
> As the lily withers leafing pale
> And the garlanding rose petals fade,

[96] See Fraenkel (1957) 420.
[97] See Scheible (1972) 53.
[98] Cf. 1 m. 5.4; 4.4.28 (where the term *aeterna lex* is applied to moral rules). The Euripus motif of 2 m. 1.2 (discussed p. 139 above) may be used to convey the sense, not merely of continuous change and instability, but also of natural law (ordered tidal movement): see Cicero, *nat. deor.* 3.10.24; cf. 2.7.19 = Posidonius F356 Theiler.
[99] See pp. 113ff. above.

The radiant glow of tender cheeks
Is ravished in a moment; no day
Has not despoiled the body's beauty (tr. Boyle).

In the picture of roses stripped of their blossoms by the stormy wind
(7f.) Boethius strikes an original note in a sequence (1ff.) that is full of
echoes of Virgil and Ovid: a reminiscence of Homer, *Il.* 6.145ff. (the
famous comparison of humans with leaves that blossom and then are
swept from the trees by the wind), and especially of the adaptation of
those lines by Marcus Aurelius (10.34), when he stresses the
impermanence of the gifts of Fortune, such as fame or popularity, and
the need to live without fear or anxiety, is likely.[100] It is precisely their
use in the latter context that gives such images their philosophical and
consolatory power, and is paralleled in Boethius. Boethius' poem,
however, lacks the explicit positive application of the image that is
apparent in Marcus: Boethius is indeed proceeding towards the same
understanding as the Stoic, but it is important for the dramatic
development of the work that he emphasizes the distressful aspects of
change in 2 m. 3.[101] The prisoner, as his words of 2.4.1f. indicate, has
not yet freed himself from the torment of misfortune. That is yet to
come, and it is an indication of Boethius' skill that in 2 m. 3 he both
points to the moral in a poem spoken by Philosophy, and suggests the
prisoner's torment by the choice of language and imagery.

If 2 m. 3 stresses the mutability of nature, the following poem evokes
such stability (*perennem*, 1; *stabilisque*, 3; *serenus*, 21) as nature may
provide. A pleasant natural site for building a house may be
treacherous (13f.), the house on a hilltop is exposed to the winds (3f., 7,
9f.), one built on sand is exposed to the wind, sea, and subsidence risks
(3f., 6, 11f.). The rock, though 'low' (*humilis*), is a secure and safe basis
upon which to build (15f.), where a house becomes a secure rampart
(*conditus quieti* / ... *robore valli*, 19f.), and one may live carefree (21f.).
Several details link these lines to the Fortune motif. It is commonplace
in Senecan tragedy, and not only there, that the heights, whether high
mountains, or houses built on lofty heights, are especially vulnerable
to the blows of Fortune, to winds or lightning.[102] Boethius' evocation of
the housebuilder who avoids the mountain top and builds on low, safe
rock is in that tradition. But the choice of site is also the choice of the
mean and avoidance of extremes: the rock is presented as the mean
between the mountain and the sandy seashore. Choice of the mean is
traditionally the choice of the wise man, and thus the housebuilder

[100] See Scheible (1972) 54f. On the passage in Marcus see Rutherford (1989) 27f.
[101] Scheible (1972) is too inclined to view Boethius in unqualified positive terms here.
[102] e.g. *Hercules furens* 199ff.; *Agamemnon* 92ff.; *Phaedra* 1128ff. (compare 1138f. with
15f. of Boethius' poem); *Oedipus* 8ff.; [Seneca] *Octavia* 896ff. See also Horace, *Odes*
2.10.9ff. and Nisbet/Hubbard 2.161f. (citing further instances).

becomes a type for the sage, in a sense more comprehensive than the Stoic one (although that, too, is included in the picture of the serenely smiling one [*serenus ... ridens*, 21f.][103] who has escaped, as much he can, from 'chance' [*sors*, 14]). For the metaphor of housebuilding in Boethius' poem is, as in Plautus, *Mostellaria* 84ff., an image of the way character is formed and expressed.[104]

The mean chosen by the sagacious builder, the rock, is, thus, avoidance of a further possibility besides the mountain: for he builds upon the rock rather than the sand. The antithesis rock-sand in a housebuilding metaphor occurs in the conclusion to the Sermon on the Mount in the Gospel of Matthew (7:24ff.); those who hear and obey Jesus' words are compared with the wise man (*phronimos*) who builds his house upon a rock, where it is impervious to the elements, while those who hear but do not obey are like the fool (*môros*) who builds upon the sand.[105] Boethius notoriously avoids explicit Christian themes and symbols, or even echoes, in the *Consolation*, but it is not unlikely that Matthew is his inspiration here, and that a blending of the Scriptural rock-sand antithesis with the Graeco-Roman motif of high-low in a context relating to Fortune occurs in 2 m. 4.[106] The *phronimos/môros* contrast in Matthew facilitates the link of the Scriptural passage with a context where the sage's prudence is being evoked. But Boethius has translated the sand image into accessible Roman terms: the reference to the risks from the sea in 5f. indicates that he is thinking of houses built on the coast, as the Romans actually did build them.[107]

2 m. 4 brings to an end the first part of the second book, and also the sequence of general 'Fortune' themes and motifs. In 2.5.1 Philosophy proffers 'stronger medicines', which initially take the form of an exposé of the valuelessness of wealth. By contrast with money, jewels, and clothes, nature is adduced as the paradigm of what is sufficient. The contrast between Fortune and its superfluous gifts, and nature's sufficiency, is developed: 'But if you wish to fill a deficiency, which is sufficient for nature, there is no need for you to ask Fortune for excessive abundance' (2.5.15). Appropriation of nature, which, it is suggested, is the aim of those fascinated by jewels and other valuables, is in fact impossible, for nature's beauty is her own:

[103] For the *serenus* cf. 1 m. 4.1ff. Calm is characteristic of God: 3 m. 9.26. Gruber (1978) 110 is right to relate it to Epicurean *galênê*; but, as he points out, it is also characteristic of the Stoic sage in Seneca, *Ep.* 59.14.

[104] Scheible (1972) 56 n. 1 noticed the relevance of the Plautus passage. For a similar extension into ethics of the theme of building a house see Horace, *Epist.* 1.10 (on which poem see Macleod [1979] 24ff.); cf. *Odes* 3.1.33ff.

[105] Scheible (1972) 56f. notes the similarity with Boethius (cf. Bieler, *CCL* edn. p. 26).

[106] Christian writers like Hilary of Poitiers (*In ps.* 126.8) and Jerome (*In Hier.* 1.6.2; 5.63.9) comment on the Matthew passage, as does Augustine, *De sermone domini in monte* 2.25.87: but there is no need to posit any such intermediary between the New Testament and Boethius.

[107] See Scheible (1972) 57. Cf. Horace, *Odes* 3.1.33ff.

Does the beauty of the countryside please you? It is a beautiful part of the most beautiful of created things. So we sometimes rejoice in the aspect of a calm sea, so also we wonder at sky, stars, moon, and sun. Are any of these things your concern, do you dare boast of the brilliance of any such things? Are you yourself adorned by spring flowers, or is it your fertility that swells with summer fruits? (2.5.11ff.).

The following Golden Age poem paints a picture of a nature which is reliable and provides adequate nourishment if it is not extravagantly misused.[108] This section of the *Consolation* develops elements of a hierarchical world-picture that is crucial to the central themes of the work. On the one hand, there is the assertion of nature's beauty as part of a beautiful creation. On the other hand, natural 'evils', such as volcanoes (2 m. 5.25f.) or floods (2.6.1), are less evil than moral defects.[109]

Yet power abused and misused is aptly evoked in the metaphors of natural catastrophes, as the argument of 2.6, developing the images of 2.6.1, asserts, and the following Nero poem, 2 m. 6, exemplifies. In it Boethius skilfully makes nature reflect the grimness of a tyrant's rule.[110] Nature can at once be the paradigm of human order, of the way we should live and the things with which we should be content, and also the symbol of human moral evil and perversion. Seen on the hierarchical scale of value, moral goodness is greater and higher than natural goods, and moral evil worse than natural evils. But nature is also a mirror, a theatre of images, in which both goodness and evil in the moral sphere may be seen to be reflected.

In a different way nature may be the point of reference against which the insignificance of human fame – the last of the specific gifts of Fortune to be discussed in Book 2 – may be measured. In 2.7 the immensity of the universe and the tiny part of the world that is supposed to be inhabited, serve to show how limited and circumscribed fame is, even fame in what appears to be the extensive Roman empire (2.7.3ff.). By the same token, individual historical periods are minimal by comparison with the span of time (2.7.13ff.). Such comparisons owe much to the elaboration of these themes in Cicero's *De re publica*, where they are to be found in its sixth book, the so-called *Somnium Scipionis* (*rep.* 6.19.20ff.). But Boethius also uses Macrobius' commentary on the *Dream of Scipio*, especially 2.5ff.[111] Following the elaboration of this theme in 2.7, the following poem epitomizes the motif in its opening lines:

[108] See pp. 179ff. below.
[109] See pp. 87f. above.
[110] See pp. 88ff. above.
[111] See Courcelle (1967) 116ff. Gruber (1978) 213ff. is, however, right to insist that Boethius also uses Cicero directly.

Quicumque solam mente praecipiti petit
  summumque credit gloriam,
late patentes aetheris cernat plagas
  artumque terrarum situm;
brevem replere non valentis ambitum
  pudebit aucti nominis (2 m. 7.1ff.).

Whoever strives only for glory with obsessive mind, and thinks that it is
the most important thing, let him consider the vast regions of the ether,
and the narrow confines of earth; he will be ashamed of the great name
that cannot fill a small space.

Thus the poem subsumes and expresses in condensed and striking
form the themes of the preceding prose section, but it does not
elaborate them.[112]

Whereas, then, the first four poems of Book 2 are unified by their
link with consolatory themes in general and the motif of Fortune in
particular, and the nature motifs are set in that context, poems 5-7 of
the book explore *inter alia* various allusive references to nature, as a
paradigm of modest sufficiency, as an image of moral, especially
tyrannical, evil, and finally as the immense background of a cosmos
where external human achievements are seen to be trivial and
insignificant.

In 2.8 Philosophy argues that, under certain circumstances, ill
fortune may be beneficial, as when it teaches its victims the fragile
nature of apparent happiness, and so may be the means of leading
them towards the true good. Furthermore, it shows us who our true
friends are. On this note the section ends, and it is followed by one of
the major poems of the work (2 m. 8). If we are to seek a direct link
between this poem and its immediately antecedent prose, then it must
surely be found in the theme of *amicitia*, which in the poem (26f.) is an
instance of the *amor* that penetrates and unifies the universe.[113] But 2
m. 8 has a far wider function in the *Consolation* as a whole. It relates
back to 1 m. 5, and that poem's concluding wish for stability and order
in human affairs (48) is now, it is suggested, to be seen as one that can
be fulfilled through the agency of *amor*.[114] But 2 m. 8 also anticipates
later thematic developments, a sequence of themes that culminates in
3 m. 9, as well as the other *amor* poem, 4 m. 6. In fact, the three poems
1 m. 5, 2 m. 8, and 4 m. 6 reinforce each other and elaborate central
themes of the work as a whole. Moreover, 2 m. 8 foreshadows the
theme whose discussion begins in the next prose (3.1): what is true
happiness, and what is true goodness?

[112] Cf. lines 15ff., where the limits of historical fame are evoked, in a passage that
parallels 2.7.13ff., just as lines 1ff. parallel 2.7.3ff.

[113] See L. Alfonsi, 'Studii boeziani', *Aevum* 19 (1945) 142-57 (here 151). Scheible (1972)
74 is too dogmatic in denying any link between the poem and its antecedent prose.

[114] See Klingner (1921) 26; pp. 125, 129f. above.

If Fortune is notoriously *instabilis* (2.8.3). then the universe is bound together by the *stabilis fides* of *amor* (2 m. 8.1). The motif of cosmic bonds underlies the poem, its *amor* is akin to Lucan's 'holy cosmic love' (*sacer orbis amor*, 4.191).[115] In other words, we are dealing with a motif that is Stoic in origin, and has a long Latin poetic tradition. The poem uses an abundance of abstract expressions for this notion of cosmic order or love.[116] And just as the first half of the poem ends with the image of

> *terras ac pelagus regens*
> *et caelo imperitans amor* (14f.),

Love ruling the earth and the sea, and commanding the skies,

so its second half concludes with *amor / quo caelum regitur* ... ('the love by which the heavens are ruled', 29f.). This *amor* unites and harmonizes the universe's variety, without removing or annulling that variety and its frequent expression in the form of contraries:

> *concordes variat vices*
> *...pugnantia semina*
> *foedus perpetuum tenent* (2ff.).

[the universe] brings about harmonious change ... the warring elements keep perpetual truce.

The last-quoted verses refer to the elements,[117] and the whole poem is strikingly reminiscent of the opening of the verse proem to Martianus Capella's *De nuptiis*, described by its most recent commentator as a hymn 'addressed to Hymenaeus, which in this case is merely another name for cosmic Eros':[118]

> *semina qui arcanis stringens pugnantia vinclis*
> *complexuque sacro dissona nexa foves,*
> *namque elementa ligas vicibus mundumque maritas*
> *atque auram mentis corporibus socias,*
> *foedere complacito sub quo natura iugatur,*
> *sexus concilians et sub amore fidem* ... (1.1, p. 1.6ff. Willis).

[You] who draw together the warring elements with secret embrace (for you join the elements through their transformations, impregnate the

---

[115] See pp. 125ff. above.

[116] 1 *stabili fide*; 2 *concordes vices*; 3 *pugnantia semina*; 4 *foedus perpetuum*; 10 *certo fine coherceat*; 13 *rerum seriem ligat*; 16 *frena*; 17 *amat*; 19f. *socia fide/pulchris motibus*; 21 *machinam*; 22f. *sancto ... foedere*; 23 *iunctos*; 25 *nectit amoribus*; 26f. *fidis ... sodalibus*. Cf. n. 48 above. See Lapidge (1980) for the tradition. Ford (1967) 61 notes the similarities between 2 m. 8.1ff. and Martianus Capella 1.1.

[117] Cf. 3 m. 9.10ff.; 4 m. 6.19ff.

[118] Shanzer (1986b) 45.

universe, and associate the breath of the mind with bodies in that pleasing bond by which nature is yoked, reconciling the sexes in loving loyalty) … (tr. Shanzer).

The term *foedus* ('bond'), part of the vocabulary of love,[119] is here and in the Boethius poem (4,23) used in both the transferred erotic sense and as a political metaphor ('covenant'), and it gains a special resonance from its ambivalence.

Significantly, the poem opens with a description of universal order

Quod mundus stabili fide
concordes variat vices (1f.).

That the universe brings about harmonious change with unwavering fidelity –

that echoes that of Fortune:

nam cur tantas lubrica versat
Fortuna vices? (1 m. 5.28f.).

For why does slippery Fortune go through so many changes?

It is even closer to the evocation of nature as a state of unstable flux in 2 m. 3:

rara si constat sua forma mundo,
si tantas variat vices … (13f.).

If the world hardly ever keeps its form, if it goes through great changes
…

The repetition of key terms (*vices, variat*) is deliberate and has a point. The 'changes' of Fortune are indeed, it would appear, haphazard and without 'law' or order. In 2 m. 3 the apparently common aspects of Fortune and nature are suggested.[120] Only now is it explicitly asserted that the *vices* of nature do indeed obey a law and exhibit a harmony. So the negative word *variat* assumes a positive connotation from its surrounding terms (*stabili, concordes*), since change in nature can be seen from two points of view, as mere mutability or as patterned change.[121]

The syntactical structure of 2 m. 8.1-12 is interesting.[122] Three noun

---

[119] See R. Reitzenstein, 'Zur Sprache der lateinischen Erotik', *Sitzungsberichte der Heidelberger Akademie der Wissenschaften*, Phil.-hist. Klasse 3/1912 (1912) 1-36 (here 9ff.); S. Lilja, *The Roman Elegists' Attitude to Women* (Helsinki 1965) 69ff.
[120] See p. 140 above.
[121] See pp. 142f. above.
[122] For the following see O'Donnell (1984) 179.

clauses introduced by *quod* ('that') form each of the first three couplets, and all are in apposition to line 13 *(hanc rerum seriem)*. There follow three further couplets in 7ff., each of which is a purpose clause dependent on *ligat* (13). These lines (especially 5ff.) give a set of pictorial images, and offer concrete physical examples, of the harmony and *amor* in nature. The syntax suggests that the six couplets proffer six examples, all independent, though together illustrative of the general principle. Thus, despite the generalized nature of 1f., Chamberlain may be right to see in these lines a reference to the seasons,[123] parallel to the fuller section in the later *amor* poem 4 m. 6, where lines 25ff. elaborate the theme of ordered seasonal change. In 2 m. 8, lines 3f. refer to the elements (the corresponding part in 4 m. 6 is lines 19ff.). In 2 m. 8.5f. day (more precisely dawn) is adduced, and complemented by 7f. which refer to night. Lines 9f. speak of the boundaries of the sea, and, again in complementary fashion, lines 11f. of the bounds of the land. Chamberlain is less convincing when he subsumes 5ff. under the general title of 'heavens'.[124] The parallel section in 4 m. 6 (1ff.) is indeed exclusively devoted to the harmony of celestial phenomena. Chamberlain wants to establish the parallelism of the two poems in order to demonstrate that the three types of consonance which are given in Boethius' *De musica* as examples of *musica mundana* – the cosmic harmony of the structure of the universe, the equilibrium of the four elements, and the cyclical nature of seasonal change – are reflected in the poems. Perhaps Chamberlain's title for 5ff. ('heavens') is misleading, for in the Platonic-Pythagorean tradition cosmic music refers not merely to the harmonic intervals determining the distances between planets, and to the movement of the stars (though that is its primary connotation), but also to the numerical structures underlying the entire universe.[125] In that sense, the boundaries of the sea and earth to which 2 m. 8.9ff. refer are in themselves an instance of balance and equilibrium (wet/dry, water/earth) in nature, and so, ultimately, an example of cosmic music. But even if the notion of cosmic music underlies 2 m. 8, it can only do so in an implicit sense: there is no explicit reference to *musica* in the poem, although, as Chamberlain writes, '... perhaps, *amor* ... becomes implicitly musical since it creates the same concord that music creates in "De musica" '.[126] For that reason – the necessarily implicit nature of the purported 'musical' connotations of the poem – Chamberlain can hardly be right to see a reference to Boethius' *musica humana* in the evocation of 'concord among peoples, spouses, and friends' in 22ff. He overemphasizes the musical aspect of the poem.[127] Moreover, as has

[123] Chamberlain (1970) 87.
[124] Chamberlain (1970) 88.
[125] See Chadwick (1981) 80ff.
[126] Chamberlain (1970) 88.
[127] Chamberlain (1970) 88. *Musica humana* in Boethius refers, in fact, to something

been remarked above, it is no more than possible that lines 1f. refer to the seasons. If we take them as a reference to the notion of ordered change in general, then their function is simply to introduce the notion, which is then exemplified in the following lines, with the instances of the elements, the alternation of night and day, and the limits of land and sea. The reference back to *De musica* may be no more than general: both the discussion of *musica mundana* in that work and the evocation of *amor* in 2 m. 8 point in complementary ways to the harmony and structure of the universe. They also use similar language to evoke it. *De musica* speaks of the *caeli machina* (1.2, p. 187.27), the poem of the *machina* that is the world (21).[128] The treatise speaks of the *varietas* of seasonal change (p. 188.11); the use of *variare* in 2 m. 8.2 has been noted above. And the general principle of balance evoked in the treatise

> So also in music we perceive that there can be nothing so excessive that it destroys its counterpart through its own excess (p. 188.19ff.)

is reflected in the common confines of land and sea in the poem (9f.). In the *De musica* passage it is clear that, although the music of the spheres exemplifies cosmic music *par excellence*, that music is first and foremost a metaphor for cosmic harmony and the underlying structure of things, based on the relation between harmonic ratios and intervals, and the structure itself. Thus Boethius uses a variety of metaphorical terms whose primary reference is to universal harmony rather than to music.[129] The explicit musical terms, such as *armonia*, though they occur, are not the most frequently used ways of evoking music in its cosmic sense. We might conclude that, although Chamberlain may strain the evidence to find references to the three types of cosmic music of *De musica* in 2 m. 8, he is none the less correct to see parallel functions for *musica* and *amor* in Boethius' world-picture.

This last conclusion suggests that it is in the Platonic-Pythagorean tradition that the sources of Boethius' notion of *amor* are to be found. That is not to deny that the Stoically influenced image of the binding of the cosmos is not a potent factor in it. There are several terminological and metaphorical indications in the poem of the influence of that tradition.[130] Lapidge is undoubtedly right to point to Lucan 4.189ff. for the metaphor of a providential *concordia* and *amor* to express the function of the Stoic *pneuma*-theory: it is not necessary to look to Proclus' concept of providential love (*erôs pronoêtikos*) for this idea.[131]

---

else, namely, the blending of soul and body, and the formation of soul and body themselves (*mus.* 1.2 [pp. 188f.]).

[128] Cf. *mus.* 1.2, p. 188.10: *machina*, referring to the unification of the elements.

[129] e.g. *coaptatio; coniungere; convenire; compaginare; committere; consentaneus* (all found in *mus.* 1.2 [pp. 187f.]).

[130] See n. 116 above.

[131] Lapidge (1980) 835 n. 55; cf. n. 50 above.

Lapidge is equally correct to see in *sanctum foedus* (22f.) the type of echo of, for example, Seneca's *sancta foedera mundi* (*Med.* 605f.) that points unmistakably to the Stoic genesis of such phrases. Scheible saw this Stoic element in Boethius' *amor* notion before Lapidge did, but she argues that in Boethius there is the additional concept of a transcendent, personal divine power which points to a source additional to Stoicism.[132] The main reason she gives, however – the idea that chaos would ensue if *amor* ceased to dominate the universe – is an inadequate one. There is no indication that in 16ff. Boethius is suggesting that either the *amor* that harmonizes the universe or the chaos that might overtake it are necessarily transcendent or external to the universe. One cannot adduce the transcendent creator God of 3 m. 9, and identify him with *amor* here.[133] Nor can the use of the metaphor of binding and reins be presumed to refer implicitly to a transcendent power: the poem suggests no more than that *amor* is the force inherent in things which harmonizes them, and without which they would cease to harmonize. Lapidge rightly points to the Stoic antecedents of this idea, and to possible poetic antecedents in Lucan (1.72ff.) and Manilius (2.804ff.).[134] But what is absent from these poetic accounts and present in Boethius is the metaphor of personalized *amor*. We must therefore go beyond the sources given by Lapidge for Boethius' precursor, but we do not have to go as far as the reality of a transcendent deity. An obvious influence is Plato's *Timaeus*.[135] There, speaking of the mixture, in a fixed proportion, of the four elements in the constitution of the universe's body by the Demiurge, Plato writes:

> ... from such constituents, four in number, the body of the universe was brought into being, coming into concord by means of proportion, and from these it acquired Amity (*philia*), so that coming into unity with itself it became indissoluble by any other save him who bound it together (*Tim.* 32c, tr. Cornford).[136]

I suggest that it is the metaphorical language of the *Timaeus* (and the *Timaeus* tradition), which does not prejudge the question of the mode of existence of the Demiurge (transcendent or otherwise) that is an

[132] Lapidge (1980) 836, anticipated by Scheible (1972) 76f., to whom Lapidge does not refer. Scheible suggests an influence like Prudentius, *Amartigenia* 236ff.

[133] Scheible (1972) 76f. avoids doing so explicitly, but that is the implication of her remarks.

[134] Lapidge (1980) 821, 835f.

[135] Seen by Dronke (1965) 400, 402, but not fully exploited by him.

[136] Gruber (1978) 228f. adduces Cicero's translation of these lines, where *philia* is translated by *amicitia* and *caritas* (Cicero, *Tim.* 15). Dronke (1965) 400 n. 43 refers to Calcidius' translation, which speaks of an *amica ratio* (p. 25.8 Waszink). Neither translator gives the term *amor*, but that term is supplied by the Latin tradition described by Lapidge (1980) esp. 835.

important influence here. It certainly facilitates the use of *amor* to refer to the *philia* of the elements, and it conveys the notion of the need for that *amor* by imagining its withdrawal in terms of a personal power's withdrawal, on his own initiative, of the cohesive force that binds things together.[137] For Calcidius, translating *Tim.* 32c, that withdrawal is only effected through the will of the Demiurge.[138] But neither Plato nor Boethius are as explicit. It is precisely at the level of metaphor that Boethius' image of cosmic *amor* is most effective. Dronke (whose article Boethius' commentators have, to their loss, ignored) has seen this: '[Boethius' and Dionysius'] point of departure here is not some abstract term that they extend by a metaphor, but a concept of incredible imaginative richness.'[139] Dronke has himself described the main currents of the poetic and mythical tradition, both in literature and philosophy, that are the essential background to Boethius. It is a tradition that includes: the Aphrodite and Eros of the Homeric hymns, Sophocles, and Euripides; the goddess of Parmenides 'who governs all things' and who 'first of all the gods ... devised Love';[140] Empedocles' Love (*Philotês*), which, with its counter-power, Strife (*Neikos*), is surely an important antecedent;[141] Lucretius' Venus; the Zeus-Eros of Pherecydes;[142] the God of the Hermetic *Asclepius*; and the divine Love of Plutarch's *Erôtikos*. Distinguishing four strands of this tradition – a divine power of love throughout the universe; an ordering power of love in the universe, in perpetual conflict with strife; the creation of the universe through a divine union in lovemaking; and a heavenly, active love, illuminating souls, and even directing the sun's movements – strands which are not mutually exclusive, Dronke does not reduce Boethius' *amor* to any or all of these, but rather sees it as a fifth alongside them, and in part formed by them.[143] The notion of an active, outgoing love is novel in the Platonic and Aristotelian traditions: elaborated in abstract terms, it is a metaphysical concept, but one richly nourished by myth. What Dronke does is provide a credible starting-point both for Proclus' providential Eros and for the *amor* of Boethius, thereby making the thesis of Boethius' dependence on Proclus unnecessary.[144] The late Neoplatonic elaboration of these ideas is undoubtedly part of the tradition exploited by Boethius.[145] His

---

[137] Cf. *desmoi* in Plato, *Tim.* 43a.

[138] Calcidius, p. 25.10 Waszink.

[139] Dronke (1965) 400.

[140] Translated by J. Barnes, *Early Greek Philosophy* (Harmondsworth 1987) 137.

[141] Cf. *bellum*, 2 m. 8.18.

[142] See G.S. Kirk/J.E. Raven/M. Schofield, *The Presocratic Philosophers*, 2nd edn. (Cambridge 1983) 62f.

[143] Dronke (1965) 398f., who also identifies this fifth strand in Proclus.

[144] See n. 50 above. To Proclus, *In Alcib.* 26.2ff. Westerink, adduced by De Vogel, Dronke (1965) 401 adds ib. 52.1ff.

[145] Cf. e.g. Pseudo-Dionysius, *De divinis nominibus* 4.10.

amor does not have to be either exclusively Neoplatonic or evolved purely from the Stoic tradition, and it is undoubtedly fed by the poetic and philosophical currents so perceptively adduced by Dronke.

Dronke suggests that Boethius is original in being the first to remove cosmic love 'entirely from its mythological frame'.[146] But it is important to realize that Boethius evolves his image of *amor* in the quasi-mythological metaphor discussed above, and that the poem 2 m. 8 does not free itself from the metaphor.[147] It is part of the poem's programmatic function that the theme of *amor* is simply superimposed on that of Fortune, anticipating the developments of Book 3, but not rising out of any progress of the argument of the work as such. The image of *amor* in the poem has complex and manifold sources and antecedents. The same diverse sources could be seen to contribute to the formation of the ideas and images in the verse proem of Martianus Capella's work quoted above.[148]

The active outgoing love of 2 m. 8 is not merely an ordering and cohesive force in the universe: it is also an object of aspiration by human beings, who, as the *Consolation* will go on to demonstrate, are endowed with free will.[149] It is thus also present in the pacts and convenants into which humans enter (22ff.), though in some of these *amor* will also be an instinctive power.[150] There is thus an element of 'ought' as well as of 'is' in the poem. Men ought to be ruled in their lives by the love which, in fact, permeates the universe. We cannot be expected to understand the full implication of the poem's final prayer (28ff.) at this stage of the *Consolation*. Neither the concept of free will nor the true nature of happiness and goodness has yet been delineated. But the poem's propaedeutic function is fulfilled. Book 3 can now turn to the theme of happiness, approached against the background of a poem which has celebrated the harmony and cohesion of the universe, and evoked suggestions of human love and concord, so providing positive images to counter the discredited and discarded persona of Fortune.

(iii) Book 3

At the beginning of the third book Boethius returns to the metaphor of medical remedies. In Book 2 there had been a gradual progression from the gentler physic of 2.1.7 to the stronger medicines of 2.5.1,

[146] Dronke (1965) 402.

[147] This is arguably more important than the poem's lack of explicit mythical colouring; cf. Dronke (1965) 403f., where he appears to suggest this.

[148] pp. 147f.

[149] See 5.2ff. Cf. Klingner (1921) 27.

[150] e.g. sexually based unions. In 2 m. 8.24f. Boethius does not differentiate between the voluntary and the instinctive elements, except in so far as *castis ... amoribus* suggests a moral and so voluntary element.

marking the transition in the argument from a general consideration of Fortune to specific examination of the nature of Fortune's gifts. Now, in 3.1.2, the prisoner feels that he is ready for 'more bitter medicines' still.[151] And Philosophy's reply announces an intensification of the intellectual level of the argument (3.1.3), and prepares the transition to Platonic metaphysics and immaterialism, increasingly dominant in the third book, but not to the exclusion of themes and attitudes, especially in the poems, that follow naturally upon those of the second. Thus it is true to say that much of the bitterness in the medical doses administered in Book 3 is contained in the prose sections. The poetry partly reflects and refracts this, but presents it in palatable measures that seem all the more acceptable for using and adapting images and metaphors, emblems and motifs, from the earlier books.

The first poem of the book, 3 m. 1, uses nature images to make the point that what is good is all the more relished and appreciated when it follows upon what is not good, or unpleasant, or negative. The nature images of lines 1-10 exemplify and prepare for the conclusion of 11ff., that insight into what is truly good most appropriately follows upon consideration of false goods:

tu quoque falsa tuens bona prius
incipe colla iugo retrahere:
vera dehinc animum subierint.

You too who look to false goods, first begin by removing your neck from the yoke; truth will then steal into your mind.

It is not explicitly suggested that this must be so, merely that this is the appropriate method for the prisoner, given his condition at the start of his treatment. At the same time, the observation is programmatic: it takes up the announcement of 3.1.7 that Philosophy will first deal with false notions of happiness and the good, so that the opposite states and conditions of genuine happiness and goodness may be recognized: the method of deducing X from its known contrary –X is introduced. This will indeed be the method adopted by Philosophy until 3.9.23, and consideration of the contrary condition of true happiness will be announced in 3.9.24.[152] But even if the method adopted is, in a sense, *ad hominem* and adapted to the prisoner's case, the nature metaphors of lines 1-10 suggest that it is not, in general, an inappropriate way to proceed: it reflects natural processes. It also reflects, as the image of the yoke in line 12 reminds the reader, the natural condition of one who is not yet liberated by philosophy.

The poem's opening picture, that of a fruitful field following upon the

---

[151] Cf. 1.5.11f. On the medical motifs see especially Schmid (1956); cf. Ch. 2, n. 7.
[152] Cf. 3.12.16.

task of weeding and eradicating scrub and fern, reverts to the pastoral metaphor of 1 m. 6.1ff., and there as here the influence of Virgil's *Georgics* is likely.[153] But the image of 3 m. 1 has its place in ethical and philosophical literature, and its use in Cicero has probably also influenced Boethius:

> ... just as a field, however good the ground, cannot be productive without cultivation, so the soul cannot be productive without teaching. So true it is that the one without the other is ineffective. Now the cultivation of the soul is philosophy; this pulls out vices by the roots and makes souls fit for the reception of seed, and commits to the soul and, as we may say, sows in it seed of a kind to bear the richest fruit when fully grown (*Tusc. disp.* 2.5.13, tr. King).[154]

In this passage, the image of preparing the soil is explicitly linked to philosophical method. The link in Boethius is implicit but no less obvious. Likewise, the mention of ferns (3) may owe at least as much to Horace's *neglectis urenda filix innascitur agris* ('when the fields are neglected, fern, which ought to be burned, springs up', *serm.* 1.3.37) where it occurs in a context about the blemish that moral defects cast on good qualities of character, as it does to its more technical agricultural context in Virgil.[155]

The second image (5f.) is closely related to the remedies metaphor of 3.1.3: honey is sweeter after one has tasted something sour.[156] A poetic antecedent has not been identified. It may be the type of consideration that leads Socrates, in the *Phaedo*, to observe that pleasure often follows closely upon its opposite, pain, and is thereby experienced all the more intensely (60bc). As with the first image, then, we should perhaps situate this second one in the tradition of philosophical metaphor.

These first two images have evoked human actions and processes, related to work and to gustatory sensations. The two which follow turn to the world of natural processes observed by human percipients:

> *gratius astra nitent ubi Notus*
> *desinit imbriferos dare sonos.*
> *Lucifer ut tenebras pepulerit*
> *pulchra dies roseos agit equos* (7ff.).

The stars shine brighter when the south wind has stopped its loud lashing rains. When the morning star has driven away the dark, beautiful day leads out the horses rosy in the dawn.

---

[153] Especially *Georg.* 1.150ff.; 2.189 (on fern as *invisam ... aratris*). See p. 133 above.

[154] Cf. Cicero, *Hortensius*, fr. 24 Mueller: see Gruber (1978) 235 for further instances.

[155] Scheible (1972) 80 seems to be over-eager to link 3 m. 1.1ff. to the *Georgics*: the link is much more obvious in the case of 1 m. 6.

[156] See p. 154 above.

Lines 7f. may echo Horace's evocation of the effects of Augustus' return to his people:

> *gratior it dies*
> *et soles melius nitent (Odes 4.5.7f.).*

The day passes more pleasantly, and the sun shines brighter.[157]

But the lines are characterized by the novel conjunction *imbriferos ... sonos*: this is a condensed description of a diverted rain-storm, of the kind usually associated with the south wind.[158] Another poem of Horace's, in fact, provides us with an extended use of the same picture, and the related theme of pleasure succeeding pain:

> *albus ut obscuro deterget nubila caelo*
> *saepe Notus neque parturit imbris*
> *perpetuos, sic tu sapiens finire memento*
> *tristitiam vitaeque labores*
> *molli, Plance, mero ... (Odes 1.7.15ff.).*

As the clearing south wind often wipes away the clouds from the overcast sky, and does not give birth to rain perpetually, so you be sensible, remember to set a limit to your gloom, Plancus, and to life's cares with mellow wine ...

What Horace suggests by the adjective *albus* ('clearing') is expressed more fully in Boethius' *gratius astra nitent* ('the stars shine brighter'). The fact that lines 9f. of Boethius' poem echo Tibullus –

> *hunc illum Aurora nitentem*
> *Luciferum roseis candida portet equis (1.3.93f.)*

May bright Dawn bring this glittering day to me, borne by her rosy horses

– has often been observed. The lines are one of a number of dawn descriptions of the *Consolation*.[159] Hitherto, these have been used to illustrate either the theme of continual change, or that of ordered change: now the sensations of agreeable light after darkness, of colour (*roseis*) after drabness, are stressed, so that the motifs of a poem like 1 m. 3 are recalled. Indeed, the cumulative effect of 7ff. – the theme of clouds clearing and light returning are those of the earlier poem – and

---

[157] See Scheible (1972) 80.

[158] See Salemme (1970/1) 71f. Cf. Nisbet/Hubbard 1.102.

[159] Cf. 2 m. 3.1ff.; 2 m. 8.5ff. Shanzer (1986b) 36f. draws attention to the apparent topos of bombastic descriptions of sunrise and sunset in the Menippean tradition. The bombast (as, indeed, the comic dimension of Menippean satire) is, of course, absent in Boethius. On *Cons. phil.* and Menippean satire see pp. 16ff. above.

the context – the recovery or restoration of mental vision – are the same. The light symbolism of 1 m. 2 and 3 (which, linked to line 12, suggests the influence of the Cave simile of Plato's *Republic*) recurs here; but it is the link with mental vision that makes these lines an apt image for the welcome apprehension of true good to which 11ff. refer.[160]

The following prose section elaborates the insight of 3 m. 1, that the capacity to desire and enjoy the good is naturally present in all humans,[161] adding that the realization of such enjoyment is universally agreed to be true happiness (3.2.2f.). Boethius subsumes the quest for the good under the laws of nature, and it is those laws that are celebrated in the following poem, 3 m. 2. What was said of *amor* in 2 m. 8 is now averred of *natura*:

> *Quantas rerum flectat habenas*
> *natura potens, quibus immensum*
> *legibus orbem provida servet*
> *stringatque ligans inresoluto*
> *singula nexu* ... (3 m. 2.1ff.).

With what powerful reins strong Nature guides all things, with what laws she in her foresight maintains the vast universe, and, binding them in a band that can not be dissolved, draws every single thing together ...

Nature, like *amor*, is a controlling, guiding, ordering, binding force.

This poem is unique among those of the *Consolation* spoken by Philosophy in being self-referring.[162] It is presented self-consciously as a song: ... *placet arguto / fidibus lentis promere cantu* ('I wish to express [the foregoing] with melodious song to the leisurely strings' accompaniment', 5f.). The words *fidibus lentis* announce the elaborate and leisurely series of images and metaphors to follow, but they also '[associate] the strings on which she [Philosophy] plays with the bonds which unite all elements of the universe'.[163] Lerer shows how the form and structure of the poem are in themselves a reflection of the order and design of nature.[164] That this, in Boethius' terms, is a musical reflection illustrates how the artistry of the *Consolation* is related to Boethius' musical theory, how instrumental music corresponds to cosmic music.[165]

Four examples from the realm of nature symbolize and explicate the general statement of the opening lines. Two are expansive, each

---

[160] See Gruber (1978) 236.
[161] Cf. esp. 3.2.4, 20.
[162] But cf. the prisoner's opening elegy, 1 m. 1.1ff.
[163] Lerer (1985) 141; cf. Gruber (1978) 243.
[164] Lerer (1985) 141f.
[165] Surprisingly, Chamberlain (1970) does not exploit the lines.

occupying 10 lines: the lion which, though tamed, reverts to its true blood-thirsty nature if once it tastes blood (7-16); and the bird which, though caged, longs to return to its native woods (17-26). Two take the form of brief vignettes of 4 and 3 lines each: the reed or switch, though bent, springs back when released to its natural position (27-30); and the sun, though it has set, returns to its place of rising (31-3). The 'moral' of these examples is more precise than that natural tendencies or processes run their habitual course.[166] In the first two examples a kind of recollection (*anamnêsis*) is at work: lion and bird have a latent memory or sense of their true nature and habitat. The theme of recollection anticipates the treatment of 3 m. 11 and 3.12, though it is as yet couched in terms that do not immediately remind one of Plato's theory, but rather illustrate the current theme, the universal innate desire for happiness. But what links these two examples to the following two is the broader notion of return. Both lion and bird revert to their natural state, or long to do so. The switch reverts to its natural position, the sun returns to rise again (32f.), and it is the theme of return that is emphasized in the poem's general conclusion:

> *repetunt proprios quaeque recursus*
> *redituque suo singula gaudent*
> *nec manet ulli traditus ordo*
> *nisi quod fini iunxerit ortum*
> *stabilemque sui fecerit orbem* (34ff.).

Everything seeks its own way back, each thing is glad at its return, nor does anything maintain the order entrusted to it unless it has joined the end to the beginning, and made its circular progress steady.

There is a natural tendency in things to return to their beginning, whether this be their normal behaviour, or their natural place or position, or whether, as in the case of the sun, regular motion is perceived to be cyclical and always return to and recommence from a beginning. We recognize that a general point of profound significance is being made, and that the motif of nature's order and law is being taken a decisive step further, with the introduction of the theme of cyclical motion, of the movement that is a return to the source.[167]

Lines 34ff. in particular give expression to the metaphor of the course of nature (*recursus*, 34).[168] Boethius stresses that this course is cyclical, and that accounts for the brief but climactic example of the sun's course, the supreme example of natural order in the

---

[166] Gruber (1978) 242 takes too limited a view of the passage.

[167] Lerer (1985) 141f. observes how 3 m. 2 foreshadows 3 m. 9.

[168] See H. Galinsky, *Naturae cursus. Der Weg einer antiken kosmologischen Metapher von der Alten in die Neue Welt* (Studien zum Fortwirken der Antike 4, Heidelberg 1968) 27ff.

Consolation.[169] The *r(e)-* repetitions of 32ff. underline the return theme.[170] The theme of cyclical change is found in Seneca:

> Mark how the round (*orbem*) of the universe repeats its course; you will see that no star in our firmament is extinguished, but that they all set and rise in alternation. Summer has gone, but another year will bring it again; winter lies low, but will be restored by its own proper months; night has overwhelmed the sun, but day will soon rout the night again. The wandering stars retrace their former courses, a part of the sky is rising unceasingly, and a part is sinking (*Ep.* 36.11, tr. Gummere).[171]

Boethius expresses the same insight, and there are many links between the Stoic letter and the poem: the use in both of *orbis* in the sense of 'cycle'; the example of the sun's course; the verb *repetere* and the use of *re-* words in general. The examples of seasonal and stellar change are, of course, familiar from other treatments of the theme in Boethius, even if they do not occur in 3 m. 2. But the detail of line 37 (the end linked to the beginning) is distinctive. Although it is reported to have been an assertion of the Presocratic Alcmaeon of Croton that 'men die because they cannot attach the beginning to the end',[172] the assertion remains obscure and difficult to interpret; it may refer to the difference between human existence and the everlasting revolutions of the heavenly bodies.[173] The theme is exploited by Boethius in 3 m. 9.12ff. and 4 m. 6.30ff.[174] There can be no doubt that in its later expressions in the work, from 3 m. 9 onwards, the motif is to be understood in the Neoplatonic, specifically Procline, context of those sections of the work.[175] But this is not yet apparent in 3 m. 2. Although the cryptic phrase 'has joined the end to the beginning' (*fini iunxerit ortum*) points towards and foreshadows its explication in the later poems, the Neoplatonic context is missing in this poem, just as the Platonic implications of the recollection theme are not yet elaborated. Boethius does not yet fully reveal in what sense the universal desire for happiness is a desire for one's source or beginning. But a theme is none the less announced.

To turn to some details of the example of 7ff. The lion example is traditional,[176] and there are signs that Boethius is indebted to its

[169] See Gruber (1978) 97f.

[170] *rursus ... repetunt ... recursus ... redituque*: see Ford (1967) 65.

[171] Note the *re-* words in this passage: *remeantium ... referent ... repetit*; cf. previous note.

[172] DK 24 B 2, tr. Barnes (n. 140 above) 90f.

[173] This view is put forward in Kirk/Raven/Schofield (n. 142 above) 347f. For a different interpretation see J. Barnes, *The Presocratic Philosophers*, 2nd edn. (London 1982) 115f.

[174] Cf. 3 m. 11.3f.

[175] See Theiler (1966) 319f.

[176] See Gruber (1978) 244.

earlier treatment in Latin poetry. One passage which seems to have influenced him is Lucan 4.237ff.:

> *sic, ubi desuetae silvis in carcere cluso*
> *mansuevere ferae et voltus posuere minaces*
> *atque hominem didicere pati, si torrida parvus*
> *venit in ora cruor, redeunt rabiesque furorque,*
> *admonitaeque tument gustato sanguine fauces;*
> *fervet et a trepido vix abstinet ira magistro.*

> So, when wild beasts have lost the habit of the woods and grown tame in a narrow prison, they lose their grim aspect and learn to submit to man; but, if a drop of blood finds its way to their thirsty mouths, their rage and fury return, and their throats, reminded of their old life by the taste of blood, swell again; their anger boils up and scarcely spares their frightened keeper (tr. Duff).

Another passage is Martial 2.75, whose first line – *Verbera securi solitus leo ferre magistri* ('The lion accustomed to endure the lashes of its uncaring master') – is echoed in Boethius' ... *metuantque trucem / soliti verbera ferre magistrum* ('... used to endure the lashes, they fear the harsh master', 9f.). But there is *variatio* and independence in Boethius' treatment of these possible antecedents.[177]

Both the example of the tamed lion (but not the detail of its reversion to savagery) and that of the caged bird are found in Epictetus 4.1.24ff.[178] Their function there is a different one from that of the Boethius poem, for Epictetus uses them as instances of lack of freedom. But the conjunction of *exempla* in both writers indicates that the examples were used as topoi in philosophical diatribe. Caged bird and lion (though not tamed) form part of a composite *exemplum* in Ovid:

> *cum bene sit clausae cavea Pandione natae,*
> *   nititur in silvas illa redire suas.*
> *adsuetos tauri saltus, adsueta leones –*
> *   nec feritas illos impedit – antra petunt (ex Ponto 1.3.39ff.).*

> Though Pandion's daughter may be well off in her cage, she strives to return to her own forests. Bullocks seek their familiar pastures, lions in spite of their wild nature their familiar lairs (tr. Wheeler).

And, in a philosophical context again, Seneca, although not referring explicitly to the bird-metaphor, speaks of the soul escaping from its cage (*cavea*) after death and ascending, presumably in flight (*in sublime secessit, Ep.* 88.34).[179] Thus the bird motif is linked implicitly

---

[177] See Gruber (1978) 244.
[178] See Scheible (1972) 82.
[179] Cf. a similar metaphor in Augustine, *Contra Academicos* 2.3.7 (on which see J. Doignon, 'L'apologue de Philocalie et de Philosophie chez saint Augustin', *Revue des*

to the Platonic theme of the soul's captivity in embodiment and its potential for return in metaphorical flight to its true home.[180] But, once again, Boethius avoids explicitly Platonizing the image in 3 m. 2. It is the type of image that would commend itself to one writing and thinking in the Stoic tradition.

The sequence of poems after 3 m. 2 and before the great hymn 3 m. 9 at the centre of the work is one of brief, sometimes almost epigrammatic statements, sparing in their use of figurative language.[181] It is only to be expected that this sequence will not greatly add to the complex of cosmic and nature imagery in the *Consolation*. But some details are worthy of discussion.

The opening image of 3 m. 3 –

> *Quamvis fluente dives auri gurgite*
> *non expleturas cogat avarus opes* (1f.)

Although the rich man in his greed may gather up the wealth that will not satisfy in an ocean of gold

– employs the picture of the *gurges* as an inexhaustible source.[182] Although Scheible adduces Prudentius as a possible antecedent, she is right to have reservations about the passage as a source for Boethius,[183] for Prudentius uses *gurges* in its other sense of a devouring whirlpool, to conjure up a different image of avarice:

> *sorbeat ut cumulus nummorum faucibus amplis*
> *gurges avaritiae ... (Amartig. 254f.).*

How the whirlpool of greed swallows piles of money with its gaping jaws
...

The next lines of 3 m. 3 introduce the theme of pearls as a symbol of extravagant wealth: the pearl-motif recurs in poems 4, 8, and 10 of the book, and is emblematic. But in 3 m. 3.3 (as in Horace, *Epodes* 8.14) the neck of the avaricious man is weighed down (*oneretque*) with the pearls, suggesting also the image of the chained or yoked neck that recurs in the work.[184] There is a further way in which the pearl-motif

---

Etudes Augustiniennes 30 [1984] 100-6). On the motif in general see P. Courcelle, art. Flügel (Flug) der Seele I, *RAC* 8 (1972) 29-65.

[180] Cf. Seneca, *Cons. Marc.* 23.1f.; *Ep.* 79.12; 92.30. See J. Doignon, 'L'âme dans l'empyrée. A propos d'un passage controverse de Sen. *epist.* 88, 34', *Hommages à L. Lerat* (Paris 1984) 114-22.

[181] See Scheible (1972) 84. The longest poem of the sequence, 3 m. 8, has 22 lines, and no other poem is longer than 10 lines.

[182] The term *gurges* can refer to salt or fresh water, usually in turbulent motion, though in poetry the sense 'whirlpool' or 'eddy' need not apply: see Thomas (1988) 2.204.

[183] Scheible (1972) 85.

[184] Cf. 1 m. 2.25; 3 m. 1.12.

here is more than an emblem of wealth and luxury: in conjunction with
the picture of vast herds of cattle in line 4, it evokes the notion of nature
extravagantly abused and misused.

In 3 m. 6 the theme of the oneness of all nature is evoked. God (8),
called the 'father of all things' (2), is the source of everything, humans,
the sun, moon, and stars. Humans are to be seen as naturally part of the
world around them, even if they have souls of heavenly origin (5). The
theme of the preceding prose has been that the fame that proceeds from
high birth is hollow. The poem, though referring to the theme, is above
all anticipatory. We are still in the middle of a discussion of the false
goods, and the negative conclusions of 3.6 about fame are now
complemented by the positive vision of nature's unity. But that positive
vision, and its central concept of a creator God who is the source of all
things, will not be elaborated until later, from 3 m. 9 onwards. The poem
points towards that later development, and so is more than a mere
interlude, or summary of what has preceded it. And once again,
although it introduces ideas that will cohere perfectly with the Platonic
themes of 3 m. 9 and following sections, this poem, like others of Book 3,
says nothing that could not have been said by a Stoic, or indeed by
philosophers, Platonic or otherwise, from Plato onwards, who subscribe
to a belief in divine providence.[185]

The 'bitter-sweet' theme has already featured in the third book, in the
image of remedies that sting the tongue but are sweet when ingested
(3.1.3), and that of honey which tastes sweeter after something bitter
has been tasted (3 m. 1.5f.). In 3 m. 7 the nature of pleasure is compared
with the sweet honey of the bee, and its aftermath with the bee's sting.
The idea is proverbial, and one need not seek for Hellenistic poetic
antecedents that may have influenced Boethius.[186] In Latin literature
he would have encountered the notion of adjacent sweetness or
pleasure, and pain or bitterness, related to honey and bees in Petronius
(56.6) and, without bees, in Juvenal (6.179ff.).[187] For Boethius is
making the same point about pleasure as Horace: *sperne voluptates:
nocet empta dolore voluptas* ('Spurn self-indulgence: pain, its price, does
harm', *epist*. 1.2.55, tr. Macleod). In 3 m. 7 Boethius employs a technique
familiar from both Greek and Latin writers, using terms that can refer
both to pleasure and to the honey-bee throughout the poem, so that
statement and simile develop in tandem. It is precisely their inter-
changeable functions that make the poem, though brief and condensed
(6 lines), a vivid and striking statement.[188]

[185] Cf. e.g. Seneca, *benef*. 3.28.1f. (referred to by Scheible [1972] 92). For Platonic and
other references see Gruber (1978) 262f.

[186] As Scheible (1972) 95 does.

[187] See Gruber (1978) 266, who also refers to Plato, *Phaedo* 91c (though there the sting
is referred to without the honey, which is essential to Boethius' point about pleasure).

[188] Salemme (1970/1) 81 n. 34. See D.A. West, *The Imagery and Poetry of Lucretius*
(Edinburgh 1969) 43ff. and index s.v. 'transfusion'. Cf. Rutherford (1989) 151f.

The prose section 3.8 summarizes the argument of Book 3 to date. False notions of happiness not merely fail to make their pursuer happy, but actually bring evil in their wake. The notion of false or misdirected vision, introduced at the beginning of the book (3 m. 1.11ff.), is subtly reintroduced, when Boethius says of beauty that is admired: '... it is not your nature that makes you seem beautiful, but the weakness of sight of those looking at you' (3.8.10). The theme is then explicitly elaborated in the following poem, 3 m. 8. It is ignorance (2) that leads on to failure in the quest for the true good (15ff.), for one is not looking in the right place. Boethius introduces the motif of the *adunaton* and modifies it, in making this point.[189] For men *do* know where to find gold, gems, fish, goats, pearls, and purple dye (3ff.), and they do not seek them in false places:

> sed quonam lateat quod cupiunt bonum,
>   nescire caeci sustinent (15f.).

But where the good they desire may be concealed, in their persistent blindness they do not know.

Gold does not grow on trees or gems on the vine, fish are not caught on mountains: these and other examples of 3ff. adopt topoi of the *adunaton* to highlight the paradox of human knowledge about physical and material things that coexists with human ignorance about what really matters – true goods.[190] Thus the natural items used figuratively in this poem link it to the earlier poems and themes of the book, and in this way the poem, like its antecedent prose, is a summary of the book thus far. Lines 21f. reiterate the themes and methodological points of the book's opening. Only one line is anticipatory. When Boethius refers to *quod stelliferum transabiit polum* ('what has gone beyond the star-bearing sky', 17) the topography becomes cosmic and Platonic, and anticipates the heavenly journey of the soul to the 'place beyond the heavens' (*huperouranios topos, Phaedrus* 247c) of 4 m. 1.

Earlier poems in the *Consolation* have evoked the controlling power in the universe, its maker, and the laws of the cosmos which are the principles of his creation, but the work's central poem, the hexametric hymn 3 m. 9, goes further, and places both the creator and his works in a specifically Platonic context. The poem draws both on the cosmology

---

(discussing a striking instance in Marcus Aurelius, *Meditations* 4.48); M.S. Silk, *Interaction in Poetic Imagery* (Cambridge 1974).

[189] On the *adunaton* motif see Curtius (1954) 105ff.; Nisbet/Hubbard 1.23, 341f., 373; E. Dutoit, *Le thème de l'adynaton dans la poésie antique* (Paris 1936).

[190] Scheible (1972) 98 observes well that the examples are of luxury goods (metals, jewels, select foods), so that Boethius sustains in this way the themes of *luxuria* and *avaritia*.

of Plato's *Timaeus* and on Proclus' Neoplatonic commentary on that dialogue.[191] The reader of Boethius' poems who is attentive to the theme of nature in them will find much in it that takes up and makes specific what has been said and suggested in earlier poems of the work.

From the beginning of the poem, the creator God is evoked as the cosmic helmsman (*gubernas*, 1) who effects movement in the universe (3): the helmsman motif takes up earlier allusions in the work (1 m. 5.25; 1.6.7, 19f.) and anticipates an important passage, 3.12.14,17, to be discussed below.[192] Cosmic helmsmanship is observable in the relations of the elements:

> *tu numeris elementa ligas, ut frigora flammis,*
> *arida conveniant liquidis, ne purior ignis*
> *evolet aut mersas deducant pondera terras* (10ff.).

> You bind the elements with numbers, so that cold and flames, dry and liquid, are counterbalanced, that fire, too pure, may not fly up and away, or heavy masses sink the earth.

The theme of the binding of the cosmos coalesces here with that of the elements as a pair of pre-eminent examples of the harmony of disparate entities.[193] Moreover, the numerical basis of elemental *concordia discors* is given an emphasis in *numeris* (10) that it has hitherto lacked in the *Consolation*: the influence of the *Timaeus* (32bc) is patent.[194] In terms reminiscent of 1 m. 3 the poem's concluding prayer is for the removal of the earthly, clouding heaviness that obscures vision and understanding:

> *dissice terrenae nebulas et pondera molis*
> *atque tuo splendore mica ...* (25f.).

> Scatter the cloudy mass of earthly heaviness, and shine in your own brightness ...

But in these lines and elsewhere in the poem there are signs of a new

[191] As Klingner (1921) 38-67 established, and Theiler (1966) 321ff. and Gruber (1978) 277ff. elaborated and confirmed. Scheible (1972) 101ff. argues for a greater direct influence of Plato and a correspondingly lesser Neoplatonic influence upon the poem's ideas and expression. A detailed analysis of all aspects of 3 m. 9 is beyond the scope of this study: see the sensitive and learned discussion of W. Beierwaltes, 'Trost im Begriff. Zu Boethius' Hymnus "O qui perpetua mundum ratione gubernas"', in *Communicatio Fidei. Festschrift für E. Biser* (Regensburg 1983) 241-51.

[192] See p. 168. On the helmsman motif see the references assembled by Gruber (1978) 278. The formative influences are Heraclitus (DK 22 B 41 and 64), Plato (*Philebus* 28d, *Laws* 709b), and Cleanthes (*Hymn to Zeus* = *SVF* 1.537, lines 2, 35).

[193] Cf. 2 m. 8.3f.; 4 m. 6.19ff. On the binding-theme see Beierwaltes (n. 191 above) 246f., 251 n. 40.

[194] In addition to number and harmony, Boethius emphasizes the proportion, relative weight, and controlled movement of the elements, all themes of the *Timaeus*.

metaphysical dimension. The earth in general is now a place of cloud and darkness by comparison with the splendours of goodness and truth. Only light and the image of the fountain can adequately suggest divine goodness:

> *da fontem lustrare boni, da luce reperta*
> *in te conspicuos animi defigere visus* (23f.).

> Grant that I may contemplate the source of goodness, grant that, having found the light, I may fix my mental vision, grown clear-sighted, upon you.

This universe is only good and beautiful in so far as it is an image of the Form of the Good (8) in the divine creator's mind (5f.). And it is only through the introspective movement of the world-soul (itself a harmonious whole, 14) upon the principle of Mind that reflected celestial movements occur:

> *in semet reditura meat mentemque profundam*
> *circuit et simili convertit imagine caelum* (16f.).

> It moves, striving to return to itself, and encircles the inmost mind, and turns the heavens in a movement that reflects its own.

In contrast with the cyclical movements of the heavenly bodies, those of humans are movements of descent and ascent, cyclical only in a sense in which all returns to source are (18ff.): the theme of the soul's cosmic journeys will be elaborated in 4 m. 1. The theme of the journey is sustained in the final litany of evocations of God at the end of the poem, where he is called the path (*semita*, 28) that leads to the truth and the goodness that he essentially is.

It is characteristic of the *Consolation* that, although 3 m. 9 initiates a specifically Platonic cosmic imagery that makes it the counterpart of the hymns of Proclus and Synesius, and is sustained in later poems (especially 3 m. 11 and 12, 4 m. 1 and 6), the use of nature motifs in a non-Platonic way continues throughout the work. The role of nature in the elaboration of Boethius' thought is transformed by the cosmic theology of 3 m. 9. But at the same time the poetic currency of the work hitherto is not rendered obsolete. Motifs and emblems, such as those of elemental harmony and light, may be metamorphosed in the *Timaeus* poem, but the sobriety of the everyday returns, and the common coin that poet and philosopher, Stoic and Epicurean, used and transmitted to Boethius is still used with purpose and precision as the argument of the work proceeds. This is nowhere more apparent than in the nature motifs of the later poems.

The next poem, 3 m. 10, takes up the theme of the misleading nature of the earth's treasures, its gold, pearls, and emeralds (7ff.). Though bright (they are evoked in words suggesting vividness and colour: *rutilante, candidis, virides*), they do not cast light upon, but rather darken the mind's sight, for their brightness is paradoxically a darkness:

> non ...
> *inlustrent aciem magisque caecos*
> *in suas condunt animos tenebras* (7, 11f.).

They would not brighten the vision, but instead bury blind minds in their own darkness.

What in previous poems were seen as symbols of greed and luxury because of the value placed upon them by men, are now seen, as it were, from an ontological viewpoint: on the scale of value that, in Platonic terms, is also a scale of degrees of being, they are emblems of earthly and even subterranean lowliness. They, if prized by the mind, drag it downwards and away from the light of truth:

> *hoc, quicquid placet excitatque mentes,*
> *infimis tellus aluit cavernis;*
> *splendor quo regitur vigetque caelum*
> *vitat obscuras animae ruinas* (13ff.).

Whatever pleases and excites minds, the earth has nourished in its deep chasms. The brightness by which the heavens are ruled flies from the dark downfall of the soul.

Here, in line 14, and also in 1f., the simile of the cave from Plato's *Republic* is influential, as are the related images of light (11, 15ff.). And the theme of the soul's fall in the *Phaedrus*, so richly exploited by the Neoplatonists, is likewise interwoven into these images (16). Yet it would be wrong to see in the symbolism of this poem an exclusively Platonic colouring.[195] The linking of earthly treasures with human degradation, and the contrasting image of the upwards gaze of the mind towards the heavenly bodies, is found in Seneca:

> She [Nature] put before our eyes no object which might stir in us the itch of greed. She placed gold and silver beneath our feet, and bade those feet stamp down and crush everything that causes us to be stamped down and crushed. Nature elevated our gaze towards the sky and willed that we should look upward to behold her glorious and wonderful works ... Nature ordained this above our heads; but gold and silver, with the iron which, because of the gold and silver, never brings peace, she has hidden away, as if they were dangerous things to trust to our keeping. It is we ourselves that have dragged them into the light of day that we might

[195] See Scheible (1972) 114.

fight over them; it is we ourselves who have attributed our own misdeeds to Fortune, and do not blush to regard as the loftiest objects those which once lay in the depths of earth (*Ep.* 94.56f., tr. Gummere, with modifications).

The poem thus combines both popular philosophizing and its imagery (the image of the haven in line 5 is another instance) with specific Platonic associations in a distinctive manner. A similar combination is found in the last lines, where the much-praised sunlight of earlier poems in the work is, as it were, put in its proper place.[196] The notion that God is a heavenly light incomparably brighter than the sun is found in Philo and later in Julian, but also in Christian writers like Clement of Alexandria and Lactantius.[197] But it is also assumed in the description of the Good in the *Republic* as the sun of the intelligible world (507ff.).[198] Furthermore, the *animae ruinas* of line 16, while undoubtedly reflecting the Platonic notion of the soul's fall, also refers to the ethical dimension of that notion as it is found in Plotinus,[199] and links the image of a spiritual fall to moral vice (here *libido*, 3) or passion in a way that echoes Stoic views and their expression.

We should not, therefore, be tempted into reading 3 m. 10 in exclusively Platonic terms. Boethius maintains through his choice of images and metaphors the links with the broader spectrum of philosophical moralizing that the earlier poems of the *Consolation* have established.

There is a comparable conjunction of Platonic and non-Platonic (or not necessarily Platonic) motifs in the next poem, 3 m. 11. The poem does not evolve out of its immediate context in the argument. The same could have been said of 3 m. 10, though there the link to the preceding prose section 3.10 is found in the idea of God's essence being identical with goodness. In the case of 3 m. 11 the themes might be said to be more generally relevant to the whole progress of the argument from 3 m. 9 onwards. There is on the one hand the reiteration of the theme of introspection and the metaphor of circular movement to denote the process of introspection:

Quisquis profunda mente vestigat verum
cupitque nullis ille deviis falli
in se revolvat intimi lucem visus
longosque in orbem cogat inflectens motus
animumque doceat quicquid extra molitur
suis retrusum possidere thesauris (1ff.).

[196] Gruber (1978) 300 perceptively notes that the same epithet *candidus* links the sunlight and those symbols of luxury, the pearls of line 10.

[197] See Gruber (1978) 300.

[198] Plato puts forward the notion that the highest principle is a metaphorical 'hyper-sun': he does not, of course, identify the Form of the Good with a supreme God.

[199] See Scheible (1972) 114.

Whoever with deep thought tracks down the truth, and does not want to be misled by any sidetracks, let him turn the light of his inner vision upon himself, bending the long straight movement, forcing it, into a circle; and let him teach his mind to hide away and hold in its treasury whatever it works upon outside.[200]

The images of sunshine and cloudy darkness to represent knowledge (or vision of the good and truth) and ignorance respectively also recur:

> *dudum quod atra texit erroris nubes*
> *lucebit ipso perspicacius Phoebo* (7f.).

What the black clouds of error recently hid will shine more sharply than Phoebus himself.[201]

There is, further, a possible reference to the theme of the earth's false riches in the correction – implicit, granted – of the idea of 'treasure' in 6: true treasures are internal, in the mind.

But what is new in this poem is the explicit elaboration of the Platonic doctrine of recollection (*anamnêsis*). Forgetfulness of the truth (which here is attributed to the soul's embodied state) is not total (9f., 13f.), learning is recalling what one has forgotten: *quod quisque discit immemor recordatur* ('what each one learns, forgetting he remembers', 16). Boethius uses two metaphors to suggest the process of recollecting. One is that of the seed of truth 'fanned' (*ventilante*, 12) by learning.[202] The other is that of the embers (*fomes*) of knowledge burning within, despite apparent 'ignorance' (13f.), just as the prisoner's initial belief in divine providence, in a state that appears otherwise ignorant, is a spark that will grow to knowledge (cf. 1.6.20).

In the following prose section the theme of divine providence is developed, and the metaphor of God as the cosmic helmsman (3 m. 9.1, 10ff.) – foreshadowed in earlier parts of the work – is reintroduced.[203] The universe is a *machina* (3.12.14) and the good or goodness (*bonum, bonitas*) is its helm or tiller (3.12.14, 17). Here the metaphor promotes the argument because it is already a familiar one from its earlier contexts, where the notion of providence was introduced in acceptable images and with persuasive associations, which now are given full argumentative corroboration. And the metaphor is itself now fully elaborated, in a way that reconciles the transcendent existence of God with the immanence of providence in the world by means of the goodness of the divine.

[200] Cf. 3 m. 9.16f.; 3 m. 2.34ff.

[201] The most recent instances have been 3 m. 9.25f. and 3 m. 10.15f.

[202] The seed and spark metaphors are blended here: cf. Seneca, *Ep.* 94.29. See Gruber (1978) 307. Scheible (1972) 117 n. 4 observes that the blending occurs, but (wrongly, in my view) attributes the mixed metaphor to Boethius' citing from memory.

[203] See p. 164 and n. 192 above. The *machina* image is also found at 2 m. 8.21.

In the concluding Orpheus poem, 3 m. 12, several of the nature themes of the book come together: vision and brightness (1f.), earth as enchainment and heaviness (3f.), descent and ascent (18f., 45ff.), the misuse of sight (49ff.), the source (1, 23). The parallelism between cosmic and human nature is sustained: Orpheus can control the former, or aspects of it, but cannot control his own human emotions and actions. Finally, the poem betrays traces of what might be called Platonic cosmic topography (of which there is more in 4 m. 1): the 'day above' (53) is probably the divine light of goodness and truth, the 'clear source of goodness' of 1f.[204]

(iv) Book 4

Four of the poems in Book 4 (4 m. 1, 4 m. 2, 4 m. 3, and 4 m. 7) are discussed in other chapters.[205] A couple of additional points should, however, be made about details of 4 m. 1 and 2 here.

In the first poem the description of God as the cosmic charioteer is found:

> *hic regum sceptrum dominus tenet*
> *orbisque habenas temperat*
> *et volucrem currum stabilis regit*
> *rerum coruscus arbiter* (4 m. 1.19ff.).

Here the lord of kings holds sway and guides the reins of the universe, and, unmoved, controls the fast chariot, the brilliant master of all things.

Much of 4 m. 1 is based on a passage of Plato's *Phaedrus*, and this description of the cosmic charioteer is based on the description of Zeus' chariot at *Phaedrus* 246e.[206] But the motif relates also to other parts of the *Consolation*. The *amor* of 2 m. 8 holds the universe on a tight rein (16), and the creator will be said to *regens flectit habenas* ('ruling guide the reins') in a later poem (4 m. 6.35). The motif of the cosmic charioteer is frequent in Philo, and, with the related topos of the cosmic helmsman, may be of Stoic origin.[207] It is not as elaborate in Boethius as it is in Dio of Prusa (*or.* 36.39ff.) or Dracontius (*De laudibus dei* 2.15ff.), where the horses represent elements, or the Hermetic writer (*C.H.* 16.7), for whom the reins represent cosmic principles.[208]

---

[204] For a detailed discussion of 3 m. 12 see pp. 188ff. below; there p. 202 on the 'day above' of line 53.

[205] 4 m. 1: pp. 201ff.; 4 m. 2: pp. 94ff.; 4 m. 3: pp. 207ff.; 4 m. 7: pp. 220ff.

[206] Quoted p. 201 below.

[207] See Lapidge (1980) 832 n. 42. Cf. Plutarch, *defect. orac.* 29, 426B = *SVF* 2.1055.

[208] See Lapidge (1980) 832f., who discusses the possible Iranian origin of this last elaboration of the metaphor.

The light-dark contrast is maintained throughout 4 m. 1. The ascending soul leaves the dark, cloudy earth behind (6.27f.), and ascends through and to a realm of light (9ff., 18, 22).

This light-realm is also contrasted with the turbulent, turbid world of the passions, suggested in the feared tyrants of 4 m. 1.29f., and also in the image of the waves whipped up by the wind, evoking the power of anger at 4 m. 2.7 in terms familiar from Lucretius (3.298) and Virgil (*Aen.* 12.831).[209]

The poems of the fourth book stand in varied relationship to their neighbouring prose sections. In general, these *prosae* are longer than those of the earlier books, and the discrepancy between their elaborately developed arguments and the, on the whole, shorter poems is more pointed than hitherto in the work. There are exceptions. The metamorphosis poem 4 m. 3 is an important and subtle extension of the argument of the preceding prose.[210] The case is different with 4 m. 4. Although both 4.4 and this poem refer back to the themes of the opening of the *Consolation* with their development of the theme from Plato's *Gorgias* of the misery and 'illness' of the wrongdoer,[211] we have no sense, when reading 4 m. 4, that we are dealing with one of the major pivotal poems of the work. Its method is rather that of the illustration of points of detail, as in the illuminated capital of a Carolingian manuscript. But like such capitals, it contains motifs of interest in themselves.

One such motif is that of the chariot of death in 3f. Whether the horses of death are winged (like those of the winds, sun, and moon), or whether *volucres* (4) simply means 'swift', is not easy to determine.[212] But in either case the representation of death's chariot seems to be without precise precedent in the poetic tradition. The winged figure of Thanatos in Greek art is not a convincing antecedent (any more than its literary counterpart in Euripides' *Alcestis* would be).[213] In the *Homeric Hymn to Demeter* 18f. Hades uses a chariot to kidnap Persephone,[214] and Homer speaks of 'Hades of the famous horses' (*klutopôlos, Il.* 5.654, etc.). But it is as likely that Boethius is here using the type of creative imagination that leads Marvell to speak of 'Time's wingèd chariot',[215] as that he is imitating or adapting a forerunner.

The implication of another vignette in 4 m. 4 is that, whereas animals

[209] Cf. 1 m. 2.4f.; 2.1.6. See also Catullus 64.97f.   [210] See pp. 207ff. below.

[211] See Gruber (1978) 342ff.

[212] In 4 m. 1.21 *volucrem currum* renders Plato's *ptênon harma* (*Phaedrus* 246e).

[213] See Scheible (1972) 141; Gruber (1978) 348. An iconographical parallel can, however, be adduced: for Hades' chariot on fourth-century BC South Italian vases depicting the rape of Persephone see K. Schauenburg, 'Die Totengötter in der unteritalischen Vasenmalerei', *Jahrbuch des deutschen archäologischen Instituts* 73 (1958) 48-78 (here 57-62); cf. I. Jenkins, 'Is there Life after Marriage? A Study of the Abduction Motif in Vase Paintings of the Athenian Wedding Ceremony', *Bulletin of the Institute of Classical Studies* 30 (1981) 137-45 (here 142).

[214] See N.J. Richardson, *The Homeric Hymn to Demeter* (Oxford 1974) 151.

[215] Andrew Marvell, *To His Coy Mistress*, line 22.

attack humans, another species and a hostile one, humans do violence
to one another (5f.). If that is so, then the lines highlight the unnatural
aspect of evil, and its degradation of human behaviour, and so are an
echo of the animal metamorphosis theme of 4 m.' 3, except that now
human violence seems somehow more degrading than 'animal'
behaviour.

The next poem, 4 m. 5, is a prelude to the explanation of the notions
of providence and fate in 4.6. Once the causes of things are known,
their power to disturb ceases (17ff). To illustrate this Boethius turns to
natural phenomena. People understand, and so are not disturbed by,
the effects of the winds, or of sun and snow (13ff.). But eclipses of the
moon (7ff.), or apparently irregular movements of certain constellations (the Bear does not appear to rise or set, Boötes sets late and only
briefly) are puzzling. Nature is demystified once it is understood, and
ignorance is, once again, compared to a cloud (21).[216] The overcoming
of fear through knowledge of nature's laws is the avowed goal of
Lucretius (1.146ff., 3.1053ff.) and of Virgil in the *Georgics*.[217] Boethius
thus allies himself to that didactic tradition, and, moreover, makes the
particular observation that even apparent irregularities in natural
phenomena are seen to be subject to law, once that law is
understood.[218]

The prose section 4.6 is the longest in the work, and at the end of it
Philosophy offers the prisoner the sweet relief of poetry (4.6.57). The
poem which follows, 4 m. 6, is the last great celebration of divine order
and cohesion in the universe, following suitably upon the detailed
account of the relation between providence and fate in 4.6. It has often
been pointed out that it is the counterpart, in metre as well as in scope,
of 1 m. 5, and it answers the questions of that poem about the apparent
discrepancy between order in nature and disorder in human affairs.
But the answer has been prepared in several intervening sections, and
among the poems 2 m. 8, 3 m. 2, and 3 m. 9 anticipate the themes of
this poem. As might be expected, key themes of the work, and key
terms, are to be found in 4 m. 6. The *foedus* (4) and *pax* (5) of the
universe, its *amor* (17, 44, 47), *concordia* (19), *ordo* (42), and *temperies*
(30) are celebrated. The creator is the cosmic charioteer (34ff.), and the
lex (37) of the universe, whose order is *stabilis* (42). The link between
cause and effect, source and product, is not rectilinear but cyclical
(30ff.), and it is through conversion as a form of love (or love as a form
of conversion) that things flow back to their cause (44ff.).

These generalizing statements – a *summa* of the cosmic themes of
the work – are varied and qualified by individual pictures from nature.
These come from three spheres: the heavenly bodies (1ff.), the

[216] Cf. 4.6.1.
[217] See Scheible (1972) 146; cf. Thomas (1988) 1.253ff. (on *Georg.* 2.490ff.).
[218] See Scheible (1972) 145f.

elements (19ff.), and the seasons (25ff.) – a range that provides Chamberlain with his most convincing example of the influence of the three types of cosmic music mentioned in the *De musica* upon the nature imagery of the *Consolation*.[219] To turn to some details. The example of the Bear in 8ff. is an interesting echo of the preceding poem, 4 m. 5.1ff. What was there presented as an example of nature not understood and so worrying to the uninitiated, is now an example of the diversity of heavenly order. In this subtle way Boethius both achieves continuity of imagery, and sustains the progression of his argument. The other examples are found in the earlier poems: the succession of night and day; Evening and Morning star appearing at irregular, if patterned times, and invariably announcing nightfall and dawn. The generalizing lines 16ff. celebrate the perpetuity of this 'mutual love' (*alternus amor*) of parts of the universe for each other,[220] and these generalizing lines mark off the first part of the poem, and their sentiment is repeated in its closing lines (44ff.), just as in the earlier 2 m. 8, lines 13ff. both divide the poem into its two parts and are reiterated in lines 28ff. The nature images put forward in this first part of 4 m. 6 stress the harmony that is discerned in irregular but ordered processes: line 13 ('with fair [*aequis*] changes of time') suggests a natural order that is equitable rather than one that is strictly regular and repetitive without variation. This *concordia discors* in nature is emphasized still further in lines 19ff. on the elements, where the 'warring' (*pugnantia*, 20) opposites of wet and dry, and cold and hot, achieve a concord that, again, is said to ensue *aequis ... modis* (19f.). So the due proportion (*temperies*, 30) found in nature is a hard-won unity: the cosmic charioteer must exercise control (*cogat*, 41) to guide the ordered motion of a potentially chaotic universe, which would not subsist without that control (39ff.).[221] The notion that universal harmony is the harmony of disparate, even opposing, entities is found in earlier poems,[222] but here it is sustained throughout the poem, and, since the theme is divine providence, it is appropriate that the sustaining power of God should be the emphasis upon which the poem concludes.

Lines 25ff. are the last expression of the seasons theme in the work. They are an example of the virtuoso attempt to evoke all four seasons in four to five lines:[223]

> his de causis vere tepenti
> spirat florifer annus odores,
> aestas cererem fervida siccat,
> remeat pomis gravis autumnus,
> hiemem defluus inrigat imber.

[219] Chamberlain (1970) 89.   [220] Cf. 2 m. 8.17, 29f.
[221] See pp. 150f. above.
[222] See p. 164 above.
[223] See pp. 114ff. above.

Through these causes in warm spring the flowering year emits its scents,
the summer heat dries the corn, autumn rich in fruit returns, winter is
wet as the rain pours down.

The individual detail of these lines is less vivid and striking than that
of the seasons motif in the second, fifth, and sixth poems of Book 1. But
Boethius is not concerned here to suggest the distinctive qualities of
the seasons. Rather he is stressing the ordered succession of opposites,
pleasant, flowering, and fruitful spring and autumn, succeeded
respectively by the burning heat of the summer and winter rains. A
rapid succession of the a–b–a–b type is called for, and that is what
Boethius provides. The seasons are purely emblematic.[224]

(v) Book 5

The theme of the first poem in the fifth book is anticipated in a single
phrase of its preceding prose section. That section has been a
discussion of the nature of chance occurrences, which concludes with
the definition:

> Chance may therefore be defined as an unexpected occurrence through
> the confluence of causes in those things done for some purpose
> (5.1.18).[225]

The metaphor of confluent causes leads into the theme of 5 m. 1, which
exploits the belief (known in antiquity to be false as early as
Herodotus) that the rivers Tigris and Euphrates rise from one and the
same source. Consequences of their confluence are imagined:

> *si coeant cursumque iterum revocentur in unum,*
> *   confluat alterni quod trahit unda vadi,*
> *convenient puppes et vulsi flumine trunci*
> *   mixtaque fortuitos implicet unda modos ...* (5ff.).[226]

[224] Cumont (n. 92 above) discusses the motif of the seasons in Roman funerary art, and
its possible links with ideas of rebirth (as expressed, for example, in Seneca, *Ep.* 36.11
[quoted p. 159 above]), and, in Christian contexts, with belief in resurrection. See further
Hanfmann (n. 16 above), and P. Kranz, *Jahreszeiten-Sarkophage. Entwicklung und
Ikonographie des Motivs der vier Jahreszeiten auf kaiserzeitlichen Sarkophagen und
Sarkophagendeckeln* (Die antiken Sarkophagenreliefs 5.4, Berlin 1984), an important
study that extends and corrects Hanfmann in many respects. Comparison of the
iconographical attributes of the individual seasons on the sarcophagi (see Hanfmann
1.134ff.; Kranz 119ff.) with Boethius confirms that Boethius is not influenced by artistic
antecedents, but rather by the Latin poetic tradition (see pp. 112ff. above). Moreover, the
function of the motif is different in Boethius and in the artistic tradition: in Boethius the
seasons reinforce the themes of order, patterned variety, and harmony of opposites; on
the sarcophagi they are (in the second century AD) nature-personifications, and later
symbols of apotheosis, as Kranz has demonstrated.

[225] Cf. 5.1.19: *concurrere ... atque confluere causas.*

[226] On *modos* (8) meaning 'appearances' see *TLL* 8.1, 1268 (post-Classical).

.If they were to come together, and be brought back into one course, and if what the water of each river carries in its flow were to unite, ships will meet, and tree trunks uprooted by the river, and their waters, now mixed, will blend appearances ruled by chance.

These lines have caused difficulties. The conditional sentence is a future condition of the less vivid kind, in which the protasis merely supposes something to be the case, and the apodosis expresses what would follow. Here, however, the change of mood to indicative in the apodosis brings home the vividly imagined consequence of the supposed confluence of the two rivers, in a way that says nothing about the realization of the condition.[227] It is thus unlikely that Boethius is referring to the actual confluence of the two rivers to form what is now the Shatt al-Arab, flowing into the Persian Gulf. We need not, therefore, speculate on the nature of this confluence in antiquity, and the information which ancient writers had about it.[228] The progress of thought of the poem is on these lines: 'The Tigris and Euphrates flow from the same source and separate. If they were to flow together again, ships and treetrunks on each river will mingle. Although this latter would seem to be the result of chance, it is in fact a consequence of the slope of the terrain and the nature of downflowing water. It is thus the consequence of laws, even if it appears to be a random process.' This interpretation leaves open the question of whether Boethius is actually referring to the real confluence of the rivers, though the subjunctives of 5f. make this less likely. The poem[229] gives a more explicit statement to the idea that apparently random processes are governed by laws – an idea found in the poems 4 m. 5 and 6 – and do not undermine the notion of order in the universe. Its imagery (especially *habenis* [11] and *frenos* [12], recalling the charioteer motif) refers back to the earlier poems, as do the abstract terms *ordo* (10) and *lex* (12). A likely poetic antecedent (and one who speculates similarly on the hypothesis of the two rivers joining) is Lucan:

> ... *quaque caput rapido tollit cum Tigride magnus*
> *Euphrates, quos non diversis fontibus edit*
> *Persis, et incertum, tellus si misceat amnes,*
> *quod potius sit nomen aquis* (3.256ff.).

[227] Cf. AG 516b.

[228] Gruber (1978) 382 is right to warn against over-interpretation of the lines, as in Scheible (1972) 157f., but he, too, assumes that they refer to the actual confluence of the two rivers. O'Donnell (1984) 245 is nearer the truth, though he reads into the lines something that is not there, namely a reference to 'an order in nature that keeps them from joining again (an event whose results would be chaotic)'.

[229] On its epigram-form see Scheible (1972) 157 n. 2: thus, despite its elegiac metre, it is not a parallel to 1 m. 1.

... and the land where the mighty Euphrates and rushing Tigris uplift their heads. They rise in Persia from springs not far apart; and, if earth suffered them to meet, who can say which of the names the waters would bear? (tr. Duff).

In the discussion of free will in 5.2 the theme of light and darkness is again exploited,[230] and it is this motif that is then developed in the ensuing poem. The opening line is an adaption of a Homeric verse[231] much favoured by the Neoplatonists, but the poem as a whole gathers together and repeats themes and images of earlier metra, especially the motif of the physical sun's inferiority to the 'true sun' (14) who is the divine creator (7). It thus reiterates what a poem like 3 m. 10 explored.[232] The final lines of 5 m. 2 (13f.) repeat the etymological pun, found in Varro and Cicero,[233] that derives *sol* from *solus*:

> *quem quia respicit omnia solus*
> *verum possis dicere solem.*

Him you could call the true sun (*solem*), because he alone (*solus*) sees everything.

The prose section that follows, 5.3, elaborates an important vexed question: how can freedom of the will be compatible with divine providence, and especially with divine foreknowledge? Both seem necessary if God is to be supreme and supremely good, if divine rewards and punishments are to make sense, and if there is to be contact on the part of humans with God through prayer. In a unique reference back to an earlier poem, the prisoner concludes that if free will and providence are not reconciled, then, as 4 m. 6.40ff. imagined, things would indeed fall apart (5.3.36).

The mood of *aporia* dominates the next poem, 5 m. 3, whose first 21 lines are a striking series of questions. The poem is spoken by the prisoner, the first to be so since 1 m. 5. It is in the same metre as that earlier poem, and commentators are right to see in it, as in 4 m. 6, a counterpart to the earlier poem. In an earlier discussion of 5 m. 3 it has been suggested that it is not the clear-cut, positive counterpart to the questionings of 1 m. 5 that is often assumed, but rather that it gives only a partial answer to the questions of the opening lines, and one that must be massively supplemented by Philosophy's exposition of the

---

[230] See pp. 190f. below.
[231] See p. 69 above.
[232] See pp. 165ff. above.
[233] Varro, *De lingua latina* 5.68; Cicero, *nat. deor.* 2.27.68 (see Pease ad loc.).

answer to this dilemma in the remainder of Book 5.[234] The partial answer of 5 m. 3 is to refer the *aporiai* to the phenomenon of forgetting, which is, in Platonic manner, said never to be total, and so always susceptible to recollection (22ff.). This reference back to earlier parts of the work is sustained by the use of key terms and metaphors. The light-dark symbolism, complete with clouds, occurs (8f., 15, 22), as do references to *foedera rerum* (1). The evocation of 'wars' (*bella*), 3) among arguments, and the notion of the *amor* (11) that drives men on to knowledge, are not direct echoes of the love-strife themes of 2 m. 8 and other poems, but the words nevertheless suggest the notions of universal concord and its possible destruction, which, as has been seen, are recalled in 5.3.36. Moreover, it is precisely the *amor* for knowledge that is striving to make the imagined order of things rationally acceptable and comprehensible, to make warring truths (3) compatible, and to see them as parts of a whole (21).[235] Lerer is thus correct to suggest that 5 m. 3 marks the internalization of the problems of the work: it is the mind and its powers that are now the focus of attention, here and in 5 m. 4.[236] Both Lerer and Gruber note the abstract language of the poem 5 m. 3.[237] But it should not be forgotten that the focus on problems of knowledge and understanding is ultimately in the service of a theory of the universe and its harmony. The reference in 20f. to the human mind's vision of the supreme mind of God is not merely to an intellectual process, but to the metaphysical basis of the universe's physical structure.[238]

The sequence from 5.4 to the end of 5.5 deals with the cognitive degrees of perception, imagination, and knowledge, and ends with an evocation of the capabilities of human reason, which can, under certain circumstances, attain the level of divine reason (5.5.12). The following poem, 5 m. 5, the last in the work, celebrates that human capability. It does so through the topos of the distinction between man's upright stance and the downcast faces (9) of other creatures. The topos is a commonplace of exhortatory philosophical literature since Xenophon.[239] Thus, at the end of the work, Boethius casts traditional popular philosophical motifs into verse, using the priamel-form in 1ff. to point the human-animal contrast.[240] Ovid is a poetic forerunner:

---

[234] See pp. 40f. above. Cf. Scheible (1972) 162; Lerer (1985) 220ff.; Curley (1987) 363ff.

[235] See Gruber (1978) 394f.

[236] Lerer (1985) 226.

[237] Lerer (1985) 224; Gruber (1978) 393.

[238] Cf. 4.6.15: see Gruber (1978) 358. On the cycle of abiding-procession-reversion in Neoplatonic metaphysics see R.T. Wallis, *Neoplatonism* (London 1972) 132f.

[239] Xenophon, *Memorabilia* 1.4.11; cf. Pease on Cicero, *nat. deor.* 2.56.140.

[240] On the priamel-form see Nisbet/Hubbard 1.2f.; Fraenkel (Ch. 5, n. 97 below) on Aeschylus, *Agamemnon* 899-902; W.H. Race, *The Classical Priamel from Homer to Boethius* (Mnemosyne Supplement 74, Leiden 1982).

pronaque cum spectent animalia cetera terram,
os homini sublime dedit, caelumque videre
iussit et erectos ad sidera tollere vultus (Met. 1.84ff.).

And, though all other animals are prone, and fix their gaze upon the earth, he gave to man an uplifted face and bade him stand erect and turn his eyes to heaven (tr. Miller).[241]

But it is striking to observe how Boethius adapts the motif to the specifically Platonic themes of ascent, transcendence, and mental vision:

haec, nisi terrenus male desipis, ammonet figura:
qui recto caelum vultu petis exserisque frontem,
in sublime feras animum quoque, ne gravata pessum
inferior sidat mens corpore celsius levato (12ff.).

This form should teach you, if you are not completely stupid through being earthbound, you who seek the sky with straining look and stretch your head up, you should also drive your mind high, that it may not be weighed down and sink deep, lower than the body raised up high.

Lerer perceptively links this aspect of the poem to the themes of transcendental aspiration and ascent of the Orpheus poem (3 m. 12).[242] But he is less convincing when he sees both as finales. 3 m. 12 is indeed the finale and climax of Book 3, but 5 m. 5 is the verse prelude to the final great argument, in prose, of 5.6, which reconciles the conflict of free will and divine foreknowledge, and to which there is no poetic conclusion.[243] We should not exploit this ending as a comment on the final status of verse, or metaphor, in the *Consolation*: after all, the later poems of the work have demonstrated how some of the profoundest problems of philosophy can be explored in verse. And even if 5 m. 5 is not a finale in Lerer's sense, it does subsume some of the work's central themes: man is no mere earthly creature, his origin and goal are heavenly, he must free himself from earthly concerns and so find true happiness and recall what is truly good. At the end, it is the privileged status of humanity in the natural world that Boethius stresses, but it is a status that can only be exercised and realized voluntarily, by the will's direction of reason to its proper objects.

[241] See Scheible (1972) 170.

[242] Lerer (1985) 227.

[243] On the question of whether this is an indication of the work's incomplete state see the discussion on pp. 28f. above.

CHAPTER FIVE

The Nature and Function
of the Mythical Motifs

Allusions to, or elaborations of, specific myths are a staple feature of
Greek and Roman poetry, particularly in its lyric forms. Myths used as
paradigms may illustrate and reinforce the general moral reflection
and evaluation that is characteristic of much poetry in antiquity. It is,
therefore, somewhat surprising that Boethius in the *Consolation* is
sparing in his use of mythical motifs. There are only three mythical
allusions in the prose parts of the work: one to the attack of the Giants
upon the gods, seen both as a symbol of the clash of arguments that can
lead to truth and of the repulsion of evil by the strength of goodness
(3.12.24f.); another to the Hydra's sprouting of new heads, compared to
the way in which new doubts and difficulties arise when one has solved
others in dealing with such important and intractable topics as
providence and fate (4.6.3); and a third to Hercules' killing of Busiris,
an example of the tyrant's susceptibility to the fate which he metes out
to others (2.6.10).

That there are so few allusions in the *prosae* is not surprising. But
Boethius is no more lavish in the poems. Apart from passing references
to Phoebus (usually equivalent to the sun), the Muses, or Bacchus' gift
of wine,[1] there is elaboration of mythical themes in four poems only:
the Golden Age motif in 2 m. 5, Orpheus' descent into the underworld
in 3 m. 12, Circe and the companions of Odysseus in 4 m. 3, and
Agamemnon, Odysseus, and Hercules in 4 m. 7. Yet the significance of
these poems must not be underestimated. They are placed at
important junctures in the work. They summarize and anticipate some
of its central themes. Finally, they relate those themes to the tradition
of which Boethius sees himself as a part: a tradition of Greek and
Roman reflective poetry, but also of the allegorical exegesis practised

---

[1] Phoebus: 1 m. 3.9; 2 m. 3.1; 2 m. 8.5; 3 m. 10.18; 3 m. 11.8; 4 m. 1.10, etc. Muses: 1 m.
1.3; 1.1.7ff.; 3 m. 11.15. Bacchus: 2 m. 5.6f.; cf. 1 m. 6.15. See also 1 m. 6.5 (Ceres); 2 m.
8.8 and 4 m. 5.10 (Phoebe).

in the Hellenistic philosophical schools as well as by the Neoplatonists.
The four poems will be examined in detail in turn, and then some
general conclusions about Boethius' use of myths will be drawn.

(i) The Golden Age (2 m. 5)

Felix nimium prior aetas
contenta fidelibus arvis
nec inerti perdita luxu,
facili quae sera solebat
ieiunia solvere glande.   5
non Bacchica munera norant
liquido confundere melle
nec lucida vellera Serum
Tyrio miscere veneno.
somnos dabat herba salubres,   10
potum quoque lubricus amnis,
umbras altissima pinus.
nondum maris alta secabat
nec mercibus undique lectis
nova litora viderat hospes.   15
tunc classica saeva tacebant
odiis neque fusus acerbis
cruor horrida tinxerat arva.
quid enim furor hosticus ulla
vellet prior arma movere,   20
cum vulnera saeva viderent
nec praemia sanguinis ulla?
utinam modo nostra redirent
in mores tempora priscos!
sed saevior ignibus Aetnae   25
fervens amor ardet habendi.
heu, primus quis fuit ille
auri qui pondera tecti
gemmasque latere volentes
pretiosa pericula fodit?   30

Happy indeed that earlier age, content with trusty fields, not ruined by
sluggish extravagance, accustomed to still hunger that was slow to come
with acorns readily available (5). They did not know how to mix the gifts
of Bacchus with clear honey, or to dip shining silken cloth in Tyrian dye.
They slept healthily on the grass (10), the flowing stream provided drink,
the tall pine shade. As yet no one cut through deep seas, or with
merchandise gathered from all over, looked, a stranger, upon foreign
shores (15). The battle trumpet was still silent then; blood shed in bitter
hate had not yet stained the rough ground. For why should anyone in
mad hostility want to be the first to brandish arms (20), when men could
see the savage wounds to come, and no recompense for blood? If only our
times might go back to the old ways! But fiercer than Etna's flames
(25) blazes the burning lust to possess. Ah, who was the first to dig up

heavy masses of hidden gold, and gems longing to remain hidden – those precious dangers? (30)

At first sight, this poem displays a striking lack of originality. Boethius evokes the Golden Age in topoi familiar to readers of the Augustan poets Virgil, Horace, Ovid, and Tibullus. So embedded is the poem in that tradition that it comes as a surprise when its closing lines (28ff.) echo those of Boethius' North African contemporary Dracontius:

viscera non terrae tantum pretiosa *metallum*
servarent, abstrusa nimis nec gemma lateret (*De laudibus dei* 2.459f.).

The rich bowels of the earth would not hold on to so much precious metal, nor would gems, deeply buried, lie hidden.

It is not inconceivable that Boethius may have known Dracontius' Christian poem, in which paradise before the Fall is depicted in familiar Golden Age terms (perpetual spring, trees flowing with honey and medicines, ib. 1.167ff.). But Boethius' poem does not employ these pictures, nor is there any Christian dimension to it. The life which he breathes into the tired clichés of the Golden Age theme is distantly related to the atmosphere of Dracontius' poem, but it is essentially a distinct life, with its own vividness.

Boethius' poem is characteristically Roman, in that it merges the historical myth of a Golden Age with the idealized depiction of primitive rural life. These two elements are linked in such different poems as Virgil's Fourth *Eclogue* and the *Georgics*, Horace's Second and Sixteenth *Epodes*, Propertius 4.1, and Tibullus 1.3 and 2.5.[2] It is misguided to attempt to distinguish them,[3] for it was quite natural for the rurally-based Roman consciousness of the late Republic and early Augustan age, torn by social, economic, and political revolution, to look back, with a mixture of nostalgia and moral concern, to the purported qualities of its ancestors, qualities which seemed essential to the renewal of contemporary society. The Hesiodic myth of a Golden Race (*Works and Days* 109ff.) and especially the Hellenistic version of Aratus (*Phaenomena* 105ff.), where Golden Age farmers work the

[2] On the Golden Age myth and motif see B. Gatz, *Weltalter, goldene Zeit und sinnverwandte Vorstellungen* (Spudasmata 16. Hildesheim 1967); K. Kubusch, *Aurea Saecula: Mythos und Geschichte. Untersuchungen eines Motivs in der antiken Literatur bis Ovid* (Studien zur klassischen Philologie 28, Frankfurt/Berne 1986); cf. the fundamental study of A.O. Lovejoy/G. Boas, *Primitivism and Related Ideas in Antiquity* (Baltimore, Md. 1935). On the motif in individual poets see P.A. Johnston, *Vergil's Agricultural Golden Age: A Study of the Georgics* (Mnemosyne Supplement 60, Leiden 1980); J.J.L. Smolenaars, 'Labour in the Golden Age: A Unifying Theme in Vergil's Poems', *Mnemosyne* 40 (1987) 391-405; M. Wifstrand Schiebe, *Das ideale Dasein bei Tibull und die Goldzeitkonzeption Vergils* (Diss. Uppsala 1981); Williams (1968) 275ff. (on Virgil's Fourth *Eclogue*); E.R. Dodds, *The Ancient Concept of Progress* (Oxford 1973) 1-25.
[3] As Scheible (1972) 59 does. Contrast Ford (1967) 46f.

earth (106, 111f.), will have both encouraged and helped to articulate such speculation.[4] Furthermore, Roman poets reflect a variant of the myth, in which the Golden Age is not the first stage of human history, but rather a period of civilized agricultural life in Latium under the rule of Saturn, following upon a brutish and uncivilized period.[5] This variant form of the myth may be influenced by Greek philosophical adaptations of the Golden Age motif, in which it evokes the earliest phase, not of human history, but of civilization proper. Thus it is not surprising to find the motif occurring in Augustan and Imperial political literature, where the coming of a new Golden Age is either predicted (for example, in Virgil's Fourth *Eclogue* or *Aeneid* 6.791ff.) or said to be realized already.

The blending of elements of the Golden Age idyll with a depiction of the life of idealized contemporary rustics[6] is especially evident in the finale of the second book of Virgil's *Georgics*:

> *O fortunatos nimium, sua si bona norint,*
> *agricolas! quibus ipsa procul discordibus armis*
> *fundit humo facilem victum iustissima tellus.*
> ...
> *alba neque Assyrio fucatur lana veneno*
> ...
> *at secura quies et nescia fallere vita,*
> *dives opum variarum, at latis otia fundis,*
> *speluncae vivique lacus, at frigida tempe*
> *mugitusque boum mollesque sub arbore somni*
> *non absunt ... (Georgics* 2.458ff.).

> How lucky, if they know their happiness,
> Are farmers, more than lucky, they for whom,
> Far from the clash of arms, the earth herself,
> Most fair in dealing, freely lavishes
> An easy livelihood.
> ...
>   wool
> Is white, not tainted with Assyrian poison
> ...
> Yet peace they have and a life of innocence
> Rich in variety; they have for leisure
> Their ample acres, caverns, living lakes,

[4] On Hesiod see M.L. West (ed.), *Hesiod: Works and Days* (Oxford 1978) 172ff. On Aratus' *Phaenomena* see N. Hopkinson (ed.), *A Hellenistic Anthology* (Cambridge 1988) 136ff. Cf. Virgil, *Georgics* 1.118ff.; 2.458ff. with Thomas (1988) 1.87ff., 244ff. (and index s.v. 'golden/Saturnian age').

[5] Virgil, *Aeneid* 8.314ff. On this idealized Saturnian Age see also Tibullus 1.3.35ff.; Ovid, *Fasti* 2.289ff.; *Amores* 3.8.35ff.; *Met.* 1.113 (see the whole section 89-112 for the Golden Age theme). Cf. *Met.* 15.96ff.

[6] These rustics are not the 'real' farmer of the *Georgics*, as Thomas (1988) 1.244f. points out.

Cool Tempês; cattle low, and sleep is soft
Under a tree ... (tr. Wilkinson).

The typical Golden (and Silver) Age motif of Justice dwelling among
such people is alluded to by Virgil (ib. 473f.): this kind of life was the
life already lived by the Sabines, by Romulus and Remus, the
Etruscans, and the early Romans, but also the life of the Golden Age
(532ff.). It is, by implication, accessible and realizable, if only one
abstracts oneself from the extravagance, desires, and ambitions of
urban life (495ff.). In other words, the Golden Age dream and idealized
primitivism are not merely retrospective and nostalgic. They are
related in some way to the contemporary situation. In the *Georgics* the
apparent conflict between the idyll of 2.458ff. and the post-Saturnian
age of Jupiter, dominated by work (*labor*), which is the real
agricultural world of the poem, is problematic. But the emphasis given
by Virgil to the rustic ideal suggests that it is not pure fantasy. If an
Augustan poet wishes to project a dreamlike vision, one that is to be a
fantasy and no more, of an ideal society, then Horace's use of the theme
of the Islands of the Blest in *Epode* 16 shows that a distinctive kind of
description was available. And in both cases the key element is concern
with the reasons for degeneration from an ideal state: what moral
defects have led to present violence and destruction? What explicit or
implicit moral reforms could lead to a regeneration of society and the
individuals in it? The function of the Golden Age motif in Augustan
poetry, whether it remains a fantastic ideal or (more usually) becomes
a model for social change, is constant: description of an ideal is both a
criterion by which to measure present ills and deficiencies, and a
means of establishing the failings which have led to the present,
experienced state.

The moral dimension of a descriptive myth of the Golden Age, or of a
sequence of ages, is already present in Hesiod, where the hubris and
impiety of the Silver race, and its inability to avoid crime because of
the way it is formed by its divine makers, are stressed (*Works and
Days* 134ff.). Aratus, despite the Stoic elements in his *Phaenomena*,
does not develop the moral aspects of the Golden Age theme in any
specifically philosophical way.[7] But the myth was clearly susceptible to
such exploitation, as its uses in later Stoicism, especially in Posidonius
and Seneca, show.[8]

To return to Boethius' poem. The commentators have established
that it is indebted, in its choice of phrasing and topoi, to several

[7] For a radical philosophical exploitation of the myth see Plato, *Politicus* 271ff.; cf. J.B.
Skemp, *Plato's Statesman* (London 1952) 82-111; W.K.C. Guthrie, *A History of Greek
Philosophy* 5 (Cambridge 1978) 193-6.
[8] See pp. 187f. below. Aristotle's pupil Dicaearchus propounded the notion of a
primitive, historical, idealized Golden Age: frr. 48f. Wehrli.

antecedents, in particular to Virgil's *Georgics*. The delights of drinking fresh water, a detail in Boethius (11), but not in Virgil or Horace, may betray the influence of Hippolytus' description of the Golden Age in Seneca's *Phaedra* (510ff.), where the motif occurs: *quam iuvat nuda manu / captasse fontem!* ('How delightful it is to grasp spring water with bare hands!', 519f.).[9] But, even if present idyll and vision of Golden Age past merge in Seneca's version, as in Virgil, Boethius' language is strikingly different from Seneca's. In fact, the force of Boethius' poem does not derive from explicit dependence upon any one source, or group of sources. He ranges through the entire spectrum of themes associated with the topos. The choice of detail, and the degree of emphasis placed upon it, are determined by the economy of the poem, by the general tendency in it to include only potentially realistic themes and details and eschew magical elements (multicoloured sheep[10] are absent, for example, and the theme of peace is the extended climax [16-22] of the description of the Golden Age),[11] and especially by the desire to establish explicit links with the preceding prose section.

To take the last point first. At the beginning of 2.5 Lady Philosophy indicates that she is resorting to 'stronger medicines' in her cure of the patient Boethius. There follows a detailed demonstration of the worthlessness of wealth. Gold, money, jewels, and clothes are discussed and dismissed: nature provides what humans need for their sustenance, and everything over and above that is superfluous (2.5.15f.). These themes provide the framework for the following Golden Age poem, in which the dangers of gold and gems are stressed (27ff.), expensive, dyed fabrics are spurned (7f.), men avoid extravagance (3), are not gluttonous (4f.), but make proper use of the earth's natural features and products for nourishment, shelter, and refreshment (2ff., 10ff.), avoiding such perversions of natural products as wine mixed with honey. The men of the Golden Age use nature appropriately and realize the potential of their human nature. They exemplify what the preceding prose passage describes in general terms (see especially 2.5.24ff.). The poem is an extended *exemplum* of the antecedent argument. The greed (*avaritia*) identified there as a hateful phenomenon associated with wealth (2.5.4) is one with the poem's 'burning lust to possess' (*fervens amor ... habendi*, 26). The phrasing and sentiment are almost a cliché of Roman poetic moralizing:

aurea quae perhibent illo sub rege fuere
saecula: sic placida populos in pace regebat,
deterior donec paulatim ac decolor aetas

[9] Cf. Lucretius 1.927f.: *iuvat integros accedere fontis / atque haurire ...* .
[10] Cf. Virgil, *Ecl.* 4.42ff. Ovid sometimes criticizes or mocks the mystique of the Golden Age: *Ars amatoria* 2.277f.; 3.113f.; *Fasti* 1.193ff.
[11] See Fraenkel (1957) 52 n. 1 on the links between the Golden Age and peace motifs.

et belli rabies et amor successit habendi (Virgil, *Aen.* 8.324ff.).

His reign was the period called in legend the Golden Age,
So peacefully serene were the lives of his subjects. It lasted
Till, little by little, the time grew tarnished, an age of baser
Metal came in, of mad aggression and lust for gain (tr. Day Lewis).

Ovid's account of the decline from the Golden and Silver Ages to the
Bronze Age is fuller in its use of moral terms:

... fugere pudor verumque fidesque;
in quorum subiere locum fraudesque dolique
insidiaeque et vis et amor sceleratus habendi (*Met.* 1.129ff.).

Modesty and truth and faith fled the earth, and in their place came
tricks, and plots, and snares, violence and cursed love of gain (tr. Miller).

Even Virgil's bees are not free from acquisitiveness:

non aliter, si parva licet componere magnis,
Cecropias innatus apes amor urget habendi
munere quamque suo (*Georgics* 4.176ff.).

Just so (if small may be compared with great)
Innate acquisitiveness impels the bees
To ply their several tasks (tr. Wilkinson).[12]

For Boethius, greed (*avaritia*), in the words of the preceding prose
passage of the *Consolation*, 'makes people hated' (2.5.4), and makes a
man, hungry for another's possessions (*alieni ... avidus*), think that he
should possess all the gold and jewels available (2.5.33).

Boethius' Golden Age poem ends with a vivid picture of the 'precious
dangers' (30) of gold and gems. It is not surprising that Roman poets
seized upon the apt image of tempting gold in their accounts of a moral
decline from primitive, ideal standards. Ovid describes the pernicious
effects of gold (and iron) thus:

effodiuntur opes, inritamenta malorum.
iamque nocens ferrum ferroque nocentius aurum
prodierat ... (*Met.* 1.140ff.).

Wealth ... was brought to light, wealth that pricks men on to crime. And
now baneful iron had come, and gold more baneful than iron ... (tr.
Miller).

On the peace theme in the Greek and Roman traditions see H. Fuchs, *Augustin und der
antike Friedensgedanke* (Berlin 1926, reprinted Berlin/Zürich 1965) 96-138, 167-248; a
recent discussion of the iconographical traditions is E. Simon, *Eirene und Pax.
Friedensgöttinnen in der Antike* (Stuttgart 1988).
[12] Cf. Ovid, *Ars amatoria* 3.541; *Fasti* 1.195; Horace, *Epist.* 1.7.85; Prudentius,
Psychomachia 478.

And Propertius:

> *aurum omnes victa iam pietate colunt.*
> *auro pulsa fides, auro venalia iura,*
> *aurum lex sequitur, mox sine lege pudor* (3.13.48ff.).

Everybody worships gold, piety is now defeated. Trust is driven out by gold, justice is on sale for gold, law falls a victim to gold, and soon decency follows, when there is no law.

The Christian poet Prudentius is in the same tradition:

> *pudor per aurum solvitur,*
> *violatur auro integritas,*
> *pax occidit, fides perit,*
> *leges et ipsae intercidunt* (*Peristef.* 2.197ff.).

Decency is destroyed by gold, innocence is corrupted by gold, peace dies, trust perishes, and the very laws are ruined.[13]

On the other hand, it is perhaps surprising that Roman poets appear to have sensed no contradiction between the term 'Golden Age' and the idea of the corrupting power of gold (except where, as occasionally in Ovid – for example, *Fast.* 1.193ff. – the term is used ironically).[14] In 2 m. 5 Boethius does not refer to the idealized primitive age as 'golden', but that may be because of the economy of his style rather than from any sense of contradiction between terminology and *exemplum*.

The *amor habendi* of line 26 of the Golden Age poem is a negative love, misguided as is the *amor* of Orpheus for Eurydice (3 m. 12.48). The characteristic condition of those who have abandoned the moderation of the Golden Age is one of perversion of the naturally good: *saevus* ('savage', 'raging') is a key word of the poem (16, 21, 25), applied appropriately to the *amor ... habendi* in 25f. For, on the scale of values proposed by Boethius, a wrong human desire is more destructive than a natural force like volcanic Etna (25),[15] just as human moral failings degrade humans to a level below that of the animals (2.5.29). Humans, possessed of the greatest powers, are capable of the greatest damage. Once again, the full meaning of the poem can only be appreciated against the background of the antecedent prose section.

If nature is treated appropriately by humans, it will be responsive: the quasi-personification of nature at the beginning of the poem – the fields are 'trusty' (2), acorns make themselves 'readily available' (4f.) –

---

[13] Cf. [Seneca] *Octavia* 425ff. (where *auri fames* in line 425 echoes Virgil, *Aeneid* 3.57). For further instances see Bömer on Ovid, *Met.* 1.141.

[14] See Bömer's remarks on Ovid, *Met.* 1.89-112.

[15] Cf. 2.6.1.

stresses this, as does the oxymoron that describes the misuse of nature involved in excavation of gold and gems: 'precious dangers' (30). Nature will be as deadly as it can be beneficent.

To understand 2 m. 5 one must, therefore, read it in the argumentational context in which it is embedded. Boethius hints at the wider context of the early part of the *Consolation* when he describes extravagance as 'sluggish' (3) and so invokes in passing the prisoner's lethargic state of the work's outset, as that state was diagnosed by Philosophy (1.2.5). That is the condition, with its attendant moral implications and consequences, from which Philosophy's arguments should cure him, so that, freed from *amor habendi*, he may appropriate the message and aspire to the moral standing exemplified in the Golden Age topos.

Lerer suggests a different kind of contextual reading of 2 m. 5.[16] According to him, poems 3-6 of Book 2 'explore the precarious balance between natural forces and the human structures built to contain them'. He reads the poems as a sequence moving from the general to the specific: 'they recreate a history of civilization'. To a certain extent, this is an apt comment. The sequence (a) Golden Age, (b) age of cultivation, navigation, colonization, and war, (c) urban cultures and their decline, is found in poems 5 and 6. But the two earlier poems explore other themes: 2 m. 3 the law of mutability in nature, and its inevitable and menacing aspects; 2 m. 4 the human attempt to build upon such stability as nature provides. These poems are indeed complementary, but the house-building of 2 m. 4 is not part of a process of civilization in the sense envisaged by Lerer. It symbolizes the attempt to come to terms with a hostile nature. Boethius cannot intend the reader to imagine that this is in a pre-Golden-Age phase. For it is overwhelmingly characteristic of descriptions of the Golden Age that men did not then live in houses,[17] but rather in natural shelters, and this is also a feature of Boethius' account (2 m. 5.10ff.). Housing is an instance of Silver Age decline (Ovid, *Met.* 1.121f.). There is no indication that Boethius wishes to diverge from this norm. The sequence of poems 3-6 cannot be read as a chronology of civilization's purported progress. The themes of these poems are related, but not in a continuous sequence: rather, poems 3 and 4, and to a lesser extent poems 5 and 6, form two complementary pairs.[18]

[16] Lerer (1985) 115f.

[17] Aratus, *Phaenomena* 106 is an exception, but that is because his Golden Age is not an original state of the human condition, but a first form of civilized life in organized communities.

[18] Lerer (1985) 115f. argues that successive literary modes – pastoral, georgic, lyrical, historical – are explored in poems 3-6 of Book 2. But his arguments are unconvincing. There is, strictly speaking, no explicit pastoral element in these four lyric poems: the Golden Age theme is appropriate to pastoral, georgic, and lyric treatment, as the Roman poetic tradition shows. If we are to think of 2 m. 6 in generic terms, historical epic would

Boethius in 2 m. 5 is not merely adapting a poetic tradition; he is also reflecting a philosophical one. He reiterates what Seneca asserts. In his account of the decline of society from early philosophical perfection, Seneca, reporting Posidonius, writes:

> This state [of fellowship] remained intact for a while, before greed tore the community apart, and brought poverty even upon those whom it had made most rich (*Ep.* 90.3).

> Greed invaded an ideal state of affairs, and, desiring to set something aside and make it its own possession, it lost everything, and reduced itself from boundless wealth to dire straits. Greed admitted poverty, and, coveting much, lost everything (*Ep.* 90.38).[19]

The context is that of a Golden Age (now considered, as by the Peripatetic philosopher Dicaearchus, as the earliest phase of civilization) in which, Seneca reports, philosophers were kings (*Ep.* 90.5).[20] It is such an idyllic age that greed (*avaritia*) disrupts. Interestingly, Seneca attempts to demythologize such thinking in *Naturales quaestiones* 5.15. *Avaritia*, he writes there, is age-old: those idealized earlier generations practised mining (although he cannot proffer an instance much earlier than the time of Philip of Macedon), and greed was the spur, then as now. It is as if the myth simply expresses in historical narrative form a truth that is perpetually relevant: greed is an ever-recurrent perversion of human nature. In *Nat. quaest.* 5.15.4 Seneca gives vivid expression to this notion. The miners assume a living death:

> Does the earth lie as heavily on any of the dead as upon those over whom great greed has thrown a mass of earth, whom it has robbed of the sky, whom it has buried in the depths where that deadly poison lurks?

In the poets mining represents the infringement of a natural boundary:

> ... *itum est in viscera terrae:*
> *quasque recondiderat Stygiisque admoverat umbris,*
> *effodiuntur opes, inritamenta malorum* (Ovid, *Met.* 1.138ff.).

---

be the most appropriate genre to which it might be related. What these poems form is a thematic sequence that has traditionally been variously treated in different generic forms. Lerer appears to confuse them with genre, and to foist upon Boethius a degree of generic self-consciousness that the poems themselves do not warrant. Cf. Klingner (1921) 117f. on the blending of various genres in *Cons. phil.*

[19] Cf. ib. 8 and 36 (where the linking of *avaritia* and *luxuria* parallels *Cons. phil.* 2 m. 5.3 and 2.5.4).

[20] On Posidonian themes in *Ep.* 90 see W. Theiler, *Poseidonios: Die Fragmente* (Berlin/New York 1982) 2.384ff.

They delved as well into the very bowels of the earth; and the wealth which the creator had hidden away and buried deep amidst the very Stygian shades, was brought to light, wealth that pricks men on to crime (tr. Miller).

sed in parentis viscera intravit suae
deterior aetas; eruit ferrum grave
aurumque ... ([Seneca] *Octavia* 416ff.).

But a more degenerate age has penetrated into its parent's vitals; it has torn out heavy iron and gold ...

Boethius in his elliptic way suggests the same, when he speaks of 'gems longing to remain hidden' (29) which avid excavators exhume. What we have here, then, is not merely traditional castigation of inventors (27), but also the reference to the reason why they are to be castigated. Infringement of natural limits is the recipe for moral disaster.[21]

For Boethius, as for his predecessors in the Latin poetic tradition, the myth of the Golden Age embodies a timeless truth and ideal. The wish for a return to old ways (23f.) is none other than an appeal for moral regeneration that will ultimately be more beneficial for the individual than longing for wealth and its possession (2.5.32ff.). Read in conjunction with the prose 2.5 the Golden Age metrum reveals how historical myth can be adapted to, and in turn help to articulate, ethical diagnosis and exhortation.

(ii) Orpheus and Eurydice (3 m. 12)

Felix, qui potuit boni
fontem visere lucidum,
felix, qui potuit gravis
terrae solvere vincula.
quondam funera coniugis   5
vates Threicius gemens
postquam flebilibus modis
silvas currere mobiles,
amnes stare coegerat
iunxitque intrepidum latus   10
saevis cerva leonibus
nec visum timuit lepus
iam cantu placidum canem,
cum flagrantior intima
fervor pectoris ureret   15
nec qui cuncta subegerant
mulcerent dominum modi,
immites superos querens

---

[21] On *avaritia* as the source of manifold moral evils see Sallust, *Catilina* 10.3f., 11.3. For Augustine's use of the theme see e.g. *City of God* 5.12.

infernas adiit domos.
illic blanda sonantibus   20
chordis carmina temperans
quicquid praecipuis deae
matris fontibus hauserat,
quod luctus dabat impotens,
quod luctum geminans amor   25
deflet Taenara commovens
et dulci veniam prece
umbrarum dominos rogat.
stupet tergeminus novo
captus carmine ianitor;   30
quae sontes agitant metu
ultrices scelerum deae
iam maestae lacrimis madent;
non Ixionium caput
velox praecipitat rota   35
et longa site perditus
spernit flumina Tantalus;
vultur dum satur est modis
non traxit Tityi iecur.
tandem 'vincimur' arbiter   40
umbrarum miserans ait.
'donamus comitem viro
emptam carmine coniugem;
sed lex dona coherceat,
ne dum Tartara liquerit   45
fas sit lumina flectere.'
quis legem det amantibus?
maior lex amor est sibi.
heu, noctis prope terminos
Orpheus Eurydicen suam   50
vidit, perdidit, occidit.
vos haec fabula respicit
quicumque in superum diem
mentem ducere quaeritis;
nam qui Tartareum in specus   55
victus lumina flexerit,
quicquid praecipuum trahit
perdit dum videt inferos.

Blessed is he who can look upon the clear source of goodness; blessed he who can loosen the chains of heavy earth. Once upon a time the Thracian poet lamented his wife's death (5). He compelled the woods to run, the rivers to stand still, with his tearful measures. The deer stood fearlessly side by side (10) with savage lions. The hare was not afraid to look upon the dog, calm already because of his song. But the flame of grief still burned in the very depths of his heart (15), nor could the measures which had subdued all else soothe their master. Complaining of the god's relentlessness he went down to the house of the dead. There he tuned coaxing songs on the sounding lyre (20), all that inspiration drawn from his goddess mother's special springs. His lament fed on uncontrollable grief, on love that doubled grief (25): he moves the underworld, and with sweet supplication begs for indulgence from the rulers of the shadowy dead. The three-headed doorkeeper [Cerberus] is amazed, captivated by the unfamiliar song (30); the goddesses who terrify the guilty, the avengers of crime, grow sad and melt in tears. Ixion does not spin on the rapid wheel (35); and Tantalus, tortured by long thirst, refuses water. While the vulture is sated with song, it does not tear at Tityus' liver. At last, 'we are overcome,' the lord (40) of the shadowy dead declares in pity: 'we grant the husband his wife to go with him, purchased by his song. But let a law set limits to the gift: until he has left Tartarus (45) he may not turn his gaze.' Who could give a law to lovers? Love is a higher law unto itself. Ah, on the borders of night Orpheus saw his Eurydice (50), lost her, and was lost.

It is you this story concerns, you who are trying to guide your mind to the day above. For he who, defeated, turns his gaze towards the cave of Tartarus (55), loses the treasure that he carries when he looks to those below.

In 5.2 Philosophy, describing how human souls, possessed of free will, none the less surrender that freedom voluntarily, says:

But their lowest degree of slavery is when, given over to vice, they have lost possession of their own reason. For when they have lowered their eyes from the light of the highest truth to inferior, darker things, all at once they are surrounded by the gloomy cloud of ignorance, they are disturbed by deadly passions, by assenting and submitting to which they sustain that slavery which they have brought upon themselves, and are somehow prisoners through their own freedom (5.2.9f.).

The highest degree of human freedom is achieved in a disembodied state prior to the soul's fall into body, when the divine mind is contemplated (5.2.8). This divine mind is equated with the 'light of the highest truth', and to turn away from it under the influence of the passions (*affectus*) is to embrace darkness, an enslavement that is tantamount to losing one's human reason (*ratio*) and becoming animal-like.[22]

The tenor of this account of the soul's dehumanization is substantially Neoplatonic, though not exclusively so: the elements of psychological conflict (*ratio* and *affectus*), of descent into body, even the antithetical light-darkness symbolism, can be fund in Cicero and Seneca, in texts where a Platonically coloured Stoicism is influential.[23] But what is chiefly interesting in the present context is the relevance of 5.2.8-10 to the interpretation given by Boethius to the Orpheus myth.[24] In the Orpheus poem 3 m. 12 the mythical narrative is framed

[22] Cf. 4.3.16.
[23] Cf. e.g. Cicero, *Tusc. disp.* 1.29.71-31.75; 1.32.79-33.80; 3.10.22ff.; *De re publica* 6.15.15ff. Seneca, *Ep.* 65.16ff.; *Marc. cons.* 25f.; *De vita beata* 4ff.
[24] As Scheible (1972) 122 has observed.

by verses (1-4, 52-8) which provide it with an interpretative context. Blessedness (1,3) consists in vision of the good (1f.), in shaking off earthly bonds (3f.), and guiding one's mind to higher things (53). For whoever turns his attention to what is lower and is dominated by it loses what is most valuable (56f.). What this thing of value is becomes clear when 5.2.8-10 is read: it is reason, the chief and characteristic human faculty. Being 'defeated' (56) by the lower is falling into the 'enslavement' of 5.2.9f. What the poem provides is the positive counterpart to descent and enslavement, missing in 5.2. Escape is possible for the soul: and escape is return to, turning towards, the light of truth, is ascent to the higher. Although the motif of chains, and that of ascent from subterranean darkness into light, recall the Cave imagery of Plato's *Republic*, the particular constellation of images and symbols here is again essentially Neoplatonic, even if, once more, Cicero and Seneca are also antecedents.[25] For the purposes of interpreting this poem the following seems clear: Orpheus is in some sense a type of the fallen or descended soul, captivated by the lower, and failing to achieve ascent towards the light of truth. Boethius' Orpheus is an *Orphée moralisé* (52).

Boethius' Orpheus poem is not an allegory, in which the various persons and objects are the strict equivalents of psychological or mental qualities. His contemporary Fulgentius provided such an allegorical interpretation of the myth, in which Orpheus and Eurydice, whose names are interpreted etymologically, represent two aspects of music – words or sounds, and harmony (*Mitologiae* 3.10). Medieval interpretations of Boethius' poem also attempted to understand it allegorically, and to find what Eurydice symbolizes. In William of Conches, for example, she is taken to represent the passional faculty of the soul.[26] But such readings are not faithful to the poem's subtlety. If one is to look for an equivalent of Eurydice in this sense on the basis of what the poem actually says, then Eurydice is most plausibly the 'best part' (*praecipuum*, 57) of Orpheus, namely that which he is endeavouring to lead upwards from the underworld. But such an

---

[25] See Gruber (1978) 86ff., 286ff., 315, 319 for the Platonic tradition of these motifs, based on exegesis and elaboration of *Republic* 514a-518b. For Cicero see e.g. *De senectute* 21.77ff. (further references in Powell's comm. [Ch. 4, n. 16] ad loc.), and for Seneca see *Ep.* 92.30ff., 65.16ff.

[26] See J.B. Friedman, *Orpheus in the Middle Ages* (Cambridge, Mass. 1970) 180f.; W. Wetherbee, *Platonism and Poetry in the Twelfth Century. The Literary Influence of the School of Chartres* (Princeton, NJ 1972) 96-8. The medieval commentary-tradition has been made immeasurably more accessible to the non-specialist by the anthology and discussions in A.J. Minnis/A.B. Scott (edd.), *Medieval Literary Theory and Criticism c. 1100–c. 1375* (Oxford 1988): for Orpheus and Eurydice in William of Conches see ib. 121; for his interpretation of *Cons. phil.* 4 m. 3 see ib. 126-30; for William of Aragon's commentary on 3 m. 12, ib. 328-36 (here Eurydice is interpreted as 'good judgement', cf. ib. 320). See also J. Whitman, *Allegory: The Dynamics of an Ancient and Medieval Technique* (Oxford 1987) 117f. (there 112-21 on allegorical elements in *Cons. phil.*).

approach is misguided. It is Orpheus' quest for Eurydice, and the attitude which it implies, that forms for Boethius the link between the details of the myth and its general significance, as given in the framing verses of the poem's beginning and end. The poem, if it is not an allegory, may none the less be a parable, illustrating certain features of the human condition, and commenting on them in the context of the stage of the work now reached: the exposé of the nature of the Good, which is identical with true happiness, and is none other than the One God (5.10 onwards).

It has been suggested above that Orpheus, seen in the interpretative context of the poetic frame of 1ff. and 52ff., is understood by Boethius to be an object-lesson in failure – and this is undoubtedly the sense of the poem. But Orpheus' failure is complex, and includes considerable success. Orpheus is a paradoxical figure. His lament (7) for Eurydice can captivate nature (7-13), but cannot assuage his own grief (16f.). Similarly, in Hades his lament is no less powerful and influential, affecting Pluto (who, exceptionally, is moved to pity, 41) and Proserpina, Cerberus, the Dirae, and the trio of notorious sinners, Ixion, Tantalus, and Tityos (and even Tityos' vulture, 38). Pluto is 'overcome' (40) by his song, but Orpheus becomes, in his failure, typical of the soul 'overcome' (56) by its passions. For Orpheus is a victim of *amor* (14f., 47f.). His grief is uncontrolled (24), despite its being measured art (17, 20f., 38). It is lament swollen by passion (24f.), and so ultimately incapable of acquiescing in divine ordinances (the 'law' of 44ff.). But Orpheus the wondrous singer almost succeeds: he reaches the borders of darkness and light (49). His failure, though unequivocal, is not abject.

Although the interpretation of the Orpheus myth in the *Consolation* is dependent upon its philosophical context, Boethius, in the narrative part of the poem (5-51), draws upon, and moves within the ambit of, the Roman poetic tradition, and betrays variously the influence of Virgil, Horace, Ovid, and Seneca.[27] Like them, he selects and

---

[27] Virgil, *Georgics* 4.453ff.; Horace, *Odes* 1.12.7ff.; 1.24.13ff.; 3.11.13ff.; Ovid, *Met.* 10.1ff.; 11.1ff.; Seneca, *Medea* 625ff. (cf. ib. 348f., 358ff.); *Hercules furens* 569ff.; [Seneca] *Hercules Oetaeus* 1031ff.; cf. [Virgil] *Culex* 268ff. The modern literature on these texts is substantial: see (apart from the standard commentaries, of which Thomas [1988] is the newest on *Georg.*, and Bömer [on Ovid, *Met.*] an unsurpassed repertory of parallels and acute observation) esp. E. Norden, 'Orpheus and Eurydice. Ein nachträgliches Gedenkblatt für Vergil', *Sitzungsberichte der preussischen Akademie der Wissenschaften*, Phil.-hist. Klasse 22 (1934) 626-83 (reprinted in id., *Kleine Schriften* [Berlin 1966] 468-532); F. Klingner, *Virgils Georgica* (Zürich/Stuttgart 1963) 193-239 = id., *Virgil* (Zürich/Stuttgart 1967) 326-63; C. Segal, 'Orpheus and the Fourth *Georgic*: Vergil on Nature and Civilization', *American Journal of Philology* 87 (1966) 307-25; D.S. Wender, 'Resurrection in the Fourth *Georgic*', ib. 90 (1969) 424-36; J. Griffin, *Latin Poets and Roman Life* (London 1985) 163-82 (see the bibliography 163 n. 2); Nisbet/Hubbard 1.148ff., 286f.; C. Segal, 'Ovid's Orpheus and Augustan Ideology', *Transactions and Proceedings of the American Philological Association* 103 (1972) 473-94; W.S. Anderson,

highlights aspects of the story's details. While he devotes significant space to three aspects of the story – the enchantment of nature (5-13), the appeasement of the underworld (29-39), and the flawed return (40-51) – it is interesting to observe the gradual lengthening of each episode: the sequence is 9, then 11, then 12 verses, with the final section given dramatic vividness by the direct speech of Pluto, and the compressed tension, with climactic asyndeton, of the closing verses 49-51. By contrast, the first two sections are unremarkable catalogues in the tradition of Latin poetic treatments of their themes. While in no sense irrelevant to the interpretation of the poem (for, as has been said, they highlight the success-in-failure of Orpheus), they are clearly upstaged by the ending, which alone yields the full moral of the story. In a not dissimilar way, Virgil devotes 7 lines (*Georg.* 4.460-6) to laments for Eurydice, 18 lines to the descent into, and enchantment of, Hades (4.467-84), and 22 lines (4.485-506) to the flawed return, with, again, direct speech, this time by Eurydice, and vivid indirect speech by Orpheus (504-5). By contrast, Ovid devotes the major part of his account (with an elaborately argued speech by Orpheus) to the persuasion and enchantment of Hades (*Met.* 10.13-49 = 37 lines), and a smaller part (10.50-77 = 28 lines) to the flawed return and its immediate aftermath. But the closest parallel to Boethius in this respect is Seneca, *Hercules furens* 569-89. If one extrapolates the three descriptive parts there, as was done with the Boethius poem above, 3 lines (572-4) are devoted to the enchantment of nature, 5 lines to the enchantment of the underworld (577-81), and 8 lines (582-9) to the flawed return. And, as in Boethius, the final section is enlivened by Pluto's direct speech, with Seneca's *tandem mortis ait 'vincimur' arbiter* ('at last "we are overcome," the lord of death declares', 583) obviously echoed in Boethius (40f.). The terse ending of Seneca's account –

> *odit verus amor nec patitur moras:*
> *munus dum properat cernere, perdidit* (588f.)

> True love hates and does not suffer delays: while hastening to look upon his gift, he lost her

– clearly influences Boethius also (48-51). For Seneca's chorus, too, Orpheus is an *exemplum*, but of success, not failure. It is the power of

---

'The Orpheus of Virgil and Ovid: *flebile nescio quid*', in J. Warden (ed.), *Orpheus: The Metamorphoses of a Myth* (Toronto 1982) 25-50; C. Neumeister, 'Orpheus und Eurydike. Eine Vergil-Parodie Ovids (Ov. *Met.* X 1-XI 66 und Verg. *Georg.* IV 457-527)', *Würzburger Jahrbücher für die Altertumswissenschaft* N.F. 12 (1986) 169-81; Segal (1983) – this article, and those on Virgil and Ovid cited above, are now incorporated by Segal into *Orpheus: The Myth of the Poet* (Baltimore, Md. 1988); Fitch (1987) 268ff.; Crabbe (1981a); Lerer (1985) esp. 154ff. (on Seneca and Boethius).

his song to overcome the underworld (569f., 590) that can be an omen
for the success of Hercules' descent and use of strength (591). And so
Orpheus' failure, which Seneca can hardly omit, is restricted to two
lines (588f.), and is the consequence of 'true love' (588). In this last
respect, Boethius is closer to Virgil, whose Orpheus is a victim of the
madness of love (*dementia, Georg.* 4.488; *furor,* ib. 4.495), even if that
madness be pardonable (4.489). Like Virgil –

> *restitit, Eurydicenque suam iam luce sub ipsa*
> *immemor heu! victusque animi respexit* (*Georg.* 4.490f.)

> he halted
> And on the very brink of light, alas,
> Forgetful, yielding to his will, looked back
> At his own Eurydice (tr. Wilkinson) –

– Boethius stresses Orpheus' loss of control (56). But Ovid, like Seneca,
emphasizes the 'lov'd not wisely but too well' aspect:

> *iamque iterum moriens non est de coniuge quicquam*
> *questa suo (quid enim nisi se quereretur amatam?) ...* (*Met.* 10.60f.)

> And now, dying a second time, she made no complaint against her
> husband; for of what could she complain save that she was beloved? (tr.
> Miller)

It is evident, then, that Boethius engages with the Orpheus myth at
two levels. It is both a paradigm for the soul's fall and flawed return or
ascent, and at the same time it is a moral fable to be interpreted in the
terms current in the poetic tradition – the power of love, whether it be
flawed or 'true', the conflict of feeling and rational control, and so on.
The links of vocabulary, verbal echoes, and similarity of structure,
outlined above, make the relation of the poem to this second dimension
no less explicit than does the philosophical frame its significance at the
first level. In choosing an interpretation of Orpheus' fate that is
influenced chiefly by Virgil, but is more forthright in its condemnation
than Virgil's tragic account, Boethius recalls the different, but no less
bleak interpretation given in the pseudo-Senecan tragedy, *Hercules
Oetaeus* 1031ff.[28] This passage puts the Orpheus myth in a
philosophical context very different from that adduced by Boethius. In
it, Orpheus learns through bitter experience – like a hero of tragedy –
that everything is subject to change and nothing lasts forever (1035,
1099). He must lose Eurydice, because she too is subject to the cosmic
law of change (1093ff.) and so must die, even a second time: *quae nata
est iterum perit* ('she who was born dies a second time', 1089). In fact,

[28] On this play see Ch. 4, n. 23 above.

the cosmic law understood by Orpheus is equated with the Stoic notion of the conflagration of the universe (1102ff.), which ends in universal death and darkness (1115). Hercules' fate, at this stage of the play, seems to parallel that of Orpheus, for Hercules (like Orpheus in Boethius [*victus*, 56]) is overcome (*devictus*, 1101). Yet the outcome, ascent to the stars as the reward for Hercules' heroic *virtus*, seems to break, at least in this exceptional case, the cycle of decay and change. Hercules represents the overcoming of the underworld (*chaos*): *agnosco agnosco victum est chaos* ('I do admit, I do, that the underworld has been overcome', 1946). It was the same *chaos* that seemed to overwhelm even the gods in Orpheus' cosmic vision (1115). Hercules achieves what Orpheus fails to do. We are in a different world from that of Boethius' poem. Even Orpheus' turning to look back at Eurydice is not ascribed to the influence of love. He does indeed forget himself (*immemor*, 1085), but rather because he cannot believe that Eurydice is actually following him (1086f.), a motif found also in the mythographers. But certain parallels between the two versions of pseudo-Seneca and Boethius can none the less be drawn.

To begin with, both poems situate the Orpheus story in a philosophical context that involves a radical reinterpretation of the myth. The philosophical context in each case, as has been seen, is quite different. But there are striking similarities in exegetical technique. Furthermore, what in Boethius is a paradigm of failure, with a frame or context that suggests what success would involve,[29] is in the *Hercules Oetaeus* a kind of diptych, in which Orpheus also represents failure, but Hercules' apotheosis, a successful ascent, symbolizes victory, the victory of *virtus*:

> *numquam Stygias fertur ad umbras*
> *inclita virtus ...*
> *... iter ad superos gloria pandet* (*HO* 1983f., 1988).

> Glorious virtue is never dragged down to the Stygian shadows ... fame will open the path to the gods on high.

It cannot be demonstrated that Boethius knew and used the *Hercules Oetaeus*, and the present argument is not concerned with establishing that the play is an antecedent of the poem. What is striking, however, is the way in which two poets, working in different traditions and distinct mediums, can elaborate a philosophical model of failure and achievement on the basis of related myths.

Boethius' knowledge and use of Seneca's *Hercules furens* is, on the contrary, well established, as has been shown above. In his perceptive discussion of the ways in which Orpheus in the *Consolation* is a figure

---

[29] See esp. Crabbe (1981a) 312-18.

for the prisoner, and a figure whereby the prisoner's progress may be measured, Lerer refers to the *Hercules furens* as a 'super-text', implicit reference to which is essential to the purport of Boethius' poem.[30] That is to say, Boethius intends us to read his poem bearing the Senecan treatment of the Orpheus myth, and the latter's role in the play, in mind. It has been observed above that Boethius' poem moves within the ambit of Virgil's Orpheus narrative in *Georgics* 4 as well. To that extent, the *Hercules furens* may not be a uniquely privileged super-text for Boethius, in the way suggested by Lerer. On the other hand, the relatively brief and concise lyric form of the Senecan and Boethius passages, and their explicit inclusion in a moralizing context, are (quite apart from the clearly similar function of Pluto's speech in both passages) indications of the importance of Seneca for Boethius, an importance that 4 m. 7, to be discussed below, underlines.

To what extent does the *Hercules furens* illuminate Boethius' poem? It has been seen that Orpheus in *Hf*. 569ff. is understood as an example of success in his enchantment of Pluto and the underworld, one whose failure to bring back Eurydice is played down and, in two lines (*Hf*. 588f.), attributed to the impetuosity of 'true love'. In this choral ode, Orpheus' success in song augurs well for Hercules' descent to Hades, and the triumph of strength or force (566, 590f.). On the surface, the chorus's optimism is justified, for Hercules returns with Cerberus, a success that upstages the outcome of Orpheus' descent. But Hercules returns to madness, crime, the slaughter of his children, and painful self-knowledge and expiation: 'Like Orpheus, but in a far more horrible

---

[30] Lerer (1985) 153ff. Allusiveness or 'intertextuality' has long been observed in Roman poetry. Fraenkel (1957) 105ff., writing on Horace's Fifth *Satire*, distinguishes between 'personal experience' and 'literary tradition' in the poem (the former is Horace's journey to Brundisium in 37 BC, the latter Lucilius' satire *Iter Siculum*), concluding that 'only the joint impact of a personal experience and a literary tradition was capable of bringing forth a particular poem' (107). In the language of the Latin rhetorical tradition there is both *imitatio* and *aemulatio* of Lucilius in Horace's poem. It is an instance of 'significant imitation' in Woodman's sense ('correspondences from which he [the writer] wishes some particular significance to emerge', D.A. West/T. Woodman, *Creative Imitation and Latin Literature* [Cambridge 1979] 154). Tarrant (1985) 18f. also distinguishes between 'isolated verbal echoes' (Woodman's 'verbal echo', op. cit. 149) and allusions 'which invite comparison': 'Sometimes the relationship between Seneca's text and an Augustan model is yet more complex: not only is the allusion meant to be observed, but the difference of tone or point of reference between the original and Seneca's revision are an integral part of Seneca's meaning' (19). Tarrant's own discussions of several passages in Seneca's *Thyestes* (see op. cit. 18 n. 88 for references) are a model of allusiveness observed; cf. also e.g. R.F. Thomas, 'Catullus and the Polemics of Poetic Reference', *American Journal of Philology* 103 (1982) 144-64; D.O. Ross, *Backgrounds to Augustan Poetry: Gallus, Elegy, and Rome* (Cambridge 1975), both referred to by Tarrant, op. cit. 19 n. 89. Crabbe (1981a) and (1981b) show what such readings of Boethius can achieve. My criticism of Lerer on the following pages is not directed against intertextuality as such, but rather against some of his attempts to detect it in *Cons. phil.*

and more culpable way, he destroys what he loves.'[31] On a deeper level, then, the comparison between Orpheus and Hercules is maintained by Seneca, but it is overshadowed by the contrast between them. The choral assumption of the superiority of force to song is questioned. Force can destroy and disturb in a way unknown to song. While both Orpheus and Hercules exemplify the inability of man to conquer death and destruction in anything but the most partial and superficial of ways, the contrast between them is stressed by Seneca. Orpheus' pacification of the underworld is genuine (575f.) if temporary, Hercules' pacification is of a different kind, and illusory.[32] The connotations of the Orpheus myth are predominantly positive for Seneca. Lerer does not differentiate sufficiently between Seneca's Orpheus and his Hercules when he sees them both indifferently as types of 'misdirected Stoic *virtus*'.[33] For, while it is true that, on a strict application of Stoic values, Orpheus in *Hercules furens* is a victim of the passion of love, and so a 'fool', Seneca does not exploit that aspect in the ode, and we cannot apply Stoic criteria automatically to his account. Whether we can do so in Hercules' case is, of course, another matter. But if Seneca influences Boethius, we must assume that it is the influence of Seneca's Hercules, as much as, if not more than, his Orpheus. Certainly, that seems the assumption made by Lerer, when he considers Orpheus to be a counterpart of the Giants assaulting heaven (3.12.24), and says of the Orpheus myth in Boethius: 'in its illogic, the story presents a pervasive disharmony, from the breaking of the bonds of marriage, through Orpheus' fervor, and finally to the mad pursuit of the dead.'[34] The insane disruption of natural harmony suggested here would be a true description of Seneca's Hercules. But does it reflect Boethius' poem? To a certain extent, it does: but Lerer's assertions need to be qualified.

To begin with, the ending of Orpheus' marriage by death is a neutral fact in Boethius. Boethius does not offer any reason for the death of Eurydice, or refer to any of the accounts of it in the tradition. It is simply the starting-point for Orpheus' grief, and is in no sense a 'disharmony' in the sense that his pursuit of his dead wife into Hades may be. That said, Orpheus is indeed, in Lerer's sense, a victim of his passion, of a misguided journey to Hades, and a failure due to *amor*. His skill – poetry and music – is flawed and misused, as Seneca's Hercules misuses his strength and courage. The apparent success that leads to deep failure, a failure accounted for in terms of the infringement of basic ethical and metaphysical principles, is what unites Orpheus in Boethius with Hercules in Seneca's play.

[31] Segal (1983) 236.
[32] Cf. Segal (1983) 235.
[33] Lerer (1985) 162.
[34] Lerer (1985) 158; cf. 159.

Lerer suggests that Boethius redirects the focus from the public, external, and physical spheres of the *Hercules furens* to private concerns, inner and metaphysical contexts.[35] In Boethius the law which Orpheus obeys is derived from the power of love: 'Boethius' hell becomes a state of mind.'[36] But despite its evident external and public form, the world of Seneca's play is no less internalized and symbolic, representing, in Segal's words, 'the monstrous within the hero's own soul'.[37] Seneca's chorus hints at this:

> *solvite tantis animum monstris,*
> * solvite, superi,*
> *rectam in melius flectite mentem* (1063ff.).

Free his soul, you gods, from such terrible monsters, guide his mind straight to a better condition.

And Hercules himself recognizes that he has somehow absorbed Hades mentally:

> *   an nondum exuit*
> *simulacra mens inferna? post reditus quoque*
> *oberrat oculis turba feralis meis?* (1144ff.).

Has my mind not yet cast off the ghosts of hell? Even after my return do the dead in their crowds wander before my eyes?

'No hell is more terrifying than that of one's own inner darkness.'[38] If Boethius rewrites the Seneca text, then that rewriting is much less radical than Lerer would have it. The contrast is not one between genuine (Boethius) and incipient (Seneca) philosophical poetry, as Lerer implies,[39] but between two kinds of poetry written in a broadly similar moralizing context, yet with a shift, in Boethius' case, to explicitly expressed Platonic values. Boethius absorbs and transmutes elements of the Senecan account, and to know that account is to be more fully receptive to the nuances of Boethius' poem. But, in a sense, the two texts complement each other. Boethius proffers an example of something that is a feature of Latin poetry since the Augustan age at least: the allusive use of an already existing poem to enrich the meaning of a newly created one. But this is no commentary on, or radical rewriting of, a pre-existing text, still less a poem which 'takes as one of its subjects the formal problems of literary execution'.[40] Such

[35] Lerer (1985) 160ff.
[36] Lerer (1985) 163.
[37] Segal (1983) 234f.
[38] Segal (1983) 236.
[39] Lerer (1985) 160.
[40] Lerer (1985) 154.

observations suggest that the dispassionate, critical attitude that Boethius may have had to the Seneca text is somehow consciously and articulately embodied in his poem, so that Seneca's text *qua* text is part of the subject-matter of Boethius' poem. But no such reference is perceptible in Boethius. Rather, he forms his own personal vision and gives expression to it against a background which is distinct from, but none the less contributes creatively to, the new work.

Boethius' Orpheus poem, as has been shown above, is embedded in a specific philosophical context, and can be fully understood only against the background of the arguments of such prose sections of the *Consolation* as 3.12 and 5.2. But the poem should also be read in the context of other, related poems of the work. Critics have pointed out the links between the Orpheus poem and the work's opening *metrum*.[41] In both the theme is, in part, the inefficacy of laments in verse (*flebiles modi*: 1 m. 1.2; 3 m. 12.7). Both have the themes of the perversion or loss of happiness (1 m. 1.21f.; 3 m. 12.1ff., 55ff.). In this respect 3 m. 12 is retrospective. At a crucial moment in the work it reiterates themes of the opening section. But the prisoner's condition has been diagnosed and the nature of true goodness and happiness outlined, and so the reason for the impotence of the kind of poetry exemplified in 1 m. 1 can now be fully understood. It is passion-dominated verse composed in a state of alienation from the Good.[42] The Muses of 1 m. 1 are, in Philosophy's words,

> they who choke the crops rich in the fruit of reason with the sterile thorns of the passions, and make men's minds used to their illness, and do not free them of it (1.1.9).

But that sick condition can now be understood in terms of Platonic metaphysics. Similarly, the misguided nature of Orpheus' love can be better appreciated against the background of the cosmic *amor* (2 m. 8) that links and controls the workings of the universe, and is also found in human institutions (2 m. 8.24f.). That poem's conclusion explicitly links natural and human *amor* with the concept of happiness, the happiness which Orpheus misguidedly forfeits:

> *o felix hominum genus,*
> *si vestros animos amor*
> *quo caelum regitur regat!* (2 m. 8.28ff.).

> O blessed human race, if the love by which the heavens are ruled should rule your hearts!

---

[41] Crabbe (1981a) 312; Lerer (1985) 154ff. Cf. Ford (1967) 88.

[42] On this Neoplatonic motif (*apostrophê, aversio*) see A.H. Armstrong, 'Salvation, Plotinian and Christian', *Downside Review* 75 (1957) 126-39; Theiler (1966) 184ff.

Furthermore, as Crabbe in particular has pointed out, the Orpheus myth is clearly understood by Boethius in terms of Platonic recollection (*anamnêsis*) and forgetting.[43] It is characteristic of earlier versions of the Orpheus story that they stress that Orpheus looks back because he is momentarily forgetful.[44] The idea does not occur in Boethius' poem. But that poem is part of a sequence where the theme of *anamnêsis* and threats to it is elaborated. The preceding poem, 3 m. 11, summarizes in poetic form the Platonic recollection doctrine and concludes:

> *quodsi Platonis Musa personat verum,*
> *quod quisque discit* immemor *recordatur* (3 m. 11.15f.).

> But if Plato's Muse sings out the truth, what each one learns, forgetting he remembers.

And the same term *immemor* occurs in the context of true Platonic ascent and recollection in the next poem, 4 m. 1:

> *huc te si reducem referat via*
>   *quam nunc requiris* immemor,
> '*haec,' dices,* 'memini, *patria est mihi,*
>   *hinc ortus, hic sistam gradum.*' (4 m. 1.23ff.).

> If the road should lead you back to this spot, for which you now search, forgetful, 'this', you will say, 'I remember, it is my native country; here was my beginning, here my feet will rest.'

Thus the Orpheus poem is part of a context where the theme of forgetting is dominant.[45] Boethius may omit the key word *immemor* at the moment of Orpheus' looking back because, seen against the background of the Platonic recollection doctrine, Orpheus is not just forgetful at that moment alone: 'His love for a woman, his grief and above all its fostering and expression in elegiac song and his descent to Hades, to all of these the term *immemor* is quite as applicable as to the failure to observe the law set by the *arbiter umbrarum*.'[46] Thus Orpheus, although he can be a figure for the prisoner, represents a stage beyond which the prisoner has already progressed, just as the work in general has progressed beyond the preoccupations of its opening sections. As Lerer writes: 'The ideas of order developed in the poetry [of Book Two] are instinctively perverted in the picture of

---

[43] Crabbe (1981a) 315f.

[44] *immemor*: cf. Virgil, *Georg.* 4.491; [Seneca] *Herc. Oet.* 1085; Martianus Capella 907.2 (p. 345.23 Willis).

[45] Cf. 4.1.1ff.

[46] Crabbe (1981a) 316.

Orpheus the poet.'[47]

To the flawed ascent of Orpheus in 3 m. 12 corresponds, as its positive antithesis, the successful ascent of the soul through the heavens in 4 m. 1. The poem cannot be understood except in relation to the account of the procession of souls in Plato's *Phaedrus*, of which it is a free poetic translation:

> Thus when it [soul] is perfect and winged it journeys on high and controls the whole world ... And behold, there in the heaven Zeus, mighty leader, drives his winged team: first of the host of gods and daemons he proceeds, ordering all things and caring therefor ... behold they climb the steep ascent even unto the summit of the arch that supports the heavens ... And now there awaits the soul the extreme of her toil and struggling. For the souls that are called immortal, so soon as they are at the summit, come forth and stand upon the back of the world: and straightway the revolving heaven carries them round, and they look upon the regions without. (*Phaedrus* 246c-247c, tr. Hackforth).

In Boethius' poem Philosophy promises the soul wings:

> *Sunt etenim pennae volucres mihi*
> *quae celsa conscendant poli;*
> *quas sibi cum velox mens induit*
> *terras perosa despicit ...* (1ff.).

> For I have swift wings with which to rise to the heights of heaven; when the quick mind has put them on, it hates the earth, looks down upon it ...

The soul progresses through its astral journey until

> *... ubi iam exhausti fuerit satis*
> *polum relinquat extimum*
> *dorsaque velocis premat aetheris*
> *compos verendi luminis.*
> *hic regum sceptrum dominus tenet*
> *orbisque habenas temperat*
> *et volucrem currum stabilis regit*
> *rerum coruscus arbiter* (15ff.).

> ... when it has exerted itself sufficiently, it leaves the furthest region of the sky, and rests on the back of the fast-moving ether, and shares in enjoyment of the holy light. Here the lord of kings holds sway and guides the reins of the universe, and, unmoved, controls the fast chariot, the brilliant master of all things.

And from its vantage point on the outer limits of the heavens the soul can safely look back on the earthly darkness which it has left behind (27f.).

---

[47] Lerer (1985) 158.

It will be evident from the sections quoted that the *Phaedrus* account informs and explains the details of 4 m. 1. It is no less clear that this poem's account of successful and blessed ascent is the counterpart of Orpheus' failure. The soul that has ascended can look upon the light (4 m. 1.18), but can also look upon the darkness with impunity and understanding (27ff.). Where Orpheus displayed lack of vision, lethargy, disharmony, alienation, and flawed insight, the ascended soul of 4 m. 1 exemplifies a vision of the truth, life, stability, homecoming (4 m. 1.25-6), and genuine perception and understanding.[48]

If the *Phaedrus* is the key to 4 m. 1, Plato's image from the *Republic* of the chained prisoners in the Cave influences the interpretation of Orpheus' condition in 3 m. 12 (1ff., 53ff.). These poems are part of a sequence in which central themes of a number of Platonic dialogues are featured: the sequence includes 3 m. 9 (*Timaeus*) and 3 m. 11 (*Meno* and *Phaedo*). 3 m. 12 may already anticipate the imagery of ascent from the earthly sphere to the divine light of truth that is characteristic of the *Phaedrus* and of 4 m. 1. For the 'cave of Tartarus' of 3 m. 12.55 may be an image of earthly existence in general, both because of the *Republic*'s Cave metaphor and by analogy with the Neoplatonic description of the sublunary sphere as Hades.[49] If that is so, then the 'day above' of 3 m. 12.53 is the divine light, the 'clear source of goodness' of 3 m. 12.1f., and the 'sublime light' of 4 m. 1.18. In other words, 4 m. 1 is the necessary complement and extension of the themes of 3 m. 12.

But, just as 3 m. 12 is to be understood both in terms of the explicit Platonic exegesis provided by Boethius in the *Consolation* and in the context of the tradition of the Orpheus myth in Latin poetry, so too 4 m. 1, while it indubitably renders essential aspects of the *Phaedrus* into poetry, also adopts the traditional Latin poetic motif of the ascent of the soul to the heavens. This motif is, of course, itself a descendant of the *Phaedrus* myth, mediated through such texts as Cicero's *Somnium Scipionis*. But it features in non-Platonic contexts and has a life of its own, so that it may legitimately be considered a tributary influence upon Boethius' poem. In Virgil's 5th *Eclogue* the dead Daphnis is described thus:

> *candidus insuetum miratur limen Olympi*
> *sub pedibusque videt nubes et sidera Daphnis (Ecl.* 5.56f.*).*

> Radiant, Daphnis admires the unfamiliar threshold of Olympus, and sees the clouds and stars beneath his feet.

The dead Pompey's soul, in Lucan's *Pharsalia*,

---

[48] See Lerer (1985) 172ff.
[49] Crabbe (1981a) 316.

> *... sequitur convexa tonantis.*
> *... illic postquam se lumino vero*
> *implevit. stellasque vagas miratus et astra*
> *fixa polis, vidit quanta sub nocte iaceret*
> *nostra dies, risitque sui ludibria trunci* (9.4, 11ff.).

sought the dome of the Thunderer ... When he had steeped himself in the true light of that region, and gazed at the planets and the fixed stars of heaven, he saw the thick darkness that veils our day, and smiled at the mockery done to his headless body (tr. Duff).

Statius apostrophizes the dead Lucan thus:

> *at tu, seu rapidum poli per axem*
> *famae curribus arduis levatus*
> *qua surgunt animae potentiores,*
> *terras despicis et sepulcra rides* ... (*Silvae* 2.7.107ff.).

But you ... lifted up in the high-flying chariot through the whirling vault of heaven, where more powerful souls rise, look down upon the earth and laugh at tombs ... (tr. Mozley, adapted).[50]

But the metaphor is not confined to the dead. Horace imagines his poetic self in celestial flight (*Odes* 2.20), and Lucan eulogizes Nero in similar terms (*Pharsal.* 1.45ff.). The motif, appropriately in view of its philosophical genealogy, is often applied to the power of knowledge ranging the universe. Thus Lucretius, of Epicurus:

> *ergo vivida vis animi pervicit, et extra*
> *processit longe flammantia moenia mundi*
> *atque omne immensum peragravit mente animoque* ... (1.72ff.).

Therefore the lively power of his mind prevailed, and forth he marched beyond the flaming walls of the world, as he traversed the immeasurable universe in thought and imagination (tr. Rouse/Smith).

These lines may have influenced Boethius' account of the prisoner's former astronomical studies:

> *hic quondam caelo liber aperto*
> *suetus in aetherios ire meatus*
> *cernebat rosei lumina solis,*
> *visebat gelidae sidera lunae* ... (1 m. 2.6ff.).

---

[50] Cf. Prudentius, *Peristefanon* 14.79f., 91ff.; *Amartigenia* 847ff. Prudentius, *Amart.* 858 '*carcareos* exosa *situs quibus haeserat* exul' may be echoed by Boethius in 4 m. 1.4 ('*terras* perosa *despicit*') and 30 ('*cernes tyrannos* exsules'); but see Ovid, *Met.* 8.183f. (quoted n. 55 below). Cf. further p. 42 with nn. 35f. above; also Rutherford (1989) 155ff.

This man, once accustomed to move freely under open skies along the paths of the starry ether, contemplated the rose-red sunlight, surveyed the light of the cold moon.

Martianus Capella prays in the same vein about the same studies:

> *da, pater, aetherios superum conscendere coetus*
> *astrigerumque sacro sub nomine noscere caelum* (2.193, p. 53.10f. Willis).

Grant, father, that I may arise to the heavenly assemblies of the gods, and know the starry sky under your sacred authority.

Manilius had envisaged his astronomical pursuits in the same manner:

> *iuvat ire per ipsum*
> *aera et immenso spatiantem vivere caelo*
> *signaque et adversos stellarum noscere cursus* (1.13ff).

It is my delight to traverse the very air and spend my life touring the boundless skies, learning of the constellations and the contrary motions of the planets (tr. Goold).

> *... nec in turba nec turbae carmina condam,*
> *sed solus, vacuo veluti velatus in orbe*
> *liber agam currus non occursantibus ullis*
> *nec per iter socios commune regentibus actus,*
> *sed caelo noscenda canam ...* (2.138ff.).

Not in the crowd nor for the crowd shall I compose my song, but alone, as though borne round an empty circuit I were freely driving my chariot with none to cross my path or steer a course beside me over a common route, I shall sing it for the skies to hear (tr. Goold, modified).[51]

It is not difficult to perceive the influence of this tradition on Boethius' poem, with its themes of liberating ascent and contemptuous looking down on the hated earth and its despised tyrannical rulers (4 m. 1.4ff., 27ff.). The vision imagery of the poem (18) is, in addition, linked to the motif of knowledge as the soul's flight.

4 m. 1 shares the triumphant mood of liberation and fulfilment that colours the poetry quoted above, and is also characteristic of the *Phaedrus* account. Is the poem's evocation of a successful flight of the soul intended by Boethius to remind the reader of the most famous unsuccessful flight in Greek myth, that of Icarus and Daedalus? Crabbe has suggested that 4 m. 1 implies a contrast between the effective flight in which Philosophy guides (4.1.9) the prisoner's mind, to which wings are affixed by her (ib.), and the failure of Daedalus to

---

[51] Cf. Manilius 2.58f.; 5.1ff.

guide the flight of Icarus to its end.[52] Crabbe argues that Ovid's accounts of the Daedalus-Icarus myth – in particular that of *Metamorphoses* 8.183ff., but also the use of the myth with reference to Ovid's own exile through Augustus' agency in *Tristia* 3.8 – have influenced Boethius here.[53] The possibility is intriguing. Daedalus is in exile, longing to return to his *patria* (*A.A.* 2.25ff.; *Met.* 8.184). He plans a heavenly journey for himself and his son: *restat iter caeli: caelo temptabimus ire* ('the path through the sky remains: we will try to go by the sky', *A.A.* 2.37). He escapes from a tyrant whose power is thus seen, after all, to be limited (*A.A.* 2.51ff., *Met.* 8.185ff.). He provides wings for himself and his son, who is to fly 'with me as guide' (*me duce, A.A.* 2.58; *Met.* 8.208). Icarus' loss of wings is described as a loss of 'chains' (*vincla, A.A.* 2.85). His fear is evoked in the following terms:

> *territus a summo despexit in aequora caelo;*
> *nox oculis pavido venit oborta metu (A.A. 2.87f.).*

Terrified, he looked down from the height of the sky upon the level sea.
Darkness fell upon his eyes, brought on by terrible fear.

In the *Consolation*, the prisoner is in exile (1.3.3, 1.5.2ff.), but Philosophy will lead him 'home' to his *patria* (4.1.8f.), loss of which is the ultimate cause of his anguish (1.5.2ff.). The prisoner is portrayed as the victim of a tyrant, and recognizing the illusory nature of the power of tyrants is part of his cure.[54] In 4 m. 1 the mind, from its heavenly vantage-point, realizes that it is the tyrants who are exiles from the true *patria* (29f.). Casting off the chains (*vincla*) which oppress the soul is one of the most urgent tasks for the prisoner to achieve under Philosophy's guidance (1 m. 2.25ff., 1 m. 4.18, 1 m. 7.29ff., etc.). Each of these items – and the other echoes of Ovid's account – serves to heighten the contrast between the misguided and failed physical flight of Icarus under Daedalus' guidance, and the true, spiritual, and successful flight of the mind under Philosophy's tutelage. Thus, for example, Icarus' loss of the wings which are *vincla* is a prelude to his fall, whereas the prisoner's loss of chains is the prelude to authentic flight. Or, to take another example, *A.A.* 2.87f., quoted above, may be echoed in 4 m. 1.4, *terras perosa despicit*[55] ('he

----

[52] Crabbe (1981a) 318ff. Her further argument (ib.) – that Boethius may here be influenced by Augustine's modification of Plotinus' *Odyssey* allegory, which discounts physical journeys (*Enneads* 1.6.8) and to which Augustine adds the example of Daedalus' flight (*Contra Academicos* 3.2.3; cf. *Confessions* 1.18.28) – shows how an antecedent in which mythical (poetic) and Neoplatonic elements are combined may have suggested to Boethius his own distinctive modification of the motif.

[53] But also (as she has pointed out to me) *Ars amatoria* 2.21ff.

[54] See Ch. 3 *passim*.

[55] Cf. Ovid, *Met.* 8.183f. *longumque perosus exsilium* (see *exsules* in line 30 of Boethius' poem).

looks down upon the earth, hating it'), and in

> *quodsi terrarum placeat tibi*
>   *noctem relictam visere,*
> *quos miseri torvos populi timent*
>   *cernes tyrannos exsules* (27ff.).

But if it should please you to contemplate the earthly night that you have
left behind, the tyrants whose ferocity wretched peoples fear you will see
as exiles.

Icarus looks down helpless, and night, in his terror, is the forerunner of
death; for the prisoner the night of earth can be observed without fear
from on high, and those below fear. The prisoner has successfully
escaped exile and can see the tyrants below as exiles.

It is perhaps significant that the details of 4 m. 1 which are closest to
the Ovid accounts in language and imagery are precisely those which
are not found in the *Phaedrus* passage which was seen above to be the
source of much of the symbolism of the poem. Like Horace, who in *Odes*
2.20 favourably compares his fame in terms of successful flight with
that of Icarus (13ff.), Boethius (but without – understandably –
Horace's insistence on Icarus' *gloria*)[56] may be here linking the
metaphor of the heavenly flight of the mind with the Daedalus-Icarus
myth.

The implications of this link extend beyond the immediate scope of
the poem. If Daedalus fails, then a human artist does – and so the
parallel with the failure of Orpheus' art in 3 m. 12 is heightened (and
possibly the failure of Circe's arts in 4 m. 3 anticipated). Only
Philosophy is the true manipulator of human resources, and only
Philosophy succeeds. And, whereas Daedalus can only propose a
middle course between the extremes of heaven and earth for Icarus
(*A.A.* 2.59ff., *Met.* 8.203ff.), Philosophy urges her protégé to aim for the
heights, and deification, the true transcending of human mediocrity.

To return to the Orpheus poem. The figure of Orpheus in Boethius is
strikingly uninfluenced by the exploitation of Orpheus in Jewish and
early Christian iconography and literary symbolism.[57] Nor has the
Orphic religious tradition contributed to Boethius' poem. Nor, despite
the poem's philosophical themes, is there any perceptible Platonic-
Pythagorean antecedent dealing with the events of Orpheus' life that
can be adduced as a substantial source for Boethius. What we have,

[56] Cf. *Odes* 4.2.2ff. and see Fraenkel (1957) 436 n. 3. Nisbet/Hubbard 2.343f. sees an
'ironic undercurrent' in Horace's remarks.
[57] On these traditions see R. Eisler, *Orphisch-dionysische Mysteriengedanken in der
christlichen Antike* (Vorträge der Bibliothek Warburg 2.2, Leipzig/Berlin 1925); C.
Murray, *Rebirth and Afterlife. A Study of the Transmutation of Some Pagan Imagery in
Early Christian Funerary Art* (British Archaeological Reports, I.S. 100, 1981) 37-63.

then, is a strikingly original creation, in which Boethius adapts
elements of the Roman literary portrayals of Orpheus to his Platonic
context. Crabbe is, however, right to link the poem to certain Platonic
themes and texts – the Cave in the *Republic*, the themes of madness and
ascent in the *Phaedrus*, and the portrayal of Orpheus in the *Symposium*
– and to see these as the starting-points of Boethius' creation.[58] It may
well be the last mentioned of these texts that influences the critical,
condemning attitude of Boethius. For the *Symposium* conjures up the
image of Orpheus as a faint-hearted musician who contrives an entrée
while yet alive to Hades because he is too cowardly to die for the sake of
love, and whose *erôs* contrasts unfavourably with that of Alcestis, so
that he ends up with a mere phantom (*phasma*) of Eurydice (*Symp.*
179d). One notes here the dual condemnation of Orpheus' art and of his
love – two negative aspects which 3 m. 12 highlights. Here is rich
Platonic material upon which the Platonist Boethius could elaborate.[59]

(iii) Circe and the companions of Odysseus (4 m. 3)

Vela Neritii ducis
et vagas pelago rates
Eurus appulit insulae,
pulchra qua residens dea
Solis edita semine   5
miscet hospitibus novis
tacta carmine pocula.
quos ut in varios modos
vertit herbipotens manus,
hunc apri facies tegit,   10
ille Marmaricus leo
dente crescit et unguibus;
hic lupis nuper additus
flere dum parat ululat,
ille tigris ut Indica   15
tecta mitis obambulat.
sed licet variis malis
numen Arcadis alitis
obsitum miserans ducem
peste solverit hospitis,   20
iam tamen mala remigies
ore pocula traxerant,
iam sues Cerealia
glande pabula verterant
et nihil manet integrum   25
voce, corpore perditis.
sola mens stabilis super
monstra quae patitur gemit.

[58] Crabbe (1981a) 314ff.
[59] Cf. Crabbe (1981a) 314 n. 16.

o levem nimium manum
nec potentia gramina,   30
membra quae valeant licet,
corda vertere non valent!
intus est hominum vigor
arce conditus abdita.
haec venena potentius   35
detrahunt hominem sibi
dira quae penitus meant
nec nocentia corpori
mentis vulnere saeviunt.

The east wind drove the sails of the Ithacan leader and his ships wandering on the sea to the island where a beautiful goddess lives, daughter of the Sun (5), who mixes new guests drinks touched with a magic incantation. When by her hand, skilled with herbs, they change into various forms, this one is disguised in the shape of a boar (10), that one, an African lion, grows teeth and claws. Another, freshly assigned to the wolves, wants to weep – and howls. Another walks tamely about the house as an Indian tiger (15). But although winged Arcadian Mercury took pity on the leader, beset as he was with many troubles, and saved him from his host's poisons (20), his oarsmen had already taken the terrible drinks, already as swine had exchanged Ceres' bread for acorns. Nothing remains unaffected (25), voice and body lost completely. Only the mind, immutable, transcendent, bewails the monstrous shapes it must endure. O hand too feeble and ineffectual herbs (30), which have the power to change the limbs, but cannot change hearts! Within the human force survives, hidden in its secret citadel. Those dreadful poisons undermine more potently (35) a man's identity that penetrate the inmost depths, and do not harm the body but, raging, wound the mind.

In the prose section 4.3 Boethius argues that the happiness of being good is its own reward, and that human goodness, which, if genuine, cannot be diminished by time or other people's efforts, is a form of deification (4.3.9f.). By analogy, wickedness is its own punishment and, since that which loses its goodness ceases to be what it was, the wicked cease to be human (4.3.14f.).[60] Boethius thereby takes up a theme of earlier parts of the work. In 2.5.28f. it is argued that misjudgement of what is good is a lack of self-knowledge that reduces man to a level below of that of the beasts. In a later section (3.7.4) it is suggested that, if bodily pleasure makes men happy, then their happiness is one with that of animals. In 4.3, however, the argument is developed and, so to speak, given a technical dimension. For it is now explicitly related to a traditional theme of Greek ethical discourse – the assumption that human behaviour which is lawless, aggressive, and generally motivated by impulse and appetite is sub-human in the

[60] The argument is typically Augustinian: see O'Daly (1987) 72ff.; G. Bonner, 'Augustine's Conception of Deification', *Journal of Theological Studies* N.S. 37 (1986) 369-86.

sense of bestial, i.e. that it is the behaviour of animals.[61] This view is linked by Plato to the Pythagorean belief in reincarnation, so that embodiment in animal form can be seen as an appropriate form of punishment for moral transgressions in a previous existence:

> [The laws of Destiny provide] that according to the character of his deprivation, he should constantly be changed into some beast of a nature resembling the formation of that character, and should have no rest from the travail of these changes, until ... he should control its irrational turbulence by discourse of reason and return once more to the form of his first and best condition (*Timaeus* 42cd, tr. Cornford).

Plato initiates a prolonged discussion in antiquity, which ranges from a symbolic and metaphorical interpretation of the reincarnation theory (we become like animals in our conduct and character if we are governed by appetite) to literal understanding of the doctrine. This gives later Neoplatonists like Porphyry and Iamblichus such problems as: does the rational soul somehow lose its powers and become inefficacious in an animal body, and how can this be? Nor are early Christian writers exempt from the discussion, whether they believe, like Origen, in reincarnation, or assume a metaphorical interpretation of it. It is against this rich background, extending from technical philosophical treatises to moral diatribe and related poetic treatments, that Boethius' views in 4.3 and the poem which follows must be considered.

In 4.3 Boethius leaves the reader in no doubt which interpretation he favours. It is the metaphorical one: the avaricious man is like a wolf, the disputatious one like a dog, the trickster like a fox, the angry man like a lion, the timid like a deer, the stupid man like a donkey, the fickle like the birds, and the lustful like a pig (4.3.17ff.). This is no real transformation in terms of change of species, but rather a case of humans transformed by vices (4.3.16).

The following poem (4 m. 3) is only fully understood against this preliminary discussion. Boethius provides a treatment of one of the episodes of the *Odyssey* most popular with moralizing and allegorizing interpreters of Homer – the Circe episode of book 10, in which Odysseus' companions are transformed into pigs when they drink Circe's drugged potions (*Od.* 10.235ff.). This appears to have attracted exegesis among the Socratics, where it exemplifies the evils to which excesses of eating and drinking may lead (Xenophon. *Mem.* 1.3.6f.).[62] Horace reflects this tradition, even if he does not make it clear whether addiction to drink, or general greediness, leads to the dreadful transformation:

[61] See K.J. Dover, *Greek Popular Morality in the Time of Plato and Aristotle* (Oxford 1974) 74f.
[62] Antisthenes' lost *Peri Kirkês* is likely to have contained similar interpretations: see Kaiser (1964) 202.

rursus, quid virtus et quid sapientia possit,
utile proposuit nobis exemplar Ulixen ...
Sirenum voces et Circae pocula nosti;
quae si cum sociis stultus cupidusque bibisset,
sub domina meretrice fuisset turpis et excors;
vixisset canis inmundus vel amica luto sus (Epist. 1.2.17f., 23ff.).

By contrast, the value of true manhood and of wisdom
is helpfully embodied in his Ulysses ...
You recall the Sirens' song and the cup of Circe:
if, like his men, he had drunk it out of greed
and folly, he'd have been unmanned by a mistress,
lived like a filthy dog or a pig in its muck (tr. Macleod).

Horace is undoubtedly drawing upon Cynic and Stoic interpretations of Circe, interpretations which are reflected in Dio Chrysostom, Cynic letters, Plutarch, and others.[63] To what extent, and in what ways, does Boethius reveal his debt to this tradition?

The structure of the Circe poem is bipartite. In the longer first section (1-28) a narrative and descriptive account of the transformation of Odysseus' companions, and of Odysseus' own escape, is given, and this account is lacking in any explicit interpretation of the events. In the shorter second section (29-39) elements of an interpretation are given, but in an oblique and somewhat puzzling manner.

It has been observed that in the first part of the poem Boethius by and large follows the Homeric account.[64] Some details, which include deviations from Homer, call for comment.

(a) Circe's beauty (4), reflecting Homer's *eüplokamos (Od.* 10.136), is not, strictly speaking, relevant to the following account, for Boethius concentrates on Circe the magician rather than the erotic temptress who became, in moralizing exegesis, the archetypal hetaera,[65] as in the extract from Horace quoted above (*sub domina meretrice*). But the reference to Circe's beauty is appropriate in a context which deals among other things with the vicious aspects of pleasure and desire (4.3.20).

(b) Boethius describes Circe as a magician skilled in herbs (9) – echoing Homer's *pharmaka lugr' (Od.* 10.236) – but also using incantations (7), a detail not used by Homer, though Circe is a sweet singer (*Od.* 10.136, 221), like those other bewitching females, Calypso and the Sirens. The influence of Virgil may be felt here, for it is precisely the power of Circe's song that is emphasized by him:

carmina vel caelo possunt deducere lunam,
carminibus Circe socios mutavit Ulixi ... (Ecl. 8.69f.).

[63] See Kaiser (1964) 202ff. for references and discussion.
[64] Scheible (1972) 137; Gruber (1978) 339.
[65] See Kaiser (1964) 201f.

Incantations can bring down the moon from the very sky; with incantations Circe transformed Ulysses' companions.[66]

Similarly, Ovid, in the most expansive Latin account of the episode (*Met*. 14.247ff.), refers to Circe's verbal magic (301f.). But it is in the Virgil passage that the ambiguity of *carmen* (song/incantation) is brought out, an ambiguity which may also be intended by Boethius and form part of his strategic attack on certain types of poetry.[67] It should, however, be added that the exegetical tradition often embroiders and elaborates Homer's account, and to add incantations to the repertoire of Circe's magic may have been a traditional part of that embroidery, and a perfectly natural one, given the practice of magical formulae and the belief that magic only becomes efficacious when the words are spoken.[68] Certainly the magical use of the *carmen* by Circe became a feature of Latin poetry, as Statius, *Theb*. 4.549ff. shows.

(c) The next detail of Boethius' poem illustrates a common elaboration of Homer's account. In Homer the companions of Odysseus are transformed into one type of animal only – swine – although wolves and lions are said to be other victims of Circe's magic (*Od*. 10.212f.). When the incident is interpreted in ethical terms, it is not surprising that animals much derided by the Greeks, namely dogs and donkeys, are added to the list.[69] To the Homeric swine, lions, and wolves Boethius adds an apparently original reference to tigers (10ff.), just as Virgil adds bears (*Aen*. 7.17), a feature followed by Ovid (*Met*. 14.255). In Boethius and Ovid the addition of tiger and bear has the same function: each poet wishes to stress the paradox of a wild and fierce animal being tame and docile (Boethius, 4 m. 3.16; Ovid, *Met*. 14.256ff.). Metamorphosed humans who become tame animals are also a feature of the Homeric account (*Od*. 10.214ff.). Here poetic *variatio* could change the tame animals into fierce ones (Virgil, *Aen*. 7.15ff.).

(d) In Homer's account the transformed humans emit animal sounds (*Od*. 10.239). Although the later tradition reflects this feature, the same concern with elaboration of the idea of humans in animal form that led to additions to the list of wild animals is apparent in the details given of the anguished transition from human to animal sounds, particularly at the moment of metamorphosis. Ovid (and this is a frequent feature of his accounts of change) also exploits this: ... *nec iam posse loqui, pro verbis edere raucum / murmur* ... ('... and I could speak no longer, but in place of words came only hoarse, grunting sounds ...', *Met*. 14.280f., tr. Miller). And Boethius, possibly influenced by Ovid, has his wolf experience a similarly disconcerting change (13f.).

---

[66] Cf. *Aeneid* 7.11f.
[67] See Crabbe (1981a) 325.
[68] See Kaiser (1964) 200 n. 12.
[69] Cf. Kaiser (1964) 202 n. 19; see also Horace, *Epist*. 1.2.26.

(e) The paradoxes of wild animals who are tame, and of animals who are aware that they can no longer emit human sounds, both serve to highlight a feature of Homer's account: the transformed humans keep their human minds (*Od.* 10.240). Boethius gives this the same prominence (27f.). And this is also the assumption of Ovid's account, in which the horror of the experience depends (as does Lucius' in Apuleius' *Golden Ass*) upon the human consciousness experiencing it (*Met.* 14.279-307).[70]

(f) Boethius' omissions are also of some significance. There is no reference to Circe's *rhabdos* or wand (*Od.* 10.238),[71] which assumes considerable importance in Ovid (*Met.* 14.278), unless the word *tacta* in verse 7 betrays some influence of this feature. The word is clearly used in that verse in the metaphorical sense 'sprinkled': the incantation is added to the drink like an extra ingredient. But *tacta* may also reveal the trace of the magical touch of the word in Ovid (*tetigit, Met.* 14.278). Circe's incantations have the same effect as the magical touch. Furthermore, although Hermes' rescue of Odysseus from his companions' fate is referred to by Boethius (17ff.), there is no mention of the means – the wonder-plant Moly – and the brief allusiveness of the reference contrasts with the elaboration of this aspect in Homer (*Od.* 10.277ff.). There is a tendency towards similar allusiveness in the case of well-known myths and their details in Hellenistic and Roman poetry: but Boethius has a specific reason for glossing over this point. He is not concerned in this poem with the virtuous exception, with an Odysseus who is untransformed, but rather with dehumanized types of wickedness, and the extent of their dehumanization. That is also the reason why he omits all reference to the restoration through the plant Moly of Odysseus' companions to their human form (*Od.* 10.393ff.). Boethius is not concerned in this poem with the way in which the wicked may be reformed.

From this and the previous points it will be obvious that Boethius' selection of features in the first part of the poem is strictly functional, with the aim of illustrating precisely those aspects upon which his interpretation will concentrate. His variations upon, and embroidery of, stock details are never undertaken for their own sake.

Boethius' interpretation of the myth, as has been indicated, is given in 29ff. Boethius concentrates on the implications of the Homeric detail that the minds of the dehumanized victims remain human (27f. – [e] above). Circe's poison may change bodies but not minds (31f.). The image of the mind in its citadel (34) echoes Cicero's account of Plato's tripartite division of soul in the *Republic*: 'Plato imagined the soul to be tripartite, and its ruling part, namely reason, he placed in the head as

---

[70] Gruber (1978) 339 thinks otherwise.
[71] Cf. *Od.* 10.293, 319.

in a citadel (*arce*)' (*Tusc. disp.* 1.10.20). This image evokes an essential and unchanging feature of mind, as a Platonist would understand it. It is therefore quite different from the Stoic image of the virtuous mind, freed from passions, as a citadel (Marc. Aurel. 8.48.3, Seneca, *Ep.* 113.27), for that refers to something which can be radically altered. This distinction is crucial to the interpretation of Boethius' poem. In 29ff. Boethius is, so to speak, taking the Circe story literally: the minds of Odysseus' companions remain unaltered. But the citadel image, inasmuch as it implies the concept of the immutable substance of the mind, introduces a specifically Platonic interpretation of the myth. When, therefore, Boethius goes on, in the poem's final lines, to contrast Circe's poison with those more deadly poisons which penetrate to man's inner self and wound the mind while leaving the body unharmed (35ff.), he is not merely moving from the literal to the metaphorical, but he is also providing the exegetical key to the first part. The contrast between physical and mental poison only makes sense if the physical is seen to symbolize the mental. What is more, Boethius is thereby offering not merely an exegesis of the first, narrative part of the poem; he is also interpreting the last part of the preceding prose section (4.3.14ff.), discussed above. This reverses a procedure which is common in the *Consolation*, where the full meaning of a poem only becomes apparent when we adduce relevant prose explications of it. Here the contrary is happening, a striking example of the varied interlock of prose and poetry in this literary form.

What the poem's concluding lines aver is that, since mind is substantially immutable, the effects of the vices do not affect its essential substance. Lines 35ff. make it clear that Boethius is referring back to the dehumanizing vices discussed at 4.3.15ff. In that section the talk was of 'losing one's human nature' (15), of 'turning into a beast' (21). The citadel image of 4 m. 3.33f. has shown that this language is not precise enough, but this only becomes fully apparent when we consider the words used by Boethius to describe the effect of moral ravages upon the mind (39). This mind can indeed be wounded by the raging passions, but it is not annihilated by them. In technical philosophical language Boethius might, like Augustine, speak of qualitative change of the mind that does not affect its essential nature. That is what the bestiality of the wicked means. And that is why, by implication, the Circe myth can serve as a model for the effect of the passions, which do not destroy the mind's nature.

This interpretation of the poem is reinforced if we situate Boethius' reflections on the myth in the context of later Neoplatonic discussions of the meaning of punitive transmigration of souls.[72]

---

[72] Gruber (1978) 339 argues against Neoplatonic influences, but does not take the evidence discussed on the following pages into account.

Plotinus appears to have accepted Plato's reincarnation beliefs literally, and to have extended the notion of punitive reincarnation to plants, so that human souls can be embodied in animals or plants (3.4.2.16ff.). But later Neoplatonists argued that if reason is not to be an accidental property of the human soul but of its essence, then it would seem to follow that a human soul cannot become the irrational soul of an animal without ceasing to exist *qua* rational soul. Thus Iamblichus argued that no soul ever abandons the level in the hierarchy to which it belongs, a view adopted by other later Neoplatonists.[73] Porphyry's views are more complex. According to the indirect tradition which reports those views, he denied transmigration of human souls to animal bodies (Augustine, *civ.* 10.30). It has, however, recently been demonstrated that passages quoted directly from Porphyry's works, in particular those transmitted by Stobaeus from the work on the freedom of the will (2.163ff.), distinguish between a primary choice of the soul before embodiment (a choice which can be envisaged as recurring countless times, as often as the soul returns to its previous, original unembodied state), in which it can opt for human or animal existence, and a secondary choice following upon the first, in which the individual type of chosen animal or human existence is adopted.[74] This view does not contradict the indirect tradition, for the soul which makes the primary choice cannot be described as a human (or animal) soul. Nor does this view exclude repeated reincarnations of a punitive kind for souls that have not lived a virtuous life: but the reincarnations will be in human form, i.e. forms of the secondary choice.

The interpreter of Porphyry's views runs up against a difficult text, and one that is directly relevant to Boethius' Circe poem. In a passage of allegorical Homeric interpretation quoted by Stobaeus (1.445ff.) Porphyry unequivocally understands Circe's transformation of the companions of Odysseus into swine as an allegory of the transmigration into animal bodies of those who have lived a life dominated by passions and pleasures.[75] Circe's island is the place where the souls of the dead are received and where rebirth begins. Deuse has argued convincingly, however, that the text cannot represent Porphyry's mature and fully-formed views.[76] Its closeness to Middle Platonic assumptions about the soul, as reflected in Plutarch,

---

[73] See R.T. Wallis, *Neoplatonism* (London 1972) 120.

[74] See W. Deuse, *Untersuchungen zur mittelplatonischen und neuplatonischen Seelenlehre*, Akademie der Wissenschaften und der Literatur, Mainz. Abhandlungen der Geistes- und Sozialwissenschaftlichen Klasse. Einzelveröffentlichung 3 (1983) 129-67.

[75] More precisely, a life dominated by the 'desiring' (*epithumêtikon*) or 'spirited' (*thumoeides*) part of the soul: the distinction, and the terminology, is taken from Plato's *Republic* 435ff. On Porphyry's method see J. Pépin, 'Porphyre, exégète d'Homère', in *Porphyre* (Entretiens Fondation Hardt 12, Geneve 1966) 231-66.

[76] Deuse (n. 74 above) 138ff.

in particular its unproblematic acceptance of the soul's ability to move from rational to irrational forms of existence, indicate that if it is Porphyrian, it represents an early, essentially pre-Neoplatonic phase of Porphyry's views, before his encounter wih Plotinus. For our purposes precise interpretation of the source of the passage's views is less important than the recognition that it represents one of a number of possible interpretations of a Homeric text based on Platonic assumptions. A similar, if not identical interpretation is offered by Pseudo-Plutarch, *De vita et poesi Homeri*, c. 126.[77] Such interpretations, however, are not merely matters of the allegorical meaning of Homer. Since Plato accepts the theory of human reincarnation into animals, understanding what he writes on the subject becomes important if, as for Porphyry and Iamblichus, that theory is unacceptable. In the solution of this dilemma the figurative or symbolic interpretation of Plato's views gains a new lease of life in later Neoplatonism.

Prior to Porphyry, the *Hermetica* and the *Chaldaean Oracles* had rejected the notion of a transmigration of human souls into animal bodies.[78] Cicero suggests that actual metamorphosis may be the equivalent of metaphorical, moral metamorphosis: 'For what difference does it make if someone changes from a human being into a beast, or exhibits the savageness of a beast in human form?' (*De officiis* 3.20.82).[79] A passage in Aeneas of Gaza suggests that both Porphyry and Iamblichus adopted a similar, metaphorical interpretation: 'They say that a man does not change into a donkey but into an asinine man, and does not change into a lion but into a leonine man' (*Theophrastos* 12.21f.). That some Neoplatonists (he does not name names) adopted a figurative as opposed to a literal interpretation of Plato's transmigration texts is confirmed by Nemesius.[80]

It is out of such a constellation of ideas that Boethius' views in 4.3 and 4 m. 3 develop. Focusing on the Homeric detail that the transformed companions retain their human minds,[81] he both excludes the view that human transmigration into animals is literally possible, and facilitates the alternative view that such talk is figurative, and does not entail complete, literal dehumanization of errant humans. For the bestiality of the types described in 4.3.17ff. depends on their human appearance and identity – they are humans, who have become *like* animals. Boethius thereby reflects not merely later Neoplatonic views – although his interest in the topic develops primarily out of

[77] See Kaiser (1964) 206; Deuse (n. 74 above) 145ff.

[78] *Corpus Hermeticum* 10.19; *Chaldaean Oracles*, fr. 160 des Places.

[79] Cf. *off.* 3.6.32.

[80] Nemesius, *De natura hominis* p. 116.2ff. Matthaei; cf. Proclus, *In Tim.* 3.294.22ff. Diehl.

[81] It is a detail upon which Porphyry *apud* Stob. 1.445ff. does not comment.

such views – but also a long tradition of metaphorical interpretations of the Circe episode.[82] Furthermore, he implicitly agrees with Augustine, for whom 'similarity in behaviour' between certain men and certain types of animal has led to the belief, mistaken as it is, in transmigration into animal forms. Augustine argues that only a metaphorical sense of transmigration is tenable, for rationality is an inalienable characteristic of the human soul (*De Genesi ad litteram* 7.10.15).[83] Augustine's discussion is in a context where he approves of, and adopts, Porphyry's figurative understanding of animal metempsychosis.

In the last line of the Circe poem the poisons which wound the mind are said to 'rage' (*saeviunt*).[84] Boethius, in using this term, links such forces for evil with other central manifestations of evil in the *Consolation*: the fickleness of Fortune, the tyrant, and unbridled natural forces. The adjective *saevus* denotes the cruelty of death which will not grant the grieving prisoner respite (1 m. 1.16), the ferocity of the north wind (1 m. 6.9), the pitiless indifference of the wheel of Fortune (2 m. 1.3), insatiable greed (2 m. 2.13), the deadly poison used by Nero (2 m. 6.17) – a direct parallel to our poem, the savage lions tamed by Orpheus' song (3 m. 12.11), and the savagery overcome by Hercules' labours (4 m. 7.15, 21). The verb *saevire* is a key term in evocations of Fortune (1.4.2), a traditional usage found in Catullus, Sallust, Horace, and Seneca, or it describes the tyrant (2.6.8), or evildoers generally (4.3.5, 4.4.1).[85] In the Golden Age poem discussed above (2 m. 5) *saevus* characterizes those qualities and events which undermine the Golden Age idyll – avarice (25), and war and violence (16.21). These terms conjure up a world in upheaval, violent and capricious, turbulent, and cruelly indifferent. The Circe poem contrasts this with the ideal of the mind, steadfast and stable in its citadel (27, 34). In opposing one key word (*saevire*) to another (*stabilis*), Boethius stresses the pivotal nature of the poem. The prisoner's own downfall and his distress at it are attributed to the fact that he 'was of unsteady step' (*stabili non erat … gradu*, 1 m. 1.22). The person dominated by passions is 'not stable or his own master' (*non … stabilis suique iuris*, 1 m. 4.16). By contrast, God is *stabilis* (3 m. 9.3). The universe, in obeying the regularity of its laws, is governed, even in change, by 'unwavering fidelity' (*stabili fide*, 2 m. 8.1). These laws (*foedera*), most evident in the celestial sphere, should also inform the earth and even men's turbulent lives (1 m. 5.42ff.: *stabiles*, 48). The

[82] Cf. e.g. Plutarch, *De esu carnium* 2, 996D; Heraclitus, *Allegoriae Homericae* 72.2ff. Buffière: see Kaiser (1964) 202f.

[83] See O'Daly (1987) 72ff.

[84] Cf. Virgil, *Aen.* 7.19, where Circe the poisoner is *dea saeva*; see further pp. 83f., 90 (with n. 49) above.

[85] See Gruber (1978) 55, 115.

cycle of cosmic change is a steady one (3 m. 2.38). God is the 'unmoved master of the world' (*stabilis ... rerum ... arbiter*, 4 m. 1.21f.), who maintains the order of things (*stabilis ... ordo*, 4 m. 6.42). By contrast, Fortune is *instabilis* (2.8.3). The stable mind is the godlike element in human beings, that part of them which links them to the governing forces of the universe. The metaphor of Circe's animal transformations typifies the extent to which insidious instability can invade man's moral centre. Lerer's observation is perceptive: 'Circe rules over a mock creation',[86] a parody of the true creation ruled over by God. If Circe's island is a microcosm of the earth, it is an earth cruelly out of joint. Crabbe compares Circe's power that is no true power with the pseudo-power of the tyrant.[87] Though her magic power appears to be great (9), in fact it is futile (29ff.). Circe's song (7) is seen to be limited in its power, as limited as are the song of Orpheus and Boethius' own poetry at the beginning of the work. But this Circe, the tyrant, the despicable poet, is also, in terms of the allegory and of the interpretation of it urged above, the deadly bringer of harm, the purveyor of moral poisons which transform a man's character and bestialize him. If the *Odyssey* is a metaphor of life's errant journey towards the goal of truth, the home of the mind, its Ithaca, then Circe represents a real and genuine obstacle of that journey. That is the purport of Plotinus' sustained allegorization of the *Odyssey* (1.6.8), where Circe symbolizes inferior pleasures. Crabbe has suggested that the Plotinus passage underlies the sequence of poems from 3 m. 12 to our Circe poem, even if its application in the Circe poem is not straightforward or even fully elaborated.[88] I shall return to this last point presently. First, however, I wish to concentrate on the motif of the errant journey.

Lerer, in pointing out that the geographical setting of the poem is emblematic and allusive, stresses the significance of the description of Odysseus' ships 'wandering (*vagas*) on the sea' (2).[89] Not only does it take up the theme of the journey from Book 2, with the attendant theme of Fortune's vagaries, but it also links up explicitly with the *vagus* motif in the work. The astronomer who defines and describes the movements of the stars pins down, so to speak, their 'wandering courses' (*vagos ... recursus*, 1 m. 2.10). The menacing and incalculable eruptions of volcanic Vesuvius characterize it as *vagus* (1 m. 4.7). The cosmic law defines the limits of earth and sea and does not allow the earth to 'wander' chaotically (*terris ... vagis*, 2 m. 8.11). In all these cases law and/or mind opposes errant disorder (in 1 m. 4 the dispassionate man remains indifferent to Vesuvius). Lerer's insight

---

[86] Lerer (1985) 189.
[87] Crabbe (1981a) 322ff.
[88] Crabbe (1981a) 318ff.
[89] Lerer (1985) 187ff.

may be developed. On the errant journey of the *Odyssey* Odysseus escapes the worst fate of his metamorphosed companions (who, significantly, lose all memory of their native land [*Od.* 10.236]): the saving of Odysseus is referred to briefly, but not exploited by Boethius (17ff.).[90] But by suppressing the theme of the loss of memory and highlighting the motif of the immutable and unaffected mind, Boethius isolates the Odysseus-like element in the companions. For it is the mind that can reactivate the memory and so provide the means of salvation and return, the end of wanderings. This is clearly not one-to-one allegory, in which each character or group of characters represents something unique and unequivocal: it is more like the use of symbol and metaphor in the Orpheus poem. By the use of *vagus*, a key term in the *Consolation*, Boethius extends and deepens the poem's symbolism in his own particular and characteristic fashion.[91] And he thereby reveals the dual influence already noted in other contexts: a specifically philosophical and Neoplatonic one, as well as a debt to the Latin poetic tradition.

This first aspect of Boethius' use of the term *vagus* has become apparent in the function of the *Odyssey* as a symbol of the soul's journey towards truth. But the term also provides a link with the specific tradition of the Circe allegory and its ramifications, in a way not hitherto noticed. In Plato's account the souls of the wicked 'wander' among tombs and graves until they are reincarnated in animal bodies (*Phaed.* 81d ff.): to wander is characteristic of the dead soul that has not reached its destination in Greek popular tradition. The souls undergo their own particular Odyssey. The motif of wandering, with its Platonic transmigration associations, links the Circe myth and what has been seen to be one of its prevalent Platonic interpretations, namely an image of the soul's animal transmigration after death. That is not, of course, the interpretation adopted by Boethius. But if the argument of the preceding pages is correct, then the Platonic tradition argues itself (if it so wishes) out of such an interpretation and into the acceptable alternative – that of the metaphorical bestialization of the soul. And that process of distancing oneself from a literal interpretation of Plato is the necessary means of reaching the acceptable alternative. Boethius is being allusive in the extreme in this most subtle of poems. In the term *vagus* he is not merely evoking *Odyssey* symbolism, but also one interpretation, which he rejects and reformulates, of the Circe episode; and he points the reader implicitly towards the complex of ideas and assumptions that provide the key to the interpretation of his poem.

[90] Plotinus, on the contrary, implies that Odysseus' recollection of his native land is the basis of his desire to return to it (1.6.8).

[91] Cf. Crabbe (1981a) 323. See Tarrant (1985) 47 with n. 161 on the motif of 'wandering' in Seneca's *Thyestes*. Cf. Segal (Ch. 3, n. 47 above).

Among recent critics Crabbe and Lerer have found the Circe poem
puzzling and unsatisfactory. For Lerer, the poem is and remains
ambivalent. Odysseus' companions are at one and the same time
wounded and unharmed. And the episode is not interpreted to its
conclusion: 'It is a profoundly unsettling poem precisely because it
offers no fixed center and no firm ending. Instead, it leaves the
Homeric story unfinished.'[92] Crabbe points out that the allegorization
of the story is incomplete, and that Boethius is aware that the Circe
episode is only partly susceptible to Neoplatonic allegorical interpretation. She concludes that Boethius solves his dilemma (which she sees
as in part caused by his having to insert the episode because he is
concerned that the run of poems from 3 m. 12 on should include a
returning Odysseus) by 'turning the myth on its head. Circe is a very
poor magician.'[93] To begin with the last point. Kaiser has shown that
the motif of the inefficacy of Circe's magic is traditional in Roman
poetry, and has a Greek antecedent in Pseudo-Theocritus 9.35f. In
Roman elegiac poetry, Circe's magic is ineffectual against, or in
comparison with, the power of true love. The diatribe tradition also
knows the motif of harmlessness, when Circe's physical powers are
compared unfavourably with the forces which poison and destroy the
mind.[94] It is likely that Boethius adopts this traditional motif not least
because it facilitates the transition in the poem from a literal to a
symbolic reading of the myth. Boethius is not embarrassed by the Circe
myth. He sees its potentially allusive, subtle meaning, to be conveyed
by the slightest of associative verbal hints. Nor is he concerned to
complete the interpretation of the myth. As has been seen above,[95] his
selection of the aspects to be treated is consistent with his purpose at
this stage of the work. It is the ravages of wickedness and the extent to
which they destroy human nature that preoccupy him. If he can in
passing convey the notion of Odysseus' salvation and the untouchable
core of the mind, then the picture is all the more complete. But the
poem is intentionally disturbing. For it is a vehicle for one of the most
difficult notions that Boethius wishes to convey in the *Consolation*: the
idea that, despite the most hideous moral corruption and dehumanization of the wicked, something uncorrupted remains in the human
being, his essentially good mind. Boethius must confront the diatribe
tradition of the bestialization of humans, which is grist to his mill, with
the belief which he truly holds and which is essential to his
understanding of Platonism. The Circe poem is the arena where these

[92] Lerer (1985) 190.
[93] Crabbe (1981a) 324.
[94] Kaiser (1964) 200; cf. Dio Chrysostom, *Or.* 33.58. For the theme in Roman elegiac
poetry see Propertius 2.1.53ff.; Tibullus 2.4.55ff.; Ovid, *Ars amatoria* 2.103ff.; *Remedia
amoris* 263ff.
[95] See pp. 210ff.

two conflicting interests meet and are resolved by means of the multiform suggestiveness of myth.

(iv) Agamemnon, Odysseus, and Hercules (4 m. 7)

Bella bis quinis operatus annis
ultor Atrides Phrygiae ruinis
fratris amissos thalamos piavit;
ille dum Graiae dare vela classi
optat et ventos redimit cruore,   5
exuit patrem miserumque tristis
foederat natae iugulum sacerdos.
flevit amissos Ithacus sodales,
quos ferus vasto recubans in antro
mersit immani Polyphemus alvo;   10
sed tamen caeco furibundus ore
gaudium maestis lacrimis rependit.
Herculem duri celebrant labores:
ille Centauros domuit superbos,
abstulit saevo spolium leoni,   15
fixit et certis volucres sagittis,
poma cernenti rapuit draconi
aureo laevam gravior metallo,
Cerberum traxit triplici catena,
victor immitem posuisse fertur   20
pabulum saevis dominum quadrigis,
Hydra combusto periit veneno,
fronte turpatus Achelous amnis
ora demersit pudibunda ripis,
stravit Antaeum Libycis harenis,   25
Cacus Evandri satiavit iras,
quosque pressurus foret altus orbis
saetiger spumis umeros notavit;
ultimus caelum labor inreflexo
sustulit collo pretiumque rursus   30
ultimi caelum meruit laboris.
ite nunc, fortes, ubi celsa magni
ducit exempli via. cur inertes
terga nudatis? superata tellus
sidera donat.   35

The avenging son of Atreus [Agamemnon], having waged war for ten years, exacted requital for his brother's lost marriage with the sack of Troy. When he wanted the Greek fleet to sail and bought winds with blood (5), he shed the father's role, and, sternly as a priest, mutilated his poor daughter's throat.

The man of Ithaca wept for his lost companions, whom savage Polyphemus, lying in his huge cave, hid in his monstrous belly (10). Yet he [Polyphemus], madly raging, blinded, paid for his pleasure with bitter tears.

His grim labours make Hercules famous. He tamed the proud

Centaurs, despoiled the fierce lion (15), shot the birds with his unerring arrows, seized the apples from under the dragon's very eyes – his left hand weighed down with metal of gold – and led Cerberus on his triple chain. A victor, he is said to have fed their harsh master (20) to the wild team of horses. The Hydra died, its poison burned up; the river Achelous, its brow disfigured, shamefully buried its face in its banks. He stretched Antaeus out on Libyan sands (25), and Cacus satisfied Evander's anger. The bristly boar flecked with its foam the shoulders upon which the vast universe would press. As a last labour he carried the heavens with unbent neck, and in turn earned (30) heaven, a reward for that last labour. Go now, you brave ones, where the high path of a great example leads! Why do you sluggishly bare your backs in flight? Earth, conquered, rewards with the stars.

After the prolonged and technical exposé of the relation and distinctions between providence and fate in 4.6, the following prose section 4.7 marks a return both to dialogue-form and to the popular philosophizing idiom of the diatribe. But, even if he now deliberately employs everyday expressions and examines them ('ill fortune', 4.7.6f.), Boethius does not eschew paradox: there is, he argues, no such thing as ill fortune, for fortune either rewards or tests the good, or punishes or corrects the wicked (2f.). Popular opinion leads to false distinctions between good and bad fortune (14ff.). It is at this level – popular but determinedly philosophical – that the conclusions of 4.7 and the following poem are pitched. Even if fortune is always good, Boethius argues, both the sage (who is in possession of virtue) and those who are progressing towards virtue must struggle with certain features of fortune. Fortune, if it is never bad, can none the less be adverse, and has to be warred against (4.7.10, 17). Life can be a struggle: 'You are fighting a bitter battle in your minds with every kind of fortune, that ill fortune may not oppress, nor pleasant fortune corrupt, you' (4.7.20). The moral struggle is also the theme of the following poem, whose opening word 'wars' (*bella*) takes up the references to war and battle of 4.7.10, 17, and 20.

The poem is in contrast with the other mythical metra already examined in that, rather than focusing upon one example or story, it treats in turn three mythical figures and some of their actions: Agamemnon is followed by Odysseus and Hercules. This has not always been found to be a merit. Thus Gruber suggested that the poem is flawed, and that only the third section, dealing with Hercules, elucidates the general points of the preceding prose section in the manner of a genuine *exemplum*.[96] Gruber finds the language and sequence of thought in the Agamemnon section 'clumsy', and suggests that the Odysseus section is not developed beyond elusive hints. He deprecates the lack of balance between the sections (7, 5, and 19

[96] Gruber (1978) 372.

verses), and speculates that the poem may be in an unfinished state. These are important criticisms, and cannot be overlooked, raising as they do the whole question of what is felt to be appropriate and successful in a poem by a late antique author. They will be dealt with in the following discussion.

Each of the three mythical sections will be considered in turn, before their relevance as *exempla* and illustrations of the concluding, generalizing lines (32ff.) and the antecedent prose section is examined.

Whereas there is a rich tradition of moralizing and allegorical interpretation clustering around the figures of Odysseus and Hercules, the person of Agamemnon attracts no such exegesis in antiquity. As Argive king and leader of the expedition against Troy Agamemnon is traditionally, even proverbially, the mighty and powerful ruler. Horace's *vixere fortes ante Agamemnona / multi* ('many brave men lived before Agamemnon', *Odes* 4.9.25f.) exemplifies his traditional function as the type of hero-king, without any appeal to the details of the *Iliad*, where he is often portrayed in a less than flattering light. Boethius highlights one of the most problematic and complex episodes in the myths regarding Agamemnon, his sacrifice of his daughter Iphigeneia at Aulis at the behest of the goddess Artemis in order to secure favourable winds for the armada to Troy. That episode, and the dilemma faced by Agamemnon – to disobey a goddess and risk disbanding the expedition, or to slaughter his own daughter – is a theme of tragedy rather than epic,[97] and is of varying importance in Aeschylus' *Agamemnon*, Euripides' *Iphigeneia in Aulis*, and Seneca's *Agamemnon*. The rich counterplay of compulsion (*anagkê*) and personal responsibility that characterizes the plays of Aeschylus and Euripides is, however, not explicitly influential in the few lines devoted by Boethius to the episode, and Scheible needs qualification when she adduces tragedy in general, and Euripides in particular, as the determining influence here.[98] A passage in Seneca's *Agamemnon* has indeed coloured Boethius' choice of language, as commentators have long observed. What is less certain is the degree to which the Seneca passage and its context are assumed by Boethius to be present in the reader's mind, and so counterpoint, as it were, his reading of our poem. In Seneca, in a dialogue-scene between the Nurse and Clytemnestra, the Nurse first recalls the consequences of the sacrifice of Iphigeneia:

---

[97] Though it featured in a poem of the epic cycle, the *Cypria*: see Proclus, *Chrestomathia* (*Homeri Opera*, OCT edn., vol. V, p. 104.12ff.). On Aeschylus' and others' treatments of the episode see E. Fraenkel (ed.), *Aeschylus: Agamemnon* (Oxford 1950) 2.96f.; the Greek religious background is discussed by H. Lloyd-Jones, 'Artemis and Iphigeneia', *Journal of Hellenic Studies* 103 (1983) 87-102.

[98] Scheible (1972) 152. It will be argued below that Boethius changes Agamemnon's dilemma from a confrontation with compulsion to an encounter with adverse fortune.

redemit illa classis immotae moras
et maria pigro fixa languore impulit (Ag. 160f.).

She [Iphigeneia] bought off the motionless fleet's delay, and roused the
sea fixed in its stagnant calm.

But for the mother Clytemnestra the sacrifice was a criminal butchery,
a justification of her plan to destroy Agamemnon:

cum stetit ad aras ore sacrificio pater
quam nuptialis! horruit Calchas suae
responsa vocis et recedentes focos.
o scelera semper sceleribus vincens domus:
cruore ventos emimus, bellum nece! (166ff.).

When her father stood at the altar (what a wedding altar!), the words of
sacrifice on his lips, Calchas shuddered at his oracular response and the
retreating flames. O house that constantly outdoes crimes with crimes!
We bought winds with blood, war with slaughter!

This version, albeit powerful and vivid, is also partisan. Boethius is at
once more brutal than Seneca in his description of the act of sacrifice (4
m. 7.7) and less evidently condemnatory (4ff.). The Senecan influence
is obvious in what Lerer has called the 'mercantile imagery' of 'bought'
(*redimit,* 5), echoing *redemit ... emimus* in *Agamemnon* 160 and 170,
just as one striking phrase in Seneca, *cruore ventos emimus* (170), is
clearly echoed in Boethius' *ventos redimit cruore* (5).[99] But it is less
obvious that the reader is intended by Boethius to find in his allusion a
reference to the whole theme of the violation and perversion of family
ties in Seneca's play, and to see in Boethius' choice of language an
unheroic Agamemnon depicted, 'a negative version of the dynamic of
reward'.[100] For what Boethius seems to be stressing in these lines and
in the first lines of the poem is the length of Agamemnon's enduring
vengeance (1) and its moral aspects: the latter dimension is
emphasized in the use of religious language (*piavit,* 3; *sacerdos,* 7).
Agamemnon endures 'shedding' the role of father (6) to act as
sacrificial priest. The pitiable nature of the sacrifice is not played
down, but this is no callous father cutting down a daughter, so much as
a sacrificer sternly and grimly (*tristis,* 6) confronting fortune. The
struggle involved is stressed both in the length of the war (1-3) and the
dilemma, subtly and allusively suggested by Boethius in the
juxtaposition of *miserumque tristis* (6), enacted at Aulis. But it would
be misguided to see Agamemnon as in the wrong here, unless we are to
assume that the triptych of the poem in some way reflects the threefold

---

[99] Lerer (1985) 192. Cf. Tarrant on Sen. *Ag.* 170, comparing it with Virgil, *Aen.* 2.116
sanguine placastis ventos et virgine caesa.
[100] Lerer (1985) 192.

division of the antecedent prose section (wicked – those progressing towards goodness – the good), and conclude that Agamemnon is the type of the wicked man punished or corrected by fortune. That may be a tempting reading, but the vocabulary of lines 1-7 of the poem at no stage reflects such a condemnatory stance: even the brutal *foederat natae iugulum* (7) is framed by the positive *tristis ... sacerdos* (6f.).

Thus, although Boethius' version follows the tradition, favoured in Latin literature, in which Iphigeneia dies at Aulis,[101] rather than that in which she is saved and a substitute animal victim is provided at the last moment by Artemis, the poem does not subscribe to the condemnatory tone of the first tradition, which extends from Lucretius' use of the episode as a lesson on the evils of superstition (*De rerum naturae* 1.82ff.)[102] to Cicero's use of it to illustrate a case where it is better to break a promise rather than commit a crime (*De officiis* 3.25.95), and Seneca's account from the mouth of a hostile Clytemnestra, discussed above. Gruber's stricture 'clumsy' seems unfair in the light of Boethius' subtle and concise recasting of a difficult example, in which the fate of Agamemnon depicted in tragedy becomes his struggle with testing fortune.

If allegorical interpretation of events in Agamemnon's life is rare, Odysseus and his adventures in the *Odyssey* are a rich quarry for ancient exegesis. This has been observed above in the discussion of the Circe poem: for Horace and his sources Odysseus is an example of what *virtus* and *sapientia* are capable (*Epist.* 1.2.17f.). Scheible rightly stresses the positive interpretation of Odysseus' actions in Plato, and in the tradition of Stoic and Neoplatonic allegory.[103] But her views should be qualified. While later interpretation of Odysseus' behaviour and character is never as negative and severe as it is among critics of Homer among the Sophists, or in Greek tragedies (such as Sophocles' *Philoctetes*), Odysseus is often portrayed as the errant wanderer on life's journey, whose goal is only reached after much deviation. This is the case with Plotinus, whose Odysseus reaches his source, his native land, only after dalliance with the blandishments of Circe and Calypso (1.6.8).[104] Odysseus thus represents the struggle to overcome vice and

[101] Aeschylus' *Agamemnon*, and the versions influenced by it, constitute a minority variant in the Greek tradition, as A. Henrichs, 'Human Sacrifice in Greek Religion: Three Case Studies', *Le Sacrifice dans l'Antiquité* (Entretiens Fondation Hardt 27, Geneva 1981) 195-235 (here 198-208), has shown.

[102] The Lucretius passage illustrates the use of the negative connotations of religious terms (... *deductast ... hostia concideret mactatu ... parentis*, 96, 99): Boethius' language illustrates their positive use.

[103] Scheible (1972) 153. See W.B. Stanford, *The Ulysses Theme. A Study in the Adaptability of a Traditional Hero*, 2nd edn. (Oxford 1963); Kaiser (1964); Buffière (1956) 365-91; R.B. Rutherford, 'The Philosophy of the *Odyssey*', *Journal of Hellenic Studies* 106 (1986) 145-62.

[104] Cf. Apuleius, *De deo Socratis* 177f. for a further positive interpretation of his wanderings, where Minerva represents his *prudentia*.

acquire virtue, as much as, if not more than, the possession of the latter. A similar ambivalence attends the two transmitted instances in which the episode treated in Boethius' poem, the blinding of the Cyclops, is interpreted by other late exegetes. In Porphyry the Cyclops is understood to represent the life of sense-perception and the act of blinding is equated with suicide, which in true Platonic manner is forbidden (*De antro nympharum* 35).[105] In the Stoically influenced *Homeric Questions* of Heraclitus a less negative interpretation is given. There (*Alleg. Hom.* 70) the Cyclops represents the savage spirit or temper (*thumos*) that must be cauterized by the sage's eloquent exhortations: the motif appears to be traditional in Homeric exegesis.[106] A negative Stoic interpretation of Odysseus' tears on Calypso's island (*Od.* 3.82f., etc.) is, however, given by Epictetus, who observes that weeping is a sign that Odysseus has not attained to the perfect goodness of the sage (3.24.18ff.).[107] It remains to be discussed whether this interpretation of Odysseus' tears is relevant to Boethius' evocation of the tears which he weeps for his lost companions in line 8 of our poem.

In Boethius' poem Odysseus' tears prompt him to heroic action, to that type of contest with fortune which the preceding prose section extols. Just as Agamemnon in the first part of the poem acts on behalf of another, Menelaus (3), so Odysseus acts to save his companions as much as himself. The parallelism is brought out by the repeated *amissos* in lines 3 and 8; and it is further stressed by the defeat of an enemy who is also a wrongdoer in each example. For Troy *ruinae* (2); for the Cyclops *lacrimae* (12). The analogies between the two heroes are stressed. Since that is so, the positive description of Agamemnon's sacrifice of Iphigenia discussed above, must be applied to the implicit, but not explicitly evalued, heroism of Odysseus. Boethius does not comment directly on Odysseus' behaviour as he does on Agamemnon's, although the description of Polyphemus (10f.) may be thought sufficiently hideous to be tantamount to praise of Odysseus' Hercules-like labour of blinding him. All this suggests that a negative or highly critical view of Odysseus is not being canvassed by Boethius, who does not appear to be appealing to that strand of the tradition referred to above. Thus Lerer's reading of this part of the poem is ultimately no more convincing than his interpretation of the Agamemnon part. The image of a over-emotional Odysseus, 'a man made captive to his tears',[108] a failure whose loss of wisdom and reason makes him like Orpheus, is not conveyed by a close reading of the text. Odysseus' tears may be felt to be problematic in view of the Epictetus

---

[105] Cf. Buffière (1956) 415f.
[106] Cf. Eusthatius 1622.55f.; Schol. on *Od.* 9.388; cf. Buffière (1956) 379 with n. 49.
[107] See Buffière (1956) 316f.
[108] Lerer (1985) 192.

passage referred to above.[109] Moreover, Boethius usually criticizes emotional outbursts and weeping, from 1 m. 1 and its criticism in 1.1 and subsequent sections of the first book, to 1 m. 7.28, seen against the context of 2.1.3 and 2.1.9ff., and Orpheus' laments in 3 m. 12.5ff. But if in 1 m. 7.25ff. and elsewhere in the earlier parts of the work Boethius seems to be advocating Stoic eradication of the emotions and impassivity, it is evident from the development of the specifically Platonic themes of Book 3 onwards that rational control of emotion, rather than its eradication, is the ideal to be aimed at. Not all tears are unequivocally to be condemned, whether they be those of the Furies softened by Orpheus' song (3 m. 12.31ff.) or the concerned tears of Odysseus in the Circe poem. Polyphemus' tears, on the other hand, are those of one justly punished, whose joy (12) was wrong and inappropriate. Thus the triptych reading of the poem explored briefly above in the case of Agamemnon,[110] although it may appear prima facie to accommodate a view of Odysseus as the man progressing towards virtue – a view that is, as has been seen, typical of the traditional exegesis – appears, once again, to be unlikely. Lerer's negative reading explores the vocabulary of 'mercantile imagery' in the Agamemnon (*redimit*, 5) and Odysseus (*rependit*, 12) sections. But to see in this imagery implicit condemnation in both cases may be to misread the tone and function of the image: there is no hint in e.g. 3 m. 12.43 that 'his wife ... purchased by his song' (*emptam carmine coniugem*) constitutes in itself a condemnation of Orpheus by Pluto, even if Orpheus' love and his song are both condemned in the poem. The verb *emere* is used because Orpheus' achievement in the terms of the mythical narrative is seen as a good thing; and consideration of the figurative usage of *emere, redimere* and related words does not reveal any distinctive negative strand that would allow us to denigrate the 'purchasing power' of Agamemnon's and Odysseus' actions in themselves. In his reading of this part of the Odysseus myth Boethius seems to place Odysseus on the side of the angels.

The Hercules[111] section occupies the largest part of the poem (13-31), and focuses upon twelve of his labours: the section is framed by two instances of the word *labor* (13,31). The linking of Agamemnon with Hercules in a sequence of *exempla* may be due to Seneca's influence. In *Agamemnon* 808ff., a choral ode which, as will be seen below,[112] has clearly influenced details of the Hercules section in Boethius' poem, the example of Hercules is evoked as an Argive hero whose exploits, it is

---

[109] Lerer does not adduce the Epictetus passage.

[110] See pp. 223f. above.

[111] On Hercules see G.K. Galinsky, *The Herakles Theme. The Adaptations of the Hero in Literature from Homer to the Twentieth Century* (Oxford 1972); Buffière (1956) 377 n. 41; Zwierlein (1984).

[112] See p. 228 below.

implied, are comparable with those of the Argive victor at Troy, Agamemnon:

> *Argos nobilibus nobile civibus,*
> *... semper ingentes educas alumnos ...* (*Ag.* 808, 810).

Argos, noble through its noble citizens ... you always produce great children.[113]

The linking of Hercules with Odysseus is, on the other hand, widespread in the poetry and mythical exegesis of the Greek and Roman traditions, beginning with the explicit comparison between their labours made by Herakles in Homer (*Od.* 11.617ff.). The Stoics link Odysseus and Hercules as types of the *sapiens*: 'For these men [Ulysses and Hercules] our Stoics declared to be sages, unconquered in their toils, despisers of pleasure, and victors over all the earth' (Seneca, *De constantia sapientis* 2.1). Seneca provides several examples of the way in which Hercules is considered by the Stoics as the *Urbild* of the sage, and indeed of the divine element in the universe, equated with nature and fate: '[Our Stoics consider] Hercules [a god] because his strength is unconquered, and when he is weary of performing labours, he will return to the fire' (*De beneficiis* 4.8.1). Seneca argues that one should not weep for the grim fates of Hercules, Regulus, or Cato: 'All of these found how, at a slight temporal cost, they might become eternal, and, by dying, reached immortality' (*De tranquillitate animi* 16.4).[114] And a similar sentiment is evoked at the end of the *Hercules Oetaeus*:

> *numquam Stygias fertur ad umbras*
> *inclita virtus: vivite fortes*
> *nec Lethaeos saeva per amnes*
> *vos fata trahent,*
> *sed cum summas exiget horas*
> *consumpta dies,*
> *iter ad superos gloria pandet* (*HO* 1983ff.).

Glorious virtue is never drawn down to the Stygian shades: live, you brave ones, and the fierce Fates will not drag you through the waters of Lethe, but, when the day is over and the final hours are to be expended, fame will open the path to the gods on high.

Boethius, who makes the upholding of the sky in place of Atlas the climax of Hercules' labours, echoes the linking of this labour with the hero's apotheosis (4 m. 7.29ff.) that is found in Seneca:

---

[113] See Scheible (1972) 153.
[114] Cf. Seneca, *De beneficiis* 1.13.2f.; *Ag.* 808ff.

> *... et posse caelum viribus vinci suis*
> *didicit ferendo; subdidit mundo caput*
> *mediusque collo sedit Herculeo polus*
> *nec flexit umeros molis immensae labor;*
> *immota cervix sidera et caelum tulit*
> *... quaerit ad superos viam (Hercules furens* 69ff.).

And, by carrying it, he learned that heaven can be conquered by his strength; he placed his head beneath the universe, and the heavens balanced on Hercules' neck, and the pain of the great weight did not make his shoulders bend; with unmoving neck he bore the stars and the sky ... he seeks a way to the gods above.

The same linking of labour and apotheosis is found in Seneca's imitator, the author of the *Hercules Oetaeus*: *quem tuli mundum peto* ('I seek the word I bore', *HO* 98). But the influence of Seneca and the Senecan tradition is not confined to these aspects of Boethius' poem. Scheible and Zwierlein have observed (following earlier commentators) that *Agamemnon* 848ff. has influenced lines 15ff. of our poem in more than one respect.[115] Not merely is there a striking sequence of verbal reminiscences, but the order of labours – Stymphalian birds, apples of the Hesperides, fetching of Cerberus – is identical. The verbal reminiscences are revealing for Boethius' poetic method. Thus the vocabulary of Seneca's descriptions of the defeat of the Amazon queen is reflected in Boethius' description (15) of the defeat of the Nemean lion:

> *vidit Hippolyte ferox*
> *pectore e medio rapi*
> spolium ... (*Ag.* 848ff.).

Fierce Hippolyte sees the spoil ripped from her very breast ...

Moreover, the Senecan sequence *spolium, et sagittis* (*Ag.* 850), which serves to link the Amazon and Stymphalian exploits, is mirrored in Boethius' *spolium ... sagittis* (15f.), which links the Nemean lion labour to the Stymphalian exploit.[116] It has long been observed that the description of the Cerberus episode in Boethius (19) is explicitly indebted to Seneca: *tractus ad caelum canis inferorum triplici catena* ... ('the dog of the underworld is dragged up to daylight on a triple chain', *Ag.* 859f.).[117] A reminiscence from a different context, referring to Phoebus, not Hercules, is observed when *figit sagitta certior missa puer* ('the boy shoots his arrow unerringly, and hits home', Seneca, *Phaedra* 193) is compared with l. 16 of Boethius' poem.

But Zwierlein has also shown that two further Senecan passages

---

[115] Scheible (1972) 154f.; Zwierlein (1984) 57ff.   [116] Zwierlein (1984) 57ff.
[117] See Bieler's *CCL* edn. ad loc.; cf. also line 18 of Boethius' poem and *Ag.* 857f.

have helped to form the substance of Boethius' poem. One is the
evocation of some of Hercules' labours at *Phaedra* 317ff. There is
identity of metre and similarity of vocabulary in Boethius (15) and in *et
minax vasti spolium leonis* ('and the menacing spoil of the huge lion',
Phae. 318).[118] And Seneca's ... *umerisque, quibus sederat alti regia
caeli* ... ('on the shoulders, on which the high court of heaven had
rested', *Phae.* 328f.) is echoed in Boethius (27f.). A similar influence of
Seneca, *Medea* 634ff. is discernible. Not merely is the exhortation *ite
nunc, fortes* (32) identical with *Med.* 650, as has long been observed,
but Seneca's description of the overcoming of Ancaeus – *stravit
Ancaeum violentus ictu / saetiger* ... ('the violent bristly boar stretched
Ancaeus out with a blow ...', *Med.* 643f.) – influences Boethius (25ff.).
These and other Senecan echoes make of this part of Boethius' poem a
cento, no less, of Senecan phrases. And yet the economy and fluency of
Boethius' writing never fails him. It is a *tour de force*, twelve labours
evoked in eighteen lines, in a sequence of cameo portraits. It reflects
Boethius' delight in artfully composed catalogues.[119] And the
disproportion in length between this section and the first two is less a
stylistic flaw than an example of elaboration for its own sake: a similar
disproportion in different contexts is observable in the massively
developed messenger-speech descriptions in Seneca's plays.[120] Virtu-
osity in an identifiable tradition is a prime aim of this type of writing.

And yet, apart from the linking of the labour of upholding the
heavens and the apotheosis of Hercules, specific links to the broader
thematic concerns of a play like Seneca's *Hercules furens* are not
immediately apparent in Boethius' poem. Zwierlein may be right to
argue that Boethius confirms the ancient interpretation of that play in
that he portrays an exemplary hero, great and good, with a cosmic role
and a deserved apotheosis, a hero who is the innocent victim of Juno,
and in no sense a victim of his own arrogance and abuse of his power
and strength.[121] Certainly Boethius' poem gives no joy to the advocates
of the latter interpretation of Seneca's play. But if we are to adduce
Boethius to interpret Seneca on the basis of this part of the poem, then
the later author provides no more than an argument from silence:
Boethius simply does not enter into such details, and the madness of
Hercules is no more a theme for him than it is for Seneca in the
Hercules passages in *Agamemnon* and *Phaedra*.[122] Now as we have

[118] Zwierlein (1984) adduces, as further parallels to line 15, *Phae.* 772 and *Herc. fur.*
1154.

[119] Cf. the underworld catalogue in 3 m. 12.29ff.

[120] Cf. *Ag.* 421-578; *Oed.* 530-658; *Phae.* 1000-1114; see Tarrant (1985) 180.

[121] Zwierlein (1984) 22ff. Fitch (1987) 15-43 is an excellent survey of the different
interpretations of Seneca's hero: Fitch's own view ('the failings of ... Hercules outweigh
his virtues and ... his madness arises from his own psyche', 21 n. 19) represents the
dominant tendency in modern critical interpretation of the play.

[122] Neither is it a theme in Seneca's *Medea* 634ff., where Hercules' quite different

seen, it is precisely those other Senecan passages which seem to have influenced Boethius as much as, if indeed not more than, the play *Hercules furens*. And that should not surprise us. For the exemplary function of the Hercules myth in those passages is closer to Boethius' concern than the elaborate exploitation of the aspect of the Hercules story dealt with in the *Hercules*, an aspect not intimately related to the labours as such, but rather a consequence of some of them. The labours contribute to the good fame of Hercules (*celebrant*, 13): that is the simple and unequivocal message of Boethius' poem. These are deeds that bring their due reward (29ff.). Juno's anger, Hercules' madness – the themes of *Hercules furens* – do not concern him. As an artist, he is interested in the elaboration of details in his description of the labours; but as a moralist he makes them all teach the same lesson. It would appear that no matter how much Senecan material Boethius uses, this has no implications for his understanding of the tragic Hercules of Seneca's *Hercules* play.

The preceding comments will underline how unacceptable Lerer's interpretation of the Hercules part of the poem is.[123] It is not really a question of Lerer's interpretation of the *Hercules furens*, which he understands differently from Zwierlein as a tragedy of arrogant pride and self-esteem. The issue is rather to what extent, if any, a reading of the Boethius poem constitutes a dialogue with Seneca's play. I take up some of the points at which Lerer feels that such a dialogue is occurring. The reference to *spolium* (15) is understood by him to be an ironical reference to the importance of the *spolia* in the *Hercules furens* for the hero's pride. But, even if one accepts Lerer's reading of the play, what plausible link is there between a possible function of 'spoils' in the play and the perfectly natural reference to them in the context of the Nemean lion labour, a reference whose phrasing, as has been seen above, is dependent upon Senecan usage in passages that do not raise the issue of the function of spoils in any interpretation of Hercules' tragic heroism? There is, furthermore, no evident link between the tone of Juno's speech in the play and Boethius' poem:[124] to suggest that Boethius' readers must be reminded of the contrast between 'Senecan harridans' (like Juno) and Lady Philosophy, and that Boethius is explicitly stressing the positive aspects of the Hercules myth against the background of Juno's speech, is to appeal to a hypothesis for which no textual evidence exists. For there is no suggested movement from the darkness of the *Hercules furens* to the alleged rehabilitation of Hercules as a philosophical *exemplum* of a righted universe in

culpability (*crimen*, 647) in venturing on the seas is shared with the other Argonauts.
    [123] Lerer (1985) 193ff.
    [124] Lerer (1985) 201. There is, of course, the influence of *Herc. fur.* 69ff. (discussed pp. 227f. above) upon lines 29ff. of Boethius' poem: but that is precisely the most positive part of Juno's prologue, and cannot be adduced in support of Lerer's case.

Boethius' poem: his Hercules is one on whom the sun never sets.

Lerer perceptively suggests that the echo of *ite nunc, fortes* (*Medea* 650) in line 32 should alert the reader to the contrast between the phrase in its original setting, where it is satirical, implying 'go and do X which has proved disastrous' – like sailing the seas – and its clearly positive connotations in Boethius, 'a benign injunction'.[125] There can be no doubt about the tone of the *Medea* exhortation, which may be aptly compared with *Medea* 1007 *i nunc, superbe* ('go now, proud one'), and the same phrase in *Hercules furens* 89, spoken by Juno, whose following words, *caelitum sedes pete / humana temne* ('seek the seats of the gods, despise things human'), are certainly apt to the Boethius context. But we cannot assume that a verbal reminiscence of this kind carries with it, so to speak, a reference to the context of its origin, and constitutes a comment on it: certainly we cannot do so when the context of the later passage affords no more explicit link to the *meaning* of the original text (or texts) than in this instance. Boethius, like all poets of antiquity, will have had a rich reservoir of remembered phrases from earlier poets. He will not necessarily have intended, when using them or adapting them, that they import their original context with them. He is, after all, not quoting, but creating from materials at his disposal. This is not to deny that such allusiveness never occurs in Latin poetry; but it operates in a different and recognizable way.[126] In fact, the influence on Boethius in *ite nunc, fortes* may be the *Hercules Oetaeus* passage referred to above, where in the context of the rewards of *virtus* and ascent to the heavens the poet exhorts *vivite fortes* ('live, you brave ones', *HO* 1984). Here theme and sentiment reinforce the verbal similarity, even if it has been seen that this is not a precondition of such reminiscences in Boethius.

It is now time to turn to the thematic links between the Hercules passage and the two preceding parts of the poem, and to consider their relevance to the poem's general conclusion (32ff.). At first sight, there is a striking lack of parallelism between the Hercules and the other sections. For Hercules is not depicted as one who invariably punishes wrongdoers in his labours, or even confronts evils.[127] What is stressed is his endurance and resourcefulness, a range of achievement that makes the hero famous and brings its reward. If a common denominator is to be sought with the portrayals of Agamemnon and Odysseus, then it is surely in the themes of endurance (prolonged also in Agamemnon's case) and readiness to do the courageous and ultimately beneficial, if terrible, deed. Resourceful confrontation with adverse fortune is the keynote theme. And that echoes the words of the preceding 4.7.22: 'For it is in your hands what kind of fortune you

---

[125] Lerer (1985) 200.

[126] See pp. 196ff. with n. 30 above.

[127] Diomedes (20f.) and possibly the Centaurs (14) are exceptions.

prefer to mould for yourselves.' Such resourceful confrontation makes every fortune 'good' (4.7.3).

While, as has been pointed out above, the moralizing interpretation of Hercules' labours is primarily a feature of Stoic exegesis, it is (as early as Prodicus' allegory of Herakles at the crossroads)[128] not exclusively so. Neither the Hercules of the Stoic Seneca's *Hercules furens*, nor the hero of the *Hercules Oetaeus*, can be understood in specifically or purely Stoic terms. The same is true of Boethius' Hercules. His Hercules is the type of the brave man (*fortis*, cf. 32) whose reward is the apotheosis described in Homer, *Od*. 11.601ff. and assumed in Sophocles' *Philoctetes* and elsewhere. It could be said that Hercules in Boethius is the traditional hero of the Greek and Roman poetic traditions, but especially when these, in the Roman context, are informed by philosophically-influenced allegory.[129] It is precisely the influence of the poetic tradition coloured by philosophical allegory, discussed briefly above[130] in the examples from Seneca and Pseudo-Seneca, which determines the parameters of Boethius' verses, especially the final, generalized lines 32ff. For those lines seem, at first sight, to refer exclusively to Hercules (34f.). It would be misguided to find here an oblique reference to the posthumous fates of Agamemnon or Odysseus. Boethius appears to be thinking primarily of his last hero. But what is said of him can be readily extended to the other two as examples of virtue: the tradition reflected in Cicero's *Somnium Scipionis*, where sidereal immortality is the lot of the great and good, may colour this finale, possibly filtered through the poetic tradition of the ascent of the soul to the heavens.[131]

The motif of ascent, which featured in the Orpheus poem 3 m. 12 and its sequel 4 m. 1, is one of a number of links in the cycle of poems that leads from Orpheus' flawed ascent to Hercules, who achieves true ascent. Lerer has pointed out further motifs which link this poem to its immediate and more distant antecedents in the work.[132] One such theme is that of loss and restitution (Orpheus, Agamemnon): struggle and reward (Orpheus, and all three heroes of 4 m. 7) is another. The theme of enchainment and enslavement is a further linking motif. Found here in line 19, it is also reflected in Hercules' 'unbent neck' (29f.) as he upholds the heavens, the antithesis of the disturbed Boethius of 1 m. 2.24ff.:

[128] Prodicus' allegory: Xenophon, *Memorabilia* 2.1.21-34 (= DK 84 B 2). See W. Schultz, 'Herakles am Scheidewege', *Philologus* 68 (1909) 489-99. Cf. Juvenal, 10.357ff. for an evocation of Hercules' labours that is coloured by Cynic and Stoic influences.

[129] For Hercules in Roman poetry from Virgil to Claudian see Zwierlein (1984) 7ff., 31ff., 46ff.; cf. Galinsky (n. 111 above) 126ff.; Fitch (1987) *passim*.

[130] See pp. 227ff. above.
[131] See pp. 201ff. above.
[132] Lerer (1985) 190ff.

nunc iacet effeto lumine mentis
et pressus gravibus colla catenis
declivemque gerens pondere vultum
cogitur, heu, stolidam cernere terram.

Now he lies, the light of his mind extinguished, his neck weighed down with heavy chains, his gaze sunk under the burden, he is forced – ah! – to look upon the mindless earth.[133]

The triumph of Hercules and the other heroes of 4 m. 7 is a moral one, earlier described as dependent upon the condition that one *nec victa libidine colla / foedis summittat habenis* ... ('should not, overcome by desire, submit his neck to the foul halter', 3 m. 5.3f.). The poetic elaboration of these motifs and images culminates in this poem, just as its exhortatory ending anticipates that of the final lines of the work, especially 'So turn vices aside, cultivate virtues, raise up your mind to honourable hopes, direct humble prayers on high' (5.6.47).[134]

A final example of the underpinning of an essentially poetic image by philosophically induced allusions is found in lines 33f. The phrase *terga nudare* is used here in the sense of *terga fuga nudare* ('to turn the back in flight'), as in Virgil (*Aen.* 5.586) and Lucan (4.713). *Inertes* ('sluggards'), further, is not used in the sense of refusal to take on a burden, but rather in the sense of moral inadequacy. Seneca's assessment of Ovid's Phaethon (Ovid, *Met.* 11.63ff.) is couched in terms which elucidate a choral ode in *Hercules furens* (125ff.) that may be also adduced to clarify our passage. Speaking of good people, Seneca writes:

Effete (*languida*) natures, and ones inclined to sleep or to a waking state that is virtually indistinguishable from sleep, are bound to the sluggish (*inertibus nectuntur*) elements ... Fire assays gold, suffering men of courage (*fortes viros*). See how high (*alte*) virtue should ascend (*escendere*): you will realize that it must not proceed on safe paths ... It is mean (*humilis*) and lazy (*inertis*) to pursue what is without risk: virtue takes the high route (*per alta virtus it*) (*De providentia* 5.9ff.).[135]

As the italicized phrases indicate, the motifs of virtuous ascent, bravery, and the overcoming of dilatory inactivity and moral sluggishness (*languida, inertibus*) are linked here as in the finale of the Boethius poem. The antithesis *fortes-inertes* is elucidated by this context.[136] The chorus of *inertes* themselves describe the same alternatives from their unheroic viewpoint in *Hercules furens* 196ff.:

[133] Cf. 1 m. 4.18.

[134] Cf. Gruber (1978) 376.

[135] Cf. Seneca, *De vita beata* 20.2. The interpretation of *terga nudare* adopted here is that of Zwierlein (1984) 34, as against Gruber (1978) 376.

[136] Cf. 1 m. 5.3 *inerti perdita luxu*.

alius curru sublimis *eat:*
me mea tellus lare secreto
   tutoque tegat.
venit ad pigros *cana senectus,*
humilique *loco sed certa sedet*
sordida parvae fortuna domus:
alte virtus *animosa cadit.*

Let another seek the heights in his chariot: may my own soil, my obscure, protective household gods, guard me. White-haired old age comes to the easy-going; the humble fortune of a little house stands on lowly ground, but is secure: spirited virtue falls from a great height.

And the poet of the *Hercules Oetaeus* evokes the same metaphor – *iter ad superos gloria pandet* ('Fame will open the path to the gods on high', *HO* 1988) – for the 'brave ones' (*fortes*, 1984) and 'glorious virtue' (*inclita virtus*, ib.).

In the case of Phaethon, Ovid and Seneca were dealing with a glorious failure; but that does not prevent Phaethon, for Seneca, being an example of the good man's confrontation of his destiny.[137] This parallel makes it all the more difficult to throw any negative light on the achievement of the heroes of Boethius' poem, whose success was fraught with terrible risks, such as are to be expected in the struggle with fortune. That is why they can be examples to Boethius and his readers (32f.).

(v) Some conclusions

What purpose does the introduction of the mythical motifs into the *Consolation* serve? From the foregoing it will have become apparent that the myths are focal points of central concerns of the work. The themes of ascent and descent, remembering and forgetting, reason and passion, loss and restoration, enchainment and liberation, impotence and action, acquire in the mythical figures of the four poems discussed a pregnant vividness that is characteristic of the use of myths as *exempla* from early Greek lyric onwards. In the person of an Orpheus, an Odysseus, or a Hercules, Boethius, like Greek and Latin poets before him, explores the complexities of human actions and provides his own characteristic analysis of those actions and behaviour.

But the mythical poems do more. It has been observed that the unique character of the *Consolation* derives from its dual quality as both a work in the Latin literary tradition and a late Neoplatonist philosophical tractate. The myths illustrate how such a symbiosis is achieved. They cannot be understood fully without reference to their immediate and more general philosophical contexts. But they are at

---

[137] Seneca, *De providentia* 5.8.

the same time a response to the mythical exploration of certain motifs – Orpheus and Eurydice, the labours of Hercules – in poets like Virgil and Seneca. Reference to those antecedents clarifies both Boethius' craftsmanship and his poetic intentions. But that is not tantamount to an explicit comment on his antecedents. Part of the pleasure to be derived from the reading of these poems is due to a recognition of the tradition of which they are part. Yet that is not the same as intended explicit dialogue with that tradition. Like all poets from the Hellenistic period onwards, Boethius depends upon his readers to accept and appreciate allusiveness. But he is not 'rewriting' any earlier poem. Rather, he is rewriting a complex tradition. With a mind and a sensibility imbued with the poetry of a Homer, a Virgil, an Ovid, and a Seneca, as well as with Plato, Cicero, Seneca's philosophical writings, and the Neoplatonists from Plotinus to Proclus, he can combine, select, allude to, elaborate on, a multifaceted spectrum of ideas, images, and intuitions. What emerges is a new artefact – a new *kind* of artefact – that can appeal and be absorbed on its own terms. This is particularly apparent in his creative metamorphosis of central myths in the literary tradition.

Postscript

Most wretched men
Are cradled into poetry by wrong,
They learn in suffering what they teach in song.
                                    Shelley, *Julian and Maddalo*

The *Consolation of Philosophy* is the work of a man whose world has been shattered. Disgraced, his family's future threatened, condemned to death, he writes a book which fulfils what Plato considered to be the philosopher's true task: to prepare himself for death (*Phaedo* 67d-e). The *Consolation* urges moral clear-sightedness and discipline upon the philosopher; it appeals to reason and exalts the life of the mind. But it also proffers meditations which are emotionally satisfying, which speak to human sensibility as well as to the intellect, to our awareness of beauty as much as to the perception of order in things. The artistic form of the *Consolation* expresses and integrates this dual perspective: its unity is the fusion of understanding and feeling. The poems of the work are an essential part of that unity. As the foregoing chapters have shown, they express some of the work's central themes, and they do so in a subtle way: through the poems themes are foreshadowed, developed, modified, and their complexities and contradictions explored and resolved. Imagery and symbolism illustrate, but are also a medium of discourse about, the *Consolation*'s main concerns. It is a work that ends with a harmonious vision of the world and our place in it: to that extent, the poetry of the *Consolation* exemplifies what Boethius saw as the musical structure of the universe. But it is also a work which gives voice to anger, despair, puzzlement, and confusion: its poetry, and the rhetorical tensions of some of its prose, express the prisoner's darker feelings and fears. Boethius is 'most wretched' and he must make his suffering bearable, but without turning his back on it and ignoring it. There will be no consolation if his sense of being wronged is not confronted.

To label the poetry of the *Consolation* 'didactic' is too simplistic a response to its many functions, unless we are aware of the importance and value of moral and metaphysical reflection and instruction in Greek and Roman cultural life, and in literature as well as philosophy. This book has explored several of the traditions of which the

Consolation is a beneficiary, and to which it contributes. It has attempted to show that a responsive reading of Boethius' work depends upon a realization of the many kinds of allusiveness in that work. Virgil, Ovid, and Senecan tragedy, no less than Plato and the Neoplatonists, Cicero's philosophical writings, and Epictetus, form the imaginative and intellectual world of the *Consolation*. In this world the art of poetry has its privileged place. We cannot know what sense Boethius may have had of writing at the end of a long tradition: it is unlikely that he saw with the clarity which historical hindsight has given us that he was, in Gibbon's words, 'the last of the Romans whom Cato or Tully could have acknowledged for their countryman'. The *Consolation of Philosophy* has often been regarded as the final chapter of ancient philosophy. This book has endeavoured to show that its cultural importance is much wider: when Boethius sought consolation in his captivity, he was also consoled by the idioms and images of Latin poetry, and his own poetry is a late and subtle flowering of that art form.

Select Bibliography

A. The *Consolation of Philosophy*: editions, commentaries, and translations

Anicii Manlii Severini Boetii Philosophiae Consolationis libri v, ed. R. Peiper (Leipzig 1871). The first modern critical edition. Its index of Seneca passages which have, or may have, influenced Boethius (228-33) is still valuable.

Boethius: The Theological Tractates and the Consolation of Philosophy, edd. H.F. Stewart and E.K. Rand (*LCL*, London/Cambridge, Mass. 1918). Prints a revised seventeenth-century translation of the *Consolation*. Replaced by the new Loeb edition of 1973, with a translation of the *Consolation* by S.J. Tester.

Boethi De Consolatione Philosophiae libri v, edd. A. a Forti Scuto = A. Fortescue and G.D. Smith (London 1925, reprinted Hildesheim/New York 1976). Annotated edition.

Anicii Manlii Severini Boethii Philosophiae Consolationis libri v, ed. W. Weinberger (*CSEL* 67, 1934). Based on a wider collation of manuscripts than Peiper's edition: a reliable text.

Boethius: Philosophiae Consolationis libri quinque, ed. K. Büchner (Heidelberg 1947, 3rd edn. 1977). A hand edition without critical apparatus, but with a useful metrical appendix.

Anicii Manlii Severini Boethii Philosophiae Consolatio, ed. L. Bieler (*CCL* 94, 1957, 2nd edn. 1984). Adds new manuscript evidence, and is, on the whole, the best edition. Greatly extends Weinberger's references to sources and parallel passages. Used in the present book: where a variant text is printed, the reader's attention is drawn to the fact.

Boethius: Trost der Philosophie, edd. E. Gegenschatz and O. Gigon (Zürich/Munich 1969, new edn. 1981). Text and German translation; stimulating introduction and useful analytical notes, mainly on the arguments of the prose passages, by Gigon. Replaces the 1949 edn. by E. Gothein.

Die Gedichte in der Consolatio Philosophiae des Boethius, by H. Scheible (Bibliothek der klassischen Altertumswissenschaften N.F. 46, Heidelberg 1972). A detailed and perceptive commentary (without text) on the poems. Cited in this book as Scheible (1972).

Kommentar zu Boethius De Consolatione Philosophiae, by J. Gruber (Texte und Kommentare 9, Berlin/New York 1978). Learned and comprehensive commentary (without text) on the entire work: an indispensable study, unparalleled in any language. Cited in this book as Gruber (1978).

Boethius: Consolatio Philosophiae, by J.J. O'Donnell (Bryn Mawr Latin

Commentaries, Bryn Mawr, Pa. 1984). Reprints Weinberger's *CSEL* text, adding brief and particularly useful notes, mainly on points of grammar and translation. Cited in this book as O'Donnell (1984).

There are many modern translations of the *Consolation of Philosophy*: that by S.J. Tester in the revised Loeb edition (see above) is, on the whole, the most satisfactory English version (cf. however J.J. O'Donnell's critical review, *American Journal of Philology* 98 [1977] 77-9). See also the Penguin translation by V.E. Watts (Harmondsworth 1969). The best modern version known to me is Karl Büchner's German translation, *Boethius: Trost der Philosophie* (Leipzig 1939, reprinted Stuttgart 1971). There is an Italian version by L. Obertello, *Boezio: La Consolazione della filosofia, Gli opuscoli teologici* (Milan 1979). For details of editions of other works of Boethius see Abbreviations, p. xii above.

B. Other authors: editions, commentaries, and translations

Standard editions of, and commentaries on, Greek and Latin authors are omitted from this list (for abbreviated titles see Abbreviations, pp. xif. above), with the exception of some works which have been cited frequently in the book. The list also includes some less readily identifiable editions, as well as the sources of translations quoted in the book.

Aeneas of Gaza. *Enea di Gaza: Teofrasto*, ed. M.E. Colonna (Naples 1958).
Anonymus Valesianus. *Excerpta Valesiana*, ed. J. Moreau, revised by V. Velkov (Leipzig 1968).
Aristotle. *The Poetics of Aristotle*, tr. and comm. by S. Halliwell (London 1987).
Ausonius. ed. S. Prete (Leipzig 1978).
—— ed. and tr. by H. Evelyn White, 2 vols. (*LCL* 1919 and 1921). This edn. follows the system of numbering the works in R. Peiper's edn. (Leipzig 1886), and I have used that system in this book.
Bion of Borysthenes. ed. J.F. Kindstrand (Uppsala 1976).
Calcidius. *Timaeus a Calcidio translatus commentarioque instructus*, ed. J.H. Waszink, 2nd edn. (Corpus Platonicum Medii Aevi, Plato Latinus 4, London/Leiden 1975).
Cassiodorus, *Variarum libri xii*, ed. A.J. Fridh (*CCL* 96, 1973).
Catullus. ed. and tr. G.P. Goold (London 1983).
Chaldaean Oracles. Oracles Chaldaiques, ed. E. des Places (Paris 1971).
Cicero. *Tusculan Disputations*, ed. and tr. by J.E. King (*LCL* 1927).
Ennodius. *Magni Felicis Ennodii opera*, ed. Fr. Vogel (*MGH* 7, 1885).
Fulgentius. *Opera*, ed. R. Helm (Leipzig 1898).
Hermetica. Hermès Trismégiste (Corpus Hermeticum), edd. A.D. Nock and A.-J. Festugière, 4 vols. (Paris 1945-54).
Hesiod. *Theogony; Works and Days*, tr. M.L. West (Oxford World's Classics, 1988).
Horace. *The Third Book of Horace's Odes*, ed. with tr. and comm. by G. Williams (Oxford 1969).
—— *The Epistles*, tr. C. Macleod (Instrumentum Litterarum 3, Rome 1986).
—— *The Art of Poetry (Ars Poetica)*, tr. D.A. Russell, in *Ancient Literary Criticism. The Principal Texts in New Translations*, edd. D.A. Russell and M. Winterbottom (Oxford 1972) 279-91.

240   *Select Bibliography*

Lucan, *The Civil War (Pharsalia)*, ed. and tr. by J.D. Duff *(LCL* 1928).

Lucretius. *De Rerum Natura*, ed. and tr. by W.H.D. Rouse *(LCL* 1924), revised 2nd edn. by M.F. Smith (1975, further revised 1982).

Manilius. *Astronomica*, ed. and tr. by G.P. Goold *(LCL* 1977).

Martianus Capella. ed. J. Willis (Leipzig 1983).

—— *A Philosophical and Literary Commentary on Martianus Capella's De Nuptiis Philologiae et Mercurii Book 1*, by D. Shanzer (University of California Publications: Classical Studies 32, Berkeley/Los Angeles/London 1986). Cited in this book as Shanzer (1986b).

Maximianus Etruscus. *Poetae Latini Minores*, ed. E. Baehrens, vol. 5 (Leipzig 1883).

Numenius. ed. E. des Places (Paris 1973).

Ovid. *P. Ovidius Naso: Metamorphosen*, comm. by F. Bömer, 7 vols. (Heidelberg 1969-86).

—— *Metamorphoses*, ed. and tr. by F.J. Miller, 2 vols. *(LCL* 1916).

—— *Tristia and Ex Ponto*, ed. and tr. by A.L. Wheeler *(LCL* 1924).

Plato. *Phaedo*, tr. with notes by D. Gallop (Oxford 1975).

—— *Phaedrus*, tr. with comm. by R. Hackforth (Cambridge 1952).

—— *Plato's Cosmology. The Timaeus of Plato translated with a running commentary* by F.M. Cornford (London 1937).

Plotinus. ed. and tr. by A.H. Armstrong, 7 vols. *(LCL* 1966-88).

Posidonius. *Fragments*, edd. L. Edelstein and I.G. Kidd (2nd edn.), and *Commentary* by I.G. Kidd (Cambridge Classical Texts and Commentaries 13-14A/B, 1988-9).

—— *Poseidonios: Die Fragmente*, ed. with comm. by W. Theiler, 2 vols. (Texte und Kommentare 10,1/2, Berlin/New York 1982).

Proclus. *In Platonis Rem Publicam commentarii*, ed. W. Kroll, 2 vols. (Leipzig 1899-1901).

Seneca. *Epistulae Morales*, ed. and tr. by R.M. Gummere, 3 vols. *(LCL* 1917-25).

—— *Moral Essays*, ed. and tr. by J.W. Basore, 3 vols. *(LCL* 1928-35).

—— *De clementia*. Translated in: *Calvin's Commentary on Seneca's De Clementia*, ed. and tr. by F.L. Battles and A.M. Hugo (Leiden 1969).

—— *Agamemnon*, ed. with comm. by R.J. Tarrant (Cambridge Classical Texts and Commentaries 18, 1976).

—— *Phaedra*, ed. with tr. and notes by A.J. Boyle (Liverpool 1987).

—— *Thyestes*, ed. with comm. by R.J. Tarrant (American Philological Association; Textbook Series 11, Atlanta, Ga. 1985). Cited in this book as Tarrant (1985).

Sextus. *The Sentences of Sextus*, ed. H. Chadwick (Cambridge 1959).

Statius. ed. and tr. by J.H. Mozley, 2 vols. *(LCL* 1928).

Tacitus. *Dialogue on Orators*, tr. M. Winterbottom, in *Ancient Literary Criticism. The Principal Texts in New Translations*, edd. D.A. Russell and M. Winterbottom (Oxford 1972) 432-59.

Velleius Paterculus. *The Tiberian Narrative (2.94-131)*, ed. and comm. by A.J. Woodman (Cambridge Classical Texts and Commentaries 19, 1977).

Virgil. *Georgics*, tr. L.P. Wilkinson (Harmondsworth 1982).

—— *Aeneid*, tr. C. Day Lewis (Oxford 1966).

C. Other works

Only works used extensively and cited in the footnotes in the form 'Courcelle (1967)' are included here. Further bibliographical information is given in the footnotes. Fuller bibliographies for Boethius can be found in Gruber (1978), Chadwick (1981), and Fuhrmann/Gruber (1984).

Alfonsi, L. (1942/3) 'De Boethio elegiarum auctore', *Atti del R. Istituto Veneto* 102: 723-7.

—— (1954) 'Boezio poeta', *Antiquitas* 9: 4-13 (German tr. in Fuhrmann/Gruber [1984] 407-21).

—— (1955) 'Storia interiore e storia cosmica nella "Consolatio" boeziana', *Convivium* 23: 513-21.

—— (1979/80) 'Virgilio in Boezio', in *La fortuna di Virgilio nei secoli.* Colloquium Vergilianum. *Sileno* 5/6: 357-71.

Baltes, M. (1980) 'Gott, Welt, Mensch in der Consolatio Philosophiae des Boethius. Die Consolatio Philosophiae als ein Dokument platonischer und neuplatonischer Philosophie', *Vigiliae Christianae* 34: 313-40.

Bark, W. (1943/4) 'Theoderic vs. Boethius: Vindication and Apology', *American Historical Review* 49: 410-26 (reprinted in Fuhrmann/Gruber [1984] 11-32).

Barnes, J. (1981) 'Boethius and the Study of Logic', in Gibson (1981) 73-89.

Barnish, S.J.B. (1983) 'The *Anonymus Valesianus* II as a Source for the Last Years of Theoderic', *Latomus* 42: 572-96.

—— (1990) 'Maximian, Cassiodorus, Boethius, Theodahad: Literature, Philosophy and Politics in Ostrogothic Italy', *Nottingham Medieval Studies* 34:16-32.

Barrett, H.M. (1940) *Boethius: Some Aspects of his Times and Work.* Cambridge (reprinted New York 1965).

Buffière, F. (1956) *Les mythes d'Homère et la pensée grecque.* Paris.

Cameron, A. (1984) 'The *Pervigilium Veneris*', in *La poesia tardoantica: tra retorica, teologia e politica.* Messina: 209-34.

Cappuyns, M. (1937) art. Boèce, *DHGE* 9: 348-80.

Chadwick, H. (1981) *Boethius: The Consolations of Music, Logic, Theology, and Philosophy.* Oxford.

Chamberlain, D.S. (1970) 'Philosophy of Music in the *Consolatio* of Boethius', *Speculum* 45: 80-97 (reprinted in Fuhrmann/Gruber [1984] 377-403).

Courcelle, P. (1944) 'Quelques symboles funéraires du néo-platonisme latin: le vol de Dédale; Ulysse et les Sirènes', *Revue des Etudes Anciennes* 46: 65-93 (reprinted in id., *Opuscula Selecta*, Paris 1984, 99-131).

—— (1948) *Les lettres grecques en Occident de Macrobe à Cassiodore.* Bibliothèque des Ecoles Françaises d'Athènes et de Rome, 159. 2nd edn. Paris (Eng. tr. *Late Latin Writers and their Greek Sources*, Cambridge, Mass. 1969).

—— (1967) *La consolation de philosophie dans la tradition littéraire: antécédents et postérité de Boèce.* Paris.

—— (1970) 'Le personnage de Philosophie dans la littérature latine', *Journal des Savants*: 209-52 (reprinted with minor changes in id., *'Connais-toi toi-même' de Socrate à S. Bernard*, vol. 3, Paris 1975, 669-707).

—— (1980) 'Le tyran et le philosophe d'après la Consolation de Boèce', Convegno Internazionale dell' Accademia Nazionale dei Lincei 45, sul tema *Passagio dal mondo antico al Medio Evo da Teodosio a San Gregorio*

Magno. Roma, 25-28 maggio 1977. Rome: 195-224 (reprinted in id., *Opuscula Selecta*, Paris 1984, 385-414).

—— (1984) *Lecteurs paiens et lecteurs chrétiens de l'Enéide. 1. Les témoignages littéraires*. Mémoires de l'Académie des Inscriptions et Belles-lettres, N.S. 4. Paris.

Crabbe, A.M. (1981a) 'Anamnesis and Mythology in the *De Consolatione Philosophiae*', in L. Obertello, ed., *Atti, Congresso Internazionale di Studi Boeziani* (Pavia, 5-8 ottobre 1980). Rome: 311-25.

—— (1981b) 'Literary Design in the *De Consolatione Philosophiae*', in Gibson (1981) 237-74.

—— See also Wilson, A.M.

Curley, T.F. (1986) 'How to Read the *Consolation of Philosophy*', *Interpretation* 14: 211-63.

—— (1987) 'The *Consolation of Philosophy* as a Work of Literature', *American Journal of Philology* 108: 343-67.

Curtius, E.R. (1954) *Europäische Literatur und lateinisches Mittelalter*. 2nd edn. Berne (Eng. tr. of 1st edn., *European Literature and the Latin Middle Ages*, London 1953).

De Lacy, P. (1948) 'Stoic Views of Poetry', *American Journal of Philology* 69: 241-71.

Dronke, P. (1965) 'L'amor che move il sole e l'altre stelle', *Studi Medievali*. Serie terza, 6/1: 389-422.

Ensslin, W. (1947) *Theoderich der Grosse*. Munich.

Fitch, J.G. (1987) ed., *Seneca's Hercules Furens. A Critical Text with Introduction and Commentary*. Cornell Studies in Classical Philology 45. Ithaca, NY/London.

Ford, S.C. (1967) *Poetry in Boethius' Consolation of Philosophy*. Columbia University thesis. Ann Arbor, Mich.

Fraenkel, E. (1957) *Horace*. Oxford.

Fuhrmann, M./Gruber, J. (1984) *Boethius*. Wege der Forschung 483. Darmstadt.

Gibbon, E. *The History of the Decline and Fall of the Roman Empire*, ed. J.B. Bury. 7 vols. London 1896-1900.

Gibson, M. (1981) ed., *Boethius: His Life, Thought and Influence*. Oxford.

Glei, R. (1985) 'Dichtung und Philosophie in der Consolatio Philosophiae des Boethius', *Würzburger Jahrbücher für die Altertumswissenschaft* N.F. 11: 225-38.

Grube, G.M.A. (1965) *The Greek and Roman Critics*. London.

Gruber, J. (1978) *Kommentar zu Boethius De Consolatione Philosophiae*. Texte und Kommentare 9. Berlin/New York.

—— (1981) 'Einflüsse verschiedener Literaturgattungen auf die prosimetrischen Werke der Spätantike', *Würzburger Jahrbücher für die Altertumswissenschaft* N.F. 7: 209-21.

Hadot, I. (1984) *Arts libéraux et philosophie dans la pensée antique*. Paris.

Hagendahl, H. (1983) *Von Tertullian zu Cassiodor. Die profane literarische Tradition in dem lateinischen christlichen Schrifttum*. Studia Graeca et Latina Gothoburgensia, 44. Göteborg.

Halliwell, S. (1986) *Aristotle's Poetics*. London.

—— (1987) *The Poetics of Aristotle*. Translation and Commentary. London.

—— (1988) *Plato: Republic 10*. With Translation and Commentary. Warminster.

Innes, D.C. (1979) 'Gigantomachy and Natural Philosophy', *Classical Quarterly* N.S. 29: 165-71.

Inwood, B. (1985) *Ethics and Human Action in Early Stoicism*. Oxford.

Jocelyn, H.D. (1973) 'Greek Poetry in Cicero's Prose Writing', *Yale Classical Studies* 23: 61-111.

Jones, A.H.M. (1964) *The Later Roman Empire, 284-602. A Social, Economic and Administrative Survey*. 3 vols. Oxford.

Kaiser, E. (1964) 'Odyssee-Szenen als Topoi', *Museum Helveticum* 21: 109-36, 197-224.

Kassel, R. (1958) *Untersuchungen zur griechischen und römischen Konsolationsliteratur*. Zetemata 18. Munich.

Kirk, E. (1982) 'Boethius, Lucian, and Menippean Satire', *Helios* 9: 50-71.

Kirkby, H. (1981) 'The Scholar and his Public', in Gibson (1981) 44-69.

Klingner, F. (1921) *De Boethii Consolatione Philosophiae*. Berlin (reprinted Zürich/Dublin 1966).

Lamberton, R. (1986) *Homer the Theologian. Neoplatonist Allegorical Reading and the Growth of the Epic Tradition*. The Transformation of the Classical Heritage, 9. Berkley/Los Angeles/London.

Lapidge, M. (1980) 'A Stoic Metaphor in Late Latin Poetry: the Binding of the Cosmos', *Latomus* 39: 817-37.

Leeman, A.D. (1963) *Orationis Ratio. The Stylistic Theories and Practice of the Roman Orators, Historians and Philosophers*. 2 vols. Amsterdam.

Lerer, S. (1985) *Boethius and Dialogue. Literary Method in The Consolation of Philosophy*. Princeton, NJ.

Liebeschütz, H. (1967) 'Western Christian Thought from Boethius to Anselm', in A.H. Armstrong, ed., *The Cambridge History of Later Greek and Early Medieval Philosophy*. Cambridge: 535-639.

Macleod, C. (1979) 'The Poetry of Ethics: Horace, *Epistles* 1', *Journal of Roman Studies* 69: 16-27 (reprinted in id., *Collected Essays* [Oxford 1983] 280-91).

Mair, J. (1981) 'The Text of the *Opuscula Sacra*', in Gibson (1981) 206-13.

Mathwich, J. (1960) 'De Boethi morte', *Eunomia* 4: 26-37 (reprinted in Fuhrmann/Gruber [1984] 33-51).

Matthews, J. (1975) *Western Aristocracies and Imperial Court, A.D. 364-425*. Oxford.

—— (1981) 'Anicius Manlius Severinus Boethius', in Gibson (1981) 15-43.

Milanese, G. (1983) 'Il *De Rerum Natura*, i *Topica* e Boezio: Due note alla *Consolatio Philosophiae*', *Maia* N.S. 35: 137-56.

Momigliano, A. (1955) 'Cassiodorus and the Italian Culture of his Time', *Proceedings of the British Academy* 41: 207-45 (reprinted in id., *Secondo Contributo alla Storia degli Studi Classici* [Rome 1960] 191-229).

Mras, K. (1914) 'Varros Menippeische Satiren und die Philosophie', *Neue Jahrbücher für das klassische Altertum* 33: 390-420.

Mueller-Goldingen, C. (1989) 'Die Stellung der Dichtung in Boethius' Consolatio Philosophiae', *Rheinisches Museum* 132: 369-95.

Obertello, L. (1974) *Severino Boezio*. 2 vols. Genoa.

O'Daly, G. (1987) *Augustine's Philosophy of Mind*. London.

O'Donnell, J.J. (1979) *Cassiodorus*. Berkeley/Los Angeles/London.

—— (1984) *Boethius: Consolatio Philosophiae*. Bryn Mawr Latin Commentaries. Bryn Mawr, Pa.

Olmsted, W.R. (1989) 'Philosophical Inquiry and Religious Transformation in Boethius's *The Consolation of Philosophy* and Augustine's *Confessions*', *The Journal of Religion* 69: 14-35.

Oltramare, A. (1926) *Les origines de la diatribe romaine*. Lausanne/Geneva.

Parsons, P. (1971) 'A Greek Satyricon?', *Bulletin of the Institute of Classical Studies* 18: 53-68.

Rand, E.K. (1904) 'On the Composition of Boethius' Consolatio Philosophiae', *Harvard Studies in Classical Philology* 15: 1-28 (reprinted in Fuhrmann/ Gruber [1984] 249-77).

Reichenberger, K. (1954) *Untersuchungen zur literarischen Stellung der Consolatio Philosophiae*. Kölner Romanistische Arbeiten N.F. 3. Cologne.

Russell, D.A. (1981) *Criticism in Antiquity*. London.

Rutherford, R.B. (1989) *The Meditations of Marcus Aurelius: A Study*. Oxford.

Salemme, C. (1970/1) 'Aspetti della lingua e della sensibilità di Boezio poeta', *Annali della Facoltà di Lettere e Filosofia della Università di Napoli* 13: 67-89.

Scheible, H. (1972) *Die Gedichte in der Consolatio Philosophiae des Boethius*. Bibliothek der klassischen Altertumswissenschaften N.F. 46. Heidelberg.

Schmid, W. (1956) 'Philosophisches und Medizinisches in der Consolatio des Boethius', in *Festschrift Bruno Snell*. Munich: 113-44.

Schmidt, P.L. (1977) 'Zur Typologie und Literarisierung des frühchristlichen lateinischen Dialogs', *Christianisme et formes littéraires de l'antiquité tardive en Occident*. Entretiens Fondation Hardt 23. Geneva: 101-90.

Schurr, V. (1935) *Die Trinitätslehre des Boethius im Lichte der 'Skythischen Kontroversen'*. Forschungen zur christlichen Literatur und Dogmengeschichte 18.1. Paderborn.

Segal, C. (1983) 'Dissonant Sympathy: Song, Orpheus, and the Golden Age in Seneca's Tragedies', *Ramus* 12: 229-51.

Shanzer, D. (1983a) 'Ennodius, Boethius, and the Date and Interpretation of Maximianus's *Elegia* III', *Rivista di Filologia* 111: 183-95.

—— (1983b) ' "Me quoque excellentior": Boethius, *De Consolatione* 4.6.38', *Classical Quarterly* N.S. 33: 277-83.

—— (1984) 'The Death of Boethius and the "Consolation of Philosophy" ', *Hermes* 112: 352-66.

—— (1986a) 'The Late Antique Tradition of Varro's ONOS LYRAS', *Rheinisches Museum* 129: 272-85.

—— (1986b) *A Philosophical and Literary Commentary on Martianus Capella's De Nuptiis Philologiae et Mercurii Book 1*. University of California Publications: Classical Studies 32. Berkeley/Los Angeles/London.

Sheppard, A.D.R. (1980) *Studies on the 5th and 6th Essays of Proclus' Commentary on the Republic*. Hypomnemata 61. Göttingen.

Silk, E.T. (1939) 'Boethius' Consolatio Philosophiae as a Sequel to Augustine's Dialogues and Soliloquia', *Harvard Theological Review* 32: 19-39.

Stein, E. (1949) *Histoire du Bas-Empire*. 2 vols. Paris.

Sundwall, J. (1919) *Abhandlungen zur Geschichte des ausgehenden Römertums*. Helsinki (reprinted New York 1975).

Tarrant, R.J. (1985) ed., *Seneca's Thyestes*. American Philological Association; Textbook Series 11. Atlanta, Ga.

Theiler, W. (1966) *Forschungen zum Neuplatonismus*. Quellen und Studien zur Geschichte der Philosophie, 10. Berlin.

Thomas, R.F. (1988) ed., *Virgil: Georgics*. Cambridge Greek and Latin Classics. 2 vols. Cambridge.

Traina, A. (1980) 'Per l'esegesi di una lirica boeziana (*cons.* 1, m. 5)', *Orpheus* N.S. 1: 391-410.

Tränkle, H. (1968) 'Textkritische Bemerkungen zur Philosophiae Consolatio des Boethius', *Vigiliae Christianae* 22: 272-86.

—— (1973) 'Philologische Bemerkungen zum Boethiusprozess', in *Romanitas et Christianitas. Studia I.H. Waszink ... oblata*, edd. W. den Boer *et al.* Amsterdam/London: 329-39 (reprinted in Fuhrmann/Gruber [1984] 52-63).

—— (1977) 'Ist die Philosophiae Consolatio des Boethius zum vorgesehenen Abschluss gelangt?', *Vigiliae Christianae* 31: 148-56 (reprinted in Fuhrmann/Gruber [1984] 311-19, omitting the 'Corollarium criticum' on 154-6).

Usener, H. (1877) *Anecdoton Holderi. Ein Beitrag zur Geschichte Roms in ostgothischer Zeit*. Bonn (reprinted Hildesheim 1969).

Viarre, S. (1975) 'L'image du naufrage dans le *De consolatione philosophiae* de Boèce', *Studia Patristica* 13 (= Texte und Untersuchungen 116). Berlin: 52-6.

Williams, G. (1968) *Tradition and Originality in Roman Poetry*. Oxford.

Wilson, A.M. (1985) 'The Prologue to Manilius I', *Papers of the Liverpool Latin Seminar* 5: 283-98 (published 1986).

—— See also Crabbe, A.M.

Wolf, C. (1964) 'Untersuchungen zum Krankheitsbild in dem ersten Buch der Consolatio Philosophiae des Boethius', *Rivista di Cultura Classica e Medioevale* 6: 213-23.

Zwierlein, O. (1984) *Senecas Hercules im Lichte kaiserzeitlicher und spätantiker Deutung*. Mit einem Anhang über 'tragische Schuld' sowie Seneca-Imitationen bei Claudian und Boethius. Abhandlungen der Akademie der Wissenschaften und der Literatur in Mainz, 1984,6. Wiesbaden.

Index of Selected Passages

This index includes references to all passages quoted and discussed, but generally omits passages that are merely cited as examples or parallels in the text and footnotes. References to the pages of this book appear in **bold** type.

General Index

This index is selective, especially in its inclusion of material in the footnotes and references to proper names. It omits names of modern scholars.

DATE DUE

UPI   PRINTED IN U.S.A.